1st edition

W9-BWQ-835

QL43'6'

ALSO BY JOHN PEARSON

**Nonfiction**
*The Last Hero*
*Arena*
*The Profession of Violence*
*The Life of Ian Fleming*
*Edward the Rake*
*The Sitwells*
*The Serpent and the Stag*
*The Selling of the Royal Family*

**Fiction**
*Gone to Timbuctoo*
*The Kindness of Dr. Avicenna*

# John Pearson

Simon & Schuster

New York   London   Toronto   Sydney   Tokyo   Singapore

# The
# Private
# Lives
# of
# Winston
# Churchill

**SIMON & SCHUSTER**
Simon & Schuster Building
Rockefeller Center
1230 Avenue of the Americas
New York, New York 10020

Copyright © 1991 by John Pearson

All rights reserved
including the right of reproduction
in whole or in part in any form.

Simultaneously published in Great Britain by Macmillan Ltd.

SIMON & SCHUSTER and colophon are registered trademarks
of Simon & Schuster Inc.

Designed by Levavi & Levavi
Manufactured in the United States of America

1   3   5   7   9   10   8   6   4   2

Library of Congress Cataloging-in-Publication Data
Pearson, John, date.
The private lives of Winston Churchill/John Pearson.
p.   cm.
Includes bibliographical references and index.
1. Churchill, Winston, Sir, 1874–1965.   2. Churchill, Winston, Sir,
1874–1965—Family.   3. Prime ministers—Great Britain—Biography.
4. Churchill family.   I. Title.
DA566.9.C5P365   1991
941.084′092—dc20
[B]                                                                        91-22435
CIP
ISBN: 0-671-63153-5

For my wife, Lynette

"Beneath the mighty oak no saplings grow"
——Randolph S. Churchill

# CONTENTS

# INTRODUCTION

This book really started many years ago when, as a young reporter, I first came in contact with Winston Churchill's son, Randolph Churchill. This was in 1966, and he helped me with a book I was writing on Ian Fleming, who had been an old antagonist of his. In Fleet Street, Randolph had a reputation as a drunk, a dangerous litigant, a brawler, and a sort of establishment buffoon. But when I saw him in his house in Suffolk, he was charm itself and very helpful. I recall an afternoon of fascinating talk that ended with my helping him dead-head roses in the garden.

This was two years before he died. He was clearly unhappy and unwell, and I drove back to London puzzled by this sad old monster and by the mystery surrounding the Churchill family.

Diana, Randolph's elder sister, had killed herself by then, but from time to time I used to see their once-beautiful youngest sister, the actress Sarah Churchill, in Chelsea. Sober, she was as charming as her brother, but drunk, she was a nightmare. Sarah's situation seemed the more alarming in contrast with the exemplary youngest sister, Mary. Happily married to the politician Christopher Soames, Mary was responsible and utterly respectable, with a large family, countless friends, and the unfeigned affection of all who knew her.

So why this appalling difference in the lives of the offspring of the man so often called the greatest Briton of his generation, if not of his whole century? In 1982, when Sarah, like Randolph before her, died of drink, the question was raised again. Why should three out of four of Winston Churchill's adult children have effectively destroyed themselves?

There seemed no easy answer. It might have been sheer coincidence, or maybe there was some deep genetic flaw within the family. Perhaps some fault resided in the Churchill marriage, or had Churchill's more-than-life-size personality contributed to his children's troubles?

It was tempting to see these three doomed Churchill children as victims of their father's genius, for there are various romantic theories that regard genius as the final flowering of a family line, fatal to all who follow. Or perhaps it was something simpler. "Great men are almost always bad men," said the great Lord Acton, who also held well-known views about the corrupting nature of power. In his day, Churchill had been extremely powerful, and possibly this had caused the trouble. It was hard to know the truth, and the only answer to the problem lay within the Churchill family itself.

This was to be the starting point from which I wrote this book. However, as I soon discovered, any attempt to understand the relationship between Churchill and his children had wider implications. There was the whole background of the family to be considered. There was the story of the Churchill marriage. There were the lives of the children and their friends and relations. And at the center of it all, gigantic key to the whole immense conundrum, stood Winston Churchill himself. It was a series of extraordinary events within his own family that helped make him what he was. And he in turn totally transformed the lives of all around him.

In describing how this happened, I have tried to write a rather different book from other works on Winston Churchill. And while attempting to avoid the pitfalls of psychobiography, I have done my best to explain something of the nature of this clever, driven, powerful, courageous, infinitely baffling Englishman.

To do so I have drawn upon the immense wealth of published material on Winston Churchill, whose stature has been matched by the vastness of the literature about him. Foremost however is the eight volume official biography, started by Randolph, and completed by Dr. Martin Gilbert. Equally valuable has been the admirable series of "Companion Volumes" of documents and letters covering Churchill's life and political career up to the Second World War. I am most grateful to the trustees of the Churchill collections at Churchill College, Cambridge, for the opportunity to consult various additional documents.

I would also like to thank the considerable number of Churchill relations, friends, and witnesses who helped me with their time and recollections. Foremost among them were Sir Winston's nephew Peregrine S. Churchill and his wife, Yvonne, for whose kindness and counsel I was immensely grateful, particularly at the beginning of my task. The omniscient Hugo Vickers is another friend I would particularly like to thank for so much early encouragement and advice. Others who were unfailingly helpful include: Mr. Michael Alexander, Mrs. Nualla Allason, Mr. Julian Amery, Lady Avon, Mrs. Natalie Barclay, Mr. Andrew Bareau, Lady Baring, Mrs. Virginia Barrington, Mrs. Judy Birkin, Mrs. Pauline Bretherton, Mr. Alan Brien, Lord Charles Spencer Churchill, Mr. John S. Churchill, Mr. and Mrs. Winston Churchill, Mr. Peter Coats, Mrs. Angela Culme-Seymour, Sir William Deakin, Mr. Nigel Dempster, Mr. Hugo Dixon, Mr. Piers Dixon, Lady Dunne, Mrs. Farelly, Sir Nigel Fisher, Mrs. Flor, Mr. Michael Foot, Mr. Alastair Forbes, Mr. Roy Foster, Mrs. Elizabeth Furze, Dr. Martin Gilbert, Sir Ian Gilmour, Lady Gladwyn, Mr. Francis Goodman, Mrs. Susan Gough, Mrs. Kay Halle, Miss Grace Hamblin, Mrs. Pamela Harrimann, Mr. Tom Hartman, Miss Joan Haslip, Mrs. Mary Huizinga, Mr. David Irving, Mrs. Edwina Kaplan, Lord Lambton, Lord Longford, Mrs. Arabella Macleod, The Duke and Duchess of Marlborough, Laura Duchess of Marlborough, Mr. Paul Medlicott, Mr. Anthony Montague Brown, Mrs. Maggie Parker, Mr. and Mrs. Kenneth Perkins, Mrs. Tanis Phillips, Miss Ellen Pollock, Mr. Patrick Proktor, Mrs. Wendy Reves, Dr. John Seale, Miss Emma Soames, Dr. Anthony Storr, Mrs. Graham Sutherland, Lady Carolyn Townshend, Mr. Michael Tree, Mr. Ralph Vickers, Mr. Alan Watkins, Lady Christine West, Mr. Peter Willes.

In addition I must thank my editors, Alice Mayhew and Susanna Wadeson, for amazing patience and unfailing competence. My friend and agent, Ed Victor, as usual made the whole book possible. Anne Hoffman, Jacqueline Williams, and Joyce Quarrie all gave invaluable help with research, as did Mathew Frankland with the illustrations. Edda Tasiemka of the remarkable Hans Tasiemka Archive was a treasury of information, and Grace Hartley was as ever the perfect secretary. My debt to my friend Peter Evans is greater than he probably realizes, and only my family will know how much I depended yet again on the calming presence of Ted Green. Finally I must thank my wife, who played so great a part in the writing of this book and who did not fail me.

J.P. 1991

# one

# Fathers, Sons, and Others

May 28, 1932, was a red-letter day in the private life of Winston Churchill—it was the day his son, Randolph, came of age. And since nothing was too good for his golden son and heir, the great man made elaborate preparations, which he could ill afford, to mark this important rite of passage.

Churchill was particularly proud of his handsome son's appearance, and the birthday portrait commissioned from Sir Philip Laszlo, the most accomplished—and expensive—royal portrait painter of the day, bears melancholy witness to the brief beauty of Churchill's dauphin. The profile is flawless, the brow regal, and the gaze from the bright blue eyes remarkably assured. Laszlo specialized in princes, and this was a portrait of a modern prince who took his inheritance for granted.

The celebration Churchill was planning in Randolph's honor consisted of an elaborate—and unusual—dinner party to be held at Claridges Hotel two and a half weeks after Randolph's actual birthday. In Churchill's eyes, young Randolph was no ordinary twenty-one-year-old but the heir to a great tradition, a young man of whom great things might be expected. To express this, Churchill himself devised the evening's theme.

Over seventy invitations were sent out for the all-male evening.

Apart from a few close friends, such as Robert Boothby, Sir Oswald Mosley (soon busily leading the British Union of Fascists), and Churchill's own scientific guru, Prof. Frederick Lindemann, the guests were to consist of great men and their sons—Max Lord Beaverbrook with "Little Max" Aitken, Lord Rothermere with the urbane Esmond Harmsworth, Lord Camrose with Seymour Berry, Lord Hailsham with Quintin Hogg, and Lord Reading with young Lord Erleigh.

One noted absentee was Stanley Baldwin, the former and future Conservative Prime Minister, who had been invited with his left-wing son Oliver. Relations between Churchill and the elder Baldwin had become strained since Baldwin joined Labour Prime Minister Ramsay MacDonald in a "national government" the year before, leaving Churchill in the political wilderness. The Baldwins had declined the invitation.

The Churchills, being Churchills, made the most of the advance publicity, which the presence of three famous press lords and their children in no way diminished. Randolph personally telephoned the "Londoner's Diary" of Lord Beaverbrook's *Evening Standard* with advance details of his birthday.

The "Diary" at the time was edited by the dissolute but well-connected former spy and flunky of the rich, Sir Robert Bruce Lockhart. That evening, having composed an appropriately servile piece about the party based on Randolph's information, Sir Robert pondered the event in his private journal: "What an amazing thing privilege and position still are in England. Here is a boy who, born in a less privileged circle, would have had to work hard and make his own way. As it is, he is lazy, lascivious, impudent, and beyond a certain rollicking bumptiousness, untalented, and everything is open to him."

In fact, the tragedy of Randolph Churchill's life was that everything was *not* open to him. And it is interesting to note that of all the sons of that privileged circle who had sat down to roast duck and champagne at Claridges on that evening of June 16, 1932, only one, Quintin Hogg—lawyer, Tory politician, and future Lord Chancellor himself—would in any way approach his famous father's reputation and achievement.

None would fail so painfully and in so many ways as Randolph Churchill. Few great men in recent history could have created such a scourge for themselves as doting Winston did with his beloved son, and few great men's sons, as loyal and loving as Randolph would remain toward his father, could have endured such desperate disappointments from their situation.

Luckily for all those confident young men and famous fathers, sitting so convivially together on that June night in their private room at Claridges, all this lay safely in the future. Reassured by the general bonhomie and a generous supply of Churchill's favorite champagne (in 1928, he had bought up all available stock of Pol Roger champagne in London), no one seemed particularly concerned about tempting fate.

Churchill himself, always at his best in congenial male company, was as sparkling as his favorite drink as he enlarged upon the evening's theme—"passing on the lamp" from one generation to the next. Referring to his precious son's prospects as a politician, Churchill spoke proudly of his verbal fluency, which he compared, in vintage Churchill style, with a machine gun: "Gentlemen, let us only hope that he accumulates a large dump of ammunition, and—er—that he learns to hit the target." (Laughter and applause.)

Churchill's theme was also expounded by an Etonian contemporary of Randolph's, the second Lord Birkenhead, who was there alone. (His father, the first Lord Birkenhead, former Lord Chancellor and Randolph's godfather and great exemplar, had died of drink some two years earlier.) The young lord then proposed a toast to Randolph's health, and to his "rise to fame."

In its way, this rise had already been spectacular. Randolph was already established as a journalist, social figure, and celebrity: He had written for Lord Beaverbrook, lectured across America, and could not wait to enter Parliament.

Like most of the guests gathered in his honor, Randolph took it for granted that his goal in life was the great pursuit of power and political success. Referring to the evening many years later, he ruefully admitted that "Had anyone told me I wouldn't soon be in the House of Commons by the time I was twenty-one, or soon afterwards, I would have thought them absolutely too ridiculous for words." Pitt the younger held office at twenty-three and was Prime Minister at twenty-five, "and I saw no reason why I should not do the same."

This extraordinary self-confidence had originated with Winston, who had been grooming and preparing Randolph for politics since childhood the way a thoroughbred is prepared for the Derby. "Politics is like prostitution and piano-playing," he once remarked. "The earlier you start the better."

Throughout his adult life Winston Churchill had been obsessed with the pursuit and exercise of political power. The thought of this power being magically passed from certain fathers to their sons was an idea that touched on one of the profoundest—and in many ways the most mysterious—elements within his extremely complex nature.

If ghosts could dine, the place of honor at the long oval table at Claridges that night would have been set aside for a small dynamic man with prominent blue eyes and a very large mustache—Churchill's own father, Lord Randolph Churchill, after whom he named his son.

Lord Randolph's life was one of the great tragedies (and cautionary tales) of Victorian politics. After a charmed ascent to the position of Chancellor of the Exchequer by the age of thirty-six, the great orator, arrogantly power-mad as only the son of a Victorian duke could be, had resigned from Lord Salisbury's government in 1886 in an ill-judged bid for the succession. He died, embittered and insane, some nine years later at the age of forty-five.

One might have thought that such an occurrence was quite enough to scare off any son from politics forever. Yet Winston had inherited his father's grand obsession.

There were already coincidences in their two careers. By the evening of Randolph's birthday dinner, Winston Churchill had occupied in succession the same two offices of state—Secretary of State for the Colonies and Chancellor of the Exchequer—that his father had held before his fall. Also, at the time of the party, Churchill was also in the midst of a political crisis—the most prolonged of his life, which would keep him firmly out of office until war began in 1939.

To most of his fellow politicians, Winston seemed politically played out. (One of his favorite guests that night, his friend Lord Beaverbrook, would soon describe him as "a busted flush.") He was out of power, (relatively) hard up, and at odds with the Conservative hierarchy. He was still feared, still potent in debate, but he was also haunted by the possibility that some unseen destiny had trapped him in the very pattern that had destroyed Lord Randolph.

Although he was a firm agnostic, Churchill had long believed in destiny. This belief gave purpose to his existence, had saved him from death (so he claimed) in countless times of danger, and had kept his unrelenting ego high above the dross of hopeless, doomed humanity. There were rare moments when he felt his destiny as an actual presence: "Over me beat unseen wings" was how he would describe the all-important stroke of luck that kept him out of Stanley Baldwin's government three years later.

Churchill's sense of destiny included members of his family, dead as well as living, and strengthened his identification with his father and his son. Asquith's daughter, Lady Violet Bonham Carter, who knew him well and had, in fact, been in love with him many years before, wrote of his obsession with his family and how its members "held pride of place within the citadel of his heart," to the exclusion of all others.

For his closest family this was a fact of life—and also something of a burden. This was particularly true for stylish Clementine, who at forty-seven still managed to appear considerably more than ten years younger than her bald and portly husband.

It is unlikely she was deeply hurt at missing out on her son's twenty-first birthday dinner. Down-to-earth by nature, she must have felt the evening's theme a touch absurd—and probably a little vulgar. She would also almost certainly have agreed with most of what Bruce Lockhart wrote about Randolph in his diary. But her disapproval never had had much effect upon her husband's princeling.

Clementine had built a personal survival route against her husband's dominating presence. Since their marriage twenty-four years earlier, she had sacrificed herself upon the altar of his greatness. She had loved him, mothered him (with the children firmly taking second place), shared in his triumphs, and seen him through his bouts of deep depression and aggressive rage when he was thwarted.

She had accepted his belief that destiny had marked him for greatness, and against her own somewhat puritanical nature, had endured his compulsive taste for extravagance and luxury—armies of servants, silk underwear, cigars, extremely good champagne, and the company of the very rich. She had learned to live with his elephantine ego, tolerate his more outlandish friends, accept his limitless capacity for work, and understand his passionate desire for power. If Clementine became neurotic and felt the need for prolonged periods away from him, it was not surprising.

More seriously at risk were the two elder daughters—twenty-two-year-old Diana and her seventeen-year-old sister, Sarah—who, as females, were also excluded from their brother's party and from the sacred bond between son and father. (The baby of the family, nine-year-old Mary, safely home in bed, was to be protected by her youth from many of the influences that were to dislocate the lives of her siblings in the years ahead.)

All the Churchill girls were pretty, with the auburn hair and blue eyes of their mother. But Diana had inherited nothing of her father's toughness. She was nervous and petite—"like a little fairy," Sarah said —and her extreme self-consciousness made her particularly vulnerable.

Sarah was tougher than her sister, with a touch of glamour that her sister lacked. She was charming, extroverted, and, like her father and her brother, tended to be intensely obstinate once she had her mind made up—hence her family nickname Mule. Outwardly, this gave her all the signs of a born survivor, but she shared Randolph's self-destructive streak; she, too, would finally fall victim to the force that drove her father forward.

Some of the extended family appeared immune to this strange family trait. Winston's younger brother, Jack, was present at the party, together with Jack's eldest son, Randolph's cousin Johnny. A tall, good-looking man with a mustache, Jack was a city stockbroker. Kind, unintellectual, easygoing, Jack worshiped his elder brother for qualities he notably lacked himself. Like his son Johnny (whose chief interests lay in acrobatics, pretty girls, and fresco-painting), Jack was essentially a private person. Whatever demons brother Winston had inherited from Lord Randolph had passed him by entirely, leaving him immune to the magnetic pull of politics.

Another guest at Claridges that night was also like a brother to Winston Churchill. Churchill treated him with notable respect, placing him directly opposite him at table. He was a small man with a thin mustache, a drooping eye, and the mark of worldly disappointment on his sallow face. This was Churchill's noble cousin, Charles Richard John Spencer-Churchill—"Sunny" to his intimates, the ninth Duke of Marlborough to the world at large. Churchill revered him as the head of his all-important family. He also loved him, warts and all, and described him as "my oldest and dearest friend."

Both had inherited their share of the depressive Churchill temperament, and both, in their early years, had shared a series of catastrophies and scandals that shook the family. All of these influences and far-off family disasters had strengthened Winston for the pursuit of power, and inspired him for a life of action. Sunny Marlborough, however, had been left profoundly scarred. He was introverted, bitter, and suspicious of anyone outside the family. Winston he loved, but he was not the sort of man to warm to Randolph.

With all the speeches and the port and the after-dinner conversation, it was midnight before Randolph's birthday party ended. And as son and father stood in the foyer of that grand hotel, bidding their guests good-night, they could congratulate themselves upon a most successful evening.

Neither could possibly have suspected that nothing would turn out as the party had suggested. Churchill's life was not drawing to its close—his years of glory still lay ahead of him—while Randolph's was already over. For that destiny in which Churchill believed was mysterious. It had its origins within the lives and legends of his ancestors. It was indissolubly linked with the tragic figure of his father, who was to haunt him all his life. It would bring him fame beyond the dreams of immortality, but it would also bring him secret anguish and destroy the lives of several who were closest to him. And, contrary to his dearest wishes, it would leave him no successors.

Behind this monolithic figure lies a hidden story. It is a stranger story than the legends and the history books admit—and it ends, as it begins, within that "citadel" of Churchill's heart, his family.

# two

# The Ancestor

Today, the paterfamilias of the Churchill dynasty stands surveying his possessions from a grandiose stone pillar set in the Oxford countryside, close to the palace named after his most famous victory. Cast in lead, with eagles at his feet, attired like a conquering Roman emperor, John Churchill, first and greatest of the dukes of Marlborough, continues to proclaim his triumphs over the armies of the French, victories that made him the greatest British general of the eighteenth century.

The palace he built was partly paid for by his grateful nation after his victory near the village of Blindheim in Austria in 1705. He called the palace Blenheim, and it was here that Winston Churchill himself was born on November 30, 1874.

One cannot overemphasize how important the Duke and his extraordinary palace were to Winston Churchill. Blenheim today is as immense, as absurdly grand as when first built—a stone-paved courtyard big enough to hold a regiment, state apartments built for the exclusive purpose of receiving royalty, four elaborate stone towers, and a great external staircase leading to a pillared entrance hall. It overwhelms rather than welcomes any visitor.

It is also quite unlike any other stately English home. From the moment it was built it was an uncomfortably ill-omened house, hated or admired but rarely loved, the scene of much noble misery and gloom, a mirage curiously at odds with the gentle landscape seven miles northwest of Oxford.

Almost without exception, great English houses traditionally reflect the settled wealth and gradually accumulated power of their owners. Not so Blenheim, which was thrown up in eight frantic, ruinously expensive years. Its principal architect, John Vanbrugh (who also came to hate it), originally found fame in the theater, and he made Blenheim first and foremost a theatrical triumph—or, as the English author Sacheverell Sitwell put it, "a private monument that is a Roman triumph and a public pantomime." Its hero was, and is, John Churchill, Duke of Marlborough.

Just as Blenheim is unique among ducal houses, so John Churchill stands unique among his peers. Like Wellington, he is that rarity, a self-made English duke; unlike even Wellington, he reached the apex of the aristocracy without an inherited title to begin with. Late in life, and against extraordinary odds, he made himself the greatest soldier of his age.

The Duke's father was the first in his family of undistinguished Dorset gentry to bear the name Sir Winston Churchill. A disappointed cavalier who lost his fortune in the sacred cause of Charles I, he was also an amateur historian whose life work, entitled *Divi Britannici,* was an impenetrable volume on the kings of England. The historian Lord Macaulay dismissed Sir Winston as "a poor Cavalier knight, who haunted Whitehall and made himself ridiculous by publishing a dull and affected folio, long forgotten, in praise of monarchy and monarch."

Neglected by his king, Sir Winston put his feelings into the family motto he invented. It would prove a shade too pat for his descendants who adopted it. It was in Spanish: *Fiel pero Desdichado,* "Faithful but unfortunate."

John Churchill was neither of these. He was a handsome man who used both battlefield and bed to promote his remarkable career in Restoration England. Macaulay says he cuckolded the king—the amiable Charles II—with the royal mistress, Lady Castlemaine, and was sharp enough to extract £5,000 from her for his services. If true this would have been a vast sum, approaching one million dollars in present-day money. Carefully invested, it was reputedly the start of what certainly became the greatest private fortune in the land.

John Churchill fought in Holland and Tangier with some distinction, but more important to his advancement was his marriage in 1677 to Sarah Jennings, bosom friend of Princess Anne, who would ascend the throne of England as Queen in 1705. When Anne succeeded to the throne, she appointed her friend's husband commander of her forces then fighting on the Continent against the French in the dynastic conflict for the mastery of Europe known as the War of the Spanish Succession.

By 1705, John Churchill, then fifty-three, had fought, intrigued, plotted, and betrayed ("ratting and reratting" as his descendant Winston called it) to reach the top. He was a time server, ruthlessly ambitious, and the most mercenary of men. He was also, by an unexpected twist of fate, a military genius. Churchill earned his fortune, dukedom, and immortality with a staggering succession of victories over the greatest military presence of his day—the united armies of France, Bavaria, and Spain led by the proudest king on earth, the Sun King, Louis XIV of France. And the first and most spectacular of these came soon after he had marched his men from Holland to the Danube. The armies met thirty miles from Vienna, and his bloody and unexpected victory saved both that city and the Holy Roman Empire from the French.

His victory at Blenheim was an extraordinary achievement and was treated accordingly. Honors and gifts were showered upon the victor: the dukedom of Marlborough, a princedom of the Holy Roman Empire, the Order of the Garter, and the former royal estate at Woodstock in Oxfordshire. A grateful Parliament voted £6,000 to build a palace there to celebrate his victory, and Churchill decided to name it after the site of the battle.

For the remainder of the war, while the Duke continued battering the French—at Ramillies in 1706, Oudenarde in 1708, and Malplaquer in 1709—Duchess Sarah commanded the horde of workmen who were rapidly creating her husband's greatest monument, the strange and all-consuming Blenheim Palace.

In the end, the palace was no protection: Marlborough was defeated—not by the French in battle but by his Tory enemies at home. They played upon the fact that Anne was tired of being dominated by her old favorite, Duchess Sarah, and that the populace at large was tired of the war. The Peace of Utrecht, signed in defiance of the Duke, returned to France almost everything he had won in battle.

At the end of 1711, his enemies publicly accused the Duke of illicitly receiving large sums of money from army contractors. Although he could show that this had been an accepted perquisite, he could not prevent his dismissal from all public offices. Instead of the triumph he expected, Marlborough's final years were passed in disgrace, and he "lingered on in surly decreptitude." The palace was finished while Duchess Sarah anxiously watched her husband's fortune being poured into it. Before it was completed, she had come to hate it, calling it "that wild unmerciful House."

The pundits of ordered eighteenth-century taste unanimously labeled Blenheim a monstrosity. Alexander Pope would compare it with a stone quarry. Horace Walpole found it overloaded with decoration and crammed with the old Duke's trophies. "It looks like the palace of an auctioneer who has been chosen King of Poland," he quipped.

Ignoring his critics and his enemies, the proud old Duke lived obstinately on at Blenheim until his death in 1722. He became more avaricious with the years and was understandably embittered and given to long bouts of melancholy. But Blenheim was, his Duchess said, "His greatest weakness." He spent on it lavishly and loved it jealously, both as his "private Habitation," and as a demonstration to the world of all he had achieved.

Blenheim was the Duke's and his alone, hung with vast Brussels tapestries depicting in detail all his greatest battles, adorned with the insignia of his countless titles, and crammed with riches garnered from his victories. It was a forbidding place to live.

Winston Churchill, who was not entirely unlike the Duke, came to be obsessed with Marlborough and compared his ancestor's building mania at Blenheim with the pharaohs' construction of the pyramids. Both, he said, were searches for "a physical monument which would certainly stand, if only as a ruin, for a thousand years."

But the pharaohs built the pyramids as tombs. The first Duke of Marlborough intended Blenheim as the birthplace for a dynasty that would bear his titles through the centuries ahead. His descendants would perpetually renew his wealth, his honors, and his grand position in society.

Such was the theory that enabled the decaying Duke to forget the politicians who had tried to destroy him. At Blenheim, he was certain, his memory would live forever. And it did. Shortly before attending Randolph Churchill's twenty-first birthday party at Claridges, the hapless Sunny, ninth Duke of Marlborough, had been sitting for the bust by the sculptor Sir Jacob Epstein that one sees today at Blenheim. Sunny had shown Epstein around his stately home, and the sculptor was distinctly puzzled by the Blenheim chapel. Instead of any sign of

Christ above the altar, there is a vast memorial in marble by another famous sculptor, Michael Rysbrack, showing the figure of John Churchill.

"What about God?" inquired Epstein.

"The Marlboroughs are worshiped here," said Sunny.

As if condemned to the worship of a god whose expectations they could never possibly fulfill, the dukes who had succeeded John have been unhappy, lesser men, cohabiting at Blenheim with a greatness they never earned and never matched. Somehow the gloom of the old Duke's final years lingered on around them. Of all the members of the family who were infected by the fatal touch of Blenheim, only Winston Churchill truly overcame it, and rose to the challenge of his overwhelming ancestor.

The Churchill depression—Winston called it "Black Dog" when it started to affect him—is one of the recurrent mysteries of the family. John himself was the victim of a markedly depressive temperament. Besides the gloom that assailed his later years, he also suffered from attacks of migraine both before and after all his battles. His ancestors fared worse: It is said that at least five subsequent dukes suffered from melancholia.

It is tempting to believe that the troubles of the Churchills were passed on genetically as a hidden part of John's legacy, but this is hard to prove. In the first place, the Marlborough Churchills did not descend in a direct male line from the first duke. His two sons died in infancy, and it was only thanks to a special act of Parliament that the dukedom traveled to his eldest daughter, Henrietta, upon her father's death.

Henrietta's only son died before her, so on her death the dukedom passed, somewhat shakily, to the son of her second sister, Anne, who had married Charles Spencer, Earl of Sunderland. This son, called Charles Spencer like his father, became the third Duke of Marlborough. Until 1817, all subsequent dukes bore the name of Spencer, then the name Churchill was tacked on to it, to revive the memory of great Duke John in answer to the *parvenu* dukedom of Wellington.

The Spencer stock was anything but melancholy. The eighteenth- and nineteenth-century Spencers, Earls of Althorp, proved to be one of the most ebullient dynasties of the British upper aristocracy. In our own time, the Spencers of the Althorp line produced the notably non-depressive Diana, Princess of Wales. But somehow the Marlborough

Spencers were infected by the gloom of Blenheim. For more than a century, the dukes who lived there were to prove themselves a resolutely sad and self-destructive lot.

The long-lived fourth Duke reigned at Blenheim for more than sixty years, from the middle of the eighteenth century. He was a great collector and outwardly had everything to make him happy: title, children, wealth, and a supremely honored position in society. But gradually the curse of Blenheim overwhelmed him. By his fifties, he was already something of a hermit, locking himself away at Blenheim to study astronomy. Soon he was dreading any outside contact with humanity.

Not long before he died in 1817, the formidable Mme. de Staël, best known for her famous salon frequented by the French romantic writers of the period, tried to gain entrance to the palace. Hearing that he had a visitor, the Duke cried to his footman, "Take me away! Take me away!" This was apparently his last recorded utterance.

After the hermit duke came his son George, one of the greatest spendthrifts of a spendthrift age. He did his best, through lunatic extravagance, to empty the first Duke's treasure chest to pay his debts. This was none too easy, since most of the fabled books and gems and paintings were still guarded by trustees. Even before succeeding to the dukedom, George could gaily lose £30,000 in an afternoon at Doncaster Races; and although this was one of many debts that he refused to pay, he remained chronically and wretchedly in debt throughout his dukedom.

The early nineteenth century was a time when a duke could get away with almost anything, but there were limits, such as when he hoodwinked the Blenheim trustees by melting down the solid gold state dinner service, presented to the first Duke by the Elector of Bavaria, and having it replaced with a cheap pinchbeck replica. But no matter what he melted down, the desperate fifth Duke could never hope to pay his debts. According to one visitor to Blenheim in the 1820s, all the servants in the palace were in fact bailiffs, which didn't do much to cheer things up.

Bankrupt and deserted by his wife (who preferred a flat at Hampton Court to her husband's house), the fifth Duke of Marlborough, according to the *Annual Register,* ended up like his father, passing "the latter years of his life . . . in utter retirement at one corner of his magnificent palace; a melancholy instance of the results of extravagance."

The unhappy reign of the fifth Duke of Marlborough ended with his death in 1840. But the seventeen years in which his son, the sixth Duke, filled the great position were not much brighter. Money remained a chronic problem, since the Marlboroughs, for all the outward splendor of the house, lacked the sort of income from their fifteen thousand acres to rival the seriously rich Victorian grandees, and Blenheim and the dukedom were expensive to maintain. No coal was found beneath the Blenheim meadows, no rich London leases buttressed the future of the line, and none of these dukes netted himself an heiress.

Hardly surprising, the Marlborough women seem as gloomy as their gloomy spouses. Two of the sixth Duke's duchesses expired in swift succession in the palace, and the third, who long outlived him in her house in London, was not mentioned in his will.

The situation brightened with the appearance on the scene of Winston Churchill's paternal grandfather, John Winston Spencer-Churchill, who succeeded to the title as seventh Duke in 1857. He was very different from his predecessors—a firm-jawed, rather solid character; a dedicated Christian; and neither a spendthrift nor a rake. His biographer has called him "a full-blown Victorian prig," but at least he was not a victim of the family depression nor of the desire to insulate himself at Blenheim from the world outside. Quite the contrary.

In 1843, he had married the equally strong-willed Frances, daughter of Lord Londonderry, by whom he swiftly had six daughters and two sons. The new duchess's uncle had been the famous Lord Castlereagh, who, as British Foreign Secretary, had dominated European politics in the crucial period after the fall of Napoleon. Afflicted with bouts of melancholy—and rumored to have been blackmailed for homosexuality—Lord Castlereagh had cut his throat in 1821.

The Londonderrys were also close friends of Benjamin Disraeli and at the center of Tory high society and politics, having a pronounced streak of political ability themselves.

Thanks to Duchess Frances, Winston Churchill would have considerably more Castlereagh blood flowing in his veins than that of his proudly claimed but very distant kinsman, John, first Duke of Marlborough. And thanks to its new ducal family, Blenheim suddenly emerged from its century-long slumbers.

# three

# Two Brothers

"I cannot be grateful enough to God for all the goodness He has shown me," John Winston piously remarked at dinner to a visiting Oxford don shortly after succeeding to the dukedom in 1860. Looking around him at his well-fed family, his liveried servants, and his splendid dining room with its frescoes by Louis Laguerre, the Duke continued, "My position here is really, of its kind, quite perfect, and if only I keep well I am thoroughly satisfied."

The ducal satisfaction was forgivable. For a brief period after his accession it seemed as if John Winston's arrival on the scene had finally repulsed the furies preying on the Marlboroughs for a century and a half.

Britain was at the zenith of the great Victorian stability; there were as yet no death duties to encroach upon the dominant position of the landed interest. A duke enjoyed the prestige of a prince within society. Supported by Disraeli's friendship, the Duke of Marlborough's political career was flourishing, and he reached the Cabinet as Lord President of the Council in 1862. Most gratifying of all was the amity of Queen Victoria herself, for whom the Marlboroughs had become "my dearest, dearest friends."

Though still no pleasure dome, Blenheim had become the home of a large and tightly knit Victorian family—Charles, Lord Blandford (born 1844 and always addressed as "Blandford"), the ducal son and heir; Lord Randolph, his younger brother (born in 1849); and their six adoring sisters: Lady Cornelia, Lady Rosamund, Lady Fanny, Lady Anne, Lady Georgiana, and Lady Sarah. They gathered in the chapel each day for morning and evening prayers, and for a while it seemed as if God was listening and the curse of Blenheim had been lifted. Then came the rumblings of disaster, as if to tell John Winston that nothing could remain "quite perfect" even for a duke.

In 1861, his picture gallery ignited—on a truly ducal scale. The whole of John Duke's great collection of Rubenses and Titians went up in smoke before anyone could save them. This was a loss the Duke could bear; he and his wife had both doubted the propriety of many of the pictures, particularly Rubens's large canvas of the *Rape of Proserpine*. More worrying was the chronic lack of money that pursued the family, as the disasters of the 1870s hit the English landed classes.

Falling rents, long-term effects of the repeal of the Corn Laws (which allowed foreign grain to undercut the produce of the Duke's own broad acres), and a succession of appalling harvests in the 1870s all made the situation worse. The Lord Chief Justice, after dining at Blenheim, said he was "prepared to share almost anything in life, but drew the line at half a snipe for dinner."

Economy was in the air. Blenheim, John Duke's great white elephant, was consuming more than it provided, and the only answer was to strip the beast of its grandiose regalia. Thanks to the precedent of other noblemen hit by the troubles of their time, the Duke was able to do what none of his predecessors had managed. He broke the legal trust controlling the contents of his palace. The saleroom beckoned, and the rape of Blenheim started.

It would continue unabated after he was dead, although John Winston squandered the greatest splendors of the Churchill patrimony: the magnificent Blenheim library (known as the Sunderland Library, it was one of the finest private collections in the land, but fetched a paltry £28,000 at auction); the fabled Marlborough gems (including the famous Roman sardonyx intaglio portrait of the Emperor Hadrian's lover, Antinous); and a number of the first Duke's pictures that had been spared the fire of 1861.

Again the Duke's faith enabled him to bear these losses with equanimity. "Lay not up treasures on earth," the Bible said. But as with the Prophet Job, John Winston's faith would soon be tested by far worse afflictions. The bitterest would come from within the bosom of the Duke's own family, for both his sons were beginning to reveal disturbing aspects to their characters—particularly the future duke, Lord Blandford, who seemed to be reverting to the Spencer-Churchill type with a vengeance. Winston Churchill's wicked Uncle Charles was, like many villains, a fascinating character. (He became the eighth Duke of Marlborough in 1883 and would be remembered as the family's legendary "Bad Duke.") Expelled from Eton at sixteen, he drank, gambled, hunted, and womanized with such abandon that even worldly old Disraeli would dismiss him as "a thorough-going blackguard."

He was both irreligious and immoral, but he was the heir to the dukedom, and the future of Blenheim rested on his slim unworthy shoulders.

Blandford's one redeeming feature was his high intelligence. He was a self-taught scientist whose moldering laboratory could still be seen at Blenheim in the 1920s, and he seems to have possessed a touch of genius, wiring up the palace for electric light, building his own dynamos, and inventing an early form of telephone.

In 1869, he did make one concession to his parents' fears about the future. He agreed to marry, cynically accepting the first young woman they suggested, twenty-year-old Lady Albertha Hamilton, daughter of the Duke of Abercorn. Known to her intimates as "Goosey," Lady Albertha was not considered overbright, but she was an uncomplicated, cheerful girl with a reputation as a sport and something of a practical joker. The old Duke must have felt that, if anyone, she could cope with his unpleasant son. But he was wrong.

After the birth of the necessary son and heir in 1871 (the future ninth Duke, Churchill's cousin Sunny, who was christened Charles Richard John Spencer-Churchill), Lord Blandford paid Goosey scant attention, and continued his experiments in adultery and electricity.

Because of the Bad Duke's terrible behavior, his younger brother, Randolph, was guaranteed the role of favored son, and made the most of it. An unhealthy child—he almost died of glandular fever at the age of ten—he was doted on by the Duchess and pampered by his sisters.

Randolph followed his brother more successfully to Eton, and then went on to Oxford, where he enjoyed the social life and considerable privileges of a young aristocrat in the unreformed university. He dressed smartly, drank excessively, and sowed the customary upper-class wild oats. Although still "delicate," he too had a touch of wildness that would reappear at intervals throughout his life.

He, too, drank, broke windows, and pursued the women of the

town. "I don't like ladies at all," he said. "I like rough women who dance and sing and drink—the rougher the better."

Randolph was also known for his biting wit; like his brother, he possessed a quick, original intelligence and unusual powers of memory. One of his party tricks was to memorize at sight a page of his favorite author, Edward Gibbon, then parrot it verbatim to his friends. Thanks to his memory and powers of concentration, he pulled himself together in the weeks before examinations, taking a respectable degree in history and law. This was considered so extraordinary for the son of a duke that great things were predicted for Lord Randolph.

What those things were, no one, least of all Lord Randolph, was quite sure. It was unheard-of for a duke's son to pursue a commonplace career or to earn himself a living. He might have joined the church, the army, or gone into politics, but none appealed to him. So, after leaving Oxford, he traveled on the Continent, learned perfect French, entered smart society, got to know the Prince of Wales, and lived at Blenheim with nothing very much to do, an aristocratic second son afflicted by the English malady of primogeniture.

Randolph's nerves were bad, his health remained "uncertain," and since he, too, had inherited more than a fair share of the Marlborough melancholy, boredom made him subject to moods of black depression during which he kept apart from everybody, read French novels, and chain-smoked Turkish cigarettes "until his tongue was sore." He could exhibit charm and wit with those he liked, but could also turn to instant upper-class hauteur when bored or with those he did not know or disapproved of. Then, in August 1873, at a ball in honor of Nicholas, the son of Czar Alexander III of Russia, this difficult young nobleman met Jennie—or as she liked to style herself, "Jeanette" Jerome. He instantly fell in love and decided to marry her. Equally impulsive, she instantly agreed.

Back at Blenheim, the news brought consternation from the family and outright opposition from the Duke—on whom Lord Randolph was financially dependent.

Not that Lord Randolph allowed this to affect him in the least. Decision made, he stuck to it, as he invariably did whenever he decided anything. It was as if some instinct urged him on toward the ideal partner to correct the inherited deficiencies of his line.

# four

# The Jeromes

Photographs of Jennie and Lord Randolph around the time they met reveal a striking contrast between the two young lovers. A short, slender figure like his brother Blandford, Lord Randolph would always be a credit to his jeweler and his tailor. But at twenty-four, he was already looking old beyond his years. With thinning hair, large mustache, and the "poppy" Marlborough eyes, as Jennie called them, he had the air of one who lived too much by his nerves—and smoked too many Turkish cigarettes.

Twenty-year-old Miss Jerome could not have been more different. Firm-browed, doe-eyed, and ample-figured, she displayed more confidence and sensuality than ladylike refinement; hers was the sort of beauty that owed more to health and energy than to gentle breeding. Her mother, rich Mrs. Leonard Jerome, late of Brooklyn, New York, and Paris, France, had taken a small villa on the Isle of Wight for the summer season, and Jennie was staying there with two unmarried sisters, Clara, then aged twenty-two, and Leonie, who was seventeen. Since the girls were presentable and pretty, they had enjoyed considerable success, but the Jeromes were not the sort of people the Marlboroughs would normally consort with. Leonard Jerome, Jennie's father, who at the time was suspiciously absent in New York, was, as the worried Duke discovered, three things no proper gentleman should be: a self-made man, a financier, and an American.

"From what I have heard," John Winston wrote anxiously to his son, "this Mr. J. seems to be a sporting, and I should think vulgar kind of man. I hear he drives about six and eight horses in New York (one may take this as a kind of indication of what the man is)."

The Duke also made it clear that "under any circumstances, an American connection is not one that we would like." It would be a considerable "coming down in pride for us to contemplate." One thing, and one alone, might still permit the Duke to forget his pride: a fortune of such magnitude that even a Duke of Marlborough would welcome the "connection." But did this vulgar Mr. J. possess it?

Lord Randolph, who to his credit thought the subject more or less irrelevant, was not sure, and the Duke made businesslike inquiries that did little to reassure him. It appeared that this mysterious American was not as rich as Lord Randolph assumed.

True, he had been a millionaire on a number of occasions, but he had also lost vast sums of money. As for the family, they were really quite ordinary.

But Leonard Jerome was far from ordinary. Born in 1819, one of seven brothers from a farming family in Syracuse, New York, he had worked his way through Princeton, entered a firm of Wall Street brokers, and in the boom years of the 1840s made himself rich enough to spend two years—from 1851 to 1853—in Italy as American consul in Trieste. His young wife, Clara, and their infant daughter, also christened Clara, accompanied him.

His wife loved Europe, but Jerome was bored, and in 1853 he brought his family back to their simple red-brick house on Henry Street, Brooklyn, where Jennie was born in 1854. Jerome was determined to make a great fortune, which he did with extraordinary dispatch.

He was a handsome man whose nerves, like his physique, seemed made of steel (a quality his daughter inherited). He was a natural gambler, a still more natural self-promoter, and had the successful gambler's flair, which showed itself repeatedly in what he called "that Wall Street Jungle" of the 1850s. He pitted his wits and money in the roughest financial trade of all—the new railways and trusts of the rapidly expanding United States.

He needed nerve. In 1855, he lost everything he owned in the collapse of the Cleveland and Toledo Railway. But within a year, he had bounced back in association with the "robber baron" Commodore Cornelius Vanderbilt and the Rothschild representative in New York,

August Belmont. Riding the wave of massive speculation that was only briefly interrupted by the Civil War, Jerome had become one of the richest speculators on the Street.

It was now that the singularity of Leonard Jerome's character revealed itself. Unlike most Wall Street millionaires, he was an enjoyer as well as an acquirer, who believed that money should be spent, not saved, and before he inevitably came unstuck in 1869, he had disposed of a reputed $10 million with more style and enjoyment than any comparable millionaire on Wall Street.

He was a many-sided hedonist. A talented amateur musician, he had a habit of adopting opera singers as his mistresses. Some were melodically exceptional, and included the "Swedish nightingale," Jenny Lind (after whom he named his second daughter), and the formidable Adelina Patti. Minnie Hauk, the first home-grown American prima donna, was reputedly his natural child.

Moving from Brooklyn, in 1860 he built himself a mansion on the corner of 26th Street overlooking Madison Square, complete with stables and a private theater. By now he had made himself a genuine celebrity. He owned an oceangoing yacht, he fished for shark, he drove a four-in-hand, and laid out Jerome Park, New York's first racecourse. In association with the even richer August Belmont, he became a founding father of the American Turf by establishing the American Jockey Club. He also found the time and money to enjoy a summer house in newly fashionable Newport, Rhode Island, and to acquire a quarter share in the *New York Times,* in which he took an active interest.

Jerome managed to maintain a happy marriage—by the old American expedient of making sure his strong-willed wife was never short of cash and letting her do exactly as she wanted.

Clara Jerome, née Hall, who claimed both genuine Iroquois Indian blood and direct descent from a lieutenant in Washington's army, was a romantic snob who had never quite got over those two years in Trieste as Mrs. Consul-General. Having given birth to a third daughter, Leonie, in 1859, she decided New York society was not for her—or for her daughters—and again embarked for Europe, where she spent her happiest, most determined years.

Paris was the city that delighted her, for in Paris rich Americans could find a *douceur de la vie* that did not exist in brash New York. There were brand-new boulevards by Baron Haussmann, operas by Jacques Offenbach and Giacomo Meyerbeer, and the most fashionable dresses in the world by M. Worth. But best of all, Paris offered Mrs. Jerome what she really loved: an Emperor and Empress whose court was always open to rich foreigners.

By the 1860s, Napoleon III (son of the great Napoleon's brother, Louis, King of Holland) had established his gimcrack Second Empire, with its rebuilt Palace of the Tuileries and cheerfully absurd revival of the protocol and splendor of the Empire of Napoleon I. "I have found the Court I want," murmured Mrs. Jerome, hoping that, with proper finishing, all her daughters might marry into the French aristrocracy.

With a true snob's single-mindedness, she made sure that she and her girls were invited not only to Their Majesties' formal receptions at the Tuileries but also to the more intimate parties of the Empress—the so-called Little Mondays at the Palace of Compiègne. It was here that fashionable Paris watched His Majesty dispatch the hunted stag—and the "beautiful Americans" had their chance to make another sort of killing.

Meanwhile, in New York, Leonard Jerome was engaging in a lethal struggle of his own as the boom years of the sixties ended. By now his luck had turned for good. There was a simultaneous default on Indiana bonds and a failure in Georgia stock. And his greatest speculation, in Pacific Mail, was also on the point of failing. The final crash occurred in the financial panic of the early 1870s.

Jerome was giving a dinner party in New York when a telegram arrived. He read it in silence but not until the food was cleared did he speak of it to his guests. "Gentlemen," he began, "the bottom has fallen out of stocks and I am a ruined man. But your dinner is paid for and I did not want to disturb you while you were eating it."

He would henceforth be most grateful for the $2 million he had signed over to his wife, since they could live on it for the rest of their lives.

By a coincidence that would be of great importance to the future Winston Churchill, the golden years of Napoleon III and his Second Empire were also numbered. The hollowness of all that imperial splendor was revealed on the battlefields of Weisenberg and Metz, when the glittering French army was crushed by the greater one of Otto von Bismarck's Prussia. The mob sacked Paris, and the Emperor fled to England, closely followed by the beautiful Jeromes.

The image that persists of Mrs. Jerome, before she stepped aboard the final train to London, is of her watching the auction of His Majesty's belongings while the Tuileries were still in flames. Practical as ever, even in disaster, Mrs. Jerome purchased part of the Emperor's dinner service, then persuaded somebody to bring it back to her apartment in a wheelbarrow. She brought it to England with her and was using it on the Isle of Wight when her daughter met Lord Randolph during Cowes Week.

# five

# A Victorian Tragedy

Faced with Lord Randolph's powerful determination to marry fresh-faced Miss Jerome, everyone involved began to weaken. Mrs. Jerome felt the second son of an English duke a pallid substitute for the romantic French aristocrat she had dreamed of having as a son-in-law. But since the France she loved was gone for good, she bowed to the force of history. Leonard Jerome, who could deny his favorite daughter nothing, also bowed to the inevitable.

John Winston, recognizing the steely nature of his son's unfortunate resolve, early in 1873 suggested "putting the idea of marriage to the test of time." "If this time next year, you come and tell me that you are both of the same mind," he told his son, "we will receive Miss Jerome as a daughter. . . ."

A year is a long time when you're in love, and the effete Lord Randolph exhibited a startling degree of ruthlessness to get his way. Then there was some inelegant but effective haggling with the amiable Mr. Jerome on the subject of a dowry for his daughter. As an American, Jerome felt a husband should support his wife. Lord Randolph felt otherwise, and not for the first time an English aristocrat proved more than a financial match for a tough New York financier. Jennie was persuaded to put pressure on Papa; and after some huffing and puffing, Lord Randolph got the promise of a settlement of £50,000 for his future wife.

The groom-to-be also managed to exploit his father's political anxieties. For some time, John Winston had been counting on his son Lord Randolph (who, as the owner of a courtesy title, could enter the House of Commons) to take the local parliamentary seat at Woodstock, which the Marlboroughs liked to think they controlled. With an election in the offing—and a despised radical showing signs of winning— Lord Randolph pressed his father to accept an earlier date for his marriage. Otherwise, he made it clear, he would refuse to enter Parliament. The Duke was most upset at the thought of forfeiting the Marlborough interest to a radical, and he agreed. Lord Randolph won by a small majority, and the marriage was allowed to proceed.

The wedding took place in the British embassy in Paris on April 15, 1874, with all the signs of a somewhat hushed and rushed affair. There was none of the splendor that an international society wedding of such wealth and standing would normally receive, no public ceremony, and little mention in the press. The Duke and Duchess were conspicuously absent.

It was typical of the bride not to have let this faze her in the least —and of her father to have made the best of things. She had a mountainous trousseau—"twenty-three French-made dresses, seven Paris bonnets, piles of delicately embroidered white underline"—and held a splendid dinner for the guests the night before the wedding. Unlike the groom's parents, the Prince of Wales's secretary, Francis Knollys, found time to attend and acted as Lord Randolph's best man and personal representative of His Royal Highness. Jennie drove to the embassy from the family apartment on the Boulevard Malsherbes in resplendent style. Her white satin wedding dress, with white malmaisons at her breast, was trimmed with Alençon lace and had several yards of billowing train. A "simple" veil of tulle covered her from head to toe, and she wore her father's wedding gift, a rope of unadorned but perfect pearls. If the Marlboroughs sent her anything it was not recorded.

Was she already pregnant? Piety says no, but the evidence suggests she might have been. Why else the rush, the discreet ceremony, and the pointed absence of the Marlboroughs—followed by a notably uncomplicated birth seven months later, of the lusty baby who was christened Winston. At the time the premature birth was accounted for by Jennie's falling while out shooting, followed by "a rather imprudent and rough drive in a pony carriage," which apparently brought on the pains of labor. A small downstairs room at Blenheim was improvised for the confinement. It would have been in character for both participants not to have allowed mere chaperones or dull convention to impede passion—and it would certainly explain much of what happened later.

Although they clearly disapproved of Jennie from the start, Lord Randolph's family maintained appearances and tried to make the best of things, but they never reconciled themselves to this fast American, nor she to them.

Lord Randolph was intensely proud of Blenheim.

"The finest view in England!" he cried out to Jennie as their carriage, pulled by loyal servants all the way from Woodstock Station, brought the honeymooners in sight of the palace. But Jennie never liked it. As good as his word, the honest Duke did his best to show Jennie the affection he had promised—not so the others. The Duchess, who would always worship Randolph, could not forgive this brazen daughter-in-law for displacing her in his affections. Her six daughters found Jennie almost everything they were not—pretty, highly talented (she was a fine pianist and spoke excellent French and German), and, thanks to her trousseau, dressed in the height of Paris fashion.

Jennie, in return, found her sisters-in-law—and Blenheim—desperately dull.

"The fact is, she complained later to her mother after a few weeks at Blenheim, "I *loathe* living here . . . and the Duchess simply hates me for what I am."

Not that she needed to endure such tedium and disapproval long. The Duke had decently paid Lord Randolph's debts, and given him £1,200 on top of the annual £3,000 he was drawing in interest on Jennie's marriage settlement. He had his seat in Parliament, his friends among the cream of metropolitan society, and now that he was married, the Duke offered him the lease on a house he owned in Mayfair.

During the first years in London, the marriage was a happy one. Baby Winston was entrusted to one of the most beloved women in his life—his widowed nanny, forty-one-year-old Mrs. Everest. Describing his parents at this period, he would later write that "with very little money on either side . . . they could only live in the smallest way possible to people in London society." But this did nothing to prevent this "poor but honest" pair from making a considerable splash in fast fashionable society—particularly the part that centered on Lord Randolph's friend, His Royal Highness, Albert Edward, Prince of Wales.

With her quick wit and cosmopolitan good looks, Jennie was

very much the sort of fashionable young matron to appeal to the Prince. But no one knows how far their friendship went. Certainly within a year of marriage there were signs of a cooling off in Lord Randolph's ardor—and one theory of his behavior a year later ascribes it to jealous anger at the Prince. Events came to a head in early 1876.

The overt cause of what occurred was the honor of that most dishonorable man—Randolph's brother Blandford. Between electrical experiments, Blandford had been conducting one of his affairs with dark-haired and passionate Lady Aylesford, mother of three young daughters and the much put-upon wife of Lord "Sporting Joe" Aylesford, crony of the Prince of Wales.

Sporting Joe had been in India tiger-shooting with the Prince when he got wind of what was happening at home. Hurrying back, and finding his wife already bearing Blandford's child, he threatened divorce proceedings, citing Blandford. The Prince, though still in India, supported him, suggesting Blandford should divorce his unfortunate Albertha and do the proper thing by Lady Aylesford.

Lord Randolph angrily became involved. It seems that Blandford had not been the first to cuckold Sporting Joe. Joe's friend the Prince of Wales had been there before him—and had written the lady highly compromising letters, which she had passed to Blandford, who showed them to his brother. Lord Randolph decided to use the letters to persuade the Prince to stop supporting the aggrieved Lord Aylesford. He warned the Prince that should he continue to agitate against Lord Blandford, the letters he had written Lady Aylesford would be given to the press. He even tried a personal appeal to the Princess of Wales, who seems not to have understood what he was talking about.

This attempt to involve his wife particularly aroused Prince Albert Edward's wrath and he challenged Lord Randolph to a duel in Amsterdam. Lord Randolph answered that he would not think of fighting with his future king, but would willingly take on a substitute.

At this point, the Prince's friends decided to intervene to stop what threatened to become a full-scale scandal. The Queen was informed, the Cabinet involved, and Lord Hartington (the future Duke of Devonshire, the discreetest man in English politics) finally made Lord Randolph see a little sense. The Prince's letters to Lady Aylesford were burned, and Blandford was not compelled to marry her. The whole unfortunate affair was more or less hushed up.

Lady Aylesford's life, of course, was ruined. A hearing before a House of Lords Committee proclaimed her son by Blandford illegitimate, and therefore incapable of succeeding to the Aylesford title. Blandford had nothing more to do with her—although she weakly permitted him to adopt their son. (Known as Guy Spencer-Churchill, he would live on at Blenheim until his death in 1923, the shadowiest of skeletons in the capacious ducal cupboard. Lady Aylesford lived out her days in Farnham Royal, short of money, deserted by her family, and never ceasing to regret the whole affair.)

Blandford, sterling villain that he was, was the one person not to be affected by the trouble he had caused. For the rest of the family the repercussions were far from over.

John Winston, deeply embarrassed over all the trouble his sons had caused the heir apparent, felt it best to leave the country for a period. (Disraeli, with his customary tact, arranged for the Duke to be appointed Viceroy of Ireland.) It was an expense the Duke could ill afford—a minimum of £20,000 a year apart from the inconvenience of closing Blenheim and transporting all the silver, plate, and servants off to Dublin Castle. But it meant that Lord Randolph, who was appointed his father's secretary, would also have a spell away from the scene of his disgrace.

The Prince of Wales, despite his fat man's geniality, could be implacable with any who offended him, and his former friend, Lord Randolph, had offended heinously. Not for nothing was the Prince the head of smart society. His ban announced, it was as if the pope had spoken. The doors of every fashionable house in London were closed to Lord Randolph and his wife. As Winston Churchill put it when he came to write his father's biography: "Powerful enemies were anxious to humiliate him. His own sensitiveness and pride magnified every coldness into an affront. London became odious to him." One wonders what "sensitive" Lord Randolph had expected. Like many of his family, he had a self-destructive streak that often made him heedless of the consequences of his acts.

There is no evidence that his father ever reproached him for the trouble he had caused. For another well-developed quality among the Churchills was an unusual sense of family loyalty, and Lord Randolph's actions could be seen as a misguided effort to protect the honor of the family.

Once in Ireland, where the Prince's ban could hardly affect them, the Randolph Churchills did not repine for long. During the Irish famine of 1877, they worked closely with the Duchess's relief fund, visiting the most afflicted parts of the country and witnessing the poverty and suffering firsthand. While Lord Randolph started to enjoy the company and conversation of Irish politicians, Jennie found other diversions.

Like her father, she was a natural rider and, fashionable as ever, soon became one of the most outstanding fox-hunting females in the country. Jennie was very much her father's daughter. In this period, she enjoyed a succession of admirers who would ride with her to hounds—such men as handsome Colonel Forster, her father-in-law's Master of Horse; the womanizing "Star" Boscowen, Viscount Falmouth, who was the Duke's assistant military secretary; and young Lord d'Abernon, whose memories reveal something of the effect she made on her admirers: "a dark, lithe figure . . . a diamond star in her hair, her favourite ornament, its lustre dimmed by the flashing glory of her eyes. More of the panther than of the woman in her look, but with a cultivation unknown in the jungle." Clearly Jennie was already a dedicated flirt, and it has often been suggested that her husband was not the father of the second son which she presented to Lord Randolph in 1880. That honor has been credited to the child's godfather, Colonel John Strange Jocelyn, who became fifth Earl of Roden shortly after, and gave the infant both his own Christian names when he was christened John Strange Spencer Churchill.

Paternity is always more or less unprovable, but despite the rumors, Colonel Jocelyn's role as father to Winston Churchill's younger brother seems improbable. Few seducers, having done the deed, would then publicly bestow both their names—and one of them such a reccognizable one—on the result. And Jennie's notably unstuffy great niece, Anita Leslie, who investigated the Jocelyn story at length, was firmly unconvinced by it. As granddaughter of Jennie's closest confidante, her sister Leonie, Anita knew much of the secret history of the family but had heard nothing of the doings of the fifth Lord Roden. What she did discover was that Colonel Jocelyn, as he was at the time when Jennie's second child was conceived, was in fact a straitlaced, Crimean veteran in late middle age who was firmly domiciled in England. It was as a friend of his near contemporary, the Duke of Marlborough, that he had been invited to stand godfather to the Duke's latest grandson, and it is hard to credit Jennie having taken someone like the aging colonel as her lover.

However, the birth of this second child did mark a most decisive change within the Churchill marriage. Shortly after, the seventh Duke's Irish exile ended, and he gratefully returned to Blenheim. The Randolph Churchills with their two young children also returned to London, with a house in fashionable St. James's Place—and it was now that Lord Randolph's political career began in earnest.

His unimpressive maiden speech in Parliament ("the speech of a foolish young man who will never come to any good" was the verdict of the influential Master of Balliol, Benjamin Jowett) gave not the slightest hint of what was soon to come. In the 1880 general election, the Conservatives were resoundingly defeated by the Liberals, and Disraeli was old and ailing. In the midst of this somewhat sorry scene, Lord Randolph saw his chance—and took it.

His was in many ways a strange ascent, for he was the odd man out in politics—erratic, often ill, scornful of his elders. But in time he vaulted from political obscurity to the position of one of the most famous—and notorious—politicians in the country. One theory has it that he was driven by the bitterness he felt against society for the treatment he received during the Aylesford affair. He was certainly ruthless—and often very funny, as he lampooned his many enemies in the political establishment, flailing his arms to make a point, jumping with anger on an official paper in the Chamber, and showing an unerring instinct for aiming at the jugular.

He was a natural showman, riding a bicycle across the terrace of the House of Commons or wearing extraordinary shoes in a debate. There was something of the guttersnipe about him, and something of the music hall performer. Known as "the Yahoo" and "Cheeky Randy," he had an instinct for publicity and reveled in it. His advent on the scene of the gentlemanly world of Victorian politics marked the introduction of a new species: the upper-class demagogue, the great political celebrity with the common touch.

Paying immense attention to the details of his dress and the delivery of his speeches, he rapidly became a star performer in Parliament, and still more on his speaking tours through the country, where mass audiences reveled in his witty repartee and fiery invective.

"Give it 'em hot and strong, Randy!" his audiences shouted—and he did. For an important part of his appeal—and his strength—was that he could wound. Drawing on some underlying source of bitterness and anger, he had discovered in the political situation of his day the perfect outlet for his remarkable but uncomfortable talents.

"I have tried all forms of excitement," he explained, "from tip-cat to tiger-shooting; all degrees of gambling from beggar-my-neighbour to Monte Carlo; but have found no gambling like politics, and no excitement like a big division."

Swiftly exploiting any situation, changing opinion as it suited him, and mocking the worn-out policies and leadership of his fellow Tories, he founded the so-called Fourth Party of Tory dissidents, free-booting critics of the government who were soon the liveliest and most effective element within the opposition.

With political success came Lord Randolph's restoration to the London scene. Relations were patched up, then totally restored with his former friend, the Prince of Wales, and it was now that the Randolph Churchills' marriage changed abruptly. Once in the fast set around the Prince of Wales, both were soon living highly liberated lives, but their love affairs posed no threat to their marriage. It was a period when divorce was inadmissible in smart society, and with the ambitious political and social life they were pursuing, Jennie and her husband were as important to each other as they had ever been and understood each other perfectly. She could provide this highly nervous, moody man with what he needed—an elegant and well-run home in London where he could work and receive his friends and allies. He could give this extroverted, dynamic woman what she wanted in return—a position of influence and status in society.

As for their private lives, they were sophisticated enough to face reality. When not traveling abroad with friends, as he often was, Lord Randolph's energies and emotions were absorbed in that "great game" —politics. Jennie had her freedom but was always careful that her friends and lovers followed the rules dictated by her situation. There must be no scandal, nothing to arouse the press or Lord Randolph's quick irascibility.

There were many ways in which a clever and attractive woman could assist a husband with her love affairs. The Prince of Wales had always been a great admirer—and Jenny certainly played a role in helping him forget that silly business with the Aylesfords.

She could also enslave financiers—for example, Baron Hirsch and Ernest Cassel—or rising politicians—such as pompous but besotted young Lord Curzon or languid, handsome Arthur Balfour. George Moore, the novelist, who called her "Black Jane," claimed to know the names of two hundred of her lovers. But Moore was Irish and a great exaggerator.

Sex and politics tend to go together, and Jennie was that particular American phenomenon, the politically ambitious married woman who is equally at ease with either. But her underlying interest was power and money. She was a lion hunter and a snob, but she was not a fool. She talked well, knew exactly what she wanted, and her preferred dinner guests were not necessarily her lovers. One such was that great receptacle of rectitude, her husband's chief and the future Conservative Prime Minister, Lord Salisbury. Another was the man for whom Lord Randolph showed consistent and outrageous enmity in debate, that "Old Man in a Hurry" as he called him, William Ewart Gladstone.

"Dear Lady Randolph," that urbane old gentleman remarked one evening after enduring a torrential drubbing from an enraged Lord Randolph in the Commons, "I do trust that dear Lord Randolph is not wearied by his *splendid* effort in the House this afternoon."

In fact, he often was—and one of Jennie's most important roles was to sustain him through his frequent periods of despondency and physical relapse. There was a particularly bad one in the summer of 1883 when for four months Lord Randolph was completely out of action with some mysterious malady. Jennie loyally supported him and served as his information service and constant source of sound advice. On one occasion, she even delivered his election speech to the electorate at Woodstock.

Jennie was also a driving force in the Primrose League, the important nationwide campaign group her husband founded to channel social and political support for the Conservatives throughout the country. For another sign of Lord Randolph's political awareness was that he sensed, as had his parents' friend Disraeli before him, the Conservatives' all-important need to attract the apparently unlikely vote of that growing and imponderable new force in politics, the working class.

With his natural arrogance, his studied dress, the privilege and glitter of his very ducal way of life, no one was more the quintessential Victorian aristocrat than Lord Randolph, and many of his most polished insults were snobbishly directed at the members of the rising middle class among the Liberals. As a nobleman, he genuinely despised the middle class, those smug inhabitants of suburban "pineries and vineries," as he called them. But he also had that invaluable alter ego of "Cheeky Randy," the hero of the public meeting and the great political performer for the common people.

Like many aristocrats, he sentimentalized the lower orders, and believed that with his common touch, he could create a union of interest between the highest and lowest in the land. "The aristocracy and the working class are united in the indissoluble bonds of a common immorality," was one of his theories, and he invented something new in politics that he airily entitled "Tory Democracy." Like most of his policies, it was never very clear exactly what it was, beyond his own brisk definition: "Tory democracy is democracy which supports the Tories."

However vague, Tory Democracy was an invaluable slogan, just as the Primrose League had now become a source of real influence throughout the country. Lord Randolph was beginning to emerge from the exuberance of opposition toward the settled aim of politics—power. Within five years of his return from Ireland, he had made himself what his son Winston would proudly call "a great elemental force in British politics." He was barely thirty-five when Gladstone's Liberal government proposed Home Rule for Ireland, and largely thanks to Lord Randolph's powerful attacks, the measure was decisively defeated by the Conservatives in the election of 1885. (This despite the fact that characteristically Lord Randolph himself had previously seemed to support some form of Irish Home Rule.)

When the Queen asked Lord Salisbury to form a new government in 1885, the time had come for Lord Randolph to enter into his political inheritance. He began with a typical show of resolution. Appointed Secretary of State for India, he gained an instant place in history by swiftly annexing the troubled state of Burma to the British Crown.

Then, after fresh elections in July 1886, Lord Randolph found himself almost at the top of what Disraeli called "the greasy pole of politics," when Salisbury made him Chancellor of the Exchequer and Leader of the Commons in this new administration.

It had been a meteoric rise. Despite uncertain health, past disgrace, countless enemies, a maverick reputation, and innumerable changes of direction, Randolph had made himself, at thirty-six, the youngest Chancellor of the Exchequer since William Pitt—and an inevitable candidate for premiership.

"There is only one place, that is the prime minister. I like to be the boss," he was to tell his friend Lord Rosebery.

Unlike Salisbury, who was nine years older and seated in that far less potent assembly, the House of Lords, Lord Randolph had his power base in the country and within the House of Commons. He was passionately ambitious, a surprisingly good administrator as well as an orator, and the only man his party had who was a match for Gladstone. Now that he had the chancellorship, all he needed was a little patience to achieve the greatest prize of all.

Inexplicably, patience seemed to be the one thing Lord Randolph suddenly lacked. Shrewd old Queen Victoria, who had known him all his life, had serious doubts about his appointment from the start: "he is so mad and odd and also he has bad health," she noted ominously in her diary. Not long after, in the months of victory late in 1886, Lord Randolph suddenly began to put at risk everything he and Jennie had worked and fought together to achieve.

He did not consult her, but for reasons of his own seemed set upon a test of strength with Salisbury. Several times that autumn he threatened to resign to get his way within the Cabinet. On each occasion he was mollified. Salisbury was a slow, strong, careful politician, and the last thing he wanted was a split within his government. But there was a limit to Lord Salisbury's patience, and in December 1886, Lord Randolph, hell-bent, it seemed, on self-destruction, overstepped it.

As with the Aylesford affair, it seemed another of Lord Randolph's acts of lunacy. Choosing an absurdly minor matter on which to stake his whole career, he suddenly objected to a War Office request to the Treasury of an additional £560,000 for the army, and delivered one more ultimatum to Lord Salisbury. His Lordship failed to support him, and on December 20, after dining with the Queen at Windsor Castle, Lord Randolph wrote Lord Salisbury his famous letter of resignation, which Lord Salisbury calmly accepted.

According to Lord Randolph's muddled explanation, he had been hoping that Salisbury would again agree to his demands. But everything he did had made this quite impossible. He may have thought that Salisbury would destroy himself by accepting the resignation of so powerful a fellow politician. If so, Lord Randolph blundered.

Aside from ensuring that his resignation letter was published in the *Times,* Lord Randolph had neglected to inform Her Majesty of his intentions, and the Queen was most offended. "The want of respect shown to me and to his colleagues have added to the bad effect which it produced," she wrote.

He even failed to inform Jennie, who learned of his decision from the *Times.* In her memoirs, she described the scene that followed.

"When I came down to breakfast, the fatal paper in my hand, I found him calm and smiling. 'Quite a surprise for you,' he said. He went into no explanation, and I felt too utterly crushed and miserable to ask for any, or even to remonstrate.

"Mr. Moore (his secretary at the Treasury), who was devoted to Randolph, rushed in, pale and anxious, and with a faltering voice said to me, 'He has thrown himself from the top of the ladder and will never reach it again!'

"Alas! he proved too true a prophet," Jennie added, but it was worse than that. The true tragedy of Lord Randolph Churchill's life was only just beginning. He was thirty-seven and still had nine tormented years to live, haunted by a sense of failure, shunned by the former colleagues who had hailed him, yet painfully intent on picking up the power he had squandered.

# six

# Family Troubles

There are conflicting opinions within the Churchill family as to the nature of the illness that began afflicting Lord Randolph in his mid-thirties and resulted in his death at the age of forty-six.

The whole distressing subject was totally ignored in his grandson Randolph's early volume of the official biography of Sir Winston Churchill. And another grandson, Winston's nephew Peregrine Churchill, Jack's son, maintains that Lord Randolph's troubles stemmed essentially from excessive medication (principally digitalis and belladonna, prescribed for nervous stress) on a constitution already weakened by the ravages of childhood glandular fever.

But other members of the family accept that Lord Randolph was in fact suffering from syphilis. His granddaughter Mary Churchill Soames, Winston's daughter, stated this unequivocally in her fascinating *Churchill Family Album,* remarking later that this was part of the received wisdom of the family. Winston himself undoubtedly believed this, too. (Among other sources, Lord Lambton told the author that as a young Member of Parliament, he clearly remembers Churchill refer quite openly to his father's syphilis in conversation. The author similarly recalls hearing Randolph speak of "my grandfather's distressing malady.")

It is, of course, impossible to prove conclusively that somebody who died in 1895 was suffering from a particular disease. It has been suggested also that Lord Randolph was afflicted with a brain tumor. (Medically this seems unlikely. The symptoms fail to match the case; his doctors never mentioned a tumor as a possibility, and a tumor would probably have killed him earlier.)

What is incontestable is that from around his mid-thirties, Lord Randolph was exhibiting symptoms suggesting the onset of an attack of secondary syphilis. He almost certainly believed that he was suffering from it, and those closest to him believed this too, going to considerable lengths to hide this desperate and shameful situation.

Despite the inevitable conspiracy of silence around his illness, there have been accounts of how Lord Randolph actually contracted what, in the days before antibiotics, amounted to a sentence of a slow, humiliating death. The most colorful—if not the most reliable—comes from the author and one-time editor of the influential *Fortnightly Magazine,* Frank Harris, who was not the most trustworthy of sources. But Harris had known both Lord Randolph and his son Winston well. He was to act as Winston's unofficial literary agent for a period, and since the story he included in his book *My Life and Loves* came originally from Louis Jennings, one of Lord Randolph's closest Oxford friends, political associates, and his literary executor, it is worth repeating.

According to Jennings, Lord Randolph got drunk one night at an undergraduate party at Oxford and woke the next morning in a filthy lodging house to find an old woman lying in the bed beside him. "She had one long yellow tooth in her top jaw that waggled as she spoke. Speechless with horror, I put my hand in my pocket, and threw all the money I had loose on the bed. I could not say a word. She was still smiling at me; I put on my waistcoat and coat and fled the room. 'Lovie, you're not kind!' I heard her say as I closed the door after me. Downstairs I fled in livid terror."

Afterwards Lord Randolph, terrified of having contracted syphilis, was treated by an Oxford doctor and was finally assured that he was safe. He may not have been, and an Oxford prostitute may have been the source of Lord Randolph's later troubles.

A more likely source, however, is that suggested by Jennie's greatniece, her sister Leonie Leslie's granddaughter, Anita. Drawing on family knowledge, she insists Lord Randolph contracted the disease not at Oxford but from a mistress he was keeping in Paris in the early 1880s.

Again, this is unprovable—and ultimately immaterial. In its nonulcerous phase, syphilis is not infectious, and is not passed on to the mother or the child through semen. So even if Lord Randolph did contract it before his marriage, there was no particular danger to his wife and sons. In all likelihood, Lord Randolph would have regarded the disease for what it was, a youthful indiscretion, and have dismissed it from his mind, genuinely believing he was cured.

But syphilis can be a time bomb of appalling consequences. Until antibiotic drugs, there was no certain way of destroying the bacillus in the blood. After years of trouble-free remission, the microbes begin a slow attack upon the central nervous system and the brain. Once this starts there is no known cure, and no escape from a slow and terrible decline that often ends with madness as the sufferer falls victim to GPI —general paralysis of the insane—the condition Lord Randolph was to die of.

From the early 1880s, he was already being treated by a Dr. Robson Roose, an expert in neurological disorders and author of a popular book entitled *Waste and Repair in Modern Life*.

Lord Randolph must have been a textbook case for Dr. Roose to study, for, to begin with, all his symptoms—sleeplessness, chronic irritability, and bouts of lethargy and deep depression—could be medically ascribed to the patient's nervous disposition and the grueling pace at which he lived his life.

But by 1885, the year Lord Randolph first entered Salisbury's government, it would seem that Dr. Roose was having his suspicions that his famous patient could be suffering from something more serious. It was then he first called in the famous London specialist in nervous diseases, Dr. Thomas Buzzard, who would care for Lord Randolph in the later stages of his illness.

There is no record of Dr. Buzzard's diagnosis, but the patient's state of health must have been causing serious concern for a doctor as eminent as Roose to bring in a specialist like Buzzard. Much of Lord Randolph's behavior at this crucial period in his career was clearly giving rise to grave anxiety.

Queen Victoria was not the only one to be worrying about his health and state of mind: so were Jennie and his mother. He was increasingly obsessional and irascible in his judgments, and suspicious of his friends. By now he was taking large amounts of digitalis as a sedative, and suffering attacks of dizziness and insomnia. The strain of late-night parliamentary sittings was becoming intolerable for this man of only thirty-five.

Lord Randolph was an educated man. His knowledge of French literature, if of nothing else, would have made him all too well aware of the dire fate syphilitic madness had brought to such writers as Verlaine, Maupassant, and Jules Goncourt. He must have known Dr. Buzzard's medical specialty; he was not the sort of man doctors lie to.

All the evidence suggests that by the summer of 1886, when he was appointed Chancellor of the Exchequer and seemed to have the highest post in government within his grasp, Lord Randolph also knew exactly what was wrong with him. His faculties were threatened. Time was running out, as his friend, Lord Rosebery must have realized.

"How long will your leadership last?" he asked him.

"Oh, about six months," Lord Randolph answered with uncanny accuracy.

"And then?"

"Why, Westminster Abbey," he replied.

There was a certain irony to his situation now: At the very moment when prodigious effort had been crowned with extraordinary success, everything was starting to collapse around him. He was heavily in debt. He and Jennie had been living increasingly above their means, having moved from St. James's to a larger establishment in Connaught Place, where they entertained in style. Lord Randolph had another house at Newmarket where, as a racehorse owner, he gambled heavily and, after some spectacular successes, lost everything. He lost still more dramatically at another of his expensive pastimes—baccarat, which he indulged in during frequent trips to Monte Carlo. He fared no better with financial speculations; his debts with the Rothschilds reached £11,000 by the beginning of the 1890s.

Simultaneously, there was an unexplained drama in his marriage, giving rise to exaggerated rumors about his private life. That October, when his battle with Salisbury in the Cabinet was intensifying, he departed hurriedly on a mysterious trip to the capitals of Europe with his friend Tom Trafford. Although he used the pseudonym "Mr. Spencer," he deceived nobody, and his every move was reported in the press. Further gossip followed. His mother suspected an affair with another woman, probably the notorious Lady Warwick, the mistress of the Prince of Wales.

This seems unlikely, and Lord Randolph's hurried journey remains unexplained. What is clear, however, is that he was going through some sort of crisis in the autumn of 1886. The responsibility for holding the family together fell on Jennie and the Duchess's attitude toward her daughter-in-law changed abruptly. Ancient animosity for-gotten, the jealous Duchess suddenly became her confidante and friend. She begged Jennie to be "patient" with Lord Randolph. She told her to forget her "jealousy" and bid farewell to her life of "flirting, gambling and fast friends." Above all, the Duchess urged her to be "responsible and wise" and to try to save her marriage.

Jennie must have done as she was told, for the marriage did not break. But her husband was in a highly nervous state, and she was powerless to prevent his resignation that December.

One explanation for his action is that he had simply had enough of politics: He was tired and sick, and when he tendered his resignation he had realized its irrevocability.

This is possible but unlikely. Lord Randolph's life was centered entirely around politics; he was intensely ambitious and had nearly reached the top. Also, after his resignation he remained in Parliament, making serious efforts to reenter Salisbury's government.

A more likely explanation is that Lord Randolph's resignation was actually a bungled bid for power, an attempt to precipitate a crisis that he hoped he could win. He had always had that great ambition for the "boss man's" role, and in a test of strength with Lord Salisbury, he still possessed a number of distinct advantages.

Lord Salisbury was in the House of Lords; Lord Randolph's power base was in the more crucial assembly, the House of Commons. Lord Salisbury lacked Lord Randolph's formidable charisma—and at this point still needed to establish full control of the Conservative party throughout the country. Lord Randolph, with the fame of his public meetings and the Primrose League behind him, was a formidable op-ponent.

With his advancing illness, Lord Randolph might have believed this to have been his only chance of rallying his supporters, toppling Lord Salisbury, and reaching that longed-for goal of Prime Minister.

It was a forlorn venture, and as a gambling man, Lord Randolph must have known the price of failure. But only when Lord Salisbury failed to topple—or even quiver on his perch—did the full extent of Lord Randolph's blunder become apparent.

His debts were mounting, and the loss of his ministerial salary of £5,000 a year made the situation worse. His party turned against him, as political parties always do to a loser, and he was bitterly attacked for his disloyalty.

This left Lord Randolph lying in a darkened room, smoking more

Turkish cigarettes than ever and muttering of comeback and revenge. Rumors of the breakup of his marriage began to reach the press. The *New York Sun* carried details of the Randolph Churchill's separation. Lord Randolph reacted angrily—and the shipwreck of his life began in earnest.

Randolph's eldest son, twelve-year-old Winston, was at boarding school at Brighton when his father's resignation was announced, and he took it badly. He was an emotional small boy, passionate and possessive, and he had been intensely proud of his father's rise to fame. Only recently, he had proudly noticed how strangers took off their hats when Lord Randolph passed, and had heard grown-ups speak of him as "Gladstones' great adversary."

Now, all that had changed abruptly. Something of the effect this had on Winston is revealed in a letter from Jennie to her husband early in 1887: "Winston was taken to a pantomime at Brighton where they hissed a sketch of you. He burst into tears—and then turned furiously on the man who was hissing behind him—and said, 'Stop that noise you snub-nosed radical!' "

Winston had been an uncontrollable, aggressive child, who at nine had already had to be removed from his first school, St. George's Ascot, for his bad behavior. The future novelist Maurice Baring, arriving at St. George's shortly afterwards, heard "dreadful legends" being told about him. "His naughtiness appeared to have surpassed anything. He had been flogged for taking sugar from the pantry, and so far from being penitent, had taken the Headmaster's sacred straw hat from where it hung over the door and kicked it to pieces. His sojourn at the school had been one long feud with authority. The boys did not seem to sympathise with him," he said.

He continued to misbehave at Brighton. "The naughtiest little boy in the world," one of his female teachers at Brighton called him. Where his brother, Jack, was easy and affectionate, Winston was very much the opposite, as first sons who are jealous of more popular younger brothers often are.

It has been suggested that he was showing all the symptoms of a child neglected by his parents, and the blame is frequently placed on the flighty, never-present figure of his mother. This is almost certainly unfair to Jennie.

By upper-class standards of the day, Winston had been treated rather well, and until he went to St. George's, he had enjoyed unusually close contact with his parents and relations. He also had the absolute devotion of an extraordinary woman—his nanny, the indomitable Mrs. Everest. "Woomie," as he called her (short for "Woman"), was a sterling character. Self-educated, intelligent, warm, and wise, Mrs. Everest mothered Winston and Jack obsessively, and even when they went away to boarding school, she was always urging Jack and "dearest Winnie" to be sure to change their socks, repeat their prayers, and eat their vegetables.

Stout Mrs. Everest was clearly the ideal mother-surrogate. But there is also evidence that far from being starved of Jennie's affection and attention, Winston's childhood owed much to his mother's presence. Some of this evidence is contained in a small appointment diary Jennie kept for the first half of 1882, when her London social life was at its height.

Throughout this period, Jennie was involved in a passionate love affair. She also had an ailing husband and an energetic social life. But the most frequent references in her diary are to seven-year-old Winston.

"Gave Winston his lessons. . . . Winston rather ill. Thought he was going to have croup." And on February 24 comes a fascinating reference for the future: "Took Winston and had tea with Blanche Hozier in her lodgings."

The headstrong Lady Blanche Hozier, daughter of the Earl of Airlie, was one of Jennie's closest friends. They had much in common. Both were fashionable beauties, both were uncomfortably married, and both were unfaithful to their husbands.

Hozier was unhealthy, irascible, and old, and Lady Blanche was currently involved with one of Jennie's former hunting friends from Ireland, a passionate pursuer of both fox and female named Bay Middleton.

By a coincidence, Jennie had also just begun the most romantic of her various liaisons, this with another great Victorian equestrian, Lord Randolph's friend, the handsome and elegant Hungarian Count Charles Rudolph Ferdinand Andreas Kinsky. Unlike Lord Randolph, Kinsky was a man of great physical strength and easy charm, and he became the hero of London society by winning the Grand National in 1886. The combination of horsemanship, European title, and great high spirits made the Count irresistible to Jennie, and their love affair became the great obsession of their lives. But as always, Jennie had her family and her position in society to consider. Her diary gives only the most guarded references to Count Kinsky.

During his childhood, Winston also had a close relationship with his father. Lord Randolph's illness must have hindered this at times and like any dedicated politician he was frequently away from home and often distracted. But this did not prevent him from taking Winston to France and Germany for holidays. On one occasion he took him to Barnum's Circus (where the concerned father refused to let him see the terrifying "Boneless Wonder," believing "the spectacle would be too revolting and demoralizing to my youthful eyes"). Later, knowing how much Winston loved tales of adventure, Lord Randolph introduced him to his friend, the famous writer Bram Stoker, future author of *Dracula*.

All these happy times ended for Winston with his father's resignation and the family troubles that ensued. His idol had collapsed, and from then on everything began to change within the family—including his father's previous concern for him. Distracted and increasingly withdrawn, Lord Randolph was already turning from his family. "You never came to see me on Sunday when you were in Brighton," Winston wrote to him accusingly just before his father's resignation.

During the months that followed, Winston's childhood ended. He was having to work hard for the examinations for Harrow school, which he would enter the following September—and simultaneously accept the loss of all that high ambition he had shared with his father.

Instead of the hero of the hour, set to become the most powerful man in Britain, Lord Randolph was increasingly seen as a failure—unpopular and sick, rejected by his party, and dependent on his strong-willed but unfaithful wife.

More than ever, Lord Randolph would be traveling abroad, but never again with Winston. Early that spring he was off to Russia, accompanied by Jennie; more and longer trips would follow in the wretched years ahead—to India, to southern Africa, and to the East. In travel he found distraction and relief, while back at home was little but disaster.

He was still in Parliament, but his pathetic efforts at a comeback brought indifference or derision from those who used to fear him. Lord Salisbury never answered his requests for the viceroyship of India or the ambassadorship to France. The debts with the Rothschilds continued to mount. The racehorses were sold; the stables followed, and then the house in Connaught Place, after which the family moved in as lodgers with the Duchess in her house in Grosvenor Square. As Lord Rosebery put it, Lord Randolph became "chief mourner at his own protracted funeral, a public pageant of gloomy years."

Feeling abandoned, Winston was miserable at Harrow and there were constant letters to his mother—begging for visits, news, and pocket money—but she had other things besides a plangent son to worry over.

No matter how bad things became, she could not leave her husband. In her situation, lovers were permissible, but the public scandal of divorce would have ruined her forever. "No public laundering of dirty linen" was the iron rule of upper-class society. Had she had money of her own, she would have had more independence, but Leonard Jerome, on whom she relied for additional financing earlier in the marriage, had become a burned-out onetime millionaire. His money was gone. All his schemes for a financial comeback had failed. He died, another disappointed man, in 1891.

All Jennie could do was wait for her husband's slow disease to take its course. Their relations were naturally erratic. He depended on her—as she had to do on him—and occasionally gave her signs of sad affection. Appearances were more or less maintained.

He seems to have tolerated her affairs, outwardly maintaining an old-world unconcern about her lovers. He continued his friendship with Count Kinsky almost to the last. It was the style, this behavior of a polished aristocrat who would not dream of letting anything as vulgar as his wife's liaisons color relations with another nobleman.

Behind the scenes, Lord Randolph's self-control was less sure. According to his brother-in-law Lord Tweedmouth (who married his sister Fanny), Jennie could irritate him unbearably, and there are references in contemporary diaries that show Lord Randolph angrily abusing her. In 1892, Jennie herself was seriously ill (with a rectal tumor) and Lord Iddesleigh (formerly his parliamentary colleague, Sir Strafford Northcote) records Randolph as "inclined to abuse his wife although her life is still said to be in danger."

Jennie made a full recovery, but Lord Randolph's decline continued as the bacillus steadily encroached upon his brain. One of the stranger side effects of the onset of general paralysis of the insane is that the sufferer frequently fails to understand how much his faculties have been impaired. Isolated, with at best a fitful contact with reality, he is buoyed by the belief that everything is normal. Lord Randolph had periods when he thought himself about to make his political comeback.

In 1893, he journeyed through southern Africa, believing he would make his fortune. Winston meanwhile continued his own depressing career at Harrow.

Although his home life was afflicted by parental misery and debt, Winston found something of a refuge in relationships with other members of his extended family. During these formative years of adolescence, he developed a strong loyalty toward his kinsmen, which continued all his life.

There was his gentle brother, Jack, six years his junior. Taller than Winston, Jack was placid, well-behaved, and rather dull. The family favorite, he was already being held up as an example to his brother, who was inclined to bully him but whom he seems to have adored. Almost from the start Winston dominated Jack, and when he allowed him to join in one of his favorite pastimes—pitched campaigns with carefully assembled armies of toy soldiers—Jack was permitted no artillery and assigned the colonial infantry so that Winston invariably won. Since Jack did not object, it was a situation that suited Winston perfectly.

Then there were the two Jerome aunts, Leonie and Clara, both of whom had followed their sister's example and married into the British aristocracy. Neither made as grand a match as Jennie, but neither had to bear the strain and horror—and excitement—of their more powerful sister's life.

Leonie had married Col. Sir John Leslie, a dependable but easygoing Irishman of Castle Leslie, in County Monaghan. Members of Ireland's long-established "Protestant Ascendancy," the Leslies were genially eccentric, and this eccentricity was passed on to Winston's cousin Shane Leslie, born in 1885. Aunt Leonie had not inherited the looks or temperament of Jennie, but she was kind to Winston, and increasingly became Jennie's confidante and principal adviser during the storms and trials of her marriage.

Jennie's other sister, Clara, was less dependable, having married one of the most spectacular young men of late Victorian society, an immensely tall and unreliable adventurer named Moreton Frewen, who spent his life pursuing fortunes that eluded him. The Frewens inhabited a picturesque but moldering ancestral home, Brede Place, near Rye in Sussex. Aunt Clara was prettier than Aunt Leonie, but less intelligent, and much of her life was spent in a curious affair with the exiled King Milan of Serbia. The Frewens' daughter, christened Clare, inherited her mother's looks and her father's fecklessness and would be a source of trouble and delight to her cousin Winston for many years to come.

But none of the Jerome relations could really hope to rival the Spencer-Churchills in the interest of the youthful Winston. In contrast to the constant strain of Lord Randolph's illness, and the anxieties of debt and of keeping up appearances, Blenheim, though having its own troubles, was a place of unassailable security. It beckoned this difficult and lonely child's imagination with historic splendor, compared with which the disappointments of Lord Randolph's life were almost insignificant. During this period, Winston became preoccupied with heroic battles and conquering generals, in particular Blenheim's great creator, John, first Duke of Marlborough.

# Seven

# Death in the Family

The years of Winston's adolescence coincided with a depressing period for all the Spencer-Churchills. Lord Randolph's miseries were only part of the misfortune now descending on this blighted family.

John Winston, seventh Duke of Marlborough, former Viceroy, and bewhiskered pillar of the Church of England, had not lived to see the triumph and disaster of his favorite son. The Duke had died in 1883. His palace declined into the gloominess it had known earlier in the century as Lord Randolph's elder brother, Blandford, cheerlessly embarked upon his tenure of the dukedom.

"He was his own worst enemy," the *Times* would write about him at his death. He picked up the nickname of "the Bad Duke" almost from the start, for at the time of his accession his maltreated wife, Goosey, Lady Blandford, was divorcing him with much scandalous publicity. This did little for what was left of his public reputation.

She felt so bitterly toward him that she refused to be known as his duchess. (For the rest of her life she would simply call herself Lady Blandford.) His mother, the old Duchess, was so distressed at the thought of this reprobate son taking over Blenheim after her worthy husband that she left the palace, never to return in Blandford's lifetime.

The member of the family who suffered most from the changed

regime was unquestionably the new Duke's nine-year-old son and heir, Charles Richard John Spencer-Churchill, who officially became Lord Blandford, a title that automatically descended to the Duke of Marlborough's heir. However, since the Duke continued to be called Blandford by all who knew him, the new Lord Blandford was to be known all his life by the nickname Sunny, the diminutive of another of the young lord's titles, Earl of Sunderland. Nothing could have been less sunny than the character and fate Charles Richard John had inherited from the dukes of Marlborough.

Born in 1871, Sunny was devoted to his mother. But he was sacrificed as part of the settlement of his parents' painfully fought divorce. As the heir to a famous dukedom, it was considered only right and proper for Sunny to be brought up at Blenheim. Thus, at the age of ten, the boy was unceremoniously bundled back to Blenheim and his father.

Sunny's maternal aunt, Lady Lansdowne, always remembered him as having been one of the most "charming and joyous" of small boys; suddenly, however, he changed, and she was alarmed to see that his good spirits seemed to have vanished. Having won him, his father almost instantly disliked him, and would either bully him or snub him. In his own words, Sunny was "given no kindness and entirely crushed" during the years his father was alive.

His cousin Winston was three years his junior, and they had played together as small boys at Viceregal Lodge in Dublin during their grandfather's term as Viceroy of Ireland. Further contact between them ended shortly after Sunny's father succeeded to the dukedom, and Lord Randolph and his brother were involved in one final, monumental feud.

As with most disagreements in the Churchill family, this one had its origins in money—or the lack of it. John Winston had set a dangerous precedent when auctioning off the Marlborough gems and his famous library. Blandford was as short of money as his father, and on becoming Duke himself, followed the paternal footsteps to the saleroom. He was not a sentimental man, and the palace was stripped of its remaining splendors, including Raphael's masterpiece, the Ansidei Madonna, and the magnificent Van Dyck portrait of King Charles I on horseback—both ended up in the National Gallery in London. Blandford, meanwhile, built himself a new laboratory at Blenheim.

Lord Randolph had not objected to his father's depredations, but those of his brother must have struck him differently. He was violently opposed to what was happening, and attempted, unsuccessfully, to stop the sales. Relations between the brothers ceased, and the ban extended to Lord Randolph's family. Winston and his brother, Jack, visited Blenheim only once more before the Bad Duke's death. This occurred during the diphtheria epidemic of 1888 when Duchess Fanny, the Bad Duke's mother, arranged for them to spend a few nights at the palace to escape the danger of infection. Apart from this, romantic Blenheim remained forbidden territory to Winston while he was at Harrow.

Winston hated Harrow from the start, and since he got no further than the lower school and refused to concentrate on anything that bored him (this included classics, mathematics, science, and all foreign languages), the legend grew around him, which he later did nothing to discourage, that he was something of a dunce.

In fact, he was extremely clever at the things he liked. He had his father's powers of concentration and had inherited the Churchill memory, winning a prize for reeling off verbatim twelve hundred lines of Macaulay's *Lays of Ancient Rome*. (The poem, with its dramatic scenes of noble heroism, war, and death in battle, was a lifelong favorite; in 1947, he would recite large sections of it over lunch to the Italian film director Mario Soldati.)

He also showed a most precocious gift for words and self-expression, which the Harrow English master evidently appreciated. One of the few things Churchill admitted that his old school taught him was "the structure of an English sentence, which is a noble thing," and as an old man, working on his memoirs, he told his assistant that it was then that he discovered "that I had this astonishing gift for writing."

But despite these few successes, Churchill himself admitted that his schooldays were the unhappiest period of his life. He was undersized and seems to have been unpopular. Sir Oswald Mosley remembered Churchill telling him, "with some resentment, how certain little beasts used to flick him with wet towels." With most of his schoolwork, he was clearly behaving like many unhappy children and simply opting out.

Temperamentally, he was sensitive and emotional, the elder son longing for paternal love and affection. But his parents were distracted and unhappy and the rigors of an English boarding school added to his misery. Mrs. Everest's letters and concern were not enough to overcome his loneliness. Winston became increasingly aggressive, and something of a bully when he got the chance. One of the famous stories of his Harrow days is of how he had the temerity to push another boy into the swimming pool. The victim was the tiny but formidable Leo Amery, athlete, captain of the school, and formidable future Tory politician. Winston gave himself away by his apology. "I mistook you for a fourth-form boy, you are so small," he said, then added, "My father too is small and he is also a great man."

The most revealing picture of this Churchill is provided by one of his contemporaries, the future pioneer and empire-builder, Col. Richard Meinertzhagen. According to him, Winston was already "precocious, bumptious and talkative." "He was," Meinertzhagen adds, "a lonely boy, usually walking by himself, but everyone in the school knew him because he was out of the ordinary." Meinertzhagen admits that, like several others, he "thought he could take liberties" with Winston, and on one occasion tried to push him off the pavement. "I cannoned into an object like a brick wall and found myself in the gutter, for he was as hard as nails and even in those days was a fierce opponent of wilful aggression." Years later, when facing a wild boar in India, Meinertzhagen saw "those same little beady eyes of warning," and as the boar prepared to charge, he had a "mental flash" of Winston Churchill.

At Harrow, Churchill's developing powers of aggression were valuable in other ways, helping him become a champion fencer—he was an unorthodox, attacking fighter—and guaranteeing his enjoyment of the warlike battles of the school army corps.

His father, however, found no joy in Winston's few accomplishments. All Lord Randolph saw in Winston was a source of trouble and expense and a reminder of his own sense of failure.

Unlike his brother, Winston always needed money and attention. And Lord Randolph came to regard him as ill-disciplined, lazy, and far too like Jennie. It is interesting that Lord Randolph's only confidante, his mother, Duchess Fanny, also strongly disapproved of her bumptious, unattractive grandson. She firmly agreed with her Randolph about young Winston's character.

She wasn't the only one to think so. One of the habits of Winston's form master was to place him in the front of the class saying, "Look at the stupidest boy at Harrow who is the son of the cleverest man in England."

Father-son relationships worsened steadily throughout Winston's later years at Harrow. Lord Randolph finally suggested that Winston (who had been thinking of the church) choose a military career and make some use of his childish love of playing soldiers and his natural aggressiveness.

Even here, however, Winston failed his father. He needed tuition for a special London crammer and three attempts before he passed the entrance examination to Sandhurst Military Academy. All of which increased his father's debt with the Rothschilds. By the time Winston finally did pass the exam, in the autumn of 1892, Lord Randolph seems to have all but washed his hands of him.

But Winston, unlike his cousin Sunny, would not let his father's attitude destroy him. He found a substitute father figure in his mother's lover, the glamorous Count Kinsky, who used to take him to the circus at Olympia, and made a fuss of him in London during school holidays. Winston purchased from his brother, Jack, a photograph of Kinsky winning the Grand National on his horse, Zoedone, to hang on his study wall at Sandhurst. And he constantly appealed to his mother for support. He argued lucidly, cajoling his "Dearest Mummy" for attention and affection throughout the time he was at school. Then at the moment when his schooldays ended, he found another world he needed.

On a November morning early in 1892, the ducal valet at Blenheim entered his master's bedroom with his customary pot of tea at the customary hour of eight o'clock. He pulled the curtains, called the Duke, and took little notice of his master's failure to respond. This was a frequent occurrence; Blandford was increasingly moody and depressed, although he appeared in perfect health for a man of forty-seven.

His Grace's moods were something of a mystery, for he seemed at last to have come to terms with life. Having stripped his palace and dispersed the proceeds, he had resolved his financial problems by following the example of an increasing number of the British aristocracy of the period.

During a visit to New York three years earlier, he had met the now aging *bon viveur,* Leonard Jerome, who had suggested a solution to his troubles: Lillian Hammersley, a widow with a heavy figure and a fortune of similar proportions. She had, explained Jerome, "Plenty of tin," and nothing would make her happier than to share it with an English duke. It was a wish that Blandford was prepared to grant her.

Ugly, good-natured, and extremely rich, Duchess Lily proved an admirable wife. She was thrilled to be a duchess, settled Blandford's debts, and indulged him lovingly. She bought him a brand-new boat house for his lake, and a massive Hammond organ for his empty picture gallery. She even did her best with her introverted stepson, Sunny, who was not particularly responsive. Nor, sadly, was her husband, who had become increasingly afflicted with the Churchill melancholy.

He never bothered to patent his electrical discoveries, still feuded with his brother, maintained a mistress, and was shunned by many of the local gentry, whose feelings he reciprocated.

Like some miserable prisoner he had taken to expressing comments on his situation on the walls of his room. "They say. What say they? Let them say," he had scrawled. And "Dust, ashes, nothing."

This sentiment was curiously apt, for when the valet returned to help his master dress, he found the tea untouched beside the figure lying in the bed. At forty-seven, Blandford, eighth and most disreputable of the dukes of Marlborough, had abruptly gone to meet his maker.

His brother was immediately informed, and that afternoon, for the first time in seven years, Lord Randolph entered his ancestral home to take charge of the situation. Despite his own illness, he behaved with admirable coolness. He reassured his nephew Sunny, who had hastened back from Oxford, where he was now an undergraduate. The young man was somewhat dazed to find himself, at twenty, Duke of Marlborough. Randolph also comforted the Duchess—with a cup of tea—before viewing his brother's corpse.

He found Blandford, as he later reported in a letter to his mother, looking "very peaceful." "His left hand," he wrote, "lies easily on his waist, but his right hand is clenched tightly on his heart. There can be no doubt that the cause of death was sudden syncope, with no one near to offer any restorative, brought on by indigestion."

Lord Randolph said the same, more briskly, to the reporter from the *Oxford Mail,* who was soon upon the scene. There could be, he added, absolutely no question of foul play in the Duke's demise. And that was that.

The Duke left nothing to his brother, Randolph, nor to his bastard son, nor to his wife (not that she needed it). But there was a large bequest of £20,000 to his final mistress, the notorious "sex goddess" of Victorian England, Lady Colin Campbell. He also made his feelings fairly clear about Blenheim: The only stipulation he insisted on about his funeral was that on no account were his remains to rest within its walls.

Some four days later, having lain in state with the ceremony and pomp prescribed for even the most unsatisfactory of dukes, Charles George, eighth Duke of Marlborough, was deposited in the spot that he had chosen—an anonymous corner in nearby Bladon churchyard. His Duchess sensibly departed for her house in Brighton, where in the course of time she met and married the heroic soldier, Lord William Beresford VC. She enriched his life as she had previously enriched the Duke's. Although legally Lady Beresford, the former Mrs. Hammersley from Brooklyn retained her title of Duchess of Marlborough. Presumably she felt that since she had paid for it she had a perfect right to keep it.

Blenheim was liberated by the eighth Duke's death. Sunny, freed from his miserable existence in his father's shadow, suddenly emerged as one of the most enviable and envied young men in England. He had the house, the title, and for the first time in his life could please himself entirely. One of his earliest guests was Cousin Winston.

The friendship between Winston and Sunny was in some ways an unlikely one, for their characters could hardly have been more different. Sunny was as shy as Winston was assertive; Sunny was a duke, Winston a penniless cadet at Sandhurst. But they had a number of important things in common. Both had suffered from their fathers' disapproval and neglect, and both had been deeply affected by traumas in the family. They were linked by blood; Winston was his cousin's heir should anything happen to Lord Randolph—as it seemed increasingly likely that it would. Above all, they shared in the extraordinary inheritance of Blenheim, and were free to enjoy it and to make the most of it together.

The vast house and its emotional legacy would affect both of them profoundly. As the ninth Duke, Sunny would remain in thrall to Blenheim all his life; he would love it jealously and dedicate himself to making good the ravages inflicted by his grandfather and father. He would even sacrifice his happiness to restore the splendor and renown of the great first Duke of Marlborough.

Winston's reaction to the house and all it represented was entirely different.

One can envision the effect of sudden contact with an ancestral house like Blenheim on an imaginative eighteen-year-old at the end of a miserable adolescence. Blenheim represented the perfect contrast and escape from his own domestic chaos and depression. It was the absolute embodiment of the sort of terrestrial greatness that Lord Randolph had failed to achieve. Stripped of its treasures, it was still the palace of a hero. With its multitude of servants it remained inordinately grand. It was witness to the power of history, proof, if proof were needed, of the enduring splendor and uniqueness of the Spencer-Churchills. Here was the ducal life *par excellence,* a most compelling blend of pomp and power, feudal privilege, tradition, and great luxury for its chosen few.

Life was expanding fast for Winston, and freedom was at hand as Lord Randolph's illness entered its final phase.

Sandhurst Military Academy was more suited to Churchill's interests and abilities than Harrow had been. He loved dressing up in uniform (a weakness that would continue almost all his life) and was absorbed by the technicalities of battle. He was companionable, and for the first time in his life began to work extremely hard. Military history—and in particular the lives of great military leaders—fascinated him. He scorned drills and team games but he loved riding, and made himself a tough and skillful horseman.

Several reasons seem to have accounted for his equestrian enthusiasm. Riding was the gentleman's activity, and Churchill was emphatically a gentleman. It was also a toughening activity. "I am cursed with so feeble a body that I can hardly support the fatigues of the day," he had written early on to Jennie. But by the exercise of willpower— particularly by forcing himself to spend long hours in the saddle—he could compel his undersized and undeveloped body to perform prodigies of strength and endurance.

There was also a subtler motive for his riding: rebellion against his father. Lord Randolph had firmly decided on the infantry for Winston, and had arranged with the Duke of Cambridge for a place in a rifle regiment. Winston, who would never see the point of walking anywhere when he could ride, entirely disagreed. He had set his heart on the cavalry.

From the letters written by Lord Randolph during Winston's time at Sandhurst, it is clear that his disapproval of his eldest son had reached obsessional proportions. Along with Mr. Gladstone and Lord Salisbury, Winston had become one of sick Lord Randolph's principal *bêtes noires.*

Docile Jack was emphatically Lord Randolph's favorite now, and he rarely missed a chance of pointing out to Winston how much cleverer and conscientious Jack was becoming. Winston was good-for-nothing, and extravagant, with "little claim to cleverness, to knowledge, or any capacity for settled work," as Lord Randolph wrote to Duchess Fanny. "He has," he added, "great talent for show-off exaggeration and make-believe."

Lord Randolph continued to attack his son. "You have demonstrated beyond refutation your slovenly, harum scarum style of work throughout your schooldays. . . . always behind-hand, never advancing in your class, incessant complaints and total want of application. . . ."

He ended by warning him that if his conduct did not improve, "my responsibility for you is over." Should he continue the "idle, useless, unprofitable life" he led at school, he would "degenerate into a shabby, unhappy and futile existence," with none but himself to blame for his misfortunes.

In June 1894, Lord Randolph had a final consultation with those two harbingers of hopelessness, Dr. Buzzard and Dr. Roose. It is not known exactly what was said—someone has neatly snipped this passage out of the letter Lord Randolph subsequently wrote to his mother—but he finally agreed to give up active life completely—for a period. Lord Randolph, it seems, was still insisting that he could be cured, provided he was free from worry (which included worries over Winston).

It was a wretched situation, with Lord Randolph caught between periods of inertia, terrible depression, and outbursts of extraordinary rage. He had gone on too long. He was a source of potential disaster to his family if the truth of his affliction ever reached the press. And in moments of violence he was dangerous.

So the family closed ranks—as only upper-class Victorian families knew how to. There was no alternative. For years now Jennie had been waiting for her freedom and her chance to marry Kinsky: She would have to go on waiting. A few of the closest, most discreet of friends could tactfully be told something of the truth—this included "old Tum" as Jennie irreverently called the Prince of Wales. The past forgiven and forgotten, His Royal Highness was to make concerned inquiries of Lord Randolph's medical condition through the Apothecary Royal, Sir Richard Quain. The doctor conveyed "such information about Lord R's condition as I think may be communicated *without indiscretion.*"

It was Dr. Roose's task to do something rather similar with Winston. In November 1894, Winston wrote from Sandhurst, "My darling Mummy—you must not be cross with me for having persuaded Roose to keep me informed as I shall never tell anyone, and it is only right that I should know." Even if Roose put him off with generalities, he would have learned the truth from Jennie in the end.

She had the hardest task of all. Everyone depended on Jennie to maintain appearances and preserve her husband's name and reputation for posterity.

In June of 1894, Randolph decided for himself the course events should take. "I know instinctively what is for my good," he told his mother, "and that a year's quiet travelling with Jennie, and a change of air and complete repose of mind is what will really benefit me. I shall pursue my travels quietly, not tiring myself and travelling with all possible comfort."

Once more, Lord Randolph was seeking diversion and escape in travel. But it must have seemed a daunting prospect for a wife to go off around the world with a husband in the throes of general paralysis of the insane. For the family, however, it was a way of keeping him out of the public eye. According to Dr. Buzzard's notes, his patient was now exhibiting marked symptoms of his illness—"tremor, faulty articulation, and successive loss of power in various parts of the frame." At times he suffered "grandiose ideas" and could be "violent of manner"; at other times "dejection and apathy" were followed by "unnatural bonhomie." As Buzzard told Sir Richard Quain, "you will understand with the uncertainty as regards the occurrence of the mental symptoms, how important it was to get the patient away."

Even on the eve of his departure, Lord Randolph was still worried that Winston might defy him and enter the cavalry. "However, I will have none of it," he told the Duchess, "and the Duke of Cambridge will be very angry if he did such things, as he put his name down for the infantry three years ago."

Lord Randolph's voyage around the world was the grim finale to his life. He was forty-six but looked a hundred. A young physician, Dr. George Keith, was in constant attendance, together with a valet.

Traveling across America, "with all possible comfort," Lord Randolph seems to have improved. But once aboard a steamer to Japan he became delusional. For a while he was sleepy and confused, then, at Yokahama, he tried to kill his valet. Dr. Keith managed to restrain him.

The journey continued to Burma, which in happier times he had annexed for Britain, then on to India, with his condition worsening all the time. That November, from Government House Madras, he managed to write in pencil to his mother, who kept the letter in a black-edged envelope on which she wrote "My Darling's Last Letter." It was in a quivering hand and largely incoherent, rambling on about the death of the Czar of Russia, his distaste for shipboard food, and a final diatribe against his old enemy, Gladstone, together with the prophecy that Ireland will never get Home Rule. There is no mention of either of his sons.

It was now that Dr. Keith decided his condition was so serious that he would have to get him back to London. Jennie must have hoped that he would mercifully die. Instead there was a slight remission and the hurrying cortege accomplished their ghastly journey up the Red Sea and the Canal to Cairo, dragging Lord Randolph with them. He could still stagger on his feet but was almost totally insane.

In a lucid moment he expressed a wish to see Monte Carlo for the last time. They took him there, but it meant little to him, and Dr. Keith, seeing that his patient was dying, insisted they return to London. They reached the Duchess's house in Grosvenor Square on Christmas Eve. Unaware of what was happening, Winston and his brother, Jack, were spending Christmas with Sunny at Blenheim.

"Lord Randolph Churchill is suffering from General Paralysis, and lies in a semi-comatose and very critical condition." This terse entry in Dr. Buzzard's case notes is dated Christmas Day, but by January 1 the patient had evidently rallied yet again, for the doctor then wrote that "under regular feeding and rest his Lordship has greatly recuperated and can now converse." He was feeble, but there seemed a chance of at least partial recovery.

This produced an anguished letter from Jennie to her sister Leonie, showing something of the strain she had endured and what had been at stake throughout the final stages of her husband's illness.

"Physically he is better, but mentally he is 1,000 times worse. Even his mother wishes now that he had died the other day. What is going to happen I can't think or what we are going to do if he does get better. Up to now the General Public and even Society does not know the real truth, and after *all* my sacrifices and the misery of these six months it would be hard if it got out. It would do incalculable harm to his political reputation and memory and is a dreadful thing for all of us."

In the same letter, Jennie mentioned her old lover, Kinsky. He had grown tired of waiting and had married a twenty-three-year-old princess. It was the end of the great romance of Jennie's life, but she refused to feel sorry for herself. Nor did she want anybody's sympathy. "I am not *quite* the meek creature I may seem to you," she told her sister. As for Kinsky, "He has not behaved particularly well and I can't find much to admire in him, but I care for him as some people like opium or strong drink although they would like not to. *N'en parlons plus.*"—Let's say no more about it.

Her real concern was the task she had set herself: ensuring the legend of her husband's greatness and playing the part expected of her. She had a bad cold, acute neuralgia, and had eaten next to nothing since their return. But she was courageous and had always had the dedication of a great actress to her role in life. Nothing could be permitted to upset the grand finale of her husband's deathbed.

Lord Randolph lingered on through most of January, and she rarely left his room, alternating the bedside watch with Dr. Keith. The house already seemed in mourning with, as Jennie's sister Clara told their other sister Leonie, "masses of Churchills who sit with the old Duchess and go one by one into Randolph's room." A Victorian death-bed was a serious family event, and both Jack and Winston were among the constant visitors.

For Lord Randolph, the horror mounted. He had taken so much morphia that it was slow to work during the attacks of inflammation of the brain, and his screams were heard throughout the house. But even now he had his lucid moments, and kept asking Jennie when they could go to Monte Carlo.

"We'll fetch your mother, and we'll all start tomorrow morning!" she told him.

By January 20, the final crisis was beginning. According to Keith's case notes, "Lord Randolph had a quiet night until 5 a.m. when his bowels moved in bed and continued moving for three quarters of an hour, very watery and offensive. His pulse began to rise until it reached 110."

The next day he suffered delusion after delusion. "At one time his pulse ran up to 140 as he tried to make himself sick but it soon fell." By the next day he was comatose after two attacks of violent mania in the night. His temperature rose, his lungs began to be affected, and at 6:15 on the morning of January 24, Lord Randolph's agony was over.

Four days later he was buried in Bladon churchyard beside the brother he had so disliked, and a memorial service was duly held for him in Westminster Abbey.

# eight

# Ambition

Lord Randolph Churchill's death brought relief to everyone concerned. In later life, Winston would piously insist how much he missed him, how he regretted not having been closer to him, and what a cruel deprivation he sustained in this early death of his famous father. As he wrote later, "All my dreams of comradeship with him, of entering Parliament at his side and in his support were ended. There remained for me only to pursue his aims and vindicate his memory."

But did it really? Deprived of a father he may have been, but one looks in vain through the mass of letters written at the time for any reference to Winston's grief. The dead man's mother, Duchess Fanny, was distracted, but if Winston wept for his father, this was one occasion in his life when his tears came privately.

Far from having shown the faintest sign of wanting Winston "at his side" in Parliament, Lord Randolph had been anxious to the end to ensure that his unruly son was assigned to oblivion in the infantry. This was one "aim" of his father that Winston did nothing to "pursue." On the contrary, and within a few days of Lord Randolph's death, Winston had his mother pen a deeply tactful letter to the grand old Duke of Cambridge, asking for permission to rescind his posting so that he could enter the 4th Hussars, the smart and expensive cavalry regiment he had his heart set on.

His Grace gracefully agreed. At a stroke, Churchill was relieved from the boring, foot-slogging, drill-dominated future Lord Randolph had tried so hard to condemn him to. Instead, he could enjoy the fashionable, romantic, splendidly accoutred life of a Victorian hussar.

According to his own account in *My Early Life,* the most exuberant of all his books, "from this moment," the future opened up "like an Aladdin's Cave." The story of his five ensuing years of soldiering and journalism reads like a happy tale of high adventure. But strangely, his own version of events does rather less than justice to his real achievement, as this undersized young aristocrat set out to push the world in his direction.

In his writing, Churchill makes his prodigious efforts sound remarkably straightforward, simply a time of high ambition, youthful spirits, and patriotic love of action. But the more one learns of the circumstances behind these high endeavors, the less straightforward any of them seem. In an unguarded moment in old age, Churchill would admit as much, referring to himself in these early days as "a freak—always that." This was in a letter to the widowed Lady Lytton, formerly Pamela Plowden, with whom he was once in love.

He failed to enlarge upon this odd admission—presumably because she knew the truth about those far-off years. But since it was then that his character was formed, and the whole pattern of his later life created, it is important to know more about this "freakish" side of the adventurous young Winston Churchill.

Once freed from restraint and paternal criticism by Lord Randolph's death, one might have expected Winston to make the most of his good fortune and simply settle down to enjoy the happy life of a hussar in that "slapdash, self-indulgent, extravagant" way his father always feared he would.

Quite the reverse occurred. Barely was he posted to his regiment at Aldershot than he began to make it clear that he found little satisfaction in the gentlemanly life of a hussar. Not yet twenty-one, he suddenly became a young man in an enormous hurry, with the most grandiose ambitions and a ruthless energy to make them work.

One of his heroes was inevitably Napoleon, and he had picked on the Emperor's famous maxim for success: *"l'art de fixer les objets longtemps sans être fatigué"* (the art of sticking to one's long-term objectives without tiring). Suddenly he seemed to have his own long-term objectives fixed with a tireless sense of purpose, and it startled everyone.

Few careerists have used connections and influence so un-ashamedly, or with such precocious flair, as Winston. Instinctively he seemed to know the value of his father's name and his mother's beauty. "This is a pushing age, and we must shove with the best," he told her, as he enlisted her support in his search for glory and adventure. She had already given him her own golden rule for self-advancement: "Do business, darling, only at the top." Totally devoid of diffidence or shyness with the great, he was to leave no gilded string unpulled, no famous door unpushed to further his ambitions.

His first priority was to enjoy some real fighting. Disappointingly, there was no prospect of this in the Hussars, who, in 1895, were tediously waiting to exchange the red-brick plains of Aldershot for the sun-baked plains of India. As a recently enlisted subaltern, Winston was expected to conform to peacetime regimental duties. As a Chur-chill he could see no point in that at all.

These were still the palmy days when English cavalry officers (unlike their other ranks) enjoyed the enviable privilege of three months' summer leave. Since the Spaniards were suppressing a colonial revolt in Cuba, why not spend this leave seeing how such things were done? For an ordinary young officer this would have been impossible, but Lieutenant Churchill was Lord Randolph Churchill's son, and Lord Randolph had always naturally enjoyed connections everywhere.

One of Lord Randolph's closest friends in politics had been Sir Drummond Wolfe, now British ambassador to Spain, and Jennie also knew the proprietor of the London *Daily Graphic*. With some judicious nagging, she was persuaded to ask them for assistance. Churchill, meanwhile, used his father's name and friendship with the great Field Marshal Lord Roberts, the hero of the battle of Kandahar, to gain entrée to the War Office, where he proposed to send back information on a new bullet being used by the Spanish forces in Cuba.

A few weeks later he was happily on his way to Cuba, via a short stay in New York, where he was briefly entertained and more lastingly inspired by one of his mother's lovers, the Tammany Hall politician and inspirational orator Bourke Cockrane.

At twenty, Churchill possessed a pronounced awareness of his own importance, which life was helping to confirm. Thanks to Drum-mond Wolfe, the Spanish Ministry of War had recommended him to their general in charge of operations, and the *Daily Graphic* had offered five guineas per article for anything he cared to write about the fight-ing.

The Cuban war fulfilled his expectations. He saw his first rebels killed in battle, and the Spaniards awarded him a campaign medal (which as a serving British officer he was not allowed to wear). He reported to the *Daily Graphic* and Whitehall, and he was even subject to a short but gratifying controversy in the London press, which criticized the presence of a British officer in a war against oppressed colonials fighting for their freedom. (He also acquired a lifelong taste for Havana cigars and a siesta in the afternoon.)

This Cuban holiday was something of a dress-rehearsal for more serious activities in the next few years, showing if nothing else, what he could do through energy and sheer persistence. From now on there is a clear impression of this small, impatient figure leaving no stone unturned, no log unrolled which could lead him swiftly on to fame and fortune.

But before this life of glory could begin there were frustrating months of home-based soldiering to be endured. During these boring months at Aldershot, something of the hidden side of Churchill's nature revealed itself, showing a little of what lay behind that galloping ambition.

Like Lord Randolph, Churchill had inherited more than his share of the family depression, and even before he left for Cuba he was secretly complaining to his mother of the "slough of despond" in which he was immersed at Aldershot. The success of his Cuban adventure changed all that—but not for long. After his return to regimental life, Churchill seemed sunk in misery and gloom as he waited for some rousing new activity to burst upon a gray horizon.

Although he had been so deeply upset at the time of his father's resignation from the Treasury, and was miserable for periods at Harrow, this is the first recorded instance of Churchill being hit by deep depression, that near-suicidal affliction which he used to call "Black Dog" and would plague him at intervals throughout his life.

Depression is an illness, but a most mysterious one. It can take many forms, and there is still no real understanding of its causes. But in Winston's case, it seems to have been triggered by his father's death —and the memory of his father recurred to him at intervals throughout his life.

This was odd, remembering how little sign of grief he showed when Lord Randolph died. On the contrary, like Jennie, Winston reacted to his father's death with understandable relief. The shame and misery of Lord Randolph's final days were over. Mother and son were free at last from "the hazard of concealing"—and from the frightful strain of coping with the poor demented victim of those last appalling months. And both had finally achieved their longed-for independence —Jennie to live the life she wanted, and Churchill to seek fame and fortune in the cavalry.

But Lord Randolph's memory began to haunt Winston. He wrote how he missed his father, how he wished that he had known him better, and from now on his father's life, career, and political beliefs would have an almost sacred significance for him.

A possible connection between Winston's unfilial reaction to his father's death and his subsequent depression is suggested by a recent "memoir on madness" from the novelist William Styron entitled *Darkness Visible*. While emphasizing the mysterious nature of depression, he puts forward a widely held hypothesis on the relationship between a certain type of chronic depression and what is termed *incomplete mourning* following bereavement of the young.

There is apparently a high incidence of cases of acute depression following the traumatic death of a parent at around the time of puberty that are not entirely explained by grief. Indeed, serious depression sometimes follows cases where the young show little outward sign of sorrow, and it is suggested that serious emotional damage can be caused by failure to accept bereavement with "the natural catharsis of accompanying grief." Without this catharsis, everything is bottled up, and a young person who already has depressive tendencies can suffer "irreparable emotional havoc" from his failure to come to proper terms with a parent's death. Abraham Lincoln, who lost his mother during childhood and exhibited symptons of incomplete mourning at the time, is cited as a classic case of this. Winston could well have been another.

Winston's memories of his father must have been a fearful burden. Not only had he gone against reiterated paternal wishes in his choice of regiment, but he also bore the knowledge of his dying father's deep and lasting disapproval. Worse still were Lord Randolph's fearsome prophecies of failure for his feckless son—"the life of a wastrel," the "shabby and futile existence" that the dying father had solemnly predicted.

Had Winston come to terms with his memories of his father through the natural processes of grief and mourning, he might have accepted what he said and been at peace. But for Winston such acceptance must have been extremely difficult. There was no grief; there was no real mourning. What there was instead was guilt and subsequent despair, the prime ingredients of Churchill's enemy, "Black Dog," which sometimes threatened him with self-destruction.

To understand this stage in Churchill's life, one must understand the power of depression and the agony endured by the true depressive. This is in a class removed from the normal person's feelings of unhappiness or of "feeling down." It brings the constant pain of utter hopelessness. It causes total isolation and despair. For the true depressive in the grip of a serious attack there is an urge to self-destruction that no logic can relieve, no outside help or medication cause to go away. This was the situation with which, at twenty-one, Churchill realized he had to cope. The agony of his depressions was almost certainly the spur that drove young Winston on. The hyperactive depressive is a well-attested psychological phenomenon. As one psychologist has put it, "many depressives deny themselves rest and relaxation because they cannot stop. If they are forced by circumstances to do so, the black cloud comes down on them."

There were, in fact, a number of activities Winston could turn to to avoid this, and the truly "freakish" thing about him was the energy and sheer resourcefulness with which he used them all. The most obvious, of course, was one he had already tried in Cuba—the sovereign anodyne of adventure and escape. He would soon turn to it again —and on countless occasions for almost the remainder of his life.

But adventure on its own was not enough to keep "Black Dog" permanently at bay. In a letter to Jennie bewailing the misery of peacetime soldiering, Churchill made a strange admission. The only way to rouse himself from the depths of depression, he said, was to read his father's political speeches, "many of which I already know by heart."

Churchill made no secret of what he was seeking when he memorized his father's words. Lord Randolph's speeches held the magic formula of political success. "I took my politics unquestioningly from him," Winston wrote. "He seemed to have possessed the key alike to popular oratory and political action." What better "long-term object" than to follow in his footsteps?

Lord Randolph was an ambiguous example for a son to follow, his whole career a tragic warning. Yet for his son, there was no alternative.

It was one thing for Churchill to decide that politics could provide true satisfaction for his driven nature, it was another to achieve political position, particularly with his regiment due to leave for garrison duties in Bangalore, India, in the autumn of 1896. Then, on the eve of embarkation, came news that the Zulu War had started in South Africa.

Here was the opportunity to repeat his performance in Cuba— on a considerably greater scale. And not only were there endless opportunities for lucrative and lively journalism, but there was also the chance to earn a medal he could wear. What's more, the fighting could lead directly to his ultimate ambition: a great career in British politics.

Once he made his name, he told his mother, he would swiftly leave the army for Westminster and, as he put it, "beat my sabre into an iron despatch box."

He was soon engaged in the same prodigies of push and pull that got him to Cuba, telling his mother he "could not believe that with all the influential friends that you possess and all those who would do something for my father's sake, that I would not be allowed to go, were those influences properly exerted."

This time influence was not enough. Jennie's friends were tired of doing favors for her overeager son, and in the end he sailed as planned for India and a bungalow in the Hussars' base camp at Bangalore.

From Calcutta he was soon writing to Jennie, saying that "if only I can get hold of the right people, my stay here might be of value." But the "right people" failed to respond like their counterparts in England, and the pushy young careerist found himself consigned to spending fourteen months in virtual exile in boring Bangalore.

His duties were minimal, his fellow officers unstimulating—so was southern India. He collected butterflies and grew roses. Bangalore had even less than Aldershot to offset his frustration.

For someone of Churchill's depressive temperament, this could have been a recipe for suicide. Instead, it proved the most formative time of his career.

For the first time in his life, his extraordinary strength of will and powers of concentration helped him ward off a recurrence of depression as he embarked upon a strict regime of physical and mental self-improvement. Acutely aware of his deficiencies, he started to re-create himself in preparation for the life he wanted. His determination was worthy of the young Napoleon himself.

In a fascinating analysis of Churchill, written in 1970, psychologist Anthony Storr notices an apparent contradiction between Churchill's character and his physique. Physically, he seemed to be "of endomorphic structure," small-boned and lightly muscled, a makeup that tends to go with qualities of carefulness, restraint, and introversion. Churchill's "love of risk," he writes, "of physical adventure, his energy and assertiveness are traits which one would expect to find in the heavily muscled mesomorph." This leads Storr to conclude that "the more one examines Winston Churchill as a person, the more one is forced to the conclusion that his aggressiveness, his courage and his dominance were not rooted in his inheritance, but were the product of deliberate decision and iron will."

This view is very much borne out by what we know of Churchill at this period.

Barely two years earlier he had complained to his mother about the "feebleness" of his body, and his difficulty getting through the day at Sandhurst. Since then, he had forcibly endured the rigors of the riding school, but on landing at Bombay had suffered a serious setback by dislocating his right shoulder, a weakness that tended to recur throughout his life.

Despite this painful disability, Churchill started playing polo as was expected of a young cavalry officer in India, but did so with his right arm strapped against his side. Polo is not a game for weaklings, its principal ingredients being sheer aggression and the will to win. Yet during his time at Bangalore, Churchill made himself one of the top polo players with the army in India.

While he was strengthening his body on the polo field, the young lieutenant was doing something rather similar with his mind. Deeply conscious of his lack of the university education his father enjoyed, he began after his siesta in the long, hot afternoons, a strenuous course of reading—not for pleasure but as a sort of mental body-building— which he pursued with much the same energy and willpower he brought to the polo field.

He read the two historians his father had approved of—Gibbon and Macaulay. History could be a source of lessons for the future, but for Churchill it was more important to use it as a model for his literary style, that rhetorical, measured, eighteenth-century language which he consciously adopted in his speech, and which would resound through English politics for the next sixty years.

His reading was deliberate and wide. It included St. Simon's memoirs, Schopenhauer's pessimistic philosophy, biographies of heroes like Napoleon and Nelson, and "that rich source of spurious erudition" Bartlett's *Familiar Quotations,* which he would recommend to Oswald Mosley, and was still using for his speeches in the House of Commons in his fifties. He had no time for anything as frivolous as fiction, for his studies were highly functional, single-minded preparation for the "great game of politics" he was determined he would play.

As further training, he began working every day on copies of the *Annual Register,* which Jennie started sending out to him. These leather-bound volumes faithfully record the great political speeches of the past, and he set himself the daily task of writing out his own speech on a particular event, then carefully comparing it with what Sir Robert Peel or Gladstone or Disraeli actually said in Parliament.

But, as he wrote to Jennie, "a good knowledge of the *Annual Register* is valuable only for its facts. . . . Macaulay, Gibbon and Plato etc. must train the muscles to wield that sword to greatest effect."

Time was passing. He was nearly twenty-three, and sharp ambition had begun to goad him once again to hurry. Back in England on leave in the spring of 1897, he made his first attempt to test himself in active politics by speaking at a Conservative and Unionist rally near Bath. He was not a particular success. Public speaking was one more accomplishment he would need to master through practice and exercise of will, but he convinced himself that the lisp inherited from Lord Randolph was no greater political impediment than it had been to his father.

His father's name and his mother's friends and influence remained his greatest assets, and he carefully cultivated both. Her friends could be useful sources of information, and it was at one of the houses of the rich and famous he would always love—in this case Goodwood House, the stately Sussex home of the Duke of Richmond and Gordon —that he learned that war was brewing on the northwest frontier. The imperial warrior, Gen. Sir Bindon Blood, as warlike as his name, was already on the borders of Afghanistan organizing what he called "a little pheasant shoot," with the Pathan tribesmen as his quarry.

Like the Cubans, these mountain people were attempting to assert their independence, and the general's shooting party, the Malakand Field Force, was a retaliatory expedition to teach these "lesser breeds" the power of the machine gun. Churchill left Goodwood House desperate to join the General.

Having already met him socially, Churchill had no difficulty with introductions: After sending a cable simply stating he was coming, he was on his way to the northwest frontier, again in search of fame and fortune, with the double role of serving as commissioned officer and as correspondent for the *London Daily Telegraph*.

This expedition marked another stage in Churchill's progress. Had he been simply a careerist, hell-bent on fame and fortune, he would have accompanied the troops as they burned the villages, made copious notes on the background and the fighting, filed his copy to the *Daily Telegraph*, and prepared to write a lively history of his experiences—all this he did, assiduously starting work on his first published book, his *The Story of the Malakand Field Force*, on returning to Bangalore.

But from the letters Churchill wrote to Jennie from the field, it is clear that career and journalism were incidental to deeper purposes. He was seeking danger for reasons of his own. In one letter he describes how, on three separate occasions, he had ridden his conspicuous white pony in front of the Pathans, "all along the front of the skirmish line where everyone else was lying down in cover. . . . Foolish perhaps," he added, "but given an audience there is no act too daring or too noble. Without the gallery things are different."

Among other things, Lord Randolph had criticized his son's "great talent for show-off exaggeration and make-believe," but on a white horse in front of the Pathans, make-believe could suddenly become reality with "an audience" to prove his bravery.

"Being in many ways a coward—and particularly at school— there is no ambition I cherish so keenly as to gain a reputation for personal courage," he wrote his mother. As it was, he had to be content with being mentioned several times in Blood's dispatches.

There was, however, more to Churchill's antics than flamboyant medal-hunting. With the depressive's urge to self-destruction, he was wagering his life against his great career, and detecting destiny in his survival.

These were important moments in his personal theater, and until old age he would grimly relish standing in positions of exaggerated danger, like his hero, Marlborough, on the battlefield.

While working on *The Story of the Malakand Field Force*, the twenty-three-year-old Churchill put aside a novel he had started writing earlier. He finished it in something of a rush in 1898, and published it a year later under the title *Savrola*.

*Savrola* is an unexpected book to have come from the pen of this bounding young careerist, and in later life, Churchill generally advised his friends against reading it. This may not have been simple modesty —as a novel, this Ruritanian political romance did little for his reputation—for at the height of his success he may have realized that it gave away far more of his inner self than he wished to be reminded of.

The plot is improbably romantic. It tells the story of a revolution in the mythical republic of Laurania led by the noble hero of the people, the young statesman Savrola, against the forces of its corrupt and aged president. After a battle in the capital, the revolution triumphs and the president is killed. But Savrola is rejected by the people he has saved, and departs for exile with the only woman he loves, the distant, beautiful Lucile, wife of the president he helped to slay.

It is tempting to find echoes here of Churchill's own situation, with Savrola superseding the dead father-figure of the failed statesman, both in his political role and in the affections of the beautiful but motherly Lucile. The story has clear unconscious parallels to Churchill's own behavior after Lord Randolph's death.

What is far more obvious is the extent to which the character of the romantic young Savrola is based upon the secret aims and great ambitions of the author. At this level, Savrola becomes a highly polished exercise in the autobiography of dreams. Make-believe mingles with reality, and against the background of this painfully romantic schoolboy tale one can hear the unmistakable voice of young Lieutenant Churchill speaking out about philosophy and politics—and, most of all, about himself.

His descriptions of the proud Savrola almost read like advertising copy for Lieutenant Churchill. "Vehement, high and daring was his cast of mind. The life he lived was the only one he could ever live; he must go on to the end. The end comes often early to such men, whose spirits are so wrought that they know rest only in action, contentment only in danger, and in confusion find their only peace."

There is more here than an ordinary description of Churchill's own driven nature. The idea of the need to hurry, spurred on by the likelihood of early death, was part of his clear identification with his father's career—and a theme that would persist until his own robust old age disproved it. More interesting still are those words that he adopts as something of a motto for Savrola. At one point in the book there is a sort of mirror-image as he describes Savrola reading Macaulay's *History of England*. "Vehement, high and daring" are precisely the words Macaulay uses to describe John Churchill, Duke of Marlborough.

The mirror-images continue. Savrola, like Churchill, is a lonely aristocrat attracted irresistibly to the cause of politics. He is the idol of the people but despises the venal middle classes. He lives alone in high-minded, studious seclusion, reading the classics, tended only by a devoted Mrs. Everest–like old nurse who cooks his food and tidies his bare apartment.

Why, Savrola muses, does he bother with the cares of politics?

"The struggle, the labour, the constant rush of affairs, the sacrifice of so many things that make life easy or pleasant—for what? A people's good! That, he could not disguise from himself, was the direction rather than the cause of his efforts. Ambition was the motive force and he was powerless to resist it."

But behind ambition lies the true depressive's vision of the world —and life itself: "Life seemed unsatisfactory," he writes. "Something was lacking. When all deductions had been made on the scores of ambition, duty, excitement or fame, there remained an unabsorbed residuum of pure emptiness."

# nine

# Faithful but Unfortunate

While Churchill was battling abroad, his favorite cousin Sunny, Duke of Marlborough, had troubles of his own at Blenheim.

In the 1880s, a dukedom was still only one step down from royalty in public estimation. Resplendent at the apex of the aristocracy, dukes inhabited the world around them much as feudal princes; deference was automatic. Society was theirs, and their position almost too grandiose for comfort.

Sunny undoubtedly enjoyed his role and worshiped Blenheim. As well as the house, he inherited an assured income of £50,000 a year, a London mansion, and fifteen thousand acres of Oxfordshire. He had stables, carriages, and servants, all in great profusion. He, if anyone, should have been able to enjoy the winnings that the lottery of birth had dealt him. But there was, inevitably, a flaw in his great inheritance. Like Cousin Winston, Sunny had also inherited the family depression, but without the lively genes of the Jeromes, which were enabling Winston to control it. In addition, there was Sunny's duty to his great inheritance. The powerful dead hand of the greatest of the Marlboroughs weighed heavily upon this young man, still in his early twenties. Scarcely were the bonfires celebrating his accession cold than he was forced to understand his lifelong obligations to his overwhelming patrimony.

As always, Blenheim needed money—in abundance. Its acreage of roof was leaking, its farms required capital investment, the interior of the house was a disgrace, and much of the famous gardens had become a wilderness. How was a conscientious duke of twenty-one to meet such inordinate expense?

Even before his nephew had succeeded to the title in 1892, Lord Randolph's thoughts had turned to a sound financial marriage for the youthful Sunny. Lord Randolph had been meeting the young French Duc de Breteuil, who had saved *his* family by marrying a very rich Miss Garner from America, and had discovered that she had a sister, "neither pretty nor ugly, but of a good disposition and intelligent." In addition, she possessed an income of £20,000 a year.

"What a good business this would be for Sunny," Lord Randolph had written to his mother. "Where is that youth? I must see him. I think this might be cooked up." This was one more project Churchill's ailing father failed to "cook up," but it shows the way the wind was blowing. Sunny's uncle Randolph and his father had both married American heiresses. Why not Sunny, too?

The young man briefly fought against the notion, and for some months after succeeding to the dukedom was rumored to have fallen in love with a beautiful young woman. But dukes like Sunny could not afford the luxury of marrying for love. The debts at Blenheim were increasing, and after the depredations of his father and his grandfather, Sunny had little left to sell—except himself. So in the spring of 1893, he forced himself to forget the girl he loved and placed himself firmly on the marriage market for the highest, most appreciative bidder.

In the 1890s, the one spot on earth where an authentic English dukedom still conveyed as much prestige as it did in England was in the country where all titles were expressly forbidden by its founding fathers. In New York, English aristocrats, like old English furniture and pictures, conveyed immense if somewhat puzzling prestige. Much of the *nouveau riche* East Coast society was intent on acquiring its social hallmark in the form of European art and titles. An emotion similar to that which in the early seventies had impelled Mrs. Leonard Jerome to Paris, now inspired Mrs. Willie Kissam Vanderbilt to take a serious interest in Blenheim and the Duke of Marlborough.

Mrs. Willie K. was wife of one of the two grandsons who inherited the vast fortune of the rough-hewn Commodore Vanderbilt, the railway king of America. A monster of snobbish self-assertion, she was obsessed with using her husband's wealth to establish her position as unrivaled queen of New York's super-rich society against her principal rival, her even richer, equally assertive sister-in-law, Mrs. Cornelius Vanderbilt II.

No holds were barred within the family as these two profoundly ugly women locked themselves like mastodons in a war of spectacular consumption that engaged the resources of the Vanderbilts throughout the 1880s. Steam-yacht was built to answer steam-yacht. A multimillion dollar New York mansion was built and crammed with European works of art only to be upstaged by an even larger New York mansion still more tightly crammed with European works of art.

Mrs. Willie K. sensed victory when, in 1888, she commissioned Richard Morris Hunt, president of the American Institute of Architects, to design her a simple "summer cottage" at fashionable Newport, Rhode Island. Her cottage, which cost $7 million, was modeled on Marie Antoinette's Petit Trianon at Versailles and decorated with the most ostentatious eighteenth-century French furnishings and works of art that the obedient Willie Kissam Vanderbilt could buy.

For ten brief weeks of that year's Newport summer season, the portly chatelaine of Marble House enjoyed her victory over her jealous rival. But Mrs. Cornelius Vanderbilt II was not so easily put down. Barely had Marble House opened its regal doors than she, too, secured the services of Richard Morris Hunt—together with the self-same workmen who had built Marble House. And by 1892, Mrs. Cornelius also had her simple "summer cottage" on Bellevue Avenue, right next door to Marble House. It was even bigger and more richly regal than its neighbor. With a touch of possibly unconscious irony it was called The Breakers.

The Breakers indirectly altered Sunny Marlborough's life, for it was in answer to her rival's house that Mrs. Willie K. first began to plan a sensational marriage for her swan-necked, seventeen-year-old daughter Consuelo.

Since earliest childhood, Consuelo had been treated like the centerpiece of her parents' collection of precious works of art. Her future role in life was preordained when she was named after Consuelo Iznaga, a friend of Mrs. Willie K.'s who married the Duke of Manchester.

Like her unassuming father, the young Consuelo was putty in her mother's hands and submitted to an education more fitting for a European princess than the daughter of a simple New York multimillionaire. She traveled extensively in Europe, was painted by the most fashionable French portrait painters of the day, and even at home conversed in French. When she occasionally rebelled or lapsed, her mother set about her with a riding crop.

Mrs. Willie K. heard of the young Duke of Marlborough's situation from an important go-between in London society of the day, the lively Lady Paget, formerly Miss Minnie Stevens of New York. It was at Lady Paget's house in Cadogan Square that Consuelo Vanderbilt met Sunny Marlborough during her stay in London in the summer of 1893.

It must have been a most uncomfortable occasion. Consuelo, very tall and shy and overshadowed by her dreadful mother, was still only a teenager. Sunny at twenty-two had been Duke for barely a year. They were placed next to each other, and one wonders what they found to talk about.

Probably not very much—Sunny was still hankering sentimentally for his forsaken love, and Consuelo, on her return to America, promptly fell in love with the rich and handsome sportsman Winthrop Rutherfurd.

None of this reached the ears of Mrs. Willie K., who was now intent upon her final coup in answer to The Breakers. All was proceeding with discreet efficiency. There was no unseemly rush, and with Lady Paget as a go-between, she could complete her negotiations with Sunny.

In the spring of 1895, Consuelo and her mother made another trip to Europe in the course of which they were invited for a long weekend at Blenheim. Consuelo, besotted now with Rutherfurd, did her best to make it clear that she was not interested in Blenheim or its duke; her mother made it clearer still that she was fascinated by them both. Lady Paget had by now completed her behind-the-scenes negotiations with Sunny, and Mrs. Willie K. invited him to Newport for September. The Duke accepted.

That summer, Mrs. Willie K. swept all before her. Rutherfurd was "persuaded" to leave Newport in a hurry. Her husband was told that no expense was too great to complete their daughter's happiness by making her a duchess, and Consuelo herself was warned that no objections to her mother's plans would be tolerated. That September, when Sunny duly came to Marble House and unromantically proposed to Consuelo in the Gothic Room, she unromantically accepted.

The high point of that autumn's Newport season was the coming-out ball at The Breakers for Consuelo's cousin Gertrude, much-loved daughter of Cornelius Vanderbilt II. That same evening, Mrs. Willie K. arranged an informal dinner party at Marble House before all proceeded to the ball. It was as dinner ended that she rose to give the news that made *her* happiness complete. Her daughter Consuelo would shortly be marrying *His Grace,* the Duke of Marlborough—and that evening it was Consuelo, not her cousin Gertrude, who was the star of Gertrude's ball.

With this final victory over her sister-in-law, Mrs. Willie K. was preparing to bow out. In fact, she had already started divorce proceedings against her inoffensive husband, and would shortly marry her Newport neighbor, Oliver P. Belmont, who was almost as rich and rather more exciting than the ill-used Willie K. But first there was Consuelo's wedding to be made the most of.

Having so carefully arranged the purchase of the Duke of Marlborough, Mrs. Willie K. needed to ensure that Willie K. would meet the bill, which of course he did, like the fond father and honest businessman he was. The transaction was not unlike the purchase of a prized European work of art, and Consuelo, something of a work of art herself, was guarded night and day.

Sunny arrived, together with his lawyers, but the Blenheim orchids sent to Consuelo failed to arrive.

The Vanderbilts had already fixed November 5 for the wedding day, but Sunny, remembering that this was Guy Fawkes Day and that Guy Fawkes had once attempted to blow up the House of Lords insisted on the sixth as "more appropriate."

"I spent the morning of my wedding day in tears and alone," the bride recalled, but this did not prevent her from being punctually delivered to St. Thomas's Anglican Cathedral on 5th Avenue in Manhattan, where the bishop of New York and the bishop of Long Island were awaiting her in the presence of a fashionable congregation. Sunny was also waiting—to receive both bride and a guaranteed annual income of $30,000.

To ensure that there was absolutely no mistake, it had also been arranged that when Willie K. Vanderbilt entered the vestry for the signing of the wedding register, he should also sign the marriage settlement.

It was here that the Marlborough lawyers proved their worth, for that all-important document gave the Marlboroughs what their palace desperately needed: a capital lump sum of $2.5 million worth of shares in the Vanderbilt-owned Beech Creek Railroad, backed by a guarantee from the New York Central. As the *Washington Post* observed, "The roof of the Marlborough Castle [*sic*] will now receive some much needed repairs, and the family will be able to return to three good meals a day."

There is a firm impression that despite so much being against it, Sunny's marriage might have had a chance had it not been for Blenheim and the dukedom. The European honeymoon proceeded amicably enough, but once the couple arrived at Blenheim, all the melancholy of that melancholy house assailed Consuelo as it had so many of her predecessors. After the comfort and luxury of millionaires' New York, she found her palace positively spartan.

"How strange that in so great a house there should not be one really liveable room," she remarked to her husband. Then she soon found the words of welcome left above the bedroom fireplace by her husband's father: "Dust, Ashes, Nothing." It might have been his verdict on her marriage.

Immediately, she and Sunny found themselves regretting the partners they might have married. Sunny felt Consuelo was failing to regard his great position in society with sufficient reverence, and Consuelo felt that Sunny was a pompous bore.

Soon they were dining every night in ducal silence, waited on by footmen in livery but eating little and finding even less to say to one another. Consuelo describes how, in these silences, Sunny "pushed his plate away . . . backed his chair away from the table, crossed one leg over the other, and endlessly twirled the ring on his little finger." In retaliation, Consuelo started knitting during dinner, and the butler read detective stories in the hall.

Somewhat surprisingly, these frigid mealtimes did not prevent Consuelo from performing her second most important task once Blenheim's roof had been repaired. It was a task that Duchess Fanny had pointed out to her in no uncertain terms when they met in the dowager's drawing room in Grosvenor Square.

Duchess Fanny was then still in mourning for her son Lord Randolph. Black lace cap on head and ear trumpet at the ready, she greeted Consuelo "with a welcoming kiss in the manner of a deposed sovereign greeting her successor."

"Your first duty," she told Consuelo, "is to have a child, and it must be a son, because it would be intolerable if that little upstart Winston ever became Duke."

This strange reference by the Duchess to the son of her beloved Randolph was a reminder of the fact that, since Lord Randolph's death, Winston was now directly in line for the dukedom. It also shows the hostility toward him in the family and how its staider members were regarding his ambitious antics.

As for Consuelo's "duty"—what her husband unromantically referred to as "providing the link in the chain"—she managed to oblige, giving birth to a ten-pound son in September 1897. The boy was duly christened John Albert Edward William. Taking the title of Marquess of Blandford, he was known henceforth as "Bert."

Consuelo was still in her early twenties, very elegant and tall, and at last free of her mother, she started to grow up. Her title, allied with her own great private income, gave her an element of independence, which she began to make the most of, and which further infuriated Sunny.

She started traveling abroad and forming friendships quite apart from her husband. There was a second son, Lord Ivor, born in 1898, but the silences at dinner lengthened. She had lovers, and there were long estrangements. Sunny grew more miserable than ever and took lovers of his own.

But the succession of the dukedom was secure for another generation, and Blenheim, thanks to Willie K. Vanderbilt, was preserved. If there were sacrifices demanded of a duke, Sunny was proud to make them, and the marriage was maintained for much the same reasons as it was originally arranged. Blenheim demanded it.

# ten

# Power and Glory

It would have been hard to find a greater contrast than between Sunny Marlborough and "that upstart," Cousin Winston. For while Sunny was so consciously the martyr, and so painfully aware of having sacrificed his happiness, Churchill was striding on in search of danger, fame, and fortune.

In the 1660s, young John Churchill had been a brash careerist firmly on the make. Winston Churchill was not dissimilar. But times had changed, and Winston's similarities to the first and greatest Duke of Marlborough made Duchess Fanny see him as an upstart and dread him succeeding to the dukedom.

A growing band of influential people shared the Duchess's feelings. Medal-hunting and blatant self-advertisement were bad form in late Victorian upper-class society. (Such things, if done at all, were done discreetly, or by the rising middle classes.) What one biographer has called "the rogue elements" in Churchill's character were generally ascribed to the unfortunate American influences in his heredity.

This was almost certainly correct. Without his mother's close support and the fresh genetic input from the Jeromes, it is hard to imagine Churchill breaking free from the doom-filled background of his father's family. But he had two great assets that made his drive and brashness always ultimately acceptable. The first was that, although socially a rebel and at odds with much of the settled social order, he remained at heart "aboriginally" conservative and patriotic, with a romantic passion and obsession with the Empire. The second was that, however angrily his enemies condemned him as a bounder, none could impugn his credentials as a gentleman. These were important facts, and Churchill employed them to extraordinary advantage.

The short period after the campaign with the Malakand Field Force on the northwest frontier is a fascinating one in which the young careerist never missed a trick. Churchill's first requirements were fame and money. (His personal extravagance, combined with Jennie's, had brought the family closer than ever to disaster. Brother Jack, instead of going on to university as he had wanted, would soon be entering a firm of stockbrokers with the backing of Jennie's friend Sir Ernest Cassel.)

Winston achieved both goals through the publication of his book on the Malakand campaign, which he wrote in five weeks flat. The invaluable Jennie produced the publisher. Churchill's "literary" uncle, Aunt Clara's wayward husband, Moreton Frewen, did a speedy and typically erratic job editing the manuscript. And the book was in the shops for the new year of 1898.

Churchill was aghast when he saw that, thanks to too much haste and Uncle Moreton's editing, the book was full of errors of typography and grammar. And his reaction shows just how vulnerable he was to the disapproving judgment of the dead Lord Randolph. In *My Early Life,* he writes of how, within his mind, he heard his father's unforgiving voice repeating "one more example of your slovenly, shiftless habits." He added bitterly that awareness of his father's certain disapproval "destroyed all the pleasure that I had hoped to get from the book," leaving only "shame that such an impertinence should be presented to the public."

He need not have worried. Despite the errors, his first published book was widely and favorably reviewed and earned him more than twice the annual salary of a subaltern. More important still, it brought its youthful author to the notice of those who mattered, in particular to Prime Minister Lord Salisbury, and to H.R.H. the Prince of Wales. Again, this was largely thanks to Jennie, who ensured that advance copies reached them with an appropriate letter from her son.

"How do I address the Prince of Wales?" he asked her.

"Address him as 'your Royal Highness,' and start each fresh paragraph with 'Sir,' " she told him.

By now he had his heart impatiently set upon the next step in his great career. Natural actor that he was, he was excited by the latest drama just about to start in the immense theater of the British Empire.

Since General Gordon had been killed by the forces of the Mahdi and his Dervish army at Khartoum in 1885, and British influence was lost through the whole of the Sudan. Now vengeance was at hand in the shape of gigantic Gen. Sir Horatio Herbert Kitchener and an army twenty thousand strong advancing slowly up the Nile with all the new technology of military destruction. Churchill had to join them.

This was not easy for a cavalry lieutenant stationed in dusty Bangalore. But Churchill had by now perfected the technique of infinite mobility, using his contacts and his dual role as journalist and soldier to propel him as and where he wanted.

It should have been straightforward to get himself assigned to the expedition. Thanks to his book's success, newspapers were willing to employ him as a correspondent. Home on leave in the summer of 1898, he was graciously received by Lord Salisbury, now in his third spell as Prime Minister. Salisbury wished to congratulate Lord Randolph's son on the publication of his book.

"If there is anything at any time that I can do which would be of assistance to you, pray do not fail to let me know," muttered the man Churchill called "the master of the British world" as they parted. Taking instant advantage, he mentioned Kitchener and the Sudan, and Lord Salisbury promised his assistance. So did another of the young man's famous readers—Albert Edward, Prince of Wales.

But Kitchener was not impressed by journalists, nor was he having bright young officers with literary pretensions thrust upon him, even by prime ministers and future kings of England. Lieutenant Churchill, on the point of leaving for the Nile, received a most emphatic negative.

"No young man should ever take no for an answer," Churchill remarked when no longer young himself. But it takes a young man of exceptional self-confidence to persist where a Prime Minister has been refused.

As always, he was in a hurry, knowing that the decisive battle for the whole Sudan was not far off. But he was also worldly enough and wise enough to sense that General Kitchener's high-handedness was causing much resentment in Whitehall. Through family connections once again, Churchill was able to exploit this, cleverly persuading the Adjutant General, whom he sat next to at a specially concocted dinner party, to assert the authority of the War Office over General Kitchener by seconding Lieutenant Churchill to the Lancers on attachment to the expedition.

Having succeeded where Lord Salisbury failed, he was swiftly on his way to Egypt with a profitable agreement to report on the expedition for the *Morning Post*.

"Life is very cheap, my dearest Mama," he wrote to Jennie, echoing *Savrola*. ". . . I have a keen aboriginal desire to kill several of these odious Dervishes & drive the rest of the pestiferous breed to Orcus, and I anticipate enjoying the exercise very much."

Before dawn on the morning of September 2, 1898, trumpeters awoke the British army bivouacked beside the Nile near the enemy city of Omdurman. Across the river, Khartoum lay in ruins, and Churchill was to witness what he later called "the most signal triumph ever gained by the arms of science over the barbarian," as General Kitchener, with heavy river gunboats, Maxim guns, and Krupp artillery, proceeded to eradicate the Dervish army.

Nine thousand enemy were killed at a cost of several hundred British and Egyptian casualties; Gordon was avenged and the *Pax Britannica* extended through the length and breadth of the Sudan. It was a signal reassertion of something in which Lieutenant Churchill passionately believed: the power of the Empire and the civilizing mission of the British race over lesser breeds beneath them.

As sheer spectacle, Omdurman was clearly unforgettable, as the two armies marched and countermarched in the desert under the "immense dome of the sky, dun to turquoise, turquoise to deepest blue, pierced by the flaming sun." And despite the unequal nature of the conflict with the unromantic technical advantage of "the British race," Churchill would remember Omdurman as a glimpse of fabled battles from the past, "the last link in the long chain of those spectacular conflicts whose vivid and majestic splendour has done so much to invest war with glamour."

He would never lose this sense of the beauty and excitement of the clash of arms—nor would he forget his vision of the warlike splendor of the Empire—and in extreme old age would fondly re-create the battle with ashtrays and cigar butts at the dinner table.

Omdurman gave him what he longed for—glory in battle and proof that the unseen hand of fate was still protecting him. Riding with the Lancers, he participated in one of the great nostalgic moments of the British army—the last full-scale charge of a regiment of British cavalry.

He had been with the Lancers on the morning of the second when they were ordered forward to engage the enemy's right wing. A massed Dervish force was unexpectedly encountered in a dried-up watercourse. The cavalry commander ordered his bugler to sound the charge. Seconds later, Churchill was spurring into the thick of the melee.

The charge proved a bungled but heroic business, producing three Victoria Crosses and the only heavy British casualties at Omdurman, with almost a quarter of the cavalry killed or wounded. Churchill was exalted by the danger. He had no consciousness of fear, and as he told his mother later, the charge passed "like a dream."

In fact, he was practical enough to fulfill his desire to kill Dervishes by purchasing, in London, the latest German Mauser automatic —what he cheerfully called "a Ripper," on account of the hideous damage it inflicted with its heavy-caliber soft-nosed bullets. Knowing he would be excused from fighting with a sword because of his damaged shoulder, he was able to use the gun to powerful effect, "despatching" several of the enemy. When the commander sounded the retreat, Churchill's instinct was to reengage. "Another fifty or sixty casualties would have made the performance historic—and have made us all proud of our race and blood."

He admitted later that the charge was strategically a futile action, which did nothing to affect the outcome of the battle, but as a demonstration of the warlike genius of the British race, it seemed to him a time of glory. It rapidly assumed an even more important inner meaning.

Writing to Jennie on the eve of battle he had said that, should he fail to return, she must calm her sorrow with what he called "the consolations of philosophy and reflect the utter insignificance of all human beings." He had returned to the depressive's theme of the worthlessness of suffering humanity. But once he had survived the risks of battle, he could feel himself exempted from this gloomy generality. He was truly "chosen" for some higher purpose, just as he had been when he faced the bullets of the Afghan tribesmen.

"I do not accept the Christian or any other form of religious belief," he solemnly informed his mother, but he was learning to create a personal religion from the miracles of his survival and the achievements of his dominating ego.

Unseen forces were involved in his ambition, raising him above the "utter insignificance" of humdrum, unredeemed humanity. There was to him an obvious pattern linking that painful moment when he damaged his shoulder landing at Bombay with the way this made him choose the Mauser when riding into battle. That choice might well have saved his life. Everything was working out, and with destiny beside him, his next priority was to write the story of the war as soon as possible.

Already hard at work on the ship that brought him home to England, Churchill had learned the lesson of his rushed book on the Malakand campaign. He would not risk ridicule again. Instead, he took his time, polishing his prose and checking all his sources. When the *River War* appeared in the late summer of 1899, it made his name as a military reporter.

Parts remain extremely readable, with the background and the excitement of the story lightening the rhetoric that came from reading too much Gibbon. Judgments are made, policies applauded or denounced with the iron-clad confidence that became the hallmark of the public Winston Churchill.

There are two other interesting precursors of the author's future in the *River War*. One is the emphasis Churchill places on that all-important charge of the British cavalry. Since it was the climax of his own experience, it has to be the climax of the book, and he uses all his literary skill to make an incidental military mistake appear the noblest of victories. This skill at slewing facts to suit his own perception of events would not desert him in the years ahead.

The second was his treatment of victorious General Kitchener. Churchill had met the general just before the battle and was snubbed by him. "A great general he may be, but he is emphatically no gentleman," Churchill told his mother. Now he wanted his revenge, and Kitchener became the first of a long and sacrificial line of generals that Churchill employed for literary target practice. In reading the *River War,* one might conclude that General Kitchener had really very little to do with the overwhelming victory he achieved at Omdurman. The charge of the heroic Lancers seems infinitely more important than the efforts of their distant and unsympathetic general; the most memorable descriptions of Kitchener come when Churchill accuses him of inhuman treatment of the Dervish prisoners and of the desecration of the grave of the Mahdi. Both accusations were denied, and neither appear in subsequent editions of the book.

•  •  •

After Omdurman, Churchill returned to his regiment in India, and it was there that, for the first time in his life, he turned his thoughts to marriage. He was twenty-five and suddenly would come to believe himself in love. But he was not a particularly successful suitor.

Love proved a difficult emotion for him to cope with and sex an irrelevant diversion from the more important matters that obsessed him. He was far from prudish, having grown up in the worldliest of male societies, and granted his inquiring mind and the romantic opportunities of cavalry officers, it is hard to believe that he remained sexually uninitiated. But perhaps he was.

Seeing one's father die in the agony of advanced syphilis would deter all but the most determined from the delights of casual sex, and throughout his correspondence and the reminiscences of those who knew him, there is no hint of any amorous adventure.

The young lieutenant's prime emotions had been directed to the pursuit of glory and his great ambitions. Sexual pleasure would have wasted precious time and energy—love for another would have made hiccups in the grand design.

When Churchill wrote *Savrola,* the best he could offer his hero was the chaste affection of aging, motherly but still beautiful Lucile, widow of the president. In his own case, Jennie—aging but still beautiful herself—remained the most important woman in his life. She provided him with all the female influence he required, and at the age of twenty-four he was still addressing her in letters as "My Dearest" and "My Darling Mama."

But Jennie was now preoccupied with her own love affair—an embarrassing passion for the boyish beauty of golden-haired George Cornwallis-West, son of her former friend and fellow society beauty Patsy Cornwallis-West. Jennie was forty-three, and at twenty-four the unresisting George was sixteen days older than her doting and still dependent son Winston.

There are signs that Jennie was trying to pare down her son's dependence, and it was at her suggestion that Winston met some friends of hers in Hyderabad, India. It was here that he fell in love with the young woman he described as "the most beautiful girl I have ever seen—bar none," fresh-faced Pamela, the highly independent daughter of the British resident in Hyderabad, Sir Trevor Plowden.

Miss Plowden was intrigued by this difficult young officer. But although they rode an elephant together through the Hyderabad bazaar, and Churchill wrote in guarded terms of marriage, the relationship failed to progress.

Miss Plowden, having had other young officers in love with her, told Churchill that she felt he was "incapable of love." He was certainly naive in his ideas of what appealed to frivolous young ladies. In the spring of 1899, he was invited to stand as Conservative candidate for the Lancashire division of Oldham, and wanted Pamela to share in the fulfillment of his great ambition. She was back in England, so he invited her to join him on the hustings. But Pamela was not enthusiastic. Oldham was a good distance from London, and since Winston had his mother, why did he need her as well?

Politically, he did extremely well; losing by a mere three hundred votes, he was convinced that next time he would win. But romantically, the by-election was a disappointment. There was no more talk of marriage. He and Pamela enjoyed each other's company, then parted on the best of terms.

Once more the great imperial stage was set for a starring role by Winston Churchill—and this time, with his books and war experience behind him, he had no need to push to get exactly what he wanted. Hostilities had started in South Africa between the Boers of the Transvaal and the British of the Cape. The cause: the vast financial interests of the gold and diamond mining companies and the dreams of British High Commissioner Lord Milner to extend dominion from the Cape to the Transvaal. Churchill had no difficulty persuading the *Morning Post* to hire him as its correspondent at a record fee of £250 a month plus generous expenses.

This time he went to war in style, sailing first class aboard the same ship as British Commander in Chief Sir Redvers Buller. He was accompanied by letters of introduction from another of Lord Randolph's old admirers, Joseph Chamberlain—now Colonial Secretary—and ample stocks of whiskey and champagne.

J. B. Atkins of the *Manchester Guardian,* one of several other journalists aboard, was intrigued by the solitary figure he encountered: "He was slim, slightly reddish-haired, pale, lively, frequently plunging along the deck with neck out-thrust, as Browning fancied Napoleon; sometimes sitting in meditation folding and unfolding his hands, not nervously but as though he were helping himself to untie mental knots."

They talked, and Atkins soon discovered Churchill's conversation matched his bold Napoleonic stance: "When the prospects of a great career like that of his father, Lord Randolph, excited him, then such a gleam shot from him that he was almost transfigured. I had not before encountered this sort of ambition, unabashed, frankly egotistical, communicating its excitement and extorting sympathy. . . . It was as though a light was switched on inside him which suddenly shone out through his eyes."

The greatest actors are distinguished not just by mastery of technique but by some instinct that attracts them to the great dramatic roles that do them justice. Churchill possessed this instinct. He had shown it in Cuba, on the northwest frontier, and at Omdurman. Now he revealed it in finished form in his various adventures in South Africa.

He was after danger, self-advertisement, and glory—and rapidly achieved all three despite the deceptive lull in hostilities, which he discovered when he landed.

Hurrying to Natal, having heard that Ladysmith was under siege, he and Atkins were offered a trip aboard an improvised armored train by an officer Churchill had known in India, Captain Aylmer Haldane. Atkins refused, saying it was his duty to report the war rather than get killed or captured by the enemy. But for Churchill, glory came before his duties to the *Morning Post;* it was the risk and the adventure offered by this crazy train that made it irresistible. As with the charge at Omdurman, this could provide the chance he needed. "I have a feeling, a sort of intuition, that if I go something will come of it," he wrote to Jennie.

The armored train, as Atkins had foreseen, became an instant target for the Boer artillery. While the engine and the rear trucks crammed with troops stayed on the tracks, the three front coaches were derailed, leaving the whole train an unmoving target for the deadly fire of the enemy. The hero's moment had arrived—and he was once more in his element.

While Haldane and his troops held off the Boers, Churchill himself took charge of the locomotive. As the bullets whistled around his head, Churchill directed the wounded driver in his efforts to free the engine from the wreckage of the front three coaches. This took time, but destiny was still protecting him, and he performed admirably. Thanks to his coolness and directions, the engine managed to break free, but Haldane and the troops were left behind. Stopping the locomotive, Churchill ran back to join them only to find the troops encircled by the Boers. Churchill attempted to escape on foot across the Veldt, but having left his trusty "Ripper" on the train, he was now unarmed, and he finally submitted to the ignominy of being taken prisoner.

Churchill was soon thanking Haldane for allowing him what he called "the star turn" of freeing the locomotive. His fellow journalists were certain to describe it, and although this might cost him his job on the *Morning Post,* the fame would certainly enhance his prospects when he stood for Parliament.

He was right, of course. His exploits made a perfect story for the British press, and while his audience at home was reading the heroic tale of his coolness under fire, he was already planning the next enthralling episode.

He and Haldane were imprisoned in a temporary camp in Pretoria with a group of British prisoners, several of whom were thinking of escape. Churchill begged to join them, but according to Haldane's subsequent account, they were not particularly keen to have him with them. He was considered too excitable and argumentative, and something of a glory-seeker. There were also worries over whether he was fit enough to make it, but he finally persuaded Haldane and a comrade to take him with them.

On the evening planned for the escape, Churchill went first, climbing through the window of an outside lavatory. As he waited in the darkness for his friends to join him, something alerted the Boer sentries, and Haldane whispered to him to return. Had Churchill been particularly concerned about the others' chances, he might have climbed back through the window and postponed his flight until he could go with them as planned.

But such a course was hardly in his nature. He was on his own and at the start of yet another great adventure. Scruffy and unshaven, with a bar of chocolate and £75 in his pocket, he made his way through the outskirts of Pretoria, rode on a goods train going east, trekked on by foot, and was finally assisted by a British coal-mine manager who hid him in his rat-infested mine, then helped him cross the frontier into Portuguese East Africa. By now the Boers were offering £25 for the British prisoner Winston Churchill, dead or alive.

From Lourenço Marques, Churchill telegraphed news of his escape to Durban in Natal so that by the time he reached there he was guaranteed a hero's welcome, which he made the most of with a carefully prepared "impromptu" speech, thanking the enthusiastic crowd who welcomed him outside Durban Town Hall. As he had foreseen, the press was eager to get his story. After a series of humiliating victories by the Boers, Churchill's escape had much the British public longed to hear: human interest and excitement, great endurance, and this plucky grandson of an English Duke outwitting a formidable opponent.

Churchill reached Durban just before Christmas, 1899. By the time the century ended, he had made himself a national celebrity.

His strange capacity for making fantasy a reality set him apart from all but the most accomplished politicians of the age. And this knack, combined with an actor's skill, caught the public eye, ensuring that anything he did was news.

During the course of this increasingly ferocious war, there would be countless acts of heroism and survival that, in comparison, made Churchill's escapade with the armored train and subsequent escape irrelevant. But Churchill's exploits were already secure in his personal mythology and would be remembered as great deeds in the hero's life. So would his subsequent adventures, about which he wrote for the *Morning Post* while serving as unpaid lieutenant with the South African Light Horse.

His charmed life continued. He was present at several of the toughest battles of the war, including the disastrous engagement at Spion Kop, where he once more witnessed the results of British generalship: the massed slaughter of his compatriots by concealed Boer infantry. But while he did not reach Ladysmith until after the siege, his powerful imagination still enabled him to write an "eyewitness" account of its liberation.

He was twenty-five and achieving the fame and fortune he had always craved. He even had his precious family around him. Jennie arrived in Durban with a hospital ship that was paid for by the committee of Anglo-American wives, which she had organized in London. Brother Jack came, too, and was wounded in the foot. Even Cousin Sunny had managed to escape the cares of Blenheim, but all that his dukedom earned him was a humble place on Lord Roberts's staff.

South Africa had made Winston's name, but the true purpose of his life—his entry into politics—was still awaiting him. This came in the autumn of 1900, when the Conservative government, cashing in on the popularity of the war at home, called for an election—the so-called Khaki Election—and Churchill hurried back to Oldham for another try.

He was "bronzed by African sunshine, close-knit by active service, and tempered by discipline and danger." This is how Churchill later described his hero, Marlborough, when he returned from *his* African adventures at much the same age two hundred years earlier, and it could easily have been applied to Winston.

He was welcomed as a hero, elected by a considerable majority, and before taking his seat at Westminster, gave a lecture tour of the United States that netted him £1,200—rather less than he expected.

In New York, where he lectured under the personal auspices of Mark Twain, the novelist not only presented him with a signed set of his collected works but also generously introduced him as "the hero of five wars, the author of six books, and the future Prime Minister of Great Britain."

# eleven

# Politics

Churchill was twenty-six. British critic Max Beerbohm remembered him around this time as having "dry hair like a wax-work, no wrinkles and the pallor of one who lived in the limelight. He also had hereditary bad manners and was courteous and brutal alternately."

Wilfred Scawen Blunt, Arabist, diarist, and poet, was kinder, describing Churchill when he took his seat in Parliament at the beginning of the new king's reign in February 1901 as "a little, square-headed fellow of no very striking appearance, but of wit, intelligence and originality."

The young M.P. was dedicated, hard-working, and, if anything, a little too self-assured. But as one of his biographers has put it, "What was difficult to see in the young Churchill was any specific objective save that of an intense and somewhat alarming personal ambition."

This was not entirely true. He did possess a clear but undisclosed objective, and he touched on it when referring to his father in his painfully rehearsed and memorized maiden speech to Parliament.

All the leading politicians of the day were there—including Arthur Balfour, Joseph Chamberlain, and Herbert Asquith. They were not attracted by Churchill, but by the eloquence of the greatest orator in Parliament, the young Welsh radical and future Liberal Prime Minister,

David Lloyd George, who had just made a passionate denunciation of the war that was still dragging on against the Boers. Drawing on his own South African experience, Churchill made a clever speech, praising the bravery of the Boers but also calling for greater efforts by the British government so as to make it "easy for the Boers to surrender, and painful and perilous for them to continue."

Pleading both for war and peace, he was applauded by both sides of the House, and his successful maiden speech established him as something more than the son of a famous man. As he sat down he thanked the House for the kindness and patience with which it had listened to him. "It has been extended to me, I know, not on my own account, but because of a splendid memory which many Honourable Members still preserve."

Since returning from South Africa, Churchill had been facing a fresh crisis in the family. Despite gossip and bitter opposition from the young man's family, Jennie was set on marrying her youthful lover, George Cornwallis-West.

Churchill and Jack were both appalled, but there was little they could do. So they made the best of things, and their mother's wedding at St. Paul's Church, Knightsbridge, on June 2, 1900, was a potent demonstration of the solidarity and sense of family of the Spencer-Churchills.

Churchill persuaded Cousin Sunny, as head of the family, to give the plump and eager bride away. The groom's family stayed absent, but the Churchills were there in force. And Winston gave no sign of objecting to a stepfather of his own age.

Jennie's marriage, however, raised other problems. Until now, as a journalist and serving soldier, Churchill had not required a settled London base, and when in London he always stayed with his mother and brother at Jennie's house in Cumberland Place.

Since this was no longer possible (two grown sons around the house would have cramped the style of the newly married lovers), Sunny offered him the lease on a house he owned in Mount Street, Mayfair, and Winston and Jack moved in together. The Mayfair house, grander than he could afford, was just around the corner from the house in Curzon Street that an earlier Duke of Marlborough had lent Lord Randolph Churchill at the start of *his* political career. The similarities did not stop there.

In *Savrola,* Churchill had described his hero's study: "A broad writing-table occupied the place of honour . . . a large bronze inkstand formed the centrepiece. It was the writing-table of a public man." He had been describing his father's old study as he remembered it from the house in St. James's Place—the scraps of paper littering the floor, papers and telegrams lying unopened on the table, and "the room lit by electric light in portable shaded lamps." (This was a reference to the time when the Churchills boasted one of the first houses in the city to be lit by electricity.)

Now in Mount Street he could re-create the study for himself, complete with his father's own impressive writing-table, big bronze inkstand, and carved oak chair, recently transferred from Cumberland Place. Also present were the portable shaded lamps and his father's precious papers. Savrola had had the works of Plato and a marble statue of the Capitoline Venus as his inspiration. Churchill had *Spy* cartoons of his father as a politician and bound volumes of his speeches. The photograph of Jennie's former lover Count Kinsky winning the Grand National, which had once held pride of place in his room at Sandhurst, had been discarded. In its place was a photograph of Lord Randolph's most successful horse, the Abbess of Jouarre (commonly known as "the abscess of the jaw"), carrying the Churchill racing colors.

It was in this shrine that he was building to his father's memory that he started on the book that would make his name in the literature of politics—the official two-volume biography of Lord Randolph Churchill. And it was here that he embarked upon the next great step in his career—making himself a successful parliamentary politician.

He had long realized that there remained one all-important weakness that he had to overcome if he was to scale the greatest heights of politics: his serious deficiency as an orator. Until now his skill had lain with the written word; he had little talent for impromptu eloquence, and he was uncomfortably aware of his lack of commanding looks and stature. He also had a slight impediment of speech, a sort of lisp, which made the enunciation of *r* and *s* difficult.

But for Churchill, life's difficulties were there to overcome. In the last five years, he had trained himself to beat his weaknesses of education and physique. Through willpower, he had formed his mind and body and made himself a champion polo player, a man of action, and a best-selling author. The skill of oratory was just a fresh accomplishment to master.

Part of the problem was simply one of practice, and during this period Churchill became a grim practitioner of tongue twisters and a great orator before his looking-glass. His speeches were painstakingly prepared, like good dramatic dialogue, and just as painstakingly committed to his actorlike memory.

But being Churchill, he could not stop there. He was absorbed by the subject, and composed his thoughts upon it in an essay that he wisely never published. Called "The Scaffolding of Rhetoric," it, like *Savrola,* provides a powerfully subjective view not just of oratory but of his innermost ambitions as a politician and the way his mind was working on this all-important subject.

For him, the orator represents "the embodiment of the passions of the multitude," which is the orator's duty to reflect. "Before he can inspire them with any emotion he must be swayed by it himself. . . . Before he can move to tears his own must flow. . . . He may often be inconsistent. He is never consciously insincere."

By developing a "striking presence," Churchill's ideal orator overcomes those personal deficiencies of which he was all too conscious in himself. "Often small, ugly or deformed, the great orator becomes 'invested with personal significance,' and 'a slight and not unpleasant stammer or impediment' can actually be of assistance in 'securing the attention of the audience.' "

Painstaking as ever, he was working out his theory of the art of rhetoric before he mastered it. Correctness of diction, the use of humor and analogy, argument and rhythm—all are carefully considered and he offers a precise description of the pattern of the wartime speeches he would deliver forty years later. "The sentences of the orator when he appeals to his art become long, rolling and sonorous," with "a cadence which resembles blank verse rather than prose."

More revealing still is the reason Churchill offers at the start of his political career for mastering the art of rhetoric.

"Of all the talents bestowed upon men," he argues, "none is so precious as the gift of oratory," for the unanswerable reason that it is the source of supreme power over all his fellow men, a power he believes to be "more durable than that of a great king." Then he continues with a sentence showing exactly how his mind is working.

The great orator, he writes, is an independent force in the world, even the setbacks of party politics fail to destroy him. "Abandoned by his party, betrayed by his friends, stripped of his offices, whoever can command this power is still formidable."

This is a description that applies, of course, to only one man, his model and the source of all his thinking on the subject of politics and power, his father.

To write a biography is to conduct a voyage of discovery around one's subject. In Churchill's case it was a voyage that lasted three whole years—the time it took to research and write the book. In the course of his work he got to know his father as never in Lord Randolph's lifetime.

Churchill was assiduous in his research, and never tired of hearing the reminiscences of his father's close associates—in particular, Sir Francis Mowatt, now head of the Civil Service, who had served Lord Randolph at the Treasury, and even more of his father's great admirer and most loyal friend, Gladstone's heir, Lord Rosebery, who was Liberal Prime Minister from 1894 to 1895. As he wrote: "I loved to hear Lord Rosebery talk about my father. I had a feeling of getting closer to my father when I talked with his intimate and illustrious friend."

Churchill was a sentimental man living in a sentimental age, so it suited him to present himself as a devoted son, piously seeking out the tragic father figure he had loved. In fact, his quest bears all the signs of an attempt to propitiate—or, as he preferred to put it, vindicate—his father's memory.

Only by acquiring Lord Randolph's powers could Winston annul the failure that his father had once predicted for him, and it was in the details of Lord Randolph's political career that Churchill found exactly what he needed for his own.

Lord Randolph was not just the model for his son's oratory; Winston found in him the day-to-day political ideas he would otherwise have lacked. During his early months as a Conservative M.P., Churchill loyally—and rarely unsuccessfully—echoed his father's policies, one of which was Lord Randolph's "Tory Democracy." "I believe in the Tory working man," Churchill insisted despite his almost total lack of contact with the working classes. And just as Lord Randolph had finally resigned over his government's additional expenditure on the armed forces, so Churchill was soon in angry opposition to *his* government's additional military expenditure.

On financial matters, it was Sir Francis Mowatt who became his mentor, teaching him the essence of Lord Randolph's views on sound —that is, highly economical—finance. For several years to come, Churchill would be the scourge of anything that hinted at military or naval profligacy.

In terms of parliamentary strategy, Churchill also used his father as his guide. Just as Lord Randolph made his name in Parliament with his breakaway "Fourth party," so Winston tried to lead an iconoclastic splinter group of wild young Tories called the "Hughligans" (named after Churchill's more respectable but less dynamic parliamentary colleague, Lord Hugh Cecil).

Churchill was soon talked about, distrusted, and feared; and parliamentary journalists, recalling Lord Randolph in his fiery prime, could hardly help remarking on the quite uncanny similarities of his son in Parliament.

One described the "startling" resemblances between "the son of Lord Randolph and that brilliant statesman. . . . He has the square forehead, and the full bold eye of his father. . . . His hurried stride through the lobby is another point of resemblance; and when something amuses him he has his parent's trick of throwing back his head and laughing heartily."

Another journalist was even more impressed by similarities of gesture. "When the young member for Oldham addresses the House, with hands on hips, head bent forward, right hand stretched forth, memories of days that are no more flood the brain. Like the father is the son in his habit of independent views on current topics, the unexpectedness of his conclusions, his disregard for authority, his contempt for conventions, and his perfect phrasing of disagreeable remarks."

Churchill would always need a role to play. Much of his genius lay in the way he would take a part that suited him, work on it, build it in whatever way he needed, and act it out with absolute conviction. He had already been Savrola and the young Napoleon, the warrior of Omdurman, and the literary recluse, writing his books late into the night. But his most rewarding role of all, which he was now so busily rehearsing, was that of his father as a famous statesman.

Once he had climbed his "scaffolding of rhetoric," it became easier. His dedication was absolute. Apart from his ambition, constant work was the surest way of staving off depression, and according to his old friend J. B. Atkins, "he gave himself entirely to work. When he was not busy with politics, he was reading or writing. He did not lead the life of other young men in London. He may have visited political clubs, but I never met him walking in Pall Mall or Hyde Park where sooner or later one used to meet one's friends. I never met him at a dinner party that had not some public or some private purpose."

He was convinced that, like his father in so many other things, he was preordained to burn out young; and soon, with an effrontery that would have been preposterous had it not been totally sincere, he was planning his Savrola-style attempt to win the leadership of one or other of the major parties.

Early in 1901, when he had been in Parliament less than a year, he was staying with his parents' old friend Cecil Rhodes. The royal ex-mistress, Lady Warwick—once rumored to have also been Lord Randolph's femme fatale—was another of Rhodes's guests. Later she recalled the twenty-six-year-old Churchill discussing his own political position after dinner.

He was, he airily remarked, "inclined to leave the Conservative leadership to Mr. Balfour, and proclaim himself a Liberal. He wanted power, and the Tory road to power was blocked by the Cecils and other brilliant Conservatives." According to Lady Warwick, Cecil Rhodes was "all in favour of his turning Liberal."

One all-important portion of Lord Randolph Churchill's political legacy was the memory of his treatment by the Tory party. From an unbiased viewpoint, Lord Randolph's own behavior more than justified the way Lord Salisbury subsequently kept him out of office.

But Churchill was not unbiased where his father was concerned, and it was easy for him to conjure up a very different scenario. In his eyes, Lord Randolph had been cruelly betrayed by the ungrateful party he had resurrected by his genius and oratory. He had resigned on a point of all-important principle, and the villain of the piece had been the leading member of the Cecil family, solid Lord Salisbury, who, having sacrificed Lord Randolph, proceeded to enjoy three unruffled terms as Prime Minister.

The Conservative leader in the Commons who, in 1902, followed Salisbury as Prime Minister was another member of the Cecil family: the deceptively lethargic-seeming intellectual Arthur Balfour. He, too, had once enjoyed Lord Randolph's friendship as an ally in the great days of the Fourth party and had then deserted him.

It was a scenario full of bitterness and high emotion that could absolve an ambitious young M.P. from ties of loyalty to a party—and a family—that had treated his father with such scant regard.

Had Balfour had the sense to offer Winston a place in his government, he would certainly have taken it. When he failed to, the young M.P. was finally convinced that he had no future in the Tory party and prepared to make the move that his career required.

It took a little time to find a convincing reason for his exit. It came early in 1903. Another of his father's former allies, Joseph Chamberlain, proposed to defend the Empire and its trade by creating tariff barriers. Although Chamberlain, the great imperialist, planned to strengthen the Empire by his measures, Churchill was vehemently against them.

For a year he campaigned vigorously against his party under the banner of free trade. Then in May 1904, he followed the logic of his interests and declared beliefs and crossed to the Liberal opposition.

It was a move that brought predictable and bitter enmity from the Conservative establishment, which followed him for many years. But at the time he barely seemed to notice—even when his former allies christened him "The Blenheim Rat."

In terms of pure ambition, Winston had acted wisely. Divided by internal disagreement over tariffs, the Conservatives had reached the end of their long monopoly of power; Balfour had lost his touch as Prime Minister; and early in 1906, the Liberals won an overwhelming victory in a general election. Churchill was returned for his Manchester constituency on a large majority and was promoted to an under-secretaryship in the Liberal government. He was thirty-one.

As deputy to the Colonial Secretary, Lord Elgin, who was in the House of Lords, Churchill had full responsibility for presenting the government's colonial policy to the Commons. And since Lord Elgin was a somewhat placid peer, the new under-secretary was in the kind of situation he loved, with permission to range freely over any subject —if not in the universe, at least throughout the great empire over which the sun still never set.

# twelve

# Love and the
# Pursuit of Power

After rejection by Miss Plowden, Churchill had been too involved with politics and journalism to worry about marriage. But now it was clear that he required a wife. Finding one, however, was not so easy, and there were several reasons for this, all of which were more or less connected with crucial elements within Churchill's character. Since these affected his relations with his friends and family throughout his life, they are worth considering.

Part of the trouble was the nature of Churchill's ceaseless quest for power. With his thoughts so firmly focused on himself and his own endeavors, he could not afford women much attention. On rare occasions when he let himself be trapped beside an attractive female at the dinner table, he tended either to ignore her or lecture her about himself.

The formidable and not unattractive social reformer Beatrice Webb recorded her impressions of him in her diary. "Went into dinner with Winston Churchill. First impression: restless, almost intolerably so . . . egotistical, bumptious, shallowminded, and reactionary, but with a certain personal magnetism. . . . More of the American speculator than the English aristocrat. Talked exclusively about himself and his electioneering plans. . . ."

Churchill's relationships with women were made more difficult still by his mood swings. On a manic up-swing he became all-powerful and needed no one, least of all a demanding and dependent woman, near him. Only his depressive down-swings saw him vulnerable and lonely, but on these occasions he learned to keep his troubles to himself.

Lord Beaverbrook, who would experience at close quarters these two extremely different sides of Churchill's personality, remarked on the unexpected charm Churchill could reveal when "down." The essence of this charm, he wrote, lay in "the simplicity of a child which no contact with the world could ever spoil." ("Churchill 'up,'" he added, was "quite a different proposition . . . on top of the wave he has in him the stuff of which tyrants are made.") So far only two women had been permitted within this vulnerable world of Winston's childhood—Jennie and his old nurse, Mrs. Everest.

One of the curiosities about *Savrola* is the contrast between the hero's lust for power and his lack of lust toward his lovely heroine. Since the heroine, Lucile, is clearly based on Jennie, this was just as well. But this also helps explain the element of chaste romanticism that lay behind his idealized concept of the other sex.

This was a point that Asquith's daughter Violet shrewdly understood. "His approach to women," she would write, "was essentially romantic. He had a lively susceptibility to beauty, glamour, radiance, and those who possessed these qualities were not subjected to analysis. Their possession of all the cardinal virtues was assumed as a matter of course. I remember him taking umbrage when I once commented on the 'innocence' of his approach to women. He was affronted by this epithet as applied to himself; yet to me he would certainly have applied it as a term of praise."

Again one is driven back upon the grim example of Lord Randolph's death. What better reason for a son to keep his sexual innocence than to avoid the trap that brought about his parent's downfall? What better impulse than to stay instead with those "innocent" memories that safely brought to mind his childhood vision of his mother— all the "beauty, glamour, radiance" that the highly sexual Jennie had exuded in the presence of her schoolboy son.

Fortunately for Churchill's peace of mind, his first two years as Junior Minister in Campbell Bannerman's Liberal government were busy and successful. As House of Commons deputy to a minister in the House of Lords, he was standing in Lord Randolph's parliamentary shoes, with responsibility to the Commons for everything relating to the colonies. The range of his activities was endless, his fortunes were ascending, "Black Dog" was safely kept at bay, and his energy and schoolboy zest for life were carrying the world before him.

From his position of power Churchill was soon poking at the dead wood in all corners of the colonial administration. "He is most tiresome to deal with," wrote the permanent Under-Secretary to Lord Elgin, "and I fear will give trouble—as his father did—in any position to which he may be called. The restless energy, uncontrollable desire for notoriety and lack of moral perception make him an anxiety indeed."

In other words, Churchill was in the sort of situation that he loved. It was ironic that now, in the summer of 1907, the woman problem should have suddenly erupted from a dangerous quarter and in an unexpected shape.

At the beginning of that year, his brother, Jack, had met Lady Gwendoline Bertie, the daughter of the Earl of Abingdon. Known as "Goonie," she was twenty-one, dark-haired, vivacious, and judging from a portrait by Sargent, romantically attractive, with an expression of alert intelligence that sly artist rarely noticed in the young English debutantes he depicted. She had led the customary sheltered life of upper-class English young ladies and on meeting handsome young Jack Churchill decided she was suddenly in love.

Jack, at twenty-six, was only just becoming established as a stockbroker. But his manly looks and simple nature, coupled with his lack of means, must have made him seem romantically appealing to this strong-willed virgin. Flattered, he returned her love wholeheartedly, and before long brought her home to meet his mother at her country house, Salisbury Place near St. Albans. It was there that Goonie met Winston.

Throughout his life, Winston had been scoring off Jack, as if in retribution for the way Lord Randolph made him his favorite during the boys' adolescence. One of the most admirable things about Jack was his total lack of resentment. He seems to have accepted uncomplainingly the way Winston had arranged an income for himself from their joint inheritance while he was in the cavalry, although there was no money for Jack to go to university. He took it for granted that Winston had inherited what brains were in the family, and seemed to have escaped the family depression. An uncomplicated soul, he hero-worshiped brother Winston. But even Jack's powers of hero worship would have been severely tested had he realized that something more than innocent affection was developing between his brother and the girl he loved.

It is hard to know how far or consciously Churchill encouraged Goonie. One can imagine Winston so dominant and so exuberant that he failed to comprehend the obvious effect that he was having on this very bright and willful girl.

One can also see, from the few extant letters she wrote him, how it was she who played up to him, striking just that note of wittily flirtatious mockery that is unerringly appealing in relationships between clever younger women and older men.

In one letter she pretended to be concerned that his official duties would bring him in contact with Mohammedans, "but please don't become converted to Islam," she implored him.

Jennie had her own suspicions of what was happening. She realized that her elder son was responding far too warmly to this young lady and may well have warned him of the situation that was developing, for quite suddenly that August Winston fled.

He had been planning an official visit to East Africa, but his decision to depart was made so hurriedly that his new secretary, the socialite man of letters Eddie Marsh, had to join him later. Jennie knew the details of his journey only after he had left. The first the eager Goonie heard about the five-month expedition was the news of his departure, which produced an anguished letter of reproach.

"It is positively cruel of Fate to determine that we should not say goodbye," nor to have had the chance to have "wined and dined" in London as they had evidently planned. "I cannot help rebelling against fate, for how entirely unreasonable it can be, considering what pleasure it should have given us."

The next day, having heard that Churchill was en route to Paris, Goonie was writing him a second shameless letter: "Dear Mr. Winston, I wish I could go with you to Paris on Sunday—I have not been there for two whole years, and I do love it so, but I don't expect I know much of your Paris, it is the other Paris, the *jeune fille* Paris that I am acquainted with."

And a week later came her final plea. "My Dear Mr. Winston, Where are you? Where have you been? Where are you going to? What are you going to do? I have lost you for a whole week, I want to find you again—you have effaced yourself from my horizon."

For the time being the effacement was complete, and Churchill's five-month absence in the British colonies of East Africa was one of those supremely happy periods in which the hero was able to submerge the cares of statesmanship and sex in the joys of travel, manly fellowship, and big-game hunting.

Writing to Jennie of rhinoceroses he had slaughtered, he noted that "the vitality of these brutes is so tremendous that they will come on like some large engine in spite of five or six heavy bullets thumping into them." Aggressive as ever, he decided that rhino made the most satisfactory adversaries outside Parliament, and while he was busy "thumping" bullets into them, he heard from Jack. During the summer, Goonie had been saying that she felt she could not promise to wait long enough for him to earn sufficient money to support a wife, but since Winston had left for Africa, something had mysteriously made her change her mind. And now she had just written to the patient Jack, saying that her love for him was even stronger than before.

As Jack put it in his letter to his brother, "she said she would sacrifice anything for her love; that her ambition for riches and everything else had all vanished and that she would wait for me. . . ."

Churchill had helped make Jack a happy man—and in return, virtue now brought rather more than traditional reward. Refreshed and resolute, Winston returned to London in mid-January 1908 to discover that the Prime Minister, seventy-two-year-old Campbell Bannerman, was on the point of retiring because of ill health (he died in April), and he was to be succeeded by the former Chancellor of the Exchequer, Herbert Asquith.

Asquith was a warm if somewhat wary admirer of Churchill. It was thanks to him that Churchill reached, at the age of thirty-three, the next decisive rung of power: his own ministry as President of the Board of Trade, with a seat in Asquith's Cabinet.

He was very much his own man with his marked abilities and fanatical capacity for work, and seemed set to reach the ultimate position of Prime Minister, which Lord Randolph once remarked was the only one worth having. Few doubted he would get there, least of all himself. But there was still the marital problem to be solved. With Jack eager to marry Goonie as soon as possible—and so break up their bachelor establishment—this was doubly urgent. Even so, the speed with which he acted was remarkable, as was the fact that he had met the girl with whom he fell in love on a previous occasion, when neither had evinced the faintest interest in the other.

It was early March, less than eight weeks after his return from

Africa, and Churchill was lying in his bath—his favorite form of relaxation—when his secretary, Eddie Marsh, reminded him that he was due at a dinner party at the home of Lady St. Helier in Portland Place.

Churchill was disinclined to make the effort. He was already late and preferred the prospect of an evening on his own. But Marsh was a friend of Lady St. Helier's. Indeed, it had been through her that he had first been introduced to Churchill, and he insisted Churchill go.

Churchill was rarely punctual anyhow, and, arriving very late, he was placed at the dinner table between Lady Lugard, the wife of the great West African explorer, and a reserved and rather beautiful young lady, Clementine Hozier, daughter of his mother's great friend.

Lady Lugard was an intelligent woman, and Churchill was particularly interested in Africa, so one might have expected him to spend the rest of dinner telling her his views, his plans, and his experiences on that fascinating continent. Instead, he turned his attention to Miss Hozier. Lady Lugard was ignored, Miss Hozier "monopolized" for the rest of the evening. With the same decision he had shown at Omdurman, Churchill's marital campaign had started.

As they discovered, he and Miss Hozier had met at a ball some four years earlier. Greatly attracted to her now, he employed his charm and knowledge of the world to powerful effect. Miss Hozier was captivated. So, it seemed, was Churchill, and the romance proceeded with much the same dispatch and energy he brought to politics.

If Churchill was acting on the rebound, he could not have picked a greater contrast in the person of the chaste Miss Hozier. Earnest, tall, shy, she had a classic beauty that was in a different class from Goonie's vivacious prettiness. Neither frivolous nor funny, she was an essentially serious person, uneducated, unsophisticated, short of money, and with a family almost as turbulent as Churchill's own.

Her father, Sir Henry Montagu Hozier, had died the year before. A largely self-made man who had ended up as secretary of Lloyds of London, he had married considerably above himself, taking as his second wife the beautiful and much younger Lady Blanche, daughter of the Earl of Airlie. He seems to have known little happiness thereafter.

There were four children of the marriage: Kitty, born in 1883; Clementine, who followed two years later; and a pair of twins, Bill and Nellie, who were born in 1888. But Sir Henry never managed to convince himself that they were all his, and this brought problems to the marriage. By the time Clementine was six, Blanche Hozier was on her own with four young children to support.

While still with Hozier, Lady Blanche had become Jennie's friend, and they had certain things in common. Both had been great beauties, both had endured disastrous marriages, and both had been unfaithful. But the similarities between them ended there.

Jennie was a born survivor. About this time, she was facing money troubles with her new husband—often referred to in her letters as "poor George." But as much the American social entrepreneur as ever, she was finding ways to keep them both in style—writing her memoirs, starting an up-market magazine, and finding houses she could fashionably redecorate and then resell at a useful profit.

Even if Lady Blanche had been capable of such resourcefulness, she would have felt such activities utterly beneath her. Born an aristocrat, she had something of the attitude of the great Whig ladies of an earlier century. She gambled, drank, spent money, and had love affairs exactly as she pleased. Later, having married beneath herself and without affection, she saw no reason to change her habits. The result had been disastrous, but Lady Blanche had also schooled herself to see disaster as something one ignored.

No one seemed to know the precise paternity of her children—except that the father was almost certainly not Hozier. One of her most dashing lovers was her brother-in-law Bertram Mitford, first Lord Redesdale. He was married to Blanche's favorite sister, Clementine, after whom she had named her second daughter, and this fed the persistent rumors that blue-eyed Bertram Mitford was Clementine Hozier's natural father.

For Clementine, life with a mother who was supported mainly by Lord Airlie was inevitably chaotic. There had been enforced migrations and a running battle with a bitter and revengeful Hozier. He had tended to appear at awkward moments, threatening to repossess the children. Partly to escape him, and partly to enjoy the cheaper living and the nearby gambling casino, Lady Blanche had finally made her home across the Channel at Dieppe, and it was there that Clementine spent much of her adolescence.

Young Clementine reacted to all this much as one might expect, disliking almost everything that Lady Blanche's way of life embodied. Hating the mess and muddle in which she had lived, she was obsessively perfectionistic in all she did, and seeing the chaos that her mother's love affairs had brought her, she was something of a puritan. Money worries could upset her deeply; gambling and drunkenness depressed her. The death of her sister Kitty at seventeen scarred her emotionally. Over the years, she taught herself to keep her feelings bottled up, but beneath the surface lay an element of rage that would burst through suddenly throughout her life.

By twenty-one she had been engaged to a wealthy civil servant nearly twice her age. Fearful, perhaps, of repeating Lady Blanche's blunder of a loveless marriage with an older man, she ended the engagement with some recriminations and a nervous breakdown. Yet she remained patently in need of certain things only a man ten years older was likely to provide: stability, a father figure able to control her, social position, and, above all, an overriding purpose to her life. Clementine was custom-built to fall in love with Winston Churchill.

Churchill's motives were not so clear, and his behavior that evening at Lady St. Helier's dinner table bears the signs of a determined act of will rather than a yielding to sudden ardor.

Clementine herself was always sensitive to suggestions that Jennie had cleverly arranged things, which she clearly had not. On the other hand, she certainly encouraged the relationship once she realized that the young woman was the daughter of her old friend. Clementine was warmly invited up to Salisbury Lodge, where she met Jack and Lady Goonie, who were making preparations for their wedding. The sight of his younger brother, suddenly so happy with the girl he might have wed himself, must have been a strong incentive for Winston to settle his own future as soon as possible.

On August 4, 1908, Jack and Goonie were married. Since the Berties were Catholic and Jack was not, this was a civil ceremony near their home at Abingdon. Winston, who had attended the ceremony, wrote Clementine about it. "We all swooped down in motor cars upon the town of Abingdon and did the deed before the Registrar—for all the world as if it was an elopement."

The bride and groom, he added, "were entirely composed & the business was despatched with a celerity & ease that was almost appalling."

Seven days later, with an even more remarkable "celerity," Winston proposed to Clementine. He did this, having carefully arranged the background, as if he were once more playing his own privately created part in history. The proposal had to take place at Blenheim, where he was shortly due to spend a few days' holiday. Cousin Sunny, as head of the family, had to play his own supporting role, so Winston persuaded him to send a pressing invitation.

Clementine had problems accepting at such short notice. She had no maid, no chaperone, and later recalled that she was "right down to her last laundered and starched dress."

But Churchill insisted she come. "I want so much to show you that beautiful place and in its gardens we shall find lots of places to talk in and lots of things to talk about."

Jennie, apprised of the situation, was hurriedly brought in to act as chaperone, and Miss Hozier, with her one clean cotton frock, arrived at Blenheim on August 10.

As good as his word, Churchill made arrangements to conduct her around the gardens the next morning for their confidential talk, but not even thoughts of marriage could make him break the habit of a lifetime. Clementine was left downstairs, until Sunny, seeing the situation and knowing Winston's habit of sleeping late, sent a message to his cousin's bedroom to bestir himself. Later, on a wet Tuesday afternoon, beside the famous lake at Blenheim, Churchill proposed to Clementine and was accepted. Never one to waste time once decisions had been made, he insisted that the wedding should be held three weeks later in London.

In contrast to Jack and Goonie's wedding at the Abingdon Registry Office, Winston and Clementine's on September 12, 1908, was a society event, with St. Margaret's Westminster filled to overflowing with the politicians and members of the aristocracy who formed so large a part of Churchill's life. Crowds of what the *Times* reporter called "people of the better sort" filled Parliament Square and the adjoining roads to cheer the groom and bride on their arrival, and in the church, the families were on parade for this all-important tribal gathering.

The bride wore ivory-colored silk trimmed with lace de Venise "lent by Mrs. George Cornwallis-West," and was given away by her sailor brother, Bill Hozier. The best man was Lord Hugh Cecil, the one-time leader of the Hughligans and a reminder of Churchill's Tory past. Churchill took his marriage vows "in a firm clear voice," while Clementine's were "all but inaudible." And when Lloyd George was invited to sign the marriage register in the vestry, the groom started talking politics to him rather than sweet nothings to his bride, thus proving the supremacy of habit over sentiment.

But the most spectacular members of the wedding must have been those two impressive ladies, once the toast and trophies of high Victorian male society and now the mothers of, respectively, the groom and the bride: Jennie, Mrs. George Cornwallis-West, and Lady Blanche, the widow of Sir Henry Hozier.

Jennie was clearly out to steal the show as she took her front-pew seat beside "poor George," who, whatever his failings, was still occasionally described as "the best-looking man in London." In addition to ensuring that the press had picked up the all-important point about the lace on the bride's dress, Jennie had also dressed to kill—in purple silk with a large hat surmounted by a dahlia.

A somewhat blousy fifty-six, Lady Blanche could not aspire to match her old friend's ample but still seductive figure—let alone her husband and her dahlia. But she did not entirely miss out. Dressed in mushroom-colored satin, she had taken care to surround herself with a phalanx of her finest-looking, most distinguished lovers.

As a widow, she was suitably escorted by her brother-in-law, the ardent Bertram, first Lord Redesdale. Just behind sat Lord Elcho's son, the handsome Hugo Wemyss, who had also intermittently enjoyed her favors, and next to him was placed the remorseless seducer, Wilfred Scawen-Blunt, who had been comforting her for many years.

To the gossip-riddled world of London society, so many of whom were present, this must have seemed a notable riposte to Mrs. George Cornwallis-West, particularly as those who were privileged to be in the know had long taken it for granted that Bertie Redesdale was, of course, the father of the lovely Clementine. Who better to be escorting his old mistress at their daughter's wedding?

However, not for the first time the gossip was inaccurate and missed the most intriguing point about the marriage. It was a point that united the mothers of the bride and groom more closely than was realized.

Back in 1892, at the beginning of her long affair with Scawen Blunt, Lady Blanche had confided in him the truth about the father of her daughters, Kitty and Clementine. It was not Sir Henry Hozier, nor was it Lord Redesdale—Redesdale had come later and was probably the father of the twins, Bill and Nellie. According to what Scawen Blunt recorded in his diary at the time, the father of the two elder girls was "the gallant Bay Middleton, superb horseman and escort to the Empress Elizabeth of Austria in the shires."

Far from being shocked or jealous, Scawen Blunt had approved of this on strict eugenic grounds. He was a great lover of horses, and it seemed sensible to him that the "valiant Blanche," as he called her, should have chosen to improve the stock with a handsome and full-blooded sportsman like Middleton rather than the spavined old Sir Henry, even if he were her husband.

Middleton, a regular army officer, was a member of a family of Shropshire gentry. His greatest claim to fame had come when he was chosen to accompany the horse-mad Empress Elizabeth on her hunting expeditions to England and southern Ireland in the 1870s. It was in Ireland that he had met Jennie, and there that they had first become close friends.

How close was anybody's guess. The Empress was known to be frigid sexually, having contracted syphilis from her husband, the Emperor of Austria. Middleton had a reputation as a rampant womanizer, and Jennie was beginning to enjoy her freedom as a very liberated woman.

By the early 1880s, when Bay Middleton appears in the entries of Jennie's London diary, he is clearly Blanche's lover, and Blanche is Jennie's most frequently mentioned female friend. When Blanche gave birth to her two daughters shortly thereafter, the worldly Jennie can have had no doubts about their true paternity.

This strange old tangle of forgotten love affairs lay carefully concealed beneath the splendor of the wedding, and one wonders whether the mothers-in-law discussed them. Probably not. Both were great believers in the status quo and keeping up appearances, and both had far too much to lose if such secrets came out even within the family. This makes it even more unlikely that they allowed a hint of this to reach their children. Certainly Winston and Clementine's daughter Mary had no idea that Sir Henry Hozier was not her true grandfather until Elizabeth Longford published her biography of Scawen Blunt in 1982.

There does remain, however, a chance that Clementine suspected that Jennie did know something. She never liked or trusted her mother-in-law—any more than she really liked or trusted her mother—and the attitudes with which she and her husband now embarked upon their marriage could not have been more different from that of the scandalous quartet to whom they owed their being.

# thirteen

# Light Fades from the Picture

After the wedding night at ancestral Blenheim, and a simpler honeymoon in Venice, the couple embarked on marriage, first in Churchill's bachelor flat in Bolton Street, then in a more spacious house on a sixteen-year lease in Eccleston Square, on the edge of Mayfair. Some were expecting Churchill, romantic man of action that he was, to lead a married life to match—sociable, extravagant, and full of high dramatic interest. Clementine, however, made it clear in one of her earliest decisive acts of married womanhood that such was not to be the case.

Before they left on their honeymoon, Churchill had innocently asked his mother to redecorate the bedroom at Bolton Street as a surprise for their return. Jennie had exercised her professional decorator's skill to some effect. The result sounds charming, but not for Clementine. "To her simple and rather austere taste, the sateen and muslin covers trimmed with bows, which decked the chairs, dressing-table and bed, appeared cheap and tawdry," writes her daughter Mary. According to the same source, Clementine regarded Jennie rather similarly: "Vain and frivolous" are the words Mary uses. It became clear that Jennie's influence, like her taste in furnishing, would not impinge on Winston's marriage. From the start, vanity and frivolity were out, simplicity and austerity would take their place—if Clementine had anything to do with it. By the standards of their group, the Winston Churchills were distinctly short of money, and it was on this note of high thinking and simple living that their marriage started.

It was to be a strangely sentimental marriage for a man of Churchill's warlike temper. The victor of Omdurman was frequently addressed as "Mr. Pug" by his strong-willed wife, whom he called "Mrs. Kat." Kat and Pug inhabited a childlike world with a private language full of furry animals.

In contrast with their fashionable friends and relations, they appear cozily middle class. Some of their visitors expressed surprise at the scenes of innocent happiness they found in Eccleston Square. On Churchill's birthday, elegant Lord Esher discovered Kat and Pug purring lovingly together on the sofa in paper hats before a birthday cake with candles. This display of affection was seen as touching and amusing, but it was also of importance to the future of their marriage. Both had been essentially lonely people despite the great activity around them. "I am a solitary creature in the midst of crowds. Be kind to me," Churchill had begged Clementine, in a flash of candor, on the eve of their marriage. As for Clementine, nothing could have been more solitary than the anxious, secluded life she led before she married.

Together they were creating something of the happy childhood neither had enjoyed and finding an exclusive, private world that offered a defense against whatever threats they felt around them. There would always be a place in their relationship into which no one else would enter. And it would be here, when needed, that Churchill would demand and find that total female love and understanding he had longed for from his mother. Clementine in turn seemed eager to dedicate herself to him and his career. The arrival of their first "Puppy-kitten" on July 11, 1909—a redheaded daughter, christened Diana—seems to have delighted Churchill.

"Is she a pretty child?" Lloyd George asked him.

"The prettiest child ever seen," the proud father answered.

"Like her mother, I suppose," said Lloyd George.

"No," said Churchill. "She is the image of me."

But regardless who Diana actually resembled—and she *did* look rather like her father—she was not permitted to intrude upon her parents' private life together.

Clementine was not naturally maternal. "Wife first and mother a very distant second" is how one of Clementine's friends described her.

It was an attitude that suited the self-absorbed husband to perfection, but it was hard to tell what damage it inflicted on his daughter. It is also difficult to judge how much Churchill's demanding nature at this time was responsible for Clementine's decided lack of interest in any of her children during their infancy. It was as if he took the children's place, leaving his wife too little affection or emotion for the others, for one of Clementine's gravest disadvantages was a weakness in reserves of energy. Again, it is hard to know how much of this was due to a neurotic weakness already present when she married, and how much to the strains of coping with her dominating husband. Certainly an element of earnestness and somewhat humorless inflexibility on her part seems to have made the problem worse.

She could be jealous and extremely prickly, and some of her husband's colleagues found her tedious. "She is, *au fond,* a thundering bore," was Asquith's unforgiving verdict—and the worldly Jennie undoubtedly agreed. Jennie's friend Mrs. Keppel, the royal mistress, seems to have enjoyed pulling ingenuous Clementine's leg, on one occasion offering her an extravagant couturier dress, which Clementine indignantly refused, and on another seriously informing her that if she was truly dedicated to her husband's political career, she should encourage him to have a mistress. (Again, Clementine was not amused.) Clementine was not a rich sophisticate like Jennie, nor a natural wit like Goonie. She was a simple, strong-willed, young aristocrat anxiously involved with her famous husband and his great career.

As for Churchill, marriage brought no change to his quest for power, nor to the rigid workaholic life it demanded. As usual, he worked late into the night, while she was inclined to retire—and rise —early. They never breakfasted together and had separate rooms from the beginning.

During these early months of marriage, it was as if Clementine had permanently banished Lord Randolph's gloomy ghost. To begin with, they went out little into smart society. As he told Clementine, it was "power and great business" that obsessed him. As president of the Board of Trade he was already a key member of the most talented peacetime government of the century—and he was barely in his middle thirties.

It was now that Churchill showed genuine sympathy with the underdog. He had been strongly influenced by reading Seebohm Rowntree's investigative book on poverty in Britain—and by memories of his experiences as a prisoner of war. Now he was in the vanguard of the great Liberal movement for social reform. Clementine, a Liberal herself, very much encouraged this. He had been converted to this admirable cause, some months before they met, through something of a "divine" revelation—as his friend C. F. Masterman makes clear in his eyewitness description of the event.

It began tempestuously. "Winston swept me off to his cousin's house and I lay on the bed while he dressed and marched around the room, gesticulating and impetuous, pouring out all his hopes and plans and ambitions. He is full of the poor, whom he has just discovered. He thinks he is called by providence to do something for them. 'Why have I been kept safe to within a hair's breadth of death,' he asked, 'except to do something like this?' "

Guided by his rival, friend, and mentor, the Welsh radical Lloyd George, Churchill swiftly made his name as a social radical and one of the founding fathers of the modern welfare state. During his three years at the Board of Trade, he skillfully employed the power he loved to establish labor exchanges, set minimum standards and conditions in sweatshops, prevent industrial exploitation of children, and begin a system of national insurance.

It was a formidable achievement and it established him as a great reformer—and also as Lloyd George's most obvious competitor for future Liberal leadership. It was an unlikely situation for the grandson of a duke; still more unlikely was his role in the Liberal battle with the Conservative opposition when the House of Lords rejected Lloyd George's so-called Peoples Budget in 1909.

Here, for the first—and last—time, was Churchill speaking out against his class and its privileges—with gusto, wit, and obvious enjoyment. At one point he seemed perfectly prepared to abolish "that feudal assembly" the House of Lords, and ridiculed the peers, those "heaven-born and God-granted legislators" in their "prejudiced chamber, hereditary, non-elected, irresponsible, and irremediable." As for the Conservatives, in one of his most memorable phrases, Churchill dismissed them all as "old doddering peers, cute financial magnates, clever wire-pullers, and big brewers with bulbous noses."

Some laughed, but others took predictable offense, and the enmity of members of his own class deepened. "I would rather be a crossing sweeper than Winston Churchill," said his onetime friend George Wyndham.

"I would like to see him and Lloyd George in the middle of twenty couple of dog-hounds," said the Duke of Beaufort.

Churchill appeared impervious to unpopularity and stayed on

sufficiently good terms with Cousin Sunny to be invited to the customary ducal Christmas at Blenheim in 1909.

It was not he but Clementine who drew out the ducal wrath against her beloved Liberal party. Shortly after, while on her own at Blenheim, she took great offense at Sunny's remarks on Prime Minister Asquith's drinking habits; harsh words were spoken, and Clementine swept out of Blenheim vowing never to return. The incident did not affect her husband's friendship with his beloved Sunny, however.

It would seem, at this point, that Churchill had everything he wanted out of life: a faithful and adoring wife, a comfortable home, a growing income from his writing, and glittering prospects. Even the "supreme power" he longed for seemed within his reach.

In February 1910, he became Home Secretary with a salary of £5,000 a year. It was an important post, responsible for police, law and order, and the day-to-day administration of the country. With this key appointment and a place in the Cabinet, everything was going as he had planned. But it was now that, unaccountably, he was hit by a mysterious crisis in his private life.

The novelist Henry James lunched with him around this time at Walmer Castle (Asquith's official residence as Lord Warden of the Cinque Ports), and that shrewd old specialist of human nature evidently spotted something in the young phenomenon that puzzled him. He did not say exactly what it was, but thinking about it later, he seems to have been uneasy about him. "I confess," James wrote, "that I am often struck at the limitations with which men of power pay the price for their domination over mankind."

In Churchill's case the price was higher than Henry James suspected. For despite his "domination over mankind," the young Home Secretary was finding himself tormented by his ancient enemy, "Black Dog."

Many years later, Churchill talked about it to his doctor, Lord Moran, making it clear how serious it had been: "For two or three years the light faded from the picture. I did my work. I sat in the House of Commons, but black depression settled on me."

Evidently, he was sometimes seriously suicidal. At railway stations, he purposely avoided the edge of the platform when an express was passing. He kept clear from the sides of ships and would not look down at the water. "A second's action would end everything. A few drops of desperation . . . ," he told Moran. The only thing that seemed to help, he said, was to "talk it over with Clementine."

It must have been hard for this outwardly confident and brash young politician to maintain his public facade. It is clear that, behind the show of bounding self-assurance, all the anxiety and sense of worthlessness associated with his father's judgment of him still persisted.

"Alas, I have no good opinion of myself," he told Clementine. "At times I think that I could conquer everything—and then again I know that I am only a weak fool." To Moran he confessed how angst had chronically oppressed him. "The mere thought that he might trip up filled him with apprehension," says Lord Moran.

Forty years later, further light was shed on the nature of this crisis from an unlikely quarter. In 1952, daughter Diana was herself afflicted by a nervous breakdown in the aftermath of which she told a friend how she had found her most sympathetic supporter in her now aged father. According to Diana, Churchill said he understood exactly how she felt, having suffered a near breakdown of his own while Home Secretary. He also told her what he thought had caused it in his case —the anguish caused by his duty to study the cases of condemned murderers so as to decide whether to mitigate or confirm the sentence.

On the face of it this sounds hard to credit. This was the man who excitedly survived the slaughter on the northwest frontier and South Africa, who purchased his "Ripper" with its soft-nosed bullets for the charge at Omdurman. In later years as war leader, he would make decisions that would affect the lives of thousands and then enjoy a good night's sleep. How could such a man have been so grievously afflicted by the fate of a few hundred common criminals? The answer is of importance to understanding Churchill's psychology and subsequent career.

Even at Harrow there had been the contrast between his two opposing personalities. The sensitive schoolboy, miserable about his parents, could transform himself into the aggressive bully shoving Meinertzhagen off the pavement. Since then, these transformations had become more frequent. Several had noticed the uncanny difference between Churchill "up"—confident, aggressive, carrying the world before him—and Churchill "down"—vulnerable, hypersensitive, and painfully aware of human suffering.

It was this second state that left him prey to the misery his congenital depression could inflict. Since coming to recognize the state of the poor, Churchill had been increasingly involved with something he had previously avoided: widespread human suffering and the misery beneath the surface of Edwardian England. This was the sort of nightmare world that he had always dreaded—the "life in the gutter" that his father had predicted as the price of failure. But worse still was the fate of the most wretched group of all with whom, as Home Secretary, he found himself involved: murderers condemned to death. The misery of their fate preyed upon his mind, and it was then that, as he put it, "the light faded from the picture."

Yet always in his times of deep depression, Churchill possessed an antidote, which he had used before and which rarely seemed to fail: aggression. His aggressive temperament had marked him out at Harrow and brought excitement and success throughout his military career. It had helped him overcome his fears of cowardice and had brought him much success in politics. Aggression was the great transformer, capable of changing the miserable depressive with his fears and weakness into the hero oblivious of danger. The astute journalist A. G. Gardiner described him now on a typical aggressive up-swing: "He is his own superman and is so absorbed in himself and in his fiery purposes that he does not pay others the compliment of even being aware of them." This was his surest antidote to melancholy—and about this time he started to return to it.

During the summer of 1910, his duties as Home Secretary made him responsible for law and order against the striking miners of South Wales. The ill-used miners and their unhappy families were the sort of people at the bottom of society who had in the past aroused the sympathy of Churchill the reformer. But once they went on strike and threatened violence, they were transformed into an enemy needing to be taught a lesson. Churchill unhesitatingly ordered in the troops.

He did not authorize the use of bayonets against the strikers, nor did he deserve the blame for the so-called Tonypandy Massacre that ensued. But there was no mistaking the energy and relish he suddenly displayed with a conflict on his hands. There was no sign of the depressive in him now—nor of any sympathy for the unhappy miners.

Then, the following year, the famous incident occurred that, while gaining him much notoriety, seemed to lift him completely out of his depression—and signaled a decisive change in the course of his life and politics.

On November 2, 1911, two shadowy figures—one of them suspected (incorrectly) of being a Latvian anarchist code-named "Peter the Painter"—were cornered by police in a house on Sidney Street in an East End slum. Shots were fired, a policeman wounded, reinforcements summoned—and the so-called Siege of Sidney Street began.

As Home Secretary, Churchill was swiftly on the scene, where he transformed a fairly simple incident of law and order into a pitched battle on the streets of London. (Photographs taken at the time show Churchill in morning coat and smart top hat, with a look of unmistakable excitement on his face.) The Horse Guards were ordered in. Artillery arrived, and Churchill, warlike feelings thoroughly aroused, suggested an assault by troops with armor-plated shields. Before this could occur the house caught fire.

Churchill gave orders to prevent the firemen from extinguishing the blaze, and the mysterious anarchists were incinerated—thus marking the conclusion of the story. Sidney Street brought Churchill considerable criticism at home and outright ridicule abroad, none of which appeared to worry him. Depression and anxieties forgotten, he was happily embarked on yet another bold aggressive upswing. When his friend C. F. Masterman asked angrily, "What the hell have you been doing now, Winston?" he cheerfully lisped in reply, "Now, Charlie, don't be croth. It was such fun."

Suddenly he seemed to be recovering his sense of fun for life in general. It was now that Churchill and his friend Lord Birkenhead— eminent lawyer, drinker, wit, and Tory statesman—founded a private dining club, which would remain a source of happiness, conviviality, and unrestrained discussion for almost the remainder of his life. Membership—by invitation of the founders only—was extended to politicians of all parties whose conversation they enjoyed. To make clear that they had no connection with a long-established gathering called "The Club," which recently had had the temerity to blackball Churchill, they simply called their group "The Other Club."

The company of friends such as Birkenhead was his favorite relaxation, and from then on, Churchill increasingly enjoyed it. What was also obvious about him, during what proved to be his final months at the Home Office, was a pronounced veering off from social questions —and from further conflict with the aristocracy—toward issues where his aggressive instincts could flourish unimpeded.

During that early summer, more labor troubles brought a clear revival of the spirit of Sidney Street, as the Home Secretary soared to new heights of bellicose activity. There was no suggestion of conciliation as Churchill, like some great commander mustering his troops, prepared to smash the transport strike threatening the nation. ("Bloody hell!" he shouted when he heard Lloyd George had settled it by deft negotiation.)

More and more, Churchill's happiness and peace of mind seemed to require the balm of conflict. Aggression cured his own deep dread of failure, and warfare, by the strangest irony of all, protected him from worry over the suffering of others.

War not only roused the noble elements he loved—adventure, courage and patriotism—it also shifted his attention from those social victims who depressed him to a new enemy that demanded all his warlike energies. Even during his period as social reformer, he had not kept himself entirely from the joys of warfare.

"Do you know," he wrote to Clementine in May 1909, during his annual two weeks on maneuvers at Camp Goring, "I would greatly like to have some practice in the handling of large forces. I have much confidence in my judgement on things, when I see clearly, but on nothing do I seem to *feel* the truth more than in tactical combinations. . . . I am sure I have the root of the matter in me—but never in this state of human existence will it have a chance of flowering—in bright red blossom."

The chance was closer than he knew. Later in 1909 he got himself invited as an observer to the German military maneuvers where he met the Kaiser and witnessed his enormous forces. "This army is a terrible engine. It sometimes marches 35 miles a day. It is in number as the sands of the sea. . . , " he told Clementine.

This first sight of the power of German militarism made an indelible impression, clearly striking chords of powerful emotion in his nature. In the same letter he admitted how much "war attracts me & fascinates my mind with its tremendous situations." Then reason intervened, and he hurried to assure his wife that "in the midst of arms" he also felt "what vile and wicked folly and barbarism it all is."

No one knows better than a drunk the horrors of the demon drink, and Churchill would never lose a deep awareness of the horrors and the dreadfulness of modern war. Yet as in the case of the drunk, his awareness of the consequences could not destroy its terrible attraction.

The summer of 1911 proved a happy time for Churchill, for it was then that he became the father of a second child—the longed-for son and heir. He was a pretty infant, with Clementine's forget-me-not blue eyes and pale blond hair. For Churchill, with his sense of dynasty, this small blond version of himself was of almost mystical importance—giving a purpose to his great ambition, forging the link in *his* dynastic chain, and also offering a chance of making further restitution to his father's memory. When it was time to christen the child at St. Margaret's Westminster, one name alone was possible: Randolph.

Just as his son was being born, the Imperial German government was completing Churchill's happiness by sending a warship to the Moroccan port of Agadir. It was an arrogant exercise in power-politics against the French, and for a moment Europe hovered on the brink of war. The crisis passed, but it revealed the danger of the Kaiser's Germany and the unpreparedness of the British fleet. In the aftermath of Agadir, Asquith decided on a new broom for the Royal Navy. In October 1911, despite his earlier impassioned opposition to more expenditure on the fleet, an exultant Churchill became First Lord of the Admiralty.

Even now he needed to believe that destiny was on his side, and he was reassured when Clementine, opening the Bible at random, hit on Psalm 107, and read: "They that go down to the sea in ships, that do business in great waters."

# fourteen

# Admiralty

Life at the Admiralty, combined with the importance and excitement of his new role, suited Churchill; an exuberant, new man was emerging—convivial, extravagant, and thoroughly enjoying rich and racy company.

This was hard on Clementine, who was missing the close, simple existence of those first years in Eccleston Square. Against the infinitely grander background of their official residence at the Admiralty, Winston's extravagance disturbed her—as did his periods away from her. His propensity to gamble particularly upset her, and on at least one occasion she erupted in a jealous rage against one of the young women —probably Herbert Asquith's daughter Violet—who were increasingly attracted by the new sociable Winston Churchill.

Her thirty-eight-year-old husband responded magisterially. Clementine should know better than to indulge in "small emotions and wounding doubts." "Your sweetness and beauty have cast a glory on my life," he told her. He was probably telling her the truth, and her fears about other women were unfounded. If nothing else, he was too busy to philander, and his truest pleasures lay in convivial male company. According to Jock Colville, Churchill's future secretary, "from 1911 onwards, Churchill's delight was to dine with F. E. Smith and sometimes Lloyd George. He would telephone to say that he was bringing them all back to dinner and it would be pleasant to have some lobsters and roast duck."

Lobsters and roast duck caused poor Clementine genuine anxiety. "The problems of housekeeping on a comparatively small budget were something that Churchill never grasped," said Colville. "She would do her best, for she did not wish to jeopardise her husband's political career or snub his friends; but she resented the late nights, the excessive consumption of brandy, the noise and the rowdiness, which were inseparable from the garrulous evenings."

Times had changed from the grim periods when he was plunged in deep despondency, and Clementine had urged him to enjoy society. It was Clementine who was now increasingly depressed, especially after a miscarriage early in 1912, which left her weak and nervous. Churchill was solicitous, but did not change his habits. Nor did Clementine. Ultimately, those who suffered most were the children, Diana and Randolph.

Clementine could barely cope with the household at the Admiralty let alone with two extremely naughty children. In the absence of a firm, reliable nanny figure such as their father had had in the person of stalwart Mrs. Everest, the children were consigned to a succession of underpaid and untrained nursemaids, who were remarkable only for the frequency with which they came and went. (Randolph's earliest memory was of him and his sister rolling together down the steps of the Admiralty in smart white coats, followed at a distance by a frantic female who was incapable of stopping them.)

Mrs. Everest would never have permitted such behavior—nor would Jennie. But in her weakened state, Clementine seems to have had little influence. Indeed, on most days she had little to do with either of her children until the evening, when they were brought down from the nursery for their parents' brief approval. Already it was their father, rather than their mother, who was their source of genuine affection and excitement, but he had little time to spare. What he did have went to Randolph rather than reserved Diana. However much Diana may have resembled her proud father at birth, in personality she was taking after her mother. Despite her naughtiness, she was already a shy and somewhat nervous child.

Randolph could not have been more different. A happy, sociable small boy, he had already become the apple of his father's eye with his blond good looks and easy nature. Churchill was entranced with him, spoiling and indulging him, as if desperate to become the sort of father he had never had himself.

With a son and heir, a place in the Cabinet, and the most exciting job in British politics, Churchill appeared to have beaten "Black Dog." It was hard to believe that barely eighteen months earlier he had been in the grip of suicidal misery.

But behind the confidence and the rediscovered zest for life, Churchill's strange psychology remained unchanged. Agadir had convinced him of what he first suspected when he saw the German army on maneuvers: A major European war was coming. With uncanny accuracy, he had actually predicted in a paper written for the government shortly before moving to the Admiralty the course events would follow.

Forseeing a major European war, it was his overriding duty to prepare his nation's sea defenses. His work revitalized the Royal Navy and offered him the antidotes he still required against depression: a patriotic cause to inspire his sense of destiny, constant activity to keep his energies engaged, and a ruthless enemy to rouse his deepest instincts of aggression.

The Royal Navy also gripped his boyish imagination. Picturing the great ironclads as "war castles foaming to their stations," he thrilled to the drama of their role, knowing that if they sank, the British Empire would swiftly follow.

As First Lord of the Admiralty, Churchill was at the center of the greatest instrument of controlled aggression in existence, and he was awed and fascinated by the concentrated firepower of the fleet. One of his key decisions was to introduce the latest fifteen-inch high-explosive naval gun. (Without it the navy would have been fatally outgunned and outmaneuvered in World War I.) Another was to change the fleet from coal to oil. This proved another crucial decision that immeasurably improved the efficiency and speed of British warships in the war to come.

Technical problems fascinated Churchill, and he was soon absorbed in the latest form of warfare—flying. He swiftly lost what he called his "Aetherial virginity" and, despite a lack of physical coordination, which always made him such a menace on the road, doggedly began his flying lessons. Only after one of his instructors had been killed did he give in to Clementine's entreaties to desist.

Fortunately, he had more important matters to attend to at the Admiralty—in particular, updating the mentality and personnel of the naval high command. He found his admirals every bit as stupid as the generals he remembered from South Africa. They were soon providing the rebellious enfant terrible of British politics with the sort of opportunity he loved: to range himself against all things old and in-grained.

He could be a fearful bully. Anyone he disagreed with rapidly became his enemy, and distinguished sailors quailed in his presence. One tried appealing to the great traditions of the navy. "Traditions! What traditions? 'Rum, sodomy and the lash,' " retorted the thirty-six-year-old former lieutenant of Hussars.

Churchill's behavior was soon bringing the naval establishment to a state of panic, but behind him lay much false bravado. Shocked by his treatment of senior officers, Admiral Sir Francis Bridgeman—backed by the future First Sea Lord, Prince Louis Battenburg—confronted Churchill about his behavior, "and was stunned to see Churchill suddenly become so melancholy and weepy that he thought he must be ill."

Churchill's meekness did not last—and neither did Admiral Bridgeman. Once he was gone, there was little to detract from Churchill's frank enjoyment of the power he wielded and the splendors that accompanied his great position.

The Admiralty itself was like a ducal principality (far too ducal for Clementine, with her continuing concern for marital economy), and the First Lord's residence was part of the impressive Admiralty establishment, on the opposite side of Horse Guards Parade to Downing Street.

As First Lord, Churchill could begin to entertain in style. More important, he could now perfect his own eccentric way of working, which he followed in the years ahead: sitting up each morning, after an ample breakfast, in the historic Admiralty bed with its gilded dolphins, the bedspread littered with official memoranda and dispatches. By dictating to his secretary, perched beside his bed, Churchill found he could deal with business with remarkable efficiency. (It was now that a critic described Churchill as "ill-mannered, boastful, unprincipled, without any redeeming qualities except his amazing ability and industry.")

Along with the splendor and comfort of the Admiralty itself went what Violet Asquith called "the sweetest of the sweets of office," the Admiralty yacht, appropriately named *Enchantress*. Constructed at great expense as the navy's answer to the royal yacht, *Victoria and Albert,* this most elegant of ships was powered by the latest steam turbines. It had a complement of a hundred sailors and a displacement of four thousand tons. It was a potent symbol of the importance and prestige of Churchill's office—and it offered him the sort of seaborne splendor only royalty or the richest of plutocrats could hope for in their private yachts.

Churchill made frequent and delighted use of the *Enchantress*, "using it not only to carry out official inspections, but also as a kind of floating hotel which he could place at the disposal of his family and friends." September 1912 saw the Churchills playing host to the Lloyd Georges aboard *Enchantress;* the following year it was Prime Minister Herbert Asquith and *his* family—all at government expense.

Churchill also used his yacht to give his mother a badly needed holiday at what was proving an awkward moment in her life. Her husband, George Cornwallis-West, had deserted her, as everyone had always said he would, exchanging strong-willed Jennie for Bernard Shaw's great leading lady, the even stronger-willed Mrs. Patrick Campbell. While Shaw's favorite actress was enjoying what she called "the comfort of the double bed after the hurley burley of the chaise longue," with Churchill's former stepfather, Churchill himself could still offer his jilted mother a free Mediterranean cruise aboard his private yacht.

"Dearest Mama," he wrote, "it would do you a great deal of good to get away from England, worry and expense for three weeks and bask a little in Mediterranean and Adriatic sunshine. . . . We start at Venice, and go round by the Dalmatian coast to Malta, Sicily, Ajaccio and Marseilles—The Asquiths are coming so you must make up your mind to get on with Margot and the PM."

Apart from the opportunity to give his wife and mother a holiday in considerable style at absolutely no expense, the three-week voyage also enabled him to exercise his charm on Herbert Asquith. It was during this cruise that the Prime Minister became particularly impressed by him. When Violet asked if Churchill was like his father, it was Asquith who replied, "No, not really. He is like no one else. He derives from no one. He is an original and most extraordinary phenomenon."

But it is Violet, clearly captivated herself, who provides the most revealing glimpse of their host on these halcyon voyages. Always incapable of relaxing on a holiday, Churchill was impatient with the sightseeing so enjoyed by Asquith, the former classical scholar. "Those Greeks and Romans, they are so overrated," he exploded. "They only said everything *first*. I've said just as good things myself. But they got in before me."

He showed the same impatience with the pleasures of the simple tourist and delivered a still more irritated retort to the harmless gushing of devoted Violet. As they stood romantically together, she recalled, "side by side against the taffrail, gliding past the lovely smiling coastline of the Adriatic bathed in sun," she casually remarked, "How perfect!" "Yes," he replied. "Range perfect—visibility perfect—If we had six-inch guns aboard how easily we could bombard . . . and details followed showing how effectively we could lay waste the landscape and blow the nestling towns sky-high."

These trips by Churchill and his friends did not escape the notice of the opposition press. "How much coal has been consumed by the *Enchantress* this year," asked the *National Review*. "How many lobsters have been eaten. How many magnums of champagne drunk?"

It is not likely that Churchill was remotely worried by what he must have considered petty carping at a time when war with Germany was imminent. He had a mission to ensure that Britain matched the German naval building program. Three years earlier he had been angrily opposed to wasting money on the fleet. Now he was even angrier that Lloyd George was seeking to restrict the naval budget.

"Winston is for 4 ships and George is for 2," Max Aitken wrote excitedly to Rudyard Kipling. "I am told Winston will stand at 4. It is said that Northcliffe is backing him to bolt from the Liberal party, and I presume form a new party. Cassel is reported to have promised him £5,000 a year. Winston's position will be rather amusing if he bolts from the Liberal party on the basis of £5,000 from Cassel." It was a trial of strength, and Churchill got his battleships.

That August, while Europe waited for the inevitable war to follow the murder of Archduke Ferdinand at Sarajevo, Churchill took one of his very rare—and very brief—holidays with the whole family, children included. He and Jack had rented two cottages on the Norfolk coast, and Churchill, with his brother and the children to support him, was soon revealing that mixture of the schoolboy and the military commander that was never far beneath the surface.

Johnny, Jack's son, remembers how "excursions to the beach were organised with military thoroughness" and the sand on the beach was marked out for a fort "of colossal dimensions."

Johnny describes how Churchill, trouser legs rolled up, supervised the battle with the sea. "Taking on impossible odds, fighting a battle he could not hope to win, intrigued him. Not until the very last moment, when all was lost and our glorious castle had vanished, were we allowed to abandon our posts."

With the Royal Navy already mobilized against the Kaiser's fleet, Churchill would soon be leading his subordinates against still greater odds, into far more hopeless situations.

# fifteen

# God Bless
# the Dardanelles

On the evening of August 14, 1914, Britain awaited the German Kaiser's answer to its ultimatum against the invasion of Belgium. That evening, the Churchills, together with Jack, Goonie, and Clementine's sister Nellie, entertained the editor of the *Times*. According to Nellie, Clementine—who was seven months pregnant at the time—"seemed crushed" by the occasion. "But Winston was elated. Perhaps 'elated' is the wrong word," she added. "Anyway, he was bursting with energy and excitement."

While Churchill was enjoying his after-dinner brandy and a good cigar, Asquith and the rest of the Cabinet, sitting in the Cabinet Room at Downing Street, waited for the Kaiser's answer. It never came. Through the open windows, the politicians heard Big Ben toll eleven (midnight in Berlin), and as its echoes died away, they sat in silence, trying to grasp the fact that Britain was at war with Germany. According to Lloyd George's secretary-mistress, Frances Stevenson, "Upon this grave assembly burst Churchill, smiling, a cigar in his mouth and satisfaction on his face. 'Well,' he said, 'the deed is done.' The dream of his life had come to pass."

This was the fateful moment for which Churchill believed destiny had been so carefully preserving him. All the other members of the Asquith government were men of peace, reforming Liberals unprepared for war and unacquainted with its grim reality. Churchill, on the other hand, was quintessentially a man of war. For three years he had thought of little else, and as he later said, "nothing could equal the sheer drama" of the days that followed. He had confounded his many enemies by having the fleet mobilized and ready as the war began (on his authority the signal "Commence hostilities" was sent that night to every British warship at 11:00 P.M. sharp). As shrewd a politician as Gladstone's old friend and biographer John Morley predicted that if there was a war Churchill would "beat Lloyd George hollow." The chance to lead his nation in the greatest war in history was finally within Churchill's grasp, and all that insatiable ambition that he had nursed since his lamented father's lamentable death would be fulfilled at last.

Instead, he failed—and his failure was so shattering and so extraordinary that it took its place among the greatest dramas of the war. It cost the lives of thousands; it precipitated the collapse of Asquith's government; and it presented Churchill and his family with a living nightmare.

What is fascinating about this great disaster is that, like its author's previous successes, its roots were firmly grounded in his strange psychology. With what we know already of his personality, much of what happened seems painfully predictable.

The outbreak of hostilities had produced in Churchill the inevitable romantic stimulus that warfare always roused in him. He had shown this spirit at Malakand, Omdurman, and in South Africa. "Everything tends towards catastrophe and collapse. I am interested, geared up and happy," he confessed to Clementine, adding candidly, "Is it not horrible to be built like this?" He was now in a unique position to "direct those great formations" in the "bright red blossom" of a major war, as he once dreamed of doing.

Savrola, his alter ego, proved himself by leaving politics to take command of his nation's forces in its time of danger. Faced by the sudden crisis of the enemy advance in Belgium, Churchill decided he would do the same. Early that October, Antwerp was about to fall to the Kaiser's armies, and for Churchill, the historian and would-be military hero, Antwerp lay at the center of a sacred zone. Within a sixty-mile radius of the city, his exemplar and ancestor, John, Duke of Marlborough, had won his three great victories of Ramillies, Oudenarde, and Malplaquet, fighting to defend this very land against the French. Now it was Churchill's chance to do the same against the Germans.

There were other motives for his decision to take charge on the battlefield. With his deep distrust of father figures—and of aged generals in particular—he saw the British forces being led by what he cheerfully described to Asquith as "dug-out trash"—a clear reference to his former enemy of Omdurman, the "ungentlemanly" and unimaginative Field Marshal Kitchener.

With the confidence of youth, he had long believed that, unlike such bemedaled incompetents, he had what he liked to call "the root of the matter" in him. He longed to prove himself a new Napoleon, and genuinely believed that destiny had saved him for the task.

As First Lord of the Admiralty, he had already thrown together what amounted to a private army of his own—the six thousand untrained, untried members of the Naval Volunteer Reserve, the so-called Dunkirk Circus, who had been uncomfortably transformed into a land-based force to defend the Channel ports. That October, in answer to Belgian calls for help, he sent these forces into Antwerp. Two days later, he entered the historic city to take charge of them himself.

This was one of the very few mistakes he ever admitted to. After the war he wrote: "I ought to have remained in London and endeavoured to force the Cabinet and Lord Kitchener to take more effective action than they did. . . . Instead I spent four or five vivid days amid the shells, excitement and tragedy of Antwerp's defence."

The phrasing of this brief confession is significant—"excitement," "tragedy," "five vivid days." This is not the language of a soldier fighting a bitter battle to defend a stricken city but of a natural actor excitedly immersed within the role of a heroic general and rising to the drama of the situation.

Churchill performed splendidly in the part. Arms outstretched, the tunic of his gold-trimmed uniform unbuttoned, he managed to harangue the citizens—in homemade French—presumably leaving them as puzzled by his eloquence as by his language. Photographers and war correspondents, equally intrigued by Churchill's garb, were told it was the full-dress uniform of an Elder of Trinity House, the historic organization traditionally responsible for Britain's ports. ("Je suis un frère ainé de la Trinité," he once told a Frenchman, who replied by congratulating him on having such a famous family.)

As German field guns intensified their barrage on the city, Churchill was so exhilarated that he cabled Asquith asking to be relieved of his ministerial position in exchange for the rank of major general. When Asquith relayed this to his Cabinet, it was greeted with what he called "Homeric laughter." Churchill was, of course, completely serious. "His mouth waters at the thought of Kitchener's armies," Asquith told his girlfriend, Clementine's cousin, young Venetia Stanley. "He declared that his political career was as nothing in comparison with military glory."

Still, the truth of the matter was that, whatever courage and panache the First Lord was displaying in beleaguered Antwerp, he was not a general but a politician. Role-player and natural actor that he was, he could act the general to perfection, but in military terms his role was farcical, for there was little he could do—except to lose a quarter of his land-based sailors as prisoners of war and then retreat from the city.

Clementine might have brought him to his senses, but she was out of action, having given birth to a second daughter, a redhead like her father, at the Admiralty on October 7. It is some indication of the warlike and dynastic way his mind was working that he insisted the child be named after Marlborough's indomitable wife, Sarah.

Churchill earned angry criticism not only from the press and opposition but from colleagues in the Cabinet. According to Miss Stevenson, Lloyd George was "rather disgusted with Winston [for] having taken untrained men over there" and for having then "left them in the lurch." Privately he told Miss Stevenson, "He would make a drum out of the skin of his own mother in order to sound out his praises." The loss of the defenseless sailors rankled with his colleagues. Asquith told Miss Stanley that they had gone "like sheep to the shambles." Churchill, however, seemed oblivious of the tragedy as only one among so many others, as the slaughter of the great campaigns in northern France began in earnest. He was still all-powerful at the Admiralty, and more than ever now his energies were needed for the day-to-day direction of the fleet.

In naval terms, these early months of war were disappointing. Instead of the triumphs Churchill dreamed of, there was a fairly mediocre showing by the Royal Navy: It bungled the battle of the Dogger Bank; it allowed a German cruiser to shell the fashionable resort of Scarborough; and it was hoodwinked by the German warships *Goeben* and *Breslau,* which passed beneath the very noses of the British fleet to hoist the Kaiser's flag in Constantinople.

The sailor king, King George V, was far from complimentary at the disappointing showing of his ships. It was in answer to these near-disasters that Churchill took advantage of racist hysteria against his German monarch's German cousin Prince Louis Battenburg to accept the Prince's resignation from his post of First Sea Lord, and to reappoint the storm petrel of the Royal Navy, seventy-three-year-old Admiral Sir John "Jackie" Fisher, in his place.

Part mountebank, part naval genius, this monkeylike old sailor had been largely responsible for starting to reform the navy during his earlier spell as First Sea Lord, when Churchill had been so vehement against the naval program. Since then, they had become good friends. With Fisher, very much a fighting admiral, now beside him at the Admiralty, Churchill was happily convinced that the chance had come for naval power to break the stalemate in the trenches of northern France, where, as he put it, the Allied armies were "chewing barbed wire."

It was an irresistible temptation for someone of his temperament to discover how the navy could be used to win the war.

"My God, this is living history!" Churchill exclaimed to Asquith's wife, Margot, "Everything we are doing and saying is thrilling—it will be read by a thousand generations, think of that! Why, I would not be out of this glorious delicious war for anything the world could give me."

Remembering himself—and Margot Asquith's reputation as a gossip—he drew up short.

"I say. Don't repeat that word, 'delicious,' but you know what I mean."

Delicious or not, it is clear that Churchill was in love with what John Maynard Keynes called "the intense experiences of conducting warfare on the grand scale which (only) those can enjoy who make the decisions." It is clearer still that he was now determined to attain his place in history, despite the recent setback he experienced at Antwerp.

It was just before the first Christmas of the war that the possibility of forcing the Dardanelles by naval power was broached at the Admiralty—reputedly by Captain William "Blinker" Hall, famous as the founding father of British Naval Intelligence. These narrowest of straits between Europe and Asia Minor, linking the Black Sea and the Mediterranean, held a magical appeal for any strategist, Churchill included.

But at the Admiralty, he had already studied and dismissed the possibility of forcing them by sea without the help of land-based forces, ("no one could expose a fleet to such perils," he wrote in 1911), and had turned instead to ancient Admiral Fisher for his masterstroke of naval strategy. Fisher had several bright ideas, including trying to establish British bases on Heligoland and the North Sea islands of Sylt and Borkum in the Baltic. All had major disadvantages—and suddenly the Dardanelles began to beckon.

Britain's great erratic Eastern ally, Russia, was calling for assistance because Turkey had joined forces with the Germans. Once the Dardanelles were forced, the Turkish capital, Constantinople, would fall, the Black Sea routes to Russia would open, and the Balkans would lie at the mercy of the Allied armies. Such was the strategist's scenario; it was the sort of grandiose masterstroke of war that Marlborough himself might have devised.

Churchill's friend C. F. Masterman graphically described how Churchill came to a decision. "In nearly every case an *idea* enters his head from outside. It then rolls around the hollow of his brain, collecting strength like a snowball. Then after whirling winds of rhetoric, he becomes convinced that he is *right;* and denounces everyone who criticises it."

This was very much the case with Churchill's swift conversion to the forcing of the Dardanelles, which came as yet another of his private revelations. Once he was sure he was right, no one could convince him otherwise. "Here," he told Violet Asquith, "we can make our way to one of the great events in the history of the world."

There were compelling reasons why the Dardanelles were particularly appealing to Churchill. One was the irresistible attraction of the great idea that he alone could grasp—thus *proving* in the face of the uncomprehending opposition of the old that he was right. What greater proof of this than to solve the problem of the war, change history, save a million lives, and bring the fearful power of Germany to its knees?

There was also a technical attraction for him in the dreamlike vision of attacking Turkey at Gallipoli. The vulnerability of land-based armies and defenses to sudden overwhelming firepower from the sea had long held an important place within his bellicose romantic fantasies.

When he wrote *Savrola,* nearly twenty years before, he ended it with a curiously prophetic scene in which the land-based forts defending the capital were shattered by the high-explosive shells of the Lauranian fleet steaming through the straits. (The fleet was commanded by an elderly, no-nonsense admiral who might have been old Admiral Fisher.) The same theme reappears in *The River War,* with Churchill's graphic description of the effect of the firepower of the Nile gunboats on the mullahs' armies. By the time he was telling Violet Asquith how to blast the Adriatic coast from the taffrail of the *Enchantress,* it is clear that the destructive power of heavy naval guns against the land was genuinely obsessing him.

This obsession became clearer still early in 1914, when his response to a threatened Unionist rebellion in Belfast was to send his North Sea fleet there with a threat to shell the city at any sign of trouble.

The awesome possibilities of destruction caused by the fifteen-inch high-explosive guns that he procured for the navy undoubtedly excited him. Later, this would change to an obsession with destruction from the air. For the moment, however, he was fascinated by the power of seaborne high explosives to destroy the balance of entrenched inertia in the static battlefields of Flanders—much as the incoming tide destroyed the sand fortresses he had built for Randolph and Johnny on the Norfolk beaches.

Once convinced, no one in politics worked faster or more effectively than Churchill, but as this small, excited man swept all before him, one saw the dangers of his eloquence, the limitations of that strange intelligence, the perils lurking in that all-powerful imagination. Above all, one saw the havoc that could be created by a role-playing melancholic with a genius for politics, an obsession with war, a belief in destiny, and a passionate desire to make his mark in history.

His inner need to prove that he was always right had made him impregnable in argument—especially on war, the subject where he really had great expertise. It finally reached the point where no one in the Cabinet was capable of arguing the very real case against the Dardanelles adventure—that it was extremely risky, that the fruits of its success were dubious, and that in terms of long-range strategy, Britain's true advantage lay not in chancy expeditions but in keeping its naval power intact and maintaining a stranglehold on Germany. (It was this strategy that finally brought the German armies to a grinding halt in 1918 despite their territorial supremacy over the Western allies.)

Churchill's nautical advisers faced the same stone wall. These were the men who should have raised the technical hazards of the operation, but he had even less difficulty overwhelming them in argument than he had with members of the Cabinet. Most notably he did this with Admiral Fisher, who was dazed and dazzled by the infinitely swifter mind of this brilliant politician, more than thirty years his junior. Temporarily suspending his instinctive disbelief about the Dardanelles proposals, Admiral Fisher gave them his assent.

In varying degrees, Chuchill dazed or dazzled everyone who mattered on the subject of the Dardanelles. Even big, slow-moving Field Marshal Kitchener was won over by Churchill's arguments, to the point of offering supporting troops when the western front could spare them. Churchill answered that the navy did not need supporting troops, being quite prepared to force the Dardanelles alone. "All the evidence now available," writes the historian of the campaign, "demonstrates the fact that Churchill initiated the Dardanelles project, and pushed it forward with vigour, overruling or ignoring the doubts and criticisms of his service advisers."

But Churchill erred. His navy could not force the Dardanelles alone. The first attempt, on February 14, failed ignominiously: The Turks were alerted and prepared, their forts resistant to the broadsides of the Royal Navy, and Sackville Carden, the commanding admiral, lost his nerve and called off the attack.

The second great attack, on March 18, though more determined, was an even worse disaster. No one had foreseen the perils of the Turkish minefields in the straits, which disabled four large Allied warships. Attempts to sweep the minefields failed. The Turkish shore batteries proved even more effective than before, and after four long days of concentrated carnage, the attempt to force the narrows by the Royal Navy was again abandoned. It was not repeated.

Yet the Dardanelles campaign was far from over. Once launched, it continued on like some great ill-fated ship with its own terrible momentum. Kitchener, by now convinced by Churchill of the strategic dividends of capturing the straits, had found the troops that he had promised—including a division of Australians and New Zealanders, as yet untarnished by the heat of battle, waiting in reserve in Alexandria. On May 5, he hurled them at the rocky beaches of the Gallipoli peninsula, which commanded the Dardanelles. The Turks had not been idle in the interval, and during the landings, twenty thousand Allied soldiers were slaughtered, machine gunned by the boatload as they landed.

This was followed by a period of astounding incompetence in the Allied high command, equaled only by the astounding courage of their troops. Opportunities were squandered; so were the lives of countless soldiers lost to dysentery and Turkish bullets under a scalding sun. Almost overnight, the masterstroke that Churchill had intended as the answer to the impasse on the western front was becoming a byword for insensate slaughter.

Back in London, an element of farce began to mingle with the tragedy. Asquith's beloved Miss Stanley announced her surprise engagement to his secretary, Edwin Montagu, leaving the Prime Minister so distraught that he felt inadequate before the crisis of the Dardanelles.

Admiral Fisher also felt inadequate, not from reasons of affection but from fears of his reputation and for the safety of his ships. Churchill remained confident that, despite the losses, victory with all its benefits could still be snatched from the rocky outcrops of Gallipoli. But with the insulation of the egotist, he had not appreciated the full extent of the problems.

On May 12, Admiral Fisher suddenly resigned, saying he was off to Scotland. In fact, the old admiral had sought refuge from his worries, first in Westminster Abbey and then in the Charing Cross Hotel. Asquith invoked the King's name to order his return, and in the ensuing uproar Fisher aired his doubts about the wisdom of the whole campaign, and also his doubts about his friend and colleague, the First Lord of the Admiralty. By now, the Tory press and opposition were in concerted clamor for the First Lord's blood.

The *Morning Post* accused Churchill of, among other things, turning "from melodrama to megalomania" in his conduct of the war. Simultaneously, the Tory leader, A. Bonar Law, offered to join a crisis coalition—with one crucial stipulation: Churchill had to leave the Admiralty. Isolated and betrayed by Fisher, Churchill clung to office with a desperation that showed where his true priorities resided. "You don't care what becomes of me," he told Lloyd George. "You don't care whether I am trampled underfoot by my enemies. You don't care for my personal reputation."

"No," Lloyd George supposedly replied, "I don't care for my own at the moment. The only thing I care about now is that we win this war."

With the Tories now in the government, nothing could keep Churchill at the Admiralty. Asquith's leaden thunderbolt descended, and on May 16, Churchill was translated from the powerhouse of the Admiralty to the stillroom of the Duchy of Lancaster. (He was to remain in the Cabinet and the Dardanelles Committee, the small group of politicians and senior officers responsible for the day-to-day running of the campaign, but his prestige and power were fatally diminished.)

Violet Asquith met him in the Commons after the announcement. She found him "silent, despairing—as I have never seen him. He seemed to have no rebellion or even anger left. He did not even abuse Fisher, but simply said, 'I'm finished.' I poured out contradictions, protestations—but he waved them aside. 'No, I'm done,' he said."

Someone else who saw him at this time was the painter William Orpen, currently engaged in what had been planned as the portrait of the victor of the Dardanelles. Churchill arrived as usual for his sitting at the painter's studio. "All he did," said Orpen, "was sit in a chair before the fire with his head buried in his hands, uttering no word." Orpen went to lunch without disturbing him, and found Winston in the same position when he returned. At four o'clock, Winston got up, asked Orpen to call a taxi, and departed without further speech.

Churchill speechless was a frightening phenomenon, and there is no disputing the misery and shock he felt at the dismissal. It was his greatest setback since his father died, and it began a period of depression even worse than the Home Office years. He was nearly forty-one, older than his father when he fell, but the parallel between their situations could not be avoided. In the words of Lord Randolph's biographer, Winston "found himself—like Lord Randolph in December 1886—completely isolated."

All was not lost. Churchill had his family to turn to, and they loyally united around him, forming the embattled "citadel of the heart" he needed. For several weeks now, Jennie had been walking across the park each morning to see him at the Admiralty and "impart something of her own vitality to sustain him." She was maternally outraged by the treatment he was receiving from his former colleagues.

So was Clementine, who had pleaded with the Prime Minister to keep her husband at his post. He alone possessed "the power, the imagination, the deadliness" to fight Germany, she insisted. Asquith, never an admirer of Clementine, described her letter as "the letter of a maniac," yet this was what she utterly believed.

Now she, too, fell into a depression. "She was so sweet but so miserable, crying all the time," wrote Edwin Montagu. "Poor Clemmie looks very sad, poor thing," added Cynthia Asquith. "She said she had always known it would happen from the day Fisher was appointed." Anger overcame Clementine's misery, and soon she was saying that her dying wish would be "to dance on Asquith's grave."

The disaster meant the loss of her home at the Admiralty, a drop in salary, and a husband in a deep depression. But the family continued to provide the stricken leader with support, including the adored Randolph and seven-year-old Diana. Later, Randolph would recall ending his bedtime prayers with "God bless Mummy and Papa. God bless the Dardanelles. And make me a good boy. Amen." Even the members of the family who found themselves serving in Gallipoli were united in their loyalty to Churchill. Jack was attached to the staff of the commander in chief, Churchill's friend and comrade from South Africa, that amiable but uninspiring general Sir Ian Hamilton. Jack's letters give a vivid picture of the chaos and the suffering of the troops, but, loyal brother and subordinate that he was, there is not a hint of criticism of Churchill's strategy behind the Dardanelles—nor of General Hamilton. Under the circumstances, this was particularly noble; for while Jack was suffering the flies and bullets of the Dardanelles, his brother and family had moved in with Goonie and the children and were sharing his comfortable house in Cromwell Road.

Clementine's brother Bill Hozier, a lieutenant aboard His Majesty's destroyer *Edgar,* was also strong for Churchill. He complained bitterly of inactivity and the lack of "ginger" in the government since his brother-in-law's demotion. As late as September, he was writing loyally to Churchill saying that the straits could still be forced provided all available warships and destroyers "blazed away like hell."

Throughout that second summer of the war, Churchill was sustained by one great hope: a crushing military victory over the Turkish army in Gallipoli, which would lead to the capture of Constantinople and vindicate his strategy. And although still suffering withdrawal symptoms after four exhilarating years at the Admiralty, he was at least being miserable in style, having rented a small country house for all the family some thirty miles from London. This was Hoe Farm, near Godalming in Surrey. With Hoe Farm, three young children, and a devoted and attractive wife barely in her thirties, life could not have been all bad for Churchill. "We live vy simply—but with all the essentials of life well understood & well provided for," he wrote Jack. "Hot baths, cold champagne, new peas and old brandy."

At this stage, Churchill still had hopes of regaining what he called "a fuller measure of control before the end of the year"—that is, getting back to power—and had started painting as a hobby. In the meantime, he was on the verge of visiting Gallipoli in person.

This was an adventure he had set his heart on, but his enemies (in this case Bonar Law and Curzon) had no intention of letting Churchill back into the limelight, and they blocked the journey on the eve of his departure. It was yet another disappointment. But by then he had written Clementine a letter to be opened in the event of his demise on the field of battle. It was most revealing.

"Randolph," he wrote, "will carry the lamp," and Clementine was not to grieve. "Death is only an incident," he continued, "& not the most important wh happens to us in this state of being. On the whole, especially since I met you my darling one I have been happy & you have taught me how noble a woman's heart can be. If there is anywhere else I shall be on the lookout for you. Meanwhile look forward, feel free, rejoice in life, cherish the children, guard my memory. God bless you."

Not only did he never reach Gallipoli, but the victory that he hoped would prove him right and bring those glittering strategic prizes of which he had dreamed never came. Instead, the generals bungled a surprise assault in early August with hideous casualties. "The golden opportunity has gone, and positions that might have been won with a little perspiration will only be gained now with blood," Jack reported.

During this crisis in his fortunes, Churchill still found time to deal with the problems of another member of his all-important family —gloomy Cousin Sunny.

Sunny, completely separated now from independent, elegant Consuelo, had become a bitter, somewhat scandalous recluse, shunned at court, unpopular with former friends in politics, and thoroughly disliked among his county neighbors. But with the war, Sunny had felt the patriotic urge to do his bit for King and Country. An admirable proportion of the Marlborough acres was ploughed up to grow potatoes for the war effort.

But potatoes were not enough; and he called on Cousin Winston and asked him to find him "something suitable" at the center of affairs. Churchill had obliged. Through the good offices of Field Marshal Kitchener, the Duke of Marlborough was appointed a war office messenger—a humble role but one that gave the Duke the right to wear a major's uniform and have an office in Whitehall. Then, as the fighting raged in Gallipoli, Sunny once again appealed to Cousin Winston in his troubles. He was in danger of being passed over for the Lord Lieutenancy of Oxfordshire.

Churchill, obsessed as always with his close relations, solemnly agreed that this would be unthinkable—a "terrible reproach to my family." He used all his powers of persuasion with the Lord Chamberlain (Sunny's uncle by marriage, Lord Lansdowne) to ensure that Cousin Sunny got the post. Sunny had already seen his uncle, who had found him "so violent and abusive . . . that anyone listening to his language would have doubted whether he was fit for any appointment requiring the possession of good manners and an even temper." But to Churchill, blood was thicker than bad manners, and he used all his influence, including enlisting the support of his influential friend, F. E. Smith (the future Lord Birkenhead) to ensure that Sunny was appointed.

For Churchill, it was a small triumph in the midst of great disasters, but for Sunny, it spelled victory over all his enemies. As he wrote to Cousin Winston, "the dirty dogs have been downed and may they now come and lick their chops in rage and annoyance." Churchill's enemies were not so easily put down—particularly that October, when the government accepted that Gallipoli was unwinnable, and he was ousted from the Dardanelles Committee, thereby losing his last scrap of influence upon the war effort. For him, this was the ultimate disgrace, the end of any hope of vindication by events. Nothing was left but resignation from the government.

There was, however, one option available to bring him out of depression and despair: Field Marshal French, the British commander in France, had already offered him the rank that he had so desired at Antwerp—that of a general commanding a brigade.

Warfare had never failed to bring an upswing of his spirits. Battle had always been his favorite way of testing destiny. "The tuning fork of death" would show if fate was with him any longer. He would forget political disgrace by once more seeking military glory.

Belloc and Scawen-Blunt toasted him with words that once celebrated Marlborough's departure: *"Malbruck s'en v'a-t-en guerre"* ("Marlborough goes off to war"). Violet Asquith sent him a copy of Kipling's "If." And the newly ennobled Canadian newspaper millionaire Lord Beaverbrook described the scene as the warrior departed for the front: "the whole household upside down while the soldier statesman was buckling on his sword. Downstairs, Mr. Eddie Marsh, his faithful secretary, was in tears. . . . Upstairs, Lady Randolph was in a state of despair at the idea of her brilliant son being relegated to the trenches. Mrs. Churchill seemed to be the only person who remained calm, collected and efficient."

In this crisis, Clementine was more admirable than Beaverbrook suspected. To save her sanity, she had already taken on war work of her own—organizing Y. W. C. A. canteens for munitions workers in North East London—and she made no attempt to stop her husband going. (The dangers for him at the front may have seemed no worse than the horrors he had lived through in the last six months in government.)

But even in Flanders, the disgrace of the Dardanelles pursued him. Although one of his early letters home to Clementine contained detailed orders for his general's uniform, it would not be needed. Faced with the anger of the Tory faithful, Asquith would not risk confirming Field Marshal French's offer of a generalship to Churchill. Had he done so—and had Churchill had the chance to play the general's role he longed for—he might well have passed the rest of the war happily in high command (how successfully is another matter). Instead, he was merely appointed to the rank of lieutenant colonel, saw service with the Guards, and was finally consigned to Royal Scots Fusiliers in charge of nothing larger than a battalion.

(On his appointment, the actor in him realized that the Fusiliers' Glengarry cap did not suit him. "Christ!" he exclaimed, catching sight of himself before a mirror. Pictures of Churchill at the front show him with a photogenic French steel helmet framing his bulldog features.)

During his brief period as a frontline infantry commander, Churchill was once again a happy man, and an undeniable success—tough, resourceful, charismatic, and courageous. With absolute assurance he would lecture on the art of laying sandbags, bridging trenches, or destroying lice. Obsessed as ever with ballistics, he enjoyed few things more than calling up a barrage of artillery at the slightest provocation (Margot Asquith always said he had "a noisy mind.") Unlike politics, this was the boyhood world of high adventure that he loved. "War is a game to be played with a smiling face," he told his dour Lowland Scots.

The adventure of war—its danger and hardship—proved an instant therapy for the Dardanelles. At forty-one, he noted proudly that "many years of luxury have not impaired the tone of my system." Of course, private luxuries of a certain sort were sent by a motherly Clementine in answer to his regular requests: a folding bath, Jaeger underwear, brandy, and a stock of very large cigars.

Soon he could write to her that "amid these surroundings, aided by wet and cold and every minor discomfort, I have found happiness and contentment such as I have not known for many months." In his letters he would sometimes use Marlborough's method of addressing his own wife, calling her "My Dearest Soul."

Battle and aggression revived Churchill's confidence and gusto. Fate even left its reassuring calling card when a chance visit to a general saved his life, as his billet was destroyed by shellfire in his absence.

By December 1915, it seemed that service at the front had saved him from depression and restored this self-appointed man of destiny, anxious for his place in history. He could now tell Clementine, "I am superior to anything that can happen to me out here. My conviction that the greatest of my work is still to be done is strong within me." Churchill was hungry to return to power. The rank of a general might have kept him happily in France, but beyond the day-to-day excitements, there was no long-term satisfaction in the duties of an infantry commander.

Clementine, however, was of two minds over her husband's desperation to return from soldiering to politics. "My darling," she wrote, "—when next I see you I hope there will be a little time for us both alone—We are still young, but Time flies stealing love away and leaving only friendship which is v. peaceful but not stimulating or warming."

In reply he made an extraordinary confession of his own desire for "tranquility." "Sometimes also I think I would not mind stopping living very much—I am so devoured by egoism tht I wd like to have another world & meet you in another setting, & pay you all the love and honour of the great romances."

Just before Christmas, Wilfred Sheridan, recently married to Churchill's cousin Clare Frewen, was killed in action. "My Darling, I don't know how one bears such things. I fear I could not bear such a blow. . . . You must come back to me my dear one," wrote Clementine to her husband in the trenches.

But she knew the full extent of feeling ranged against him, having in his absence kept in touch with political life in London—even dining quite politely with the Asquiths. He might well be safer in Flanders than staging a comeback in Westminster.

In May 1916, Clementine's doubts notwithstanding, Churchill relinquished what he called "the rough fierce life under the Hammer of Thor" in France, believing that the time had come to return to search for power and destiny in London. But Clementine was right, the stigma of the Dardanelles persisted, and he found himself a political untouchable, suspected (correctly) of designs on Asquith's faltering government —he was unemployable, untrusted, and unhappy.

For more than a year he hung in limbo, witnessing the terrible attrition of a war he no longer had a part in. When the grim disaster of the Somme was added to the old disaster of the Dardanelles, and Asquith's government was ousted at the end of 1916, it was not the scion of warlike Marlborough who succeeded but the humbly born ex-pacifist and Little Englander, Lloyd George, who now received the chance of making history.

According to Lord Beaverbrook, throughout this period Churchill remained "a character depressed beyond the limits of description." Eddie Marsh described him as being "like Beethoven deaf."

The one who saw the full extent of his misery was, naturally, Clementine. Many years later, talking to Birkenhead's son Freddie, she admitted, "The worst part of our life together was the failure of the Dardanelles expedition. W. was filled with such a black depression that I felt that he would never recover from it, and even feared at one time that he might commit suicide."

One would like to think that he was troubled by the death toll of the Dardanelles, but there is little evidence that he was seriously haunted by the loss of so many lives pursuing that strategic dream he started. This was war and he had taught himself to close his mind to death in battle. During this period he visited no hospitals to see the wounded, made no contact with the widows, and remained majestically apart from the misery of others.

Except in that painful period as Home Secretary, when the anguish of murderers got through to him, his lonely insulation from the lives of ordinary people was total. So was the great aristocrat's aloofness. H. G. Wells was not unfair when he described Churchill as believing "quite naively, that he belongs to a peculiarly gifted and privileged class of beings to whom the lives and affairs of common men are given over, the raw material of brilliant ideas."

Still less does Churchill seem to have been troubled by the thought that his great idea to force the straits was less than brilliant. During the years ahead, much time and energy would be spent demonstrating his intense conviction that he had been right about the Dardanelles. Others could be blamed—and were: his old enemy, slow-moving, unimaginative Kitchener; drunken Asquith, "Supine, sodden but supreme" as he privately described him; and of course the origin of all his troubles, Admiral Fisher, whom he would call "the dark angel of the Service." But there remained one crucial actor in this gruesome tragedy he could never bring himself to blame: himself. And it is this that makes his state of suicidal misery so revealing.

It was Beaverbrook who gives the clue to what was happening. "His thoughts," he wrote, "turned inwards as if he was anatomising his own soul."

Remembering the course of Churchill's life ever since his father died, it is not hard to appreciate his soul's torment. Political power, military glory, a place in history—all protected him against the deep depressive misery that any setback, coupled with Lord Randolph's judgment, unfailingly produced. Churchill's essential attitude to life had been summed up in a chance remark he made to Violet Asquith. "We are all worms," he said resignedly, "but I intend to be a glowworm."

As a glowworm, high above the wormlike mass of dull humanity, Churchill had been happy: hence his unabashed delight in power, his joy in battle, and his exultation at the prospect of his place in history. Hence, too, his lonely misery when all this vanished in the debris of the Dardanelles.

Power, with its splendid consolations, was denied him, as was military glory and the chance of shaping history. Hope was lost. The glowworm lost its light. "Black Dog" in all its awfulness descended.

Churchill himself described something of the pain of his inactivity. "Like a sea-beast fished up from the depths, or a diver too suddenly hoisted, my veins threatened to burst from the lack of pressure." And in the small book from which this is taken, he also described the antidote he used to save his sanity.

He called his book *Painting as a Pastime,* but once adopted as a pastime, Churchill's painting rapidly became a source of true salvation. Quoting an American psychologist, he described himself as suffering from chronic worry, "a spasm of the emotion; the mind catches hold of something and will not let it go." Painting proved the one activity that could divert his mind from what he called worry's "convulsive grasp," and he described how a painter's wife, the glamorous Hazel Lavery, gave him his first true lesson in the art by teaching him not to fear his canvas. " 'Painting! But what are you hesitating about?' she said. 'Let me have a brush—the big one.' Splash into the turpentine, wallop into the blue and white, frantic flourish on the palette—clean no longer—and then several large, fierce strokes and slashes of blue on the absolutely cowering canvas. Anyone could see that it could not hit back. No evil fate avenged the jaunty violence. The canvas grinned in helplessness before me. The spell was broken. The sickly inhibitions rolled away. I seized the largest brush and fell upon my victim with berserk fury. I have never felt any awe of a canvas since."

Ever since childhood, Churchill had been turning to aggression to dispel depression. Now he found in art the ideal way of sublimating this aggression. And he learned, too, to curb his anxieties, to cope with "Black Dog" as best he could, and to wait. Then, in the early summer of 1917, patience and painting were rewarded. The new Prime Minister, Lloyd George, summoned his old colleague from misery and exile. On July 12, 1917, Churchill was readmitted to the Cabinet, and his task suited his energies—if not his original ambitions. The "man of war" as Baldwin called him, was made Minister of Munitions.

# sixteen

# Lullenden

On a peaceful summer afternoon in
1918 a group of Royal Flying Corps mechanics waited by a staff car on
the perimeter of a former meadow, now officially a "flying station," just
outside the Surrey village of Godstone. Less than a hundred miles away
across the English Channel the last throw of the German High Command was about to be bloodily repulsed by the Allied armies on the
western front, but none of this disturbed the rural calm of a Saturday
afternoon in southern England.

The aircraft the men were waiting for was late, but finally they
heard the staccato buzzing of an engine and saw a biplane come in low
across the trees, circle the airstrip, then make a bumpy landing on the
freshly mown grass. Before the propellor had stopped, a bulky figure
in a sheepskin coat had heaved himself out of the passenger cockpit
and the car had started off to pick him up. The driver knew from
experience that Churchill was invariably in a hurry.

Forty minutes earlier, Churchill had been driven in a very large
Rolls-Royce to the aircraft from his headquarters at the Château Fou-
quienberg, just behind the Allied lines near Amiens. He referred to the
place as "Chateau Fuck and Bugger," and the Rolls had been specially
lent him for his spell in France by his great friend "Benny," Duke of
Westminster. "You might tell Winston in answer to his wire that I only

have a shut Rolls at present, if that's any use to him," Westminster told Churchill's secretary when he asked if he could lend him an open Rolls on his appointment as Minister of Munitions in Lloyd George's government in July 1917.

It seemed a typically casual arrangement, but the use of this personal Rolls-Royce exemplified the optimistic and flamboyant mood with which Churchill undertook his duties as the war was ending. After the personal disaster of Gallipoli, the months spent recovering from deep depression, and active service at the front, he was back where he knew he belonged—in power. His morale and confidence seemed entirely restored now that he was once again in office. His task, as Lloyd George knew when he appointed him, was one that matched his ingenuity and boundless energy. Present at every major battle to ensure that the guns had their munitions, he was a warlord once again. He loved the role, bullying the generals and thriving on the breath of battle. Half seriously, Clementine had called him "a Mustard Gas fiend, a Tank juggernaut and a Flying terror," but at least he was no longer the gray-faced husband she remembered, with the doom of the Dardanelles across his brow.

A few days before he landed on that meadow outside Godstone, Churchill had spent a day at the front with the seventy-two-year-old French Premier, the white mustachioed George "Tiger" Clemenceau. (This indefatigable old statesman was a man after Churchill's heart, insisting on getting as close as possible to the fighting and clearly relishing all the risks of war.) Now Churchill was back to make his personal report to the Prime Minister that Monday morning. In the meantime, there was the weekend to enjoy at his new country house only seven miles away, where the whole family was awaiting the returning hero, who would descend like Mars, the god of war, in time for a very good dinner.

Clementine had always wanted what she called "a country basket" where her three "kittens" would be safe and healthy in the middle of the war. Although essentially an urban being who tended to get bored with country pleasures, she felt Jack's house in Cromwell Road was no place to bring up the children, particularly now that the German zeppelins had started bombing London. Diana was eight, Randolph six, and Sarah three. Jack's two boys, Johnny and Peregrine, were six and three. There was nothing to prevent them all, Goonie included, from living happily together if Clementine could find a place big enough for the two families. It had to be close enough to London for Winston's politics and friends, and for Jack when he was home on leave from France.

Churchill loved the English countryside for short periods, provided the sun was shining. The chance arose to buy a farmhouse of their own in the Sussex farming country near East Grinstead. It was called Lullenden and seemed as peaceful and romantic as its name.

It is hard to reconcile the family's accounts of Lullenden with the house as it exists today. During the two years Churchill actually owned it, it was still very much Lullenden Farm, and Sarah simply called it "a small farm outside East Grinstead." But small it was not. Today, it is emphatically Lullenden Manor—a very beautiful, distinctly grand, late Tudor, stone-and-timbered Sussex country mansion with some sixty acres of fields and woodland. (In 1990, it was sold for £2 million.)

When Churchill bought it, Lullenden was still very much a working farm managed by a bailiff, but it was clearly more elaborate than he and Clementine had bargained for. It was one more example of the boring problems of extravagance that Churchill's demanding way of life would always land them in. He could ignore the problems, but Clementine worried as she always did when the farming failed to pay, the bills piled up, and his decreased salary since leaving the Admiralty failed to cover them.

This apart, Lullenden appeared ideal: a country haven in the middle of the war where the grown-ups could lead the sort of comfortable country-house existence they took for granted. And there was no shortage of local girls to cook, clean, and act as nursemaids for the children. There were seven bedrooms, a dining room to seat eighteen, and a galleried seventeenth-century drawing room. Lloyd George, Sir Ernest Cassel, the press proprietor Lord Ridell, and the American lawyer, diplomat, and businessman Bernard Baruch were among the weekend visitors.

But for the Churchill children, this period at Lullenden was anything but gracious living. It was here that patterns for their future were established and the collective character of the family itself took shape around the legend and occasional exciting presence of the over-life-size statesman who made his flying visits to be with them.

Everyday life at Lullenden was primitive. A barn had been converted to provide the children with communal sleeping quarters, well away from the adults. They drank water from the pond and untreated milk from the local cows. Their only weekday supervision came from the Sussex nursemaids, who were even less effective than the Admiralty

House domestics had been in quelling Randolph and Diana. One of the few events they all remembered was the arrest of a German prisoner of war, working on the farm, for poisoning the water after they were all infected by a mystery illness. Local diversions of this sort were rare, and in effect, at Lullenden, the children lived two quite separate lives. For most of the time they were simple little savages, uncontrolled and rather undernourished, playing their games, attending the village school, and wandering at will around the farm. Throughout the week the grown-up members of the family would be away in London—Lady Goonie had her social life, which continued much as usual with friends like the Asquiths and the Horners, and Clementine, following a line of wartime duty to match that of her husband, continued her work organizing her YWCA canteens.

Only on weekends did adult life impinge on Lullenden. Then and only then would the children be spruced up and brought together for contact and conversation with their elders in the drawing room before their bedtime. This apart, they were left to their own devices in a world already largely ruled by Randolph. It was a very different world from that sentimental dream of Clementine's of what country kittens should be up to.

At seven, Randolph was already showing signs of the emergent monster who would terrorize his enemies—and friends—for the remainder of his life. Peregrine, who was a somewhat gentle child, remembers his cousin as "a most dreadful bully. He would defend us to the death against the village children, but life in the nursery with Randolph could be bloody hell."

Randolph was tough and confident, already showing a total disregard for any sort of criticism or punishment from outsiders. Peregrine remembers him taking dares to confess to frightful misdemeanors he had not committed for the sheer pleasure of showing he could take any punishment his nurse could give him. One of the Lullenden domestics, presumably goaded beyond endurance, filled his mouth with mustard. Randolph screamed—but swallowed it.

He was the children's inevitable ringleader, and Johnny still has memories of the terrible behavior he had engaged in with this small, diabolical boy: how on one occasion Randolph egged him on to tip the contents of his chamber pot out of his bedroom window, not telling him that Prime Minister Lloyd George was sitting below. (Lloyd George, according to his recollection, was used to the rain of his beloved Wales and took no notice of the extra drops of moisture in the air.) On another occasion Randolph had the bright idea of shutting the infant Peregrine and Sarah inside a model caravan that had been presented to the children by rich Lord Ridell and letting it run off down a hill. (The children emerged more or less undamaged.)

If none of the hired help at Lullenden was any match for Randolph, how could the children be? Johnny, an artistic, easygoing child, had found his role as the joker of the family. Red-haired Sarah was a rather sickly, elfin infant who had no doubt already picked up the glandular tuberculosis that would dog her childhood. As for Diana, she was already showing signs of retreating into herself in the midst of this rambunctious family. She was a pretty, doll-like child, but whereas Randolph seemed to have been born with one skin too many, Diana already had one too few and secretly resented Randolph's domination.

Churchill's lightning appearances made a deep impression on all the children. Neither Johnny nor Peregrine had any particular recollection of their unassuming father when he returned on leave from France, but with Uncle Winston it was different.

He was always marvelous with very young children—one of those adults who loves them in theory, plays great games with them, overexcites them, and then has abruptly had enough. But to them he was glamorous and fun. Peregrine remembers playing "bears" with him and being chased by a growling Churchill through a tunnel made of piled-up picture canvases. Another game he played at Lullenden was called "gorilla," in which he would jump down on the unsuspecting children from the trees.

Churchill's presence served to liven up the humdrum life at Lullenden in other ways. His arrival would invariably spell important guests for the weekend, together with the chauffeurs, guards, and extra servants who accompany the great in time of war. Lullenden would come to life as a proper country house and, however briefly, all the children had a glimpse of the status and excitement Churchill would always generate around himself. He was unlike anybody else—and no one was more impressed by his effect than Randolph. The strange, intense relationship between father and son was starting. Clementine's influence on Randolph at this time was minimal. Wisely, she tended to ignore what she could not control. But between Winston and Randolph there was growing mutual adoration, which nothing could shake, as when Randolph learned his father's role in the Dardanelles.

At the local school there was one village boy who would not play with him because, the boy explained, he was Winston Churchill's son, and Winston Churchill was responsible for his father's death at the Dardanelles. Puzzled by this, Randolph asked his mother what the boy had meant. When she told him, he was completely unabashed. Instead, as he would relate the story later, he felt extremely proud to have a father who "was a boss man who could order other fathers about" so easily. This echoes Lord Randolph's remark to Lord Rosebery that the only position worth having in life was "the boss man's." A true Churchill, Randolph was already thinking much the same.

If Randolph's admiration for his father was straightforward, Churchill's feelings for his son and heir were more involved. It was as if the infant Randolph was already filling a mysterious vacuum in his father's complex nature.

Randolph was a beautiful child, and Churchill must have been extremely proud of the press photographs of him dressed up as a page at the St. Margaret's Westminster wedding of Venetia Stanley and Asquith's former secretary Edwin Montagu in July 1915. With fair hair and angelic countenance, five-year-old Randolph could have been a young medieval prince.

He was also very bright and, like his father, was never at a loss for words. The combination of looks, intelligence, and precocious confidence struck chords in the sentimental side of Churchill's nature. They also appealed to his pride and passion for his family, for Churchill always had the old-fashioned aristocrat's firm conviction of the primacy of the Churchills, an eighteenth-century sense of dynasty and breeding, setting the members of the family high above ordinary humanity.

This sense of dynasty in Churchill found full expression at the end of 1918. Peace came in mid-November, and a few weeks later the whole tribe of Spencer-Churchills enjoyed the first Christmas of the peace together in fine old feudal style at Blenheim Palace. For the first time since before the war, Jack and Winston with their wives and children joined Sunny Marlborough and his sons, Bert, Lord Blandford, and Lord Ivor Churchill, to bring that somber house alive in a burst of unaccustomed celebration.

The festivities that year were on a truly ducal scale: a great bonfire close to the Column of Victory with its brooding statue of the omnipresent first Duke of Marlborough; an effigy of one of Blenheim's most honored former guests, the German Kaiser, thrown to the flames; and a whole ox roasted in the courtyard for family and friends and favored members of the tenantry. Bert was now twenty-one, and everyone had much to celebrate—with the exception of the Duke, who seemed more crushed and miserable than ever.

The contrast between Sunny and Winston had never been more marked; Churchill was at his ebullient best—or worst—having ended the war with his reputation more or less patched up after the horrors of the Dardanelles. At forty-four, he had begun to put on weight, which suited him, and he had just received the finest Christmas present anyone could give him: the knowledge that his political star was still ascending. Cashing in on the nation's gratitude for victory, Prime Minister Lloyd George had smartly called a snap election three weeks earlier, which his coalition government had won. Churchill himself had been elected for the constituency of Dundee with his majority increased, and Lloyd George had promised him promotion in the government.

After his success as Minister for Munitions, Churchill had dreamed of returning to his old position at the Admiralty. It would have laid aside the ghost of the Dardanelles for good, and, besides, he loved the navy; Admiralty House would also have been an invaluable London base for his growing family. He and Clementine now possessed no settled London home, and she had just presented him with one more kitten to be taken care of. It was another daughter, which was probably just as well. A son might have complicated his relationship with Randolph, who was there to carry on the line, and Churchill enjoyed the easier devotion of his daughters.

This latest one was pretty, equable, and redheaded. She would be christened Marigold, but in accordance with the code of private whimsy in the family was already known as "the Duckadilly."

Alas, the family would not be making its home at the Admiralty, but the alternative was almost as good. By the time Churchill reached Blenheim for Christmas, he had exciting news for Clementine about his future. Lloyd George was offering him a more important role, tailor-made to suit his talents: combined responsibility for war and air within the new administration. Churchill had heard rumors that certain generals were horrified by the prospect, which must have pleased him, for he truly enjoyed horrifying generals. The War Office would offer him continued scope for his martial instincts and immense capacity for work, while the official salary of £5,000 a year would be useful with his ever-growing family commitments.

The future settled, Churchill could now happily relax for a few nostalgic days in the splendor of what he looked upon as his true ancestral home with a circle of his closest friends and members of his precious family around him.

Clementine was less entranced. She had never forgotten—or forgiven—Sunny for the way he once insulted her at Blenheim, and the little she had heard about his private life could not have particularly endeared him to her. Nor was she at ease amid these great tribal gatherings of Churchills. She knew the sentimental importance Churchill himself attached to them, and for his sake endured them—as she endured so many other things within their marriage. But she had never felt at home at Blenheim, which had none of the coziness and comfort she really liked about a house. She hated the horseplay and the late nights and the drinking all the men indulged in, and she profoundly disapproved of the rumors of loose living that had grown up around the house. Since Sunny and the Duchess parted, Blenheim had become the sort of place mothers advised their daughters to beware of.

Luckily for Clementine's peace of mind, there was one noted absentee from this year's party—her particular family bête noire, another of her husband's favorite relations: his extremely rich and lecherous cousin Ivor Guest, second Baron Wimborne, who was enjoying a brief period of unaccustomed splendor holding court in Dublin Castle as the last Viceroy in Ireland. The eldest son of the steel magnate, the first Lord Wimborne, who had married Sunny's devoted sister Cornelia, Ivor had inherited his father's fortune with little of the family intelligence or charm.

Only the year before he had been ill-advised enough to attempt nocturnal rape on another of Blenheim's Christmas visitors, the beautiful and unassailable Lady Diana Manners. Forewarned of Blenheim's reputation, let alone what she already knew about Lord Wimborne, Lady Diana had gone to bed with a loaded service revolver, which proved sufficient to calm his lordship's ardor when he burst into her room on his midnight foray. Never one to place discretion before the chance of a thoroughly good story, Lady Diana afterward made sure everybody heard about the incident, and this year the Wimbornes had not been invited (nor had Lady D.).

But the rest of the family was there in force, including Sunny's mother, the ill-used but indestructible Goosey, Lady Blandford, now in her seventy-eighth year, and his indomitable old aunt, Lady Sarah Wilson, who had been at Mafeking. Several grand local families like the Duffs (descendants of the Dukes of Fife) and Birkenheads had also been invited, so that altogether with their personal maids and valets, more than a hundred extra faces thronged the palace, bringing a resurgence of its prewar splendor. The nurseries and corridors were loud with children. Something like forty indoor servants were on hand to guarantee the stately running of this stateliest of homes. Christmas dinner, though cold (the kitchens being far away from the dining room), was eaten off the Marlborough gold plate and served by footmen wearing powdered wigs and the red and silver-braided Marlborough livery. There were good cigars and very good champagne and the family appeared united with all the living generations in their legendary habitat.

This was what Churchill really loved, the essence of the ducal world he always felt he belonged to.

After Churchill's own experience at the center of a European war, the first Duke of Marlborough had become even more of a source of inspiration to him than ever. What greater pleasure than to be returning to his palace at the conclusion of the sort of conflict Marlborough himself had once enjoyed?

Churchill's nephew Johnny has described a particular "Blenheim smell" remembered from his childhood visits, "like the weighty smell of locked-in history." The past was alive in this enormous house with its dusty tapestries and old brocade, its hordes of silent, deeply deferential servants, and the footmen and gamekeepers in their eighteenth-century velvet coats.

With his old green topcoat and awareness of the dignity of his position, Sunny might easily have been an eccentric eighteenth-century nobleman—and so might his most unlikely friend Lord Birkenhead, wildest, wittiest, and most bibulous of politicians.

Birkenhead was one of Winston's oldest friends in politics, cofounder of the Other Club, and one of the few men capable of standing up to him in an argument. With Birkenhead as his verbal sparring partner, Winston was guaranteed the sort of political talk late into the night that he enjoyed, while with his brother Jack, recently returned from France, he could relive the memories of boyhood.

Winston and Jack organized the children, re-creating the games of their own youth, the most popular of which was "French and English." This was played in the great hall, with the children lining up as rival armies. Winston commanded the English, and Jack (as always in the past) the French. Battles were fought, prisoners taken and released, and according to Birkenhead's daughter Eleanor, the two grown men "took such a passionate interest in the game, and played so roughly that they soon scattered the children, conducting some violent struggle of their own that resembled nothing so much as American football."

Winston apparently was one of those disturbing adults who enter a little too exuberantly into the remembered joys of childhood. Of all the children, only Randolph seems to have truly enjoyed such rough play, but then, Randolph was always inventing dangerous games of his own.

Somehow he managed to emerge unbeaten and unbowed after having pushed a nursemaid named Isabel into the bathtub, fully clothed, when she threatened to bathe him. What else did nursemaids expect? He also took immense delight in climbing up to slap a marble Venus on the bottom for a dare. What else was Blenheim's antique statuary for?

Clementine had baby Marigold to attend to while Churchill, as usual, chose to see almost any outrage Randolph managed to commit as one more sign of robust independence. He would not have thought of quelling him. The other children tired much more easily, and then they would sprawl together on the bear-skin rugs in the Long Library and listen to the Duke's organist, Mr. Perkins, play on Blenheim's mighty Willis organ.

This first Blenheim Christmas of the peace was a time everyone remembered as a last glimpse of a world now gone for good. But while the guests were eating, drinking, and enjoying this most pagan festival, there was one melancholy stranger in their midst, a small man in his late forties, "slight, and frail-looking, with beautiful manners," as Lady Eleanor remembered him—the Duke himself. He was a lonely, isolated figure now, and in contrast with his cousin Winston, one sees how unenviable was the fate he had inherited with his dukedom. He had fared badly in the genetic lottery, and the curse of his unhappy house was still pursuing him.

Sunny had sold himself irrevocably for his inheritance when he had married Consuelo Vanderbilt. The Vanderbilt money, and the regular annual 4 percent he still received from the original marriage settlement, had enabled him to do what he conceived to be his duty to his ancestor's voracious palace. The leaking roof had been repaired, two of the state rooms sumptuously restored with gilt French wainscoting, and he was about to embark on ambitious plans to make the exterior of the palace even grander by building a series of elaborate formal terraces, à la Versailles, to connect the palace with the lakes.

It had become something of an obsession with his locked-in

nature to enhance the setting of the dukedom and to maintain the dignity and splendor of his great position. It was a humorless, slightly mad obsession that had grown worse with age. Lord Birkenhead was one of his few friends with the wit to try to make him occasionally unbend, but Sunny was too far gone in dukedom to be aware of everyday reality.

Nothing in his blighted life worked very well, apart from Blenheim—and even here his mania to preserve his house cocooned within the past made it more than ever like a well-run mausoleum once the Christmas guests had gone.

One gets a clear impression of the airless atmosphere of Blenheim in the twenties from one of its visitors, the French Duchess of Clermont-Tonerre.

> I heard the fire crackling in my room without having seen it lighted, the curtains were drawn in my room without my being wakened, and . . . by eight o'clock in the morning the lawn was rolled, the dead leaves removed and the flowerstands filled with fresh flowers.

After a day or two of this, even the Duchess found "the majestic silence of those great mute corridors" getting on her nerves, and she was not the only one. In her otherwise nostalgic memories of Blenheim Christmases, Lady Eleanor Smith includes one episode that reveals a touch of nightmare barely concealed behind the dignity and splendor.

> One day, at Blenheim, a housemaid went mad. She ran through the state rooms, screaming, stalked by grim, powder-headed footmen. It was just before dinner. Her screams rang through the vast rooms, and they were so terrible that I will never forget them. They reminded me of a hare's screams. Finally, she ran to the furthest state room, and there, in the darkness, she was cornered. Four footmen carried her away; she attacked them furiously, and the powder flew from their hair like clouds of snow. They bore her across the huge hall [and] through green baize doors, behind which her anguished cries were no longer heard. That same night she was removed to a lunatic asylum.

This was the world the Duke had made his life's mission to preserve, and it had brought him little but that private bitterness reflected in the down-turned mouth and set expression on his pallid features. As Winston had told Clementine when Sunny and Consuelo separated before the war, his cousin was "absolutely dependent upon feminine influence of some kind for the peace and harmony of his soul"—yet his character and situation had made it all but impossible for him to find it.

There was a sort of grim poetic justice over what had happened to him since he sold himself to Mrs. Vanderbilt and saved Blenheim by marrying her daughter Consuelo. Twenty years later, he was as much the victim of his house as ever, and the cost of maintaining and improving it made him still dependent on the income from his marriage settlement. Any attempt to end the marriage by divorce, without Consuelo's cooperation and assent, could have forfeited not just the income but the capital as well. It was a risk he could not take. And beautiful, rich Consuelo had not the faintest intention now of doing anything to make life easier—let alone more pleasurable—for her husband.

She had a splendid house in London and would soon begin to build another, even more beautiful, at Eze sur Mer, near Monte Carlo, in the South of France. Like the Duke, she had her lovers, but unlike him, she was remarkably discreet. She still enjoyed her title, and she undoubtedly enjoyed annoying Sunny. After those early indignities of marriage, it was understandable.

So Sunny was stuck until Consuelo decided she would free him —if she ever did. He had his consolations. One of the most attractive of them was a former friend of Consuelo's, the beautiful, sophisticated Gladys Deacon from Boston, friend of Rainer Maria Rilke, Marcel Proust, and Charles de Montesquieu. Since well before the war, Sunny had shared Gladys's favors with many of her other lovers, who had included the successful but dubious aesthetic pundit Bernard Berenson, the great sculptor Auguste Rodin, and the President of France. As beautiful as ever, by 1918 she was secretly approaching forty and was as eager to become a duchess as Sunny was to make her one. This, however, did not suit Consuelo, and that "peace and harmony of his soul" that Sunny thought he would find by marrying Miss Deacon sadly eluded him.

Nor did Sunny find comfort in either of his sons, both of whom were adding to his Christmas cup of bitterness. At twenty-one, his heir, the egregious Bert, Lord Blandford, gave every sign of being vastly stupid, which Sunny was not. Bert was extremely tall, largely incoherent, and generally irresponsible. Sunny blamed his deficiencies upon the Vanderbilt strain, which was probably unfair. Having just left the

Life Guards, Bert was having an affair with an actress and there was considerable speculation in the press that he would either marry her or be heavily sued for breach of promise. Neither prospect could have added to the Christmas spirit.

Sunny's other son, Lord Ivor Churchill, could not have been more different from his brother, but he presented the Duke with other problems. As short as Bert was tall, as intelligent as his brother was stupid, Ivor was very much Consuelo's favorite, and he spent more time with her than he ever did at Blenheim. He was highly civilized, already something of a connoisseur of furniture and modern painting, and as precious and refined as Bert was insensitive and boorish. (Bert's character, it was often said, derived largely from the fact that Consuelo had rejected him for Ivor.) Cynthia Asquith, who had a motherly crush on Ivor around this time, described him as "a mannikin," as delicate as a porcelain "figure de Limoges"; while his Oxford contemporary Henry "Chips" Channon, who admired his style and cleverness, detected a fatal touch of melancholy and lack of purpose in his life.

Shortly after leaving Oxford, Ivor seemed to have had some sort of breakdown, and for many years he was psychoanalyzed by Dr. Ernest Jones, Freud's biographer and the leading Freudian in Britain, who must have found the young nobleman a fascinating subject. Freud would have made much of Lord Ivor's close relationship with the powerfully appealing figure of Consuelo and his difficulty in relating to Sunny.

So, all in all, poor Sunny's lot was not a happy one. Perhaps the only person who appreciated what he had done and sacrificed for Blenheim was Cousin Winston. Churchill was the only one who really shared Sunny's obsession with the ancestral palace, for the family traditions it enshrined, and for the dukedom. He always demonstrated unfeigned respect for the reigning Duke as head of the family—as well as maintainer of the honors and title of his hero, ancestor, and source of inspiration, John, first Duke of Marlborough.

But whereas Sunny's devotion to Blenheim had helped to ruin his life, making him a bitter introverted character, Blenheim's influence had had the opposite effect on Winston. At times he might almost have been the first Duke reincarnate, with the same unbridled love of power and enjoyment of luxury and great activities. Sunny was maintaining the tradition of the Marlboroughs for him to draw on, but Sunny's role as Duke of Marlborough was essentially an unrewarding task. The family melancholy afflicted him, and the older and more miserable he got, the more truly ducal Cousin Winston seemed to be—immensely confident and bellicose and reveling in the one thing Sunny never would possess, what Churchill himself has called "that greatest of elixirs": power.

# seventeen

# To Russia with Love

Not long before the Armistice, Siegfried Sassoon, the war-hero-turned-pacifist and poet, had had a bizarre encounter with Churchill, who was then still Minister of Munitions. While recovering from service at the front, Sassoon had become an overnight celebrity with his book *Counterattack,* and Churchill himself seems to have been disturbed by the power of Sassoon's anti-war poetry—and by its potential danger to national morale. Somewhat cynically, he had already tried to compromise Sassoon by offering him a desk job in his own ministry. When this failed, Churchill decided to employ his powers of personal persuasion on the sensitive young officer.

He knew all about Sassoon from his secretary, Eddie Marsh: that he was a member of a prominent Anglo-Jewish family and kinsman to Lloyd George's private secretary, the wealthy Liberal politician Sir Philip Sassoon; also, that he was a great country-lover, horseman, patriot, and manifestly not a coward. Through Marsh, Churchill arranged a meeting so that he could "have it out with him" on a subject still engaging Churchill's energies and passionate excitement.

The meeting started comfortably enough. Churchill seemed "almost boyish" as he talked about the war, and Sassoon began to feel that he "would have liked to have had him as my company commander in the frontline."

But then, as so often with Churchill, what began as a discussion soon became a monologue. Sassoon felt tongue-tied as, "pacing the room, with a big cigar in the corner of his mouth, he gave me an emphatic vindication of militarism as an instrument of policy and stimulator of glorious individual achievements and social progress."

"Head thrust well forward and hands clasped behind his back," Churchill the orator had taken over, leaving the poet more or less forgotten.

"Transfixed and submissive in my chair, I realised that what had begun as a persuasive confutation of my anti-war convictions, was now addressed, in pauseful and perorating prose, to no one in particular."

Other visitors and business now forgotten, the rhetoric flowed on. When it finished, Sassoon emerged from the great man's presence shaken and baffled.

Had Churchill been entirely serious, he asked himself? Could he have meant it when he insisted that "war is the normal occupation of man"?

Having experienced modern war in all its horror, he found it inconceivable that anyone could honestly believe this after four long years of conflict. But Churchill had been plain, and Sassoon concluded: "It had been unmistakeable that for him war was the finest activity on earth."

To set such a man in charge of the War Office with overall responsibility for the armed forces when the war was over was the sort of joke to be expected of Lloyd George, but he should have known Churchill better than to take such a risk. Just as it seemed that he would be Secretary of State for War without a war, Churchill promptly found one.

The Russian Revolution of 1917 had left the victorious Western allies in an awkward position. The Bolsheviks had been abetted originally by the German High Command, and the revolution swiftly led, as the Germans had hoped, to Russia's withdrawal from the war. The Russian royal family was killed and civil war had broken out between the Bolsheviks and groups from the old Imperial army. French and British forces, which had been fighting the Germans with their Russian ally, remained on Russian soil to help the White Army.

Among the Western powers, the general feeling was to disengage and leave the Russians to get on with it. Europe was sick of bloodshed, and few wanted yet another war. But Lenin and the Bolsheviks were proclaiming worldwide revolution against capitalist oppression. The

Communist Bela Khun had established his government in Budapest. Even in Britain, there was widespread discontent following the war, and the red flag threatened postwar Europe. There were arguments for supporting the anti-Bolsheviks in Russia and crushing the revolution in its infancy.

Most Western statesmen hedged their bets. The United States opted for withdrawal, but France favored intervention, and Lloyd George seemed to waver. Not so his Secretary of State for War.

From the beginning of the Russian Revolution, Churchill had felt passionate about the Bolsheviks; it is clear that they offended the profoundest elements within his nature. He saw Czar Nicholas as a tragic hero and Lenin as beneath the range of civilized contempt—"a plague bacillus" that had infected Russia with "the foul baboonery" of communism, "a monster crawling down from his pyramid of skulls." Lenin, he remarked, almost converted him to Christianity; only the most atrocious depths of hell were fit to receive so terrible a man.

Although he felt strongly about the revolution, Churchill, in fact, knew very little about the aims and characters of those involved. He fulminated against the revolution as the work of "a group of international semitic conspirators" despite the fact that Trotsky was the only Jew among the Soviet leaders. Of all the causes of the Russian Revolution, a conspiracy of evil Jewish gentlemen was the least convincing even then.

"Before all things, he desires a dramatic world with villains—and one hero," H. G. Wells once wrote, and Lord Beaverbrook described Churchill at the War Office in the spring of 1919 as striding up and down the room on little feet and "tingling with vitality. Bold and imaginative in the sweep of his conceptions, prolific of new ideas, like a machine of bullets and expelling his notions in much the same manner." When Asquith's daughter Violet Bonham Carter asked about his latest policy, Winston answered, "Kiss the Hun and kill the Bolshie."

Throughout the spring of 1919, Churchill set out to do just that. Lloyd George's preoccupation with the peace conference in Paris left Churchill a free hand at the War Office, and he was clearly on a high as he mounted his campaign in the Cabinet, Parliament, and press against the monsters he so vividly created in his powerful imagination.

It was good theater, and a vintage Churchill one-man show. On the pretext of covering their ultimate withdrawal, he was soon ordering the British forces in Archangel to advance. He kept the White Russian general Alexei Denikin supplied with money and surplus British war matériel and proposed the annexation of the Caspian Sea by the Royal Navy and the use of poison gas against the enemy. When it looked as if the Communists were crumbling, he even talked of "going out there to ride a white charger" into Moscow at the head of the Czarist forces. His friend Lord Ridell said half jokingly that Winston dreamed of being Czar himself.

Perhaps he did, or possibly he dreamed of beating his old hero, Napoleon, to the gates of Moscow. Thanks to this dream, by late spring of 1919, Britain was on the brink of war. Or as Lloyd George put it, Britain was in "a state of war" with the Soviets, but had no intention of actually "making war" upon them.

Churchill had no such reservations. "If we don't put our foot on the egg, we shall have to chase the chicken round the world's farmyard," he remarked.

But mutiny was already breaking out among British forces in Murmansk, the White Russians were in chaos, and Churchill's scant support at home was fading. Long before the winter of 1920 started, he was having to admit the failure of his great campaign as the "intervention" against the Soviets collapsed.

The star was eager but the show was ending. He would not be riding into Moscow, nor making Europe safe from communism. It was an ignominious failure, which ended with Lloyd George demoting him from the War Office to responsibility for the colonies early in 1921. By then the Bolshevik revolution was even haunting Churchill within the safety of his precious family. It was at a weekend gathering of Churchills at Templeton, the Roehampton mansion of his rich cousin Freddie Guest (second son of Aunt Cornelia) early in September 1920 that Churchill's nephew Johnny heard the beginning of a scandal that suddenly shook the family.

"I was a child, just home from school, and I was fascinated to hear a terrific commotion from the drawing room. There was my uncle Winston, beside himself with rage, and Lord Birkenhead, who seemed to be trying to calm him down. But Uncle Winston went on shouting, 'Clare's in Russia. Clare's in Russia with those filthy Communists. She's mad, I tell you. Mad! It's absolutely typical of Clare, but this time she's really gone too far. I'll not forgive her.' "

For the rest of the weekend, chaos reigned as the gathered Churchills tried to decide what on earth to do about their cousin, who at that moment was in Moscow with the "hairiest Bolshevik baboon" of all, Vladimir Ilyich Lenin.

Clare Sheridan, then aged thirty-five, was the widowed daughter of Jennie's sister Clara and her handsome husband, Moreton "Mortal Ruin" Frewen. Churchill's aunt Clara was a true Jerome, with much of Jennie's extravagance and energetic charm. Incurably romantic, Clara had even managed to maintain her marriage while conducting a long affair with the most improbable of lovers, Milan Obrenovich, the dispossessed King of Serbia. Her husband, Churchill's uncle Moreton, seems to have been more than a match for her. Inventor, speculator, spendthrift, and philanderer—"every woman I have ever enjoyed has been completely paralysed by the vigour of my performance"—he was probably the most unreliable man in England, as Churchill had discovered years before when Uncle Moreton edited the proofs of *The Malakand Field Force*.

Golden-haired, dramatic Clare inherited her parents' beauty— and most of their other qualities as well. Her marriage to Wilfred Sheridan, a descendant of the playwright, had ended with his death in action. Since then, she had indulged her artistic temperament as a sculptress and achieved considerable success.

Much of this was due to the support of her cousin Winston, who was fond of her and helped promote her work. She sculpted him, and several of his friends had also sat for her, including Lord Birkenhead, Lord Reading, and the egregious Freddie Guest.

By the summer of 1920, Churchill and his friends were seeing much of Cousin Clare. She had started an affair with the fifty-two-year-old Lord Birkenhead, who was now Lord Chancellor of England and happily infatuated. When Jennie heard what was going on, she laughed and told her that although Birkenhead was married, he was just the sort of man Clare needed to "perk her up."

According to Clare's grandmother, Mrs. Frewen, who also knew of the affair, Churchill was equally complacent. "He adores Clare, thinks she can do no wrong after all she has suffered and he is devoted to Lord B.—you know how he always stands by his friends. So whatever scandal these two create together is in Winston's view no scandal —they are 'splendid,' and whatever they feel like doing is 'perfect.' So there it is. . . ."

On weekends, Lord Birkenhead collected Mrs. Sheridan from her studio in his Rolls and brought her back to Templeton, where she also had a studio, so that love and sculpture could continue their idyllic course among the Churchills. Clementine's views about what was going on were not recorded.

Clare was industrious as well as romantic, and Agnew's Gallery in Bond Street had promised her a one-woman exhibition before Christmas if she produced portraits of enough celebrities to make a show.

Since the failure of Winston's intervention policy in Russia, Lloyd George had invited a Russian trade delegation to visit London, and although Churchill indignantly refused to have anything to do with them, Clare remarked casually, "What fun to add a Bolshevik to my Agnew exhibition!"

This chance remark was reported to Lev Borisovich Kamenev, the leader of the Russian delegation, who was smart enough to see the publicity potential of a close relation of the dreaded Winston Churchill doing portrait busts of Russian leaders for a Bond Street show. He met Clare, flattered her (which was not difficult), and promised her that if she came to Moscow, he would guarantee her introductions to the leading members of his government.

She must have known that Kamenev's brother-in-law was Leon Trotsky, the creator of the Red Army, who was second only to Lenin as her cousin Winston's archenemy. She had also recently agreed to join Churchill and the Lord Chancellor for a cruise aboard her lover's yacht. But not for nothing was she Moreton Frewen's daughter. An adventure such as this was irresistible. So was the thought of adding the notorious face of Lenin to her other portraits—it would make her famous. Secretly she took the train to Stockholm, then journeyed on to Moscow, leaving her cousin and the jilted Birkenhead aboard their yacht, wondering what could possibly have happened. They found out when they returned to Templeton—and Johnny was there to witness the result.

Clare, in the meantime, was blithely unconcerned with the furor she had roused at home. Thanks to Kamenev's influence, she was lodged—in considerable discomfort—in the official guest house on the Sofiskaya Embankment (now the British embassy), and various leading Bolsheviks were produced to sit for her. The notorious Grigori Evseyevich Zinoviev, President of the Third Communist International, was succeeded by the most feared man in Moscow, Felix Edmundovich Dzerzhinsky, a leading organizer of the original Bolshevik coup d'état and head of the Soviet secret police, the Cheka. (Clare found him to be pale, undersized, and sickly, and he explained that eleven years in prison had destroyed his health, a compliment he was repaying his ancient enemies in spades.)

Then it was Lenin's turn. The sittings took place in his office in the Kremlin, and they were curiously peaceful and relaxed. While Lenin worked away in silence at his desk—"I have no interest in art, but you can work here as long as you don't disturb me"—the indomitable sculptress tried doing justice to the head of the most powerful man in Russia. Although Lenin spoke English, it was not until the bust was nearly finished that she coaxed a little conversation from him.

"Your cousin, Winston Churchill, he must be pleased with you!" he said, with what could have been a touch of unexpected wit.

"Is he hated in Russia?" she inquired.

To which Lenin answered that Churchill was the Russian people's greatest enemy, since "all the force of your Court and your army lie behind him."

She replied that although Churchill was Minister for War, the Court had little actual power in England. Lenin, who seemed very conscious of King George's hatred of the Bolsheviks for murdering his Russian royal cousins, would not accept this.

"It is a pose to say the King does not count. He counts very much. He is the head of the army, and he is the bourgeois figurehead. Churchill is backed by him."

This apparently ended the singular conversation. Asked for an opinion of the finished bust, Lenin's secretary dutifully pronounced it "good."

"I like a fast worker," Lenin said. And that, after shaking hands, was that.

Before leaving Russia, Clare was determined to complete her gallery of leading Bolsheviks with a portrait bust of Trotsky—and it was this that brought a romantic grand finale to her visit.

From the start, she found Trotsky a more responsive subject than Comrade Lenin. The scholarly-looking figure with the pince-nez spectacles was commander in chief of an army of five million men, which was in the process of mopping up the remnants of the White Russians Churchill was supporting in the Crimea. Still, he found the time to meet her in the white-pillared ballroom of the Soviet Ministry of War.

Clare would not forget the sessions that ensued each evening in that ballroom as she worked on the "magnetic" features of her favorite Bolshevik. Did he really kiss her frozen hands and warm them by the fire? Did he really tell her that "even when your teeth are clenched and you are fighting with your work *vous etes encore femme*"? And when the bust was finished, could she have resisted him amid the damask-covered walls of her lonely bedroom when he murmured that "a woman like you could be a whole world to a man"?

This was the story as she told it to her niece Anita Leslie many years later, and according to this version, it was touch and go whether she should accompany her latest lover on campaign in the Crimea. "C'est à vous de décider," he told her with his arms around her.

Luckily for Churchill back in London, Cousin Clare placed art and duty over the promptings of her heart, and she headed homeward with her sculptures and her memories.

As it was, it was embarrassing enough. Through its secret agents, the British government was kept informed of what went on in Moscow, and the doings of this close relation of the Secretary of State for War were naturally reported back to London. "Poor Winston, Lloyd George chaffs him terribly in the Cabinet about you," Clare's cousin, the literary Shane Leslie, informed her. Lloyd George was not remarkable for delicacy in sentimental matters, and would not have missed so obvious a chance to embarrass the strongest critic of his reconciliation policy with Russia. And Churchill was notoriously touchy over any scandal that involved his family.

He was extremely angry for a while. According to Shane Leslie, he seriously proposed having his cousin placed in quarantine on her return, and not unnaturally, he refused to meet her. So did her father, who complained that, thanks to Clare, he was now unable to show his face at the White's Club bar. The royal family were reported "scandalised." According to Clare's own account, the only Churchill to support her was Jennie, who supposedly told her, "You're so like me really—I would have loved to do it in your place."

(Perhaps she would, and certainly her niece's escapades were very much in character with the headstrong and romantic Jennie, who had recently married for the third and final time—to a lonely Colonial official named Montagu Porch, who was three years younger than her eldest son. Although apparently delighted with her gentle husband, Jennie had no intention of being Mrs. Monty Porch, and made it known that she was to be addressed as Lady Randolph Churchill. "My boys asked me to," she said.)

Clare soon discovered that life in London was impossible. Far from making her fortune as she had hoped, the sculptures of her Bolsheviks were little more than competent and did nothing to advance her own artistic reputation. With her family and most of her former friends, including, not surprisingly, Lord Birkenhead—giving her the coldest of cold shoulders—she wisely headed for a lecture tour in the States, where her tales and talents were appreciated. (In Hollywood she sculpted her next sitter—Charlie Chaplin.)

When she had safely left the shores of England, Churchill sent her a letter. Given the circumstances, it was one of the most tolerant he ever wrote. He was not a man for bearing grudges, particularly not with women he was fond of, and he was genuinely fond of Cousin Clare.

It had been, he said, impossible for him to meet her on her return from Russia, "fresh from the society of those I regard as fiendish criminals." But that did not mean that he no longer regarded her with affection, and he earnestly wished her "success and happiness in a right way." She could always count upon his friendship and, more important still, his kinship, and he trusted they would meet again when there was "a healthy gap between you and an episode which may then have faded and to which we need neither of us ever refer."

Clare's departure for the United States overlapped Churchill's departure from the War Office early in 1921—and with this vanished any further serious concern for what went on in Russia. Having brought Britain to the brink of war to indulge his dreams of conflict with the Bolsheviks, he washed his hands of them. Never one for lingering on the field of failure, he had found himself fresh enemies closer to home to keep him happily involved in politics and "man's normal occupation"—war.

The new ministry to which Lloyd George had shifted him was one he had occupied earlier in his ministerial career: Secretary for the Colonies. Although the shift was seen as a demotion, the workaholic Churchill soon immersed himself in complex new responsibilities, which were a welcome contrast to the snows and gloom of Russia.

Almost his first task was to impose the British government's proposed settlement on Palestine, in accordance with the promise made in 1917 by former premier A. J. Balfour to set up a Jewish national home there. At the Cairo conference, early in 1921, he accomplished this with a speed and firmness much applauded at the time and commemorated ever since in unceasing Arab-Jewish conflict.

History would be no kinder to him over his swift solution to another problem awaiting him at the Colonial Office—the transformation of Turkish Mesopotamia, conquered by the British in 1918, into the modern Arab kingdom of Iraq. Anxious to safeguard British oil interests at minimum expense, Churchill selected malleable King Faisal for the newly created Iraqi throne backed by British arms and influence. Rather than rely on large, expensive troop detachments, Churchill devised a policy of swift retaliation by British armored cars and RAF bombers against troublesome Iraqi villages as "a deterrent to the unruly tribesmen," most of them members of the harshly treated Kurdish minority, who opposed Baghdad.

It was a policy that set a chilling precedent for the future of this unhappy country. His old Harrow contemporary, Richard Mein-ertzhagen, now British military adviser on Middle East Affairs, wrote to him anxiously of rumors he had heard of the use of poison gas against rebellious tribesmen. But Churchill had never been sentimental about rebellious tribesmen. Far from condemning the use of poison gas against them, his reaction was to authorize "the construction of such bombs at once. . . . In my view they are a scientific expedient for sparing life which should not be prevented by the prejudices of those who do not think clearly." Luckily the rest of the cabinet failed to share Churchill's "unprejudiced" views on chemical warfare, and despite his enthusiasm for the use of poison gas, he never got the chance to be the first to use it to suppress the Kurds.

But as Colonial Secretary, Churchill's main preoccupation during 1921 was not Baghdad but Dublin. Here too as a warrior politician he had already had his chance to make his contribution to the miseries of Ireland. While Secretary for War, Churchill had devised the plan for what he called a "Special Emergency Gendarmerie" of a thousand for-mer servicemen to give backbone to the harassed Royal Irish Constab-ulary, which was facing growing violence and disorder. Swiftly drafted into Ireland, in khaki uniforms and black military belts, his thousand troops acquired the nickname of the "Black and Tans" and rapidly became a byword for organized brutality and British government-backed terror in retaliation of the murderous activities of the Irish Republican Army (IRA).

Churchill was soon strongly urging ruthless war against the Irish revolutionaries—which included retaliatory murder, the destruction of much of the city of Cork, and the proposed bombing and machine gunning from the air of the revolutionary Sinn Fein meetings. Only when it became clear that such a policy was pushing Ireland to the verge of anarchy did he change course and opt for the granting of dominion status to a new Irish Free State. Under this plan, only Prot-estant Ulster in the North would remain part of mainland Britain.

These proposals were neither simple nor particularly popular in Dublin or in London, and their acceptance finally owed much to Chur-chill's vigorous espousal, in particular to the ruthless way he faced the Irish delegates with the alternatives of settling or facing all-out blood-shed.

The Irish Treaty, signed at the end of 1921, was hailed as a triumph for the conciliatory powers of Lloyd George and the skilled advocacy of Lord Birkenhead. It was also a considerable success for Churchill, whose ministerial responsibility it was, and whose ruthlessness and energy, both in Ireland and in the House of Commons, had helped to bring it to fruition.

The settlement, however temporary, of Palestine, Iraq, and Ireland helped restore Churchill's tattered credibility after the failure of his Russian policy. This made 1921 a year of spectacular recovery for him; indeed, he judged it one of the most successful of his whole career. His only serious regret was that it had not been crowned with that "great office of state" he had always set his heart on, his father's old position at the Treasury. Churchill's rage on hearing that Lloyd George had entrusted it to the pedestrian Sir Robert Horne in succession to Austen Chamberlain widened the rift between the two and was proof of the extent to which his powerful ambitions were reviving.

What was particularly remarkable about Churchill's political recovery in 1921 was that he achieved it in the face of a succession of family disasters and private tragedies. All were unforeseen and might have been expected to divert if not prostrate a man of Churchill's naturally depressive temperament. But the reverse occurred. Aggression and political success sustained him, so that the tragedies that now befell him and his family barely appeared to interrupt the brisk momentum of his days.

The first sign that Churchill's private life was threatened came from Clementine, who in the last months of 1920 was clearly heading for a nervous breakdown.

Behind the cool and carefully controlled exterior, Clementine was always nervously at risk. Even before her marriage, there had been a long period of prostration after she ended her engagement with her older suitor, and throughout her life she was afflicted by dramatic outbursts of hysteria, which could be followed by lethargy, depression, and a sudden inability to cope with life.

Much of her trouble lay in chronic insecurity, which seems to have had its origins in her fatherless and insecure girlhood.

Although not the easiest of husbands, Churchill, the confident, ambitious older man, had offered her the reassurance she needed, and she determined early on to place him and his great career before family and children. She had stuck to this with all the dedication of her own romantic nature, sharing his triumphs and seeing him through times of deep depression. He relied upon her for encouragement and advice. She must have known that clever people, such as the Asquiths and even the vivacious Goonie, sometimes mocked her earnestness behind her back, but it barely mattered. Her lack of learning and sophistication could be seen as a virtue.

"Just becos' I am ordinary & love you I know what is right for you & good for you in the end," she wrote to Churchill on one occasion. Convinced of this, she could be reassured of her importance as the handmaid of the superman, guiding his destiny with simple intuition and helping him against his enemies.

But supermen can be erratic husbands. Churchill "up" was egotistical and self-absorbed. Once on the warpath, he had little need of anyone—apart from enemies and allies.

This was the side of Churchill that Clementine distrusted. One of her constant plaints toward the end of his time as Minister of Munitions had been that he should turn from "Hunnish" violence toward the paths of peace. "Can't the men munition workers build lovely garden cities?" she had asked him with a touching faith in Churchill's own pacific nature. But while he was smiting the Bolshevik baboon and scourging the disaffected Irish, Clementine's vision of "lovely garden cities" faded. So did her favorite role of guardian and guide of her aggressive husband.

It was unfortunate that this had had to coincide with a period when they were homeless and Clementine was having to accept the hospitality of cousin Freddie Guest at Templeton. Young Randolph had just gone off to boarding school, and lacking any close maternal feeling for Sarah or Diana, she must have felt vulnerable and lonely in the midst of Churchill's rich relations and overpowering friends—Birkenhead and Beaverbrook—whose influence she never trusted.

It was then that Clementine's troubles started: lassitude and hysterical outbursts followed by attacks of hopelessness. These may have been either a cry for help or a way of attracting Churchill's sympathy. If so, they seemed to work, and late that summer Churchill took her on an unusually lengthy holiday, first to the obliging Bend'or, Duke of Westminster's palatial house in Normandy, which Churchill loved, and then to Italy. It was an unusual concession to Clementine for Churchill to tear himself away from hunting boar with Bend'or and instead stump around the sights of Florence; and on their return they were due to leave resplendent Templeton for the London house that Clementine so badly wanted. No. 2 Sussex Square was a comfortable, capacious, cream-stucco mid-Victorian house near Marble Arch. Jennie had discovered it.

The property seemed ideal, and Clementine's troubles should have been over now that she had her own home near the park. There would be servants, the sort of drawing room she wanted, and a proper nursery where a nursemaid could tend baby Marigold. At nearby Notting Hill there was a girls' high school where Sarah and Diana could attend as day-girls, and Churchill could have his study and his library and entertain his friends and ride down Rotten Row for exercise.

But at Sussex Square the troubles of the Churchills were far from over. The girls were sickly and Clementine's depression and listlessness persisted. At eight years of age, the once bonny Sarah had changed into what she herself later described as a "listless little old lady." After Christmas, she and Diana were packed off to a boardinghouse in Broadstairs, accompanied by a maid named Annie. Marigold was left in London with the nursemaid, and Churchill, more concerned than ever for his wife, took her to the South of France to stay with rich Sir Ernest Cassel at his luxurious villa outside Nice.

Clementine's illness was becoming increasingly mysterious. It was certainly serious enough to rouse her husband's deep concern, and he urged her to observe her doctor's advice to the letter, avoid undue exertion, stay in bed, and "subordinate everything in yr life to regathering yr nervous energy and recharging yr batteries."

In mid-January, as soon as Winston returned to London, Clementine, who stayed in France, achieved a startling recovery. Moving on from good but dull Sir Ernest to younger friends with a villa nearer Cannes, she was soon lunching out, enjoying a most untypical flutter at the casino at Monte Carlo, and all but winning the local tennis championship.

From London, Churchill, now on the death list of the IRA and guarded by a Scotland Yard detective, was writing anxious letters. "I do hope you will soon see sunshine & preen yr poor feathers in it." But Clementine, no longer molting, had spread her wings and was thoroughly enjoying life—suggesting that her troubles were essentially bound up with Churchill and the family, and that the surest cure was a period apart.

This was something she was able to do, and she went on energetically recharging batteries in the warmth of the Riviera while Churchill and the children, back in London, soldiered on as best they could. She had further treats in store. In early March, Churchill collected her from

Nice and took her on to Cairo with Eddie Marsh and fascinating Col. Thomas E. Lawrence (of Arabia) for the signing of the Palestine Treaty. This was followed by a visit to Jerusalem, much enjoyed by Clementine, before returning to the girls in rainy Sussex Square after an almost three-month absence.

But although she appeared recovered, Clementine was far from cured, and for many years to come that winter's strange neurotic pattern would reappear. Her hysterical attacks were accompanied by lowered vitality and deep depression, leaving the doctors baffled and only able to suggest another holiday. Since the problem became part of Clementine's existence, Churchill and the family accepted it and learned to live with it.

Indeed, they would learn to cope rather well without her for long periods, thanks to the servants and to Churchill's self-reliance. Churchill himself always seemed extremely sympathetic to his wife's neurosis. Perhaps his own experience of depression made him understand what she was suffering, and he rarely complained about her absences. They may, in fact, have suited him. Anything was better than a weepy and neurotic wife as a companion, and he made sure nothing interfered with life as he wished to live it. Impregnably involved in politics and with a support staff that included a valet, secretaries, and a detective, he was happy in his own unshakable routine. Whenever Clementine was absent, he would write her loving sentimental letters signed by Mr. Pug.

Clementine, while certainly not feigning her attacks, seems to have increasingly relied upon them to escape the strains of life with Churchill. All who knew her were impressed by her sense of duty and her dedication to her home and husband. But it was also clear that the dedication and involvement placed a growing burden on her rigid nature.

He was supremely selfish, and there were things about that remorselessly self-directed life that Clementine had grown to dislike. She loathed his buccaneering friends, his monologues, his personal extravagance that left so many bills worryingly unpaid, and the bewildering ups and downs of his political career. All brought an element of chaos to the perfect life she longed for. But she had learned that there was next to nothing she could do to make him change—even communication between them on such subjects was extremely hazardous.

Clementine was not a weak-willed woman. "Had she been a man," insists her secretary, Grace Hamblin, "you would have called her the strong silent type." And such a type is always liable to collapse rather than complain. So it was that, in the midst of all her troubles, no one seemed to notice that Randolph was becoming a young monster. The other children had problems, too. Diana was introverted and neurotic, Sarah suffered from tuberculosis, and baby Marigold, suffering from bronchial infections all winter, was at risk.

Whatever the nature of Clementine's illness, it can hardly have been helped by the tragedy that greeted her on her return from Cairo and Jerusalem in April 1921. At thirty-two, her only brother, profligate and handsome Bill Hozier, formerly of the Royal Navy, had blown his brains out in a hotel room in Paris. Clementine was badly needed in Dieppe to help her sister Nellie cope with a grief-stricken Lady Blanche and to make arrangements for the funeral. In the small expatriate community of Dieppe, a suicide created a considerable scandal, and the normally rambunctious Lady Blanche was incapable of coping with it. She struck Clementine as "shrunk and small."

For Clementine, so recently the victim of nervous illness herself, the irrational suicide of such a close relation must have been particularly harrowing. One possible explanation for his death was that it was linked with gambling anxieties. Addictive gambling seemed to run in Clementine's family. Like Bill, Clementine's sister Nellie and their mother, Lady Blanche, were chronic gamblers, and Clementine apparently believed that all had inherited a "gambling gene" and that it had ruined their lives. What, she had to wonder, was in her own heredity? Knowing her mother as she did, she must have had her doubts about her paternity—along with fears that she, too, had inherited whatever streak of instability had brought her brother to a suicide's grave.

In arranging for the funeral it at first appeared that the local chaplain would deny Bill a proper burial. Believing that Churchill's attendance would change the chaplain's mind, Clementine begged her husband to find the time to come across to France.

"Oh Winston my Dear, do come tomorrow & dignify by your presence Bill's poor suicide's funeral," she implored him. He promised that he would, and the funeral was specially delayed for him.

The arrival at Dieppe of the Cabinet minister in black topcoat aboard the afternoon ferry ensured that his brother-in-law at least received a dignified and Christian burial.

Soon after Bill Hozier's funeral, Churchill himself had to face bereavement, and it was as unexpected as Bill's death. Since her remarriage,

Jennie seemed to have taken on a fresh lease on life, making her appear a great survivor from a richer age. "She was still a handsome woman, her dark eyes had lost none of their sparkle with the passing of the years, and the shape of her face was always admirable," wrote her friend the Duchess of Sermoneta, with whom she spent part of that spring in Rome. While the self-effacing Mr. Porch had vanished on a business trip to Africa, the sixty-seven-year-old Jennie, her white hair à la Pompadour, enjoyed herself with all her old vivacity.

She still made money out of property. Only a year before she had sold a house in Berkeley Square for £35,000—"a clear profit of £15,000"—and spent as lavishly as ever. After her trip to Rome she went to stay with another grande dame from an earlier age, Lady Frances Horner, at her house at Mells in Somerset, and while wearing a pair of highly fashionable shoes bought in Rome, slipped on the stairs and broke her ankle. Gangrene set in. Churchill was summoned to the hospital as next of kin, and the leg was amputated.

"Please make sure you have cut high enough," she told the surgeon.

She soon seemed to be recovering. "My poor departed leg served me well for 67 years & led me into some very pleasant walks," she wrote philosophically to her former admirer Lord Curzon. But on the morning of June 29 she called her nurse.

"I think my hot water bottle's burst," she said. In fact, the main artery had hemorrhaged, and late that afternoon the placards for the London evening papers were announcing the sad death of Lady Randolph Churchill.

Mr. Porch was reported to be heartbroken. He hurried back to London on a ship from Lagos as her two sons set about making funeral arrangements. On July 3, thirty-five years after Lord Randolph's death, Jennie was buried beside him in Bladon churchyard, with the name her sons had wanted, Lady Randolph Churchill, on her tomb. Her second husband, George Cornwallis-West, had sent a wreath "for auld lang's syne." Nobody mentioned Mr. Porch (whose boat failed to arrive in time), and Shane Leslie described Jack and Winston standing "like widowers" beside the grave. Both were in tears and Winston threw a spray of crimson roses on the tomb.

"I do not feel a sense of tragedy but only of loss," Winston wrote to Curzon.

But more tragedy was in store for him—and Clementine. The beginning of August saw their family again split up, with Churchill staying on in London, Clementine up at Eaton Hall with the Duke and Duchess of Westminster for a tennis tournament, and all four children—including two-and-a-half-year-old Marigold—once again packed off to Broadstairs in the charge of a solitary and inexperienced young French nurse-governess.

With Churchill, as with Clementine, there was a marked difference between the deeply sentimental way they referred to the "kittens" in their letters, and how they treated them. Churchill was not the man to waste his precious weeks away from politics on seaside holidays "bunged up with brats," and the deeply unmaternal Clementine seems to have felt much the same.

Presumably, then, nobody noticed that Marigold was suffering from a throat infection when she went to Broadstairs. It was, however, serious enough for Randolph to comment on it in a letter to his mother on August 2, but it was nearly another two weeks before anything was done. Only when Marigold lay in bed with septicemia was Clementine summoned by the anxious governess.

Action finally ensued. Churchill arrived soon after Clementine with a London specialist, but in the days before antibiotics there was little in the way of treatment—except to await the outcome of the illness. In this dramatic situation, Clementine was diligent in bedside duties, sitting up all night beside her stricken daughter. But it was too late, and on August 23, with both parents by her bedside, Marigold died. According to what Churchill told daughter Mary "Clementine in her agony gave a succession of wild shrieks, like an animal in pain."

But nothing was permitted to deflect the Churchills from their plans. They had already arranged to go with the children to another ducal home, Westminster's house at Loch More in Sutherland, for two weeks, and afterward Churchill was due to spend another fortnight on his own with the Duke of Sutherland at Dunrobin Castle. Dukes could not be disappointed, and the Churchills made the best of things. Marigold was buried at Kensal Green cemetery, the family had their holiday at Loch More, and then, barely two weeks after Clementine had lost her youngest daughter, Churchill left her, as arranged, for the pleasures of Dunrobin Castle.

While Clementine was back at Sussex Square arranging for the children to return to school, Churchill found time from his painting to write another deeply sentimental letter, expressing tender thoughts about their "sweet kittens" and the hurt he was feeling for Marigold. Hardly surprisingly, Clementine was soon exhibiting symptoms of lassitude again. Churchill, however, was buoyed up by political success throughout that autumn, and immediately after Christmas had arranged to accompany Lloyd George, with whom relations were more or less restored, on yet another trip to the Riviera.

Clementine was to be permitted to join her husband in the South of France a few days later. She was, in fact, delayed by yet more illness in the family. There was an influenza epidemic, and Marigold's demise had taught her the danger of entrusting sick children to the servants. So it was not until the end of January that she succeeded in joining her husband in Cannes, just when he was almost ready to return to London for the start of the new parliamentary session. Since Clementine had planned to stay on in France for a little more "recharging," this meant that they had only a few brief days together—but it was enough time to create a replacement for their lost and much lamented kitten.

# eighteen

# The Chartwell Dream

At £5,500, the property had hung on the market for more than a year even though it was something of a bargain, for in 1922 house prices this close to London had sunk to their lowest since the war. It was comprised of some sixty unkempt hillside acres on high ground close to the village of Westerham in Kent, a once grand but decidedly derelict high-Victorian villa built around the inner core of an earlier small farmhouse, and a spring at the bottom of the hill—the Chartwell. The house, in turn, had inherited the name Chartwell Manor.

It needed an optimistic buyer, for it was not a cheerful-looking place. Dry rot had rampaged through the woodwork, and damp from the overhanging trees had "slimed the walls with green." According to its future architect, the unloved house had "grown weary of its own ugliness so that the walls ran with moisture and creeping fungus tracked down the cracks and crevices."

Its best feature was the view. On a clear day one could see for miles across the profoundly boring but romantic-sounding stretch of southern England known as the Weald of Kent. It was the sort of view a commanding general would appreciate—and so did Winston Churchill from the moment he clapped eyes on it.

He would be forty-eight that November and was at the start of another period of upheaval for himself and his family, for there was

"A full-blown Victorian prig." John Winston, seventh Duke of Marlborough, with his second son, Lord Randolph Spencer-Churchill.

2

The man Disraeli called "a thorough-going blackguard." Winston Churchill's Uncle George, eighth Duke of Marlborough, more commonly known as "the Bad Duke."

Blenheim Palace, begun in 1705 as both home and monument for the triumphant first Duke of Marlborough —"an uncomfortably ill-omened house, hated or admired, but rarely loved, the scene of much noble misery and gloom."

3

"Chief mourner at his own protracted funeral." Lord Randolph Churchill, aged forty-four, affected by encroaching madness.

"A dark, lithe figure . . . a diamond star in her hair . . . its lustre dimmed by the flashing glory of her eyes. More of the panther than the woman in her look." Lady Randolph in her prime.

"Links in the chain." The Vanderbilt heiress Consuelo, as Duchess of Marlborough with her two sons, John Albert Edward William, Lord Blandford, future tenth Duke of Marlborough (commonly known as "Bert") and her favorite, the future connoisseur-perfectionist, Lord Ivor Churchill.

Was this Winston Churchill's true father-in-law? Captain W. G. "Bay" Middleton, great horseman, "rampant womaniser," and according to strong evidence, the father of Clementine Hozier, future wife of Winston Churchill.

"A keen aboriginal desire to kill several of these odious Derivishes." Winston Churchill, a lieutenant in the 4th Hussars, at the time of the Charge at Omdurman.

"Christ!" Churchill said when seeing himself in the Glengarry cap he should have worn as Lieutenant Colonel with the Royal Scots Fusiliers in France in 1916. Instead he adopted the French *poilu*'s steel helmet which flattered his bulldog features.

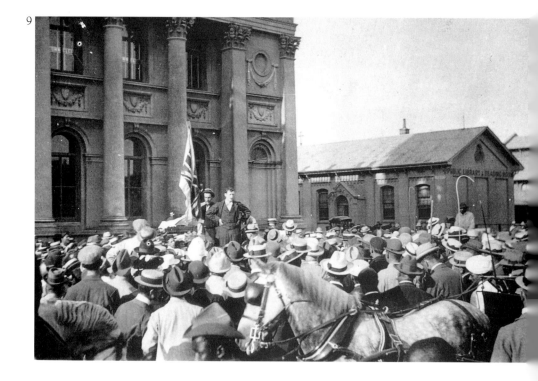

Winston's "oldest dearest friend," Sunny, nineth Duke of Marlborough.

"Hero of five wars, author of six books, and the future prime minister of England"—Winston is given a hero's welcome at Durban after his escape from Boer captivity.

Churchill and Clementine on Armistice Day, 1923. "War attracts me and fascinates my mind with its tremendous situations," he told her.

also dry rot in the Liberal government in which he had been Colonial Secretary since February 1921. He was in angry disagreement with the current intention of his Prime Minister, Lloyd George.

The P.M. wanted to offer not just recognition but a £4 million trading loan to the very men Churchill had tried so desperately to topple, those "Semitic conspirators" as he called them, the Bolshevik leaders of the U.S.S.R. And from his cousin, the former Liberal Chief Whip, the wealthy Capt. Freddie Guest (known in political circles as the "the Paying Guest"), he unquestionably knew more than enough about Lloyd George's involvement in the widespread scandal of the sale of honors to ruin him had he felt inclined.

Churchill strongly disapproved of the blatant offering of titles in return for contributions to Lloyd George's party funds, but he did not denounce his chief in public. He and the old "Welsh Wizard" had been through too much together for this to have been a possibility.

Suffice to say that by that all-important autumn of 1922, both Churchill and the electorate at large were profoundly disillusioned with the postwar spell of Lloyd George and the Liberal party. Churchill's attentions had been increasingly—and lucratively—involved in authorship as he prepared to write the first volume of his war memoirs, for which he had already garnered a useful £5,000 advance from his publisher, together with a further offer of £3,000 for serial rights from the *Times* of London.

In addition, Churchill had also just enjoyed one of those strokes of sudden luck that traditionally light up the lives of hard-pressed members of the aristocracy. That spring his childless Londonderry cousin Lord Vane Tempest had perished in a railway accident in Wales. The victim owned an Irish castle that, for want of any closer heirs, descended somewhat casually to Cousin Winston, who in turn, having little use for Irish castles, had sensibly disposed of it for £20,000. As so often in the past, his friend and patron good Sir Ernest Cassel, the Jewish multimillionaire and onetime crony and financial aide of King Edward VII, had been advising him on his investments. (Unlike "Semitic conspirators," Semitic bankers had their uses.)

Now for the first time in his life, Churchill possessed a private income of some £4,000 a year and had more than £20,000 in the bank. This was independence on a scale he had never known before. Should the government crumble, and Churchill's ministerial salary go with it, he and Clementine and the family could live in the style and comfort to which they had grown accustomed—provided they were sensible.

Such was profoundly Clementine's dream and her intention—if

she had anything to do with it—and she pleaded for tranquillity and common sense.

"Now that the sharp edge of financial anxiety has been removed, if only we could get a little country home within our means, and live there within our means, it would add great happiness and peace to our lives," she wrote to her husband in September 1922.

By then, however, Churchill had a very different dream.

The Churchills had been to Chartwell Manor the year before and had turned it down. They had done so partly on the grounds of cost —Lord Vane Tempest's railway accident was still some months away. But it was also far from Clementine's dream of the "little country place within our means." It was a moldering semi-ruin that instantly appalled her. Churchill, however, had not dismissed it completely, and as summer faded he was being carried forward on a dangerously optimistic mood swing in his private life—as so often happened when he found himself apart from his wife.

Clementine, at thirty-seven, was pregnant for the sixth and final time, as something of a consolation and replacement for poor Marigold. Churchill was, as always, profoundly sentimental at the *idea* of childbirth and children. "I think a great deal of the coming kitten—it will enrich your life." But he was not one for the realities of pregnancy and parturition, and took elaborately selfish steps to ensure that neither impinged upon his pleasures or his peace of mind. The child was due in mid-September. Clementine was to spend July in Barnstaple in Devon with her sister-in-law, Lady Goonie, and then go on to Frinton just before coming back to London for the birth. Churchill, his "monstrous ego" free and unencumbered, floated happily away to be with those he most enjoyed—the powerful and very rich.

First he visited Lloyd George at his newly purchased country house at Churt in Surrey; then he spent some golden days at his favorite "hotel" on the Riviera—Maxine Elliot's ever-open villa, Château l'Horizon, on the doorstep of his beloved casino at Monte Carlo. But even he could not avoid returning for a few days to Britain for the birth. Almost immediately afterward, Churchill intended being back in France at Benny Westminster's Château Mimizan in Normandy for the wild-boar hunting, "where you can join me as soon as you are fit," he wrote generously to Clementine.

En route to London he spent a night with yet another very wealthy friend amid his very grand surroundings—the exotic Jewish politician, Lloyd George's Parliamentary Private Secretary, Sir Philip

Sassoon, who had built himself an extraordinary red-brick palace with
a moorish courtyard at Port Lympne, Sassoon's estate near New Rom-
ney, just inland from the coast of Kent.

During this visit, Churchill met Port Lympne's architect, a fashionable, neo-Georgian revivalist named Philip Tilden, who specialized
in homes for wealthy politicians and who, by a coincidence, had just
been working on Lloyd George's house at Churt.

With his £20,000 in the bank and that view from Chartwell in
his memory, Churchill's ambitions ballooned far beyond the boring
little country house Clementine wanted. The passion for grand houses
is notoriously contagious, and without his wife's restraining presence,
he was seeing more grand houses than were good for him. If Lloyd
George could have a country mansion, he could go one better. If
Sassoon could entertain the great in style, think how much better
Churchill could do it if he only had the sort of country place he
needed.

Churchill's imagination, boosted as it always could be by a surge
of confident good living, was already picturing the Port Lympne–style
dream house he could so splendidly create at Chartwell—the lakes he
could construct like those at Blenheim, a study and a generous dining
room to entertain his friends, a setting for the near-ducal luxury his
happiness required, and of course, a studio for his painting, a heated
swimming pool for exercise, a private cinema like Sassoon's in which
he could relax, a library, a garden for Clementine, and the chance for
all and sundry to enjoy those views across the Weald of Kent.

Churchill discussed much of this with Tilden but said nothing of
his plans when, next day, back in London, he was reunited with his
decidedly neglected wife, who was entering the last few days of pregnancy. She also knew nothing of his trip to Chartwell two days later,
when the architect confirmed that the house would need virtual re-
building. Nor did she know that, shortly afterward, he summoned a
Mr. Marshall from the estate agents Knight Frank and Rutley to the
Colonial Office in Whitehall, and against the awesome background of
his study, used all the Churchillian powers of rhetoric to persuade the
agent to accept an offer of £4,500 for the house. Mr. Marshall, however, knew his trade, and Churchill finally agreed to pay £5,000 for
Chartwell Manor.

"Let us beware of risking our newly come fortune on operations
which we do not understand," Clementine had warned him. But with
her baby imminent, she could be kept safely in the dark about the

mystery tour her now-elated husband organized for Randolph, Sarah, and Diana. Swearing them all to secrecy, he made them excited conspirators in his latest venture as they rambled through the dank, deserted house and overgrown shrubberies at Chartwell.

"Do you like it?" he inquired.

Later, Sarah would remember having felt "delirious" about the place. "Oh, do buy it! Do buy it!" she exclaimed.

"Well, I'm not sure," he said, not admitting that everything was settled.

By the time Clementine was gratefully delivered of yet another daughter, to be christened Mary, on September 14, the contract for Chartwell Manor was irrevocably signed. As Clementine recovered, she was apparently still unaware that her cross—and Churchill's dream— of Chartwell had begun.

According to her secretary Grace Hamblin, Clementine never entirely forgave Winston for the underhanded way in which he purchased Chartwell. For her, this left a sort of stigma on the house, and much as she did her best to cope with it, she never really liked it.

By the time she found out about the fait accompli, there was not a great deal she could do about. More than anyone she knew the power of her husband's determination, and no sooner had he signed the deeds than he was conveniently involved in another crisis, making any anger that she felt more or less irrelevant.

For some time, Churchill had been suffering chronic indigestion. Serious eater, steady drinker, and something of a hypochondriac to boot, he had often complained of the problem in the past; with the work load he was bearing—and his worries for his political future with a general election looming—it would have been surprising if his harshly treated stomach did not rebel.

Since summer, he had also been complaining of acute pains in his side; that October, three days before Lloyd George's government collapsed, his doctor diagnosed appendicitis. Churchill's appendix was removed on October 23, at the King Edward VII Hospital for Officers.

Though still recuperating from what was at that time a major operation, Churchill could not postpone his fight to save his parliamentary seat for the Scottish city of Dundee. Gamely and very bravely, everything considered, Clementine largely fought it for him.

It was a situation that showed her at her best. However intolerable he could be to live with, and whatever the strains and disappointments in their private life, in one thing she would never waver: her loyalty toward her husband and his great political career. Although as a life-long Liberal she was by no means personally convinced of the rightness of his recent warlike policies, particularly against the Turks, she went as his champion and proxy to the cold, unwelcoming election.

It was a forlorn endeavor. Dundee, like the rest of the country, had swung decisively against the Liberal Lloyd George government of which Churchill was a member, and Clementine had a tough time justifying him. But this tall, shy woman with her tweed coat and her English accent did her best, as she later told her husband, to present him to the Scottish voters in the unlikely guise of "a Cherub Peace Maker with little fluffy wings around your chubby face" at a number of profoundly hostile meetings.

Just before polling day he arrived in person and, as always, stole the show. Even in illness he was still the old accomplished actor; a wan and weakened figure in overcoat and large black hat, he was carried to the meetings in a special chair. It made a gallant picture for the press photographers—the wife freshly risen from the childbed, the husband from the sickbed—but it failed to work. When the results of the election were announced on November 23, Churchill was out by ten thousand votes to his Conservative opponent, and Lloyd George's government was out as well. For the first time since 1904, Britain had a Conservative government led by a new Prime Minister, the Canadian A. Bonar Law.

"In the twinkling of an eye," said Churchill ruefully, "I found myself without an office, without a seat, without a party and without an appendix." But the defeat at Dundee was not entirely a joke. For almost the next two years Churchill would be out of Parliament and power, and for his career it was a setback second only to the disaster of the Dardanelles.

He was in something of a mess politically, a dominating figure stranded by his failed allegiance to the Liberals. To have any hope of power his only course was to "re-rat" as he put it, back to the Conservatives where his instincts, as well as his interests, increasingly resided. Even for him this proved a difficult maneuver, as he knew he had to overcome the deep distrust and fear that he aroused among the old-guard Tories. But he did not feel dejected.

There was no evidence of "Black Dog" now, still less of failing confidence. Instead, with Clementine happily beside him, he departed for the South of France, where he rented a villa called appropriately Le

Rêve d'Or, the dream of gold. While Clementine played tennis (she was a good, enthusiastic player), he engaged a secretary and dictated the first volume of his memoirs, *The World Crisis,* in three months flat.

With its sweep of narrative, its powerful romantic rhetoric, and Churchill's personality on every page, *The World Crisis* is in a class apart from any other memoir of World War I. He made no pretense that this was calm unbiased history. The theme and center of the book was a passionate defense of his actions over the Dardanelles.

He was not overscrupulous in rearranging facts and misrepresenting his opponents—so much so that the conclusion of modern historians (in particular that of Robin Prior, the young Australian historian who has written a full-length study of *The World Crisis,* is that its value is essentially literary rather than historical. But at the time, *The World Crisis* was most effective in its primary purpose—that of rehabilitating Churchill's wartime reputation. There was another fascinating point about the book that John Maynard Keynes would shrewdly notice. Churchill's essential criticism of the conduct of the war had been the absence of what Keynes called "that supreme combination of the Warrior-King-Statesman which is apparent in the persons of the great conquerors of history."

As far as Churchill was concerned, the blunders of the war had stemmed from blunders of leadership, a constant failure to engage politics and strategy under a unified decisive command. Churchill's two greatest heroes—John, Duke of Marlborough, and Napoleon— were examples of the sort of ideal wartime leadership he had in mind, and the Churchillian concept of the warrior-king-statesman leading an undivided nation in time of war would not be left to molder in his memoirs.

Churchill seems to have enjoyed the bouts of long dictation that produced his book. He once said that he looked on any book he was writing as "a companion." It was the ideal friend who could not answer back as, large cigar in hand and brandy and soda on his desk, he walked back and forth, long into the night, regaling his attentive secretary with his own uninterrupted version of events from his extraordinary memory.

Certainly the composition and the great success on publication that autumn of *The World Crisis* did much for Churchill's private happiness. He was still out of Parliament, but he had firm plans for the future. The next volume of his memoirs was waiting to be written, and that overgrown hillside outside Westerham was claiming his attention.

Aside from the view, to Churchill, the most exciting feature of dilapidated Chartwell Manor was the very thing that most appalled the careful Clementine: its ruinous condition. He could respond to architectural splendor, but as Tilden put it, he "would not allow the sentimental appreciation of beauty to obscure practical essentials." The existing house with its high-pitched gables and long windows facing out toward the shrubbery was simply one more enemy to be demolished.

The core of the oak-beamed farmhouse could remain; oak beams appealed to him. Around them he was planning the extraordinary red-brick fortress of the house one sees today. It was a fairly massive undertaking, for the house was effectively turned around to take advantage of the view and a new four-story wing constructed. There were to be long French windows going out onto the garden, a brick terrace that he called his "palanquin," and, in the center of the house, his high-beamed study, with his bedroom conveniently leading off. Chartwell was to be a center for his work, his friends, and all the members of his family. Such was, at any rate, the plan.

Relations between Churchill and his architect were doomed to be fractious. Tilden, a fussy man, was not the sort of character to appeal to Churchill, and as he soon discovered, the new Lord of Chartwell Manor was hardly the sort of client he was used to. Most of the busy, wealthy men Tilden had worked for were grateful to entrust the details of their future home to his expertise; such was not the case with Churchill, who rarely met an expert without fairly swiftly knowing more than he did on his chosen subject.

Once Churchill was safely back from France, Tilden would be summoned at a moment's notice out to Chartwell. The great man, invariably late, would roar up in his big black Wolseley, chauffeur at the wheel. Then, in the heavy boots he had worn on the western front, Churchill would plod around his property, with Tilden trying to keep up.

As in everything he set his mind to, Churchill was deeply, often maddeningly, involved with what was going on, "laying bricks, trying experiments with baths, and theorising about matters which most men have taken for granted all their lives, but to which in some miraculous fashion, he managed to give a new turn of thought."

As a result of this, Chartwell started to emerge as a decidedly eccentric house. It was very much its owner's personal creation, for although he made a show of trying to include a reluctant Clementine in the operation, keeping her painstakingly informed of what was happening, it was not in her nature to disguise her disapproval of the whole endeavor.

The purchase of Chartwell, coinciding as it did with the birth of their final child, conclusively changed the setup of the family and altered much within the Churchills' marriage.

Had Clementine had the sort of house she wanted, the story might have turned out differently. It would have been emphatically her house as well as his, and at this crucial period in her life, the planning and creation of the sort of country home she had hoped for could have been a bond between them. Instead, the reverse was happening, and her husband's "Chartwell Dream" was emphasizing something of a rift within their lives.

Had she been moving into the sort of convenient establishment she wanted, she could have organized her life around her husband and her brand new baby. Life would have been quite undemanding, money would not have been a constant worry, and there might have been a chance for the sort of order and perfection she enjoyed in her surroundings.

Instead, the whole family was now involved in this exhausting and extravagant grand enterprise of Churchill's of which she alone so strongly disapproved, for Churchill had kept the children closely involved with all he did at Chartwell. One of his earliest activities was to build them all a tree house in the garden. A nearby house called Bosey Rigg (inevitably rechristened "Rosy Pig") was rented for the summer, and for the three children all the excitement centered inevitably around their father and his fascinating playground. Clementine tended to become the odd one out as the children joined an exuberant Churchill laying bricks, leveling the terrace, and damming the waters of the stream at the botton of the hill to make a lake.

It was just after Mary's birth and the purchase of Chartwell that the Churchills hit upon their own solution to the problems raised by Clementine's continuing depressions and the complexities of Chartwell. It was clear that she simply could not cope with Churchill *and* a brand new baby. But Clementine's spinster cousin Maryott "Moppett" Whyte was poor and practical and good, and she had trained at that academy of well-adjusted upper-class British babyhood, the Norland School of Nursing. A fully qualified Norland Nanny, Cousin Moppett was looking for a job.

In effect, she took the baby over, nursing and mothering the infant Mary with the devotion and expertise that Clementine could never manage. Maybe it was heartless, but it was eminently practical; Clementine had never been particularly maternal. As Churchill's cousin Anita Leslie said, "Clementine was more deeply tied to her husband than to her offspring, and she herself said that she did not have sufficient energy to support them all."

Instead, Cousin Moppett and the two-month-old baby moved into Bosey Rigg; Clementine was given a period of respite in which she could try to cope with life and with her husband; and Mary, most fortunate of all the Churchill children, was to enjoy what all the rest disastrously lacked: a stable, ordered childhood, more or less insulated —thanks to rocklike, unshakable Miss Whyte—from the dangerous emanations of her father's genius.

Somewhat surprisingly, considering the scale of the work and Churchill's constant interference, Chartwell was ready to move into by early 1924.

It had been a busy spring for all the family, with Churchill's political fortunes dramatically reviving. Since the Conservative defeat in 1923, there had been a minority Labour government, supported by the Liberals, in power. Although theoretically still a Liberal himself, Churchill considered the behavior of his old party in abetting socialists a national disgrace "not dissimilar from missionaries assisting cannibals." This confirmed his strengthening conviction that his future— and his only hope of power—lay on the right in politics, and he prepared himself for a fresh crusade against an enemy at home: socialism.

For Churchill, Ramsay MacDonald's Labour party was little different from "those bloodstained Bolsheviks who killed the Tsar." Worse still, they were totally "un-English [with] not the slightest idea of fair-play or sportsmanship." Accordingly, in February 1924, Churchill placed himself firmly in the role of the great opponent of the Left by standing as an independent anti-Socialist in a parliamentary by-election at Westminster.

It was the sort of knockabout political extravaganza Churchill thrived on. Undeterred by an official Conservative candidate against him, he organized such Conservative celebrities as Balfour and Birkenhead to speak on his behalf, together with a stand-up cast of jockeys, dukes, and chorus girls. On polling day, Churchill drove around the constituency with all his family in a coach and four. There was noise, immense publicity, and although he lost by a whisker, this memorable by-election returned him firmly to the map of politics.

Clementine, as always when it came to politics, had been with him throughout the ten days of the campaign. With Chartwell it was different. Here she coolly kept her distance, as if intent on still showing her disapproval of the whole enterprise. Within a few weeks of the Westminster by-election, her excited husband was ready to take charge of his splendid new domain. Clementine left him to get on with it— alone—and chose this moment to visit her aged mother in Dieppe.

After a lifetime of strained relations, it cannot have been a particularly exhilarating holiday for Clementine. The once-beautiful Lady Blanche had lost her looks and was obviously ill, after years of gambling and drink and crazy living. Even so, for Clementine, Dieppe could offer a release from the tensions of the Churchill family. "I am enormously and unbelievably tired and the strong air makes me drunk with sleep," she wrote to Churchill.

Her husband's state of mind could not have been more different as moving-in day dawned, and by the evening of April 17, 1924, tired but triumphant, he sat down in the absent Clementine's bedroom to write her a battlefield report.

He had commanded the troops in person—the three children; his bodyguard, Sergeant Thompson; a gardener; and six laborers from Westerham. Two van loads of furniture arrived from the house at Sussex Square, "the weather was delicious," and they were out, "toiling all day like blacks in dirty clothes and only bathing before dinner."

Apart from installing the furniture, they had also started turfing what he called "the plateau" and the bank beneath the house. He sounded like an extremely happy man, "drinking champagne at all meals and buckets of claret and soda in between." As he concluded in his letter, "Only one thing lack these banks of green, The Pussy Cat who is their Queen."

# nineteen

# Paradise on Earth

On November 5, Guy Fawkes Day, 1924, Churchill was summoned from his London house in Sussex Square to 10 Downing Street by the new Prime Minister, Stanley Baldwin. He came punctually for once, clad in top hat and the astrakhan-collared topcoat he had worn at Sydney Street, knowing the importance of this interview to his career.

Two days earlier, the minority Labour government had fallen to the Tories in a landslide election, and Baldwin was back at the head of a Conservative administration with an absolute majority.

After his busy two-year absence, Churchill was also back as a member for the highly convenient Conservative constituency of Epping on the suburban northeast fringe of London. He was still not officially a Conservative, having fought the election as an anti-Socialist "constitutionalist," but Baldwin had ensured that his party had not opposed him. The long march from the Liberals to the rewarding foothills of the Right was all but over.

"I am what I have always been—a Tory Radical," Churchill insisted; in fact, he was poised to return to the party where he started and where power, with all its pleasures, now resided.

Seven years Churchill's senior, Baldwin, the former iron manufacturer from Worcestershire, was his political antithesis; ruminant where

Churchill was flamboyant, soberly shrewd where Churchill tended to be brilliantly erratic, he was to give Britain fourteen years of soporific leadership. By the end of it (he was succeeded by Neville Chamberlain in 1937), Baldwin, "the quiet man at the top," would embody much that Churchill politically detested. But for the moment, Baldwin alone could offer Churchill what he wanted.

Churchill knew the strength of his position. In two weeks he would be fifty, but he possessed more experience of government than Baldwin and the rest of the Conservative leadership put together. The Westminster by-election had reconfirmed his status as a national celebrity, while the force of his anti-Socialist invective during the campaign had convinced his enemies, inside as well as outside the Conservatives, that he was still the most dangerous, and the most eloquent, single presence on the uninspiring scene of British politics.

"Unique, wayward and exciting, a man with a particular glamour of his own," Harold Macmillan called him now, and Baldwin knew how risky it would be to leave so powerful a figure outside the folds of the faithful much longer.

Churchill also knew. "I have no intention of joining the government except in some great position," he assured Clementine, and when ushered into Baldwin's presence made himself very much at ease. While the two men chatted, he produced a large cigar.

"Do you mind the smoke of a cigar?"

"No," said Baldwin, and as Churchill ignited his Havana, Baldwin pulled out the stubby pipe that was *his* trademark. Through a cloud of retaliatory pipe smoke Baldwin posed his all-important question.

"Are you willing to help us?"

"Yes. If you really want me."

There was a pause, more puffing at his pipe, then Baldwin said, "Will you be Chancellor of the Exchequer?"

This was a genuine surprise, a greater position than even Churchill had been hoping for. (In fact, Baldwin had offered it because Neville Chamberlain had just refused it.)

"Will the bloody duck swim?" was the way Churchill later said he felt like answering. Instead, recalling the formality of the occasion, he replied like the politician he was: "This fulfils my ambition. I still have my father's robes as Chancellor. I shall be proud to serve you in this splendid office."

According to varying accounts, Churchill's eyes then may or may not have filled with tears. Probably they did. He had a lachrymose tendency when moved emotionally, and this was clearly one of the most emotional moments of his whole political career.

There was the joy of power again, a great state office, the house next door to Baldwin's house in Downing Street as his official residence, and a salary of £5,000 a year. No lover pining for the return of his beloved could have felt a keener satisfaction than Churchill did at the prospect of heading the Treasury, of having responsibility for the nation's economy.

But as his reply made clear, there was more to it than this. Nearly forty years before, Lord Randolph's appointment to the chancellorship marked the pinnacle of his doomed career. Now the strange drama that tormented and inspired Churchill through his long political career seemed to have run its course.

He would speak piously of his delight at being able to vindicate Lord Randolph by his appointment to his father's former office, but it is hard to see what vindication he was offering his father's memory. It was himself he was absolving—rather late in life—from those never-forgotten moments when the sick Lord Randolph had ignored him, cast him in the role of failure, consigned him to the infantry, and issued such dire warnings for his future.

Now he had proved him wrong—and in the most effective way he could. What better answer could he give his unforgiving father than to reach that self-same "splendid office" that had once distinguished him?

Churchill had also justified his mother's faith all those years ago when she carefully preserved Lord Randolph's robes of office after his resignation, as if intent on showing even then that her son had a duty to succeed where her husband failed.

With great skill—and unfaltering determination—Churchill had somersaulted himself back to the power that meant so much to him. And as he entered the Treasury and set himself to master the intricacies of his forthcoming budget, he was already standing out, as Asquith said of him, "like some Chimborazo or Everest among the sandhills of the Baldwin Cabinet."

The Treasury was really not the place for Churchill. Finance was not his forte—either publicly or privately—any more than it had been his father's, who was equally extravagant and who once admitted that he never understood "those damned dots" in the Treasury accounts.

But in April 1925, an exuberant Churchill had the private satisfaction of achieving the one important act Lord Randolph had signally failed to accomplish during his time as Chancellor: the presentation of his budget. Top-hatted and with large cigar he drove from Downing Street holding Gladstone's original Chancellor's dispatch box to present *his* budget in the House of Commons.

The Churchill succession was continuing. As a boy of twelve, Churchill had watched his father's speeches from the gallery. Now, fifteen-year-old Randolph was sitting in the front row of the gallery with Clementine beside him.

As a sheer performance, Churchill's first budget speech must have made them very proud. This was Churchill witty, Churchill lucid, and Churchill dominating the House as no other politician could have done. Baldwin told King George V that Churchill had risen "magnificently to the occasion," showing "not only consummate ability as a parliamentarian, but also all the versatility of an actor."

But although this first budget speech was hailed as a triumph, confirming Churchill's dominant position in the government, it also managed to enshrine what he himself would come to think of as the greatest blunder of his whole career, which would dog him and the nation for the rest of his five years in office. Again like his father, Churchill had little time for the "dismal science" of economic theory, and inspired by considerations of national prestige he returned the pound sterling to the old-fashioned gold standard at prewar parity.

The result, which Churchill does not seem to have foreseen, despite loud warnings from economists like John Maynard Keynes, was a prolonged deflation of the whole economy. The high rate of the pound priced British goods out of world markets. Unemployment rose, wages fell, and hardship and widespread working-class bitterness led directly to the catastrophic general strike of 1926.

Because of this, Churchill's period as Chancellor must count as a considerable disaster—and one of the very few that he would finally accept as such. He was not given to self-recrimination, but years later, over dinner, he remarked: "everyone said that I was the worst Chancellor of the Exchequer that ever was. And now I'm inclined to agree with them. So now the world's unanimous."

A less self-confident and self-obsessed statesman would have resigned in the face of the disaster he had created. But Churchill, being Churchill, rose cheerfully above the nation's troubles and thoroughly enjoyed his tenure in office. He could dominate his gray colleagues in the Cabinet with his cleverness and wit, while his eloquence and personality made him a star performer in the House of Commons.

In the light of what happened later, it is ironic that in this period he was keen to cut spending on defense in order to lower taxation. The air force suffered badly, and only determined opposition by a group of admirals saved the navy.

The general strike brought forth his warlike zeal against the strikers. Natural journalist and propagandist that he was, he jumped at the chance Baldwin gave him to create his own official newpaper—the sensational and tendentious *British Gazette,* which he edited and masterminded for the government throughout the strike, and which enjoyed a circulation of two million by the time it finished.

Throughout his time as Chancellor, Churchill showed constant ingenuity in the fine print of his budgets, and was said to have worked out his best schemes in his bath. While lying there he must have mused upon the whole extent of government, for during these years in office, he would blithely range across the jealously protected interests and responsibilities of all the other ministers, the Prime Minister included. This secretly infuriated Baldwin, who was not as somnolent and stupid as he seemed. As his government neared its end in 1929, Baldwin swore that he would not be including Churchill in any future administration.

But Churchill had the thickest skin in politics, and was simply unaware of the antagonism he aroused by his suggestions. He loved power and he loved Parliament. He enjoyed the chance to wear his father's robes of office on ceremonial occasions. All the photographs taken of him during this period show the round and smiling face of a satisfied and happy man whose private life was working out exactly as he wanted. The key to this happy situation largely lay with Chartwell, and it is now one sees exactly why Churchill had ignored his wife's pleas for a simpler establishment. He did not want a tasteful, cozy country home, but something very different and infinitely more ambitious—a proper setting for his egocentric life-style and a house to satisfy the various demands of his career and totally demanding personality.

Both as a man and as a politician, Churchill was uncomfortably unique—and so was Chartwell. It both reflected him and suited him, offering contentment to his restless nature and the facilities he needed for his powers to function unimpeded. This would become more so with the years, finally making Chartwell, as its historian has called it, "the most important country house in Europe."

But as Clementine knew from the beginning, there was also an element of absurdity about her husband's Chartwell dream, this grandiose and inconvenient establishment that exhausted her and which she knew they could not afford to run. For as so often in his life, Churchill was using all his ingenuity and energy in an attempt to make reality conform to his imagination, and there were elements within the Chartwell fantasy that simply could not work.

Just as becoming Chancellor of the Exchequer marked the fulfillment of a dream that had haunted him since adolescence, so his Chartwell dream had its origins in Blenheim and the ducal world he had known as a boy.

Everything fitted in with this. Once he had built his two lakes at the bottom of the hill, the vista from his long French windows would match the not dissimilar view across the lakes at Blenheim—the one his father boasted of to Jennie as "the finest view in England"—and whatever the expense, Churchill demanded many of the features of a substantial country mansion: stabling for his ponies, a home farm for the animals he loved, spacious rooms where he could dine happily with men of influence and power, cottages for his retainers, pools for his pet fish, and grounds laid out with terraces and walks and gardens where the grandson of a duke could feel at ease.

Chartwell was becoming a sort of tiny principality where Churchill could truly be himself. Reverting to his Spencer-Churchill ancestry, he was like some energetically eccentric eighteenth-century Whig grandee, with everything he wanted around him. Once the lakes and terraces were finished, there was the long brick wall around the kitchen garden to be built. This kept him busy for the next three years. Then came a cottage for the gardener and an original heating system for his outside swimming pool to think about. He had his painting studio, his oak-beamed study, and his library. Boredom would never be a problem —nor should "Black Dog" return in such surroundings.

During the blazing August of 1925, Churchill went to visit Blenheim. But Blenheim had lost its magic, and Cousin Sunny was almost as miserable as ever. He should not have been, for he was now entirely free from Consuelo. Four years earlier she had fallen in love with the romantic Jacques Balsan, a French flying ace. In order to marry him, she had agreed to an amicable settlement with Sunny. (Since Sunny was now a Catholic, and the Balsan family was also Catholic, the marriage had to be dissolved by the Vatican, which it was—on the grounds that Consuelo had been coerced into marrying Sunny.)

Nothing now prevented Sunny from making the beautiful Gladys

Deacon his Duchess, which he did in Paris in the spring of 1921. "We are both awfully poor," he told reporters. "Just say I gave the bride a motor-car as a wedding present."

To start with, the new couple was happy. Sunny completed his precious terraces, and Gladys tried to bring a touch of European art and culture back to Blenheim.

Among her guests was Lytton Strachey, who coveted the place. "I wish it were mine. It is enormous, but one would not feel it too big. The grounds are beautiful too, and there is a bridge over a lake that positively gives one an erection." H. G. Wells arrived one Saturday and danced with the Duchess—"a most comic business" according to Prof. Frederick Lindemann, who was present. And she invited Marcel Proust to stay. (When the great novelist replied he was too ill, Sunny said he wouldn't mind at all if he stayed in bed.)

But none of this social life lasted. The marriage, like most things in Sunny's life, soon went sour. Gladys had three miscarriages in fairly swift succession, the last allegedly brought on when Sunny, "in an ungovernable rage," had struck her at a Brighton hotel.

Then, with a final touch of the grotesque, his Duchess's face was starting to collapse before his eyes. Years before, desperate to preserve her beauty and perfect the shape of her nose, Gladys had had paraffin wax injected beneath the skin. Now the wax was slipping inexorably toward her jaw.

By the summer of 1925, Sunny and Gladys were living separate, angry lives, which must have suited Churchill, who never liked her any more than she did him. (The Churchills had always preferred Consuelo, and had wisely kept in touch with her. They often stayed with the Balsans at their glamorous new house at Eze, or at the château they had bought in Normandy.)

As Sunny's second marriage started to collapse, all Gladys's maternal instincts turned to breeding spaniels, and she encouraged them to foul the Blenheim carpets to annoy her husband. He kept away from her, devoting all his energies to building fountains and yet more terraces to enhance the only thing he really loved—his house.

Cousin Winston, fresh from similar construction work at Chartwell, could advise him. So could the ingenious Professor Lindemann, who loved dukes and great houses, and who was going back to Chartwell after the weekend. The writer and politician Harold Nicolson made up the trio, and the three of them drove back to Chartwell, with Churchill at the wheel.

According to Nicolson, Churchill was thrilled to return to Chartwell after Blenheim. Far from envying Sunny any longer, "Winston was so delighted with his house that it was a pleasure to witness his enthusiasm," wrote Nicolson. "He considered it his paradise on earth."

It was an expensive paradise, as perpetually busy, Churchill needed servants to maintain mometum. At one point there were eighteen on the Chartwell payroll, and when Clementine became alarmed at the expense, Churchill told her, "servants exist to save one trouble, and should never be allowed to disturb one's inner peace."

It was a very ducal definition of the role of a domestic, and once again there seems something deeply nostalgic in Churchill's need to have servants perpetually on hand to do his bidding. His valet, Inches, had to call him punctually at eight each morning, bring him his breakfast in bed with all the morning papers, run and prepare his bath and dry him afterward, help him dress, and even tie his tie and lace his shoes. Churchill's demands upon this faithful man did not cease there, for he was on call seven days a week; besides his valet, Churchill required the services of at least two full-time secretaries and a research assistant, together with housemaids, footmen, gardeners, and associated building laborers, who also had to be on hand.

Churchill was immensely organized, but he would always need people around him who would act as obedient extensions of his will. It was a pattern he would steadily develop, so that by the time the war broke out in 1939, he had perfected the routines of work and relaxation that he had devised for himself at Chartwell, together with the personnel and friends required to make them function.

The friends were as important as the servants, for Churchill was a social animal whose ideas of entertaining were very similar to those of his parents: extremely good food, excellent champagne, vivid personalities, and conversation fundamentally concerned with politics.

His greatest friend, apart from Sunny Marlborough, was still Lord Birkenhead, the Lord Chancellor. But with Chartwell, a new sort of follower appears upon the scene. Churchill had always had people he relied on, who appeared dependent on him, showing all the signs of unquestioning loyalty. Eddie Marsh, litterateur and civil servant, who had been his official secretary before the war, was the first of them. He was devoted to his master, finding in Churchill an excitement and affection lacking in his highly social life; in return, Churchill frequently invited him to Chartwell, picked his highly cultivated brain, and used him as a sort of resident literary adviser.

A very different figure, who would soon adopt a similar role in matters scientific, was the rich, tennis-playing polymath from Oxford, Frederick Lindemann. Snobbish and remote, this Alsatian teetotaler hardly seemed the sort of character whose company Churchill would enjoy, but they became devoted, and "the Prof," with his famous slide rule and academic manner, became something of a fixture during long weekends at Chartwell.

So did the even more improbable self-made financier and news-paperman Brendan Bracken, who arrived at Chartwell one summer afternoon in 1924, introduced himself to Churchill, and for the re-mainder of his life was devoted to him, acting as stimulant, factotum, clown, and faithful friend.

These three men would all be of immense importance to the efficient running of Churchill's life. All unmarried, highly talented outsiders, they were lonely men who seemed to find a purpose in the strange regime Churchill was building around himself at Chartwell. They would be joined by others in the years to come, acting as cour-tiers, advisers, ministers in exile to the potentate of Chartwell.

Such were the important elements of Churchill's Chartwell Dream, but there was an impossible side to it as well. "For everyone except my uncle," Churchill's nephew Peregrine insists, "life at Chart-well was continual chaos."

As at Lullenden, Churchill's attempts at farming were doomed to failure. His herd of handsome belted Holstein cows would never pay, the pigs contracted lice, the chickens foul-pest, and the swans he had carefully imported for his lakes were killed by foxes.

More serious, as Clementine foresaw from the beginning, was the expense. Churchill had overspent wildly on the project. The building costs alone were £19,000—this on top of the original purchase price, so that around the time of his appointment as Chancellor, he had all but bankrupted himself, and would presumably have had to sell the house.

The chancellorship saved both him and Chartwell, for in addition to the ministerial salary of £5,000 a year, it meant that he and Clemen-tine could move into the Chancellor's official London residence in Downing Street and sell the house in Sussex Square, which they did for £10,750. This gave them breathing space, although the never-ending costs of Chartwell were still draining their resources as the gold standard produced similar effects on the national economy.

Churchill refused to be depressed on either score. As Chancellor, he continued to devise ingenious new taxes that did little for the nation's underlying malady, and he was equally resourceful as he began to grapple with his personal finances. Yet here he was more successful, as he turned to journalism to pay for Chartwell and ensure, as he put it, that he "would never be unable to drink a bottle of champagne and offer another to a friend."

Churchill's reliance on popular journalism as a way to pay the bills would be of great importance, for it meant that he increasingly treated politics and journalism as complementary activities. Knowing everyone, and having an opinion on absolutely everything, he was a natural journalist who could dictate an effortless two thousand words on almost any subject without so much as getting out of bed.

As a political celebrity, anything he wrote was news, and at half a crown a word he became one of the highest-paid journalists of his day. This was to be a crucial source of power as well as income, guaranteeing that his views stayed at the center of debate whatever his relations with the government. Popular journalism also developed Churchill's flair for mass communication. Like his father, this most insulated aristocrat was adept at sensing the feelings of the common people he almost never met—or really cared about.

On the other hand, knowing where his bread and butter came from, Churchill took considerable care to cultivate the leading press proprietors. Since the war, he had a close if turbulent relationship with the Canadian proprietor of the *Express*, Max Lord Beaverbrook. ("Some take drugs. I take Max," Churchill muttered, explaining the uneasy friendship.) In some respects, the two men were similar: Both were bullies when the need arose, both were nonconformists in the inside world of politics, and both were obsessed with the pursuit and exercise of power. As high-powered egomaniacs, they tended to distrust each other as much as they generally enjoyed each other's company. For Churchill, simpler and more lucrative journalistic friendships were those he carefully pursued with Lord Rothermere of the *Daily Mail*, and the future Lord Camrose of the *Daily Telegraph*.

All were entertained at Chartwell, where dinners graced by barons of the press had a habit of resulting in ideas for articles. Churchill never missed a deadline, and in a good year managed through his journalistic efforts to augment his income by up to £20,000.

For Churchill, though, money earned was money to be spent. Wage bills and maintenance costs at Chartwell were heavy, while in food and drink, both for himself and for his many guests, Churchill was more prepared than ever to "be satisfied with the very best."

At Chartwell, the result was a life of intermittent luxury, unpaid tradesmen's bills, and periodic family discussions on economy. Within months of moving in, Churchill was already contemplating renting the whole house for £80 a week. This came to nothing, but he could always manage to dismiss his money problems as airily as his spend-thrift Marlborough ancestors. Clementine, so different from him in this as in so many other things, never managed to forget them.

# twenty

# The Happy Family

Clementine's troubles obviously ran deeper than mere pique at the way her husband had ignored her wishes when he purchased Chartwell. At this period, she frequently appears a remote, unhappy figure both as wife and mother—nonmaternal and chronically exhausted—despite the fact that she was totally involved with her husband and was the object of his deep affection.

Although she had all the domestic help she needed, she remained unnaturally aloof from her baby daughter, Mary, and was quite prepared to leave the admirable Miss Whyte as virtual foster mother in her place. She had also stayed aloof from Churchill's plans to build his dream house.

As for the three elder children, Clementine's unconcern could verge on positive neglect. In her relations with the teenage Randolph there was no hint of the rapport that wayward Jennie had maintained with the youthful Winston. Thirteen-year-old Randolph had gone off to Eton in September 1924, but it was Churchill, not Clementine, who took charge of everything to do with this event.

Far from putting any pressure on him to go to his old school, Harrow, Churchill simply left the choice of school to his son, who chose Eton. Churchill remained the most tolerant and concerned of fathers where Randolph was concerned. (He even asked Birkenhead's

son Freddie to make sure that Randolph did not suffer corporal punishment at Eton. This did not prevent him from being swiftly beaten,
as he was "bloody awful all round"—"the kind of comprehensive verdict," as his friend Michael Foot would put it, "which others who had
dealings with him were always searching for.")

Clementine's relations with Sarah and Diana were little better
than those she had with Randolph. Sarah described Clementine as
"formidable," and both girls seemed in awe of her and kept their
distance. Diana, despite her garrulous exterior, appears to have suffered badly from the way her elegant mother seemed to ignore her. In
many ways she was more like Clementine than any of the other children, introverted and emotional, which only exacerbated the antagonism between them.

Contact with Sarah was easier, thanks to her sunnier nature, but
they were far from close. On the edge of adolescence, Sarah was just
recovering from the illnesses that dogged her childhood, and was
changing from a redheaded waif into something of a beauty. She had
her father's toughness and a streak of independence that enabled her
to cope better than Diana with their distant, temperamental mother.
Yet if Clementine did have a favorite it was Sarah—when she saw her.

Hardly surprisingly, the children were closer to their father than
to their mother and saw him as their hero and greatest source of
excitement and amusement. As far as the children were concerned,
Clementine, as her daughter Mary put it, was "not a fun maker."

When Lady Blanche died suddenly in March 1925, Churchill was
preparing for his next financial budget, and Clementine was forced to
go to the funeral in Dieppe alone. To make up for his absence, he
wrote her one of his cheering letters, saying "what a true mother, and
grand woman" Lady Blanche had been. He was, he added, "proud to
think her blood flows in the veins of her children."

It is hard to think that Clementine agreed, having spent so much
of her life steeling herself against those very weaknesses that had
helped destroy her mother—weaknesses Churchill, at a distance,
found appealing.

More than ever, Clementine appeared the total opposite of Lady
Blanche: painfully self-controlled; a rigid perfectionist in food, dress,
and surroundings; and always vulnerable against those elements of
chaos and excess that were an integral part of life with Winston.

Cruelly tested as it often was, her self-control would sometimes
crumble. Then she would suddenly erupt in such a rage that, as Jock

Colville, Churchill's future secretary, noted, "the tallest of trees would bend. . . . When her nerves were stretched," he added, "she sometimes turned on Winston with vitriol in her voice and the flashing eyes of fury."

On one of these occasions she made family history by hurling a dish of spinach at him (it missed). But her anger was not confined to members of the family, and she would verbally lash out unexpectedly at any of her husband's friends. The effect was awesome. "You know, Clemmie dropped upon him like a jaguar out of a tree," said Churchill, describing one of Clementine's surprising reactions.

According to his niece Clarissa, Jack's daughter, Churchill's reactions to these outbursts was to "take no notice, keep his head down and carry on with whatever he was doing." But tantrums invariably left Clementine weakened and depressed, for just as she could not control them, so they were contrary to the sense of order and decorum she believed in. She was at heart a kindly puritan, and away from all the strain and tension of her family the kindness showed.

Bertrand Russell's cousin Conrad met her on holiday in Wales during the summer of 1924, when Churchill was once more hunting the Duke of Westminster's wild boar in Normandy. Clementine did not particularly enjoy pursuing boar or dining with the Duke. Instead, accompanied by ten-year-old Sarah, she spent a few days in a small hotel beside the sea.

Russell, an intimate of the Asquiths and reputedly the lover of Diana Cooper, was the only other guest, and his summing up of Clementine to his sister Flora catches something of her loneliness, as well as the condescension with which the Asquith circle still regarded her.

"Mrs. C.," he wrote, "is highly friendly and quite incredibly chatty. I'm afraid I find her a bore and she has a common sort (but an amicable sort) of mind."

The Churchills' marriage had been stranger than most people realized. For Clementine, but not for Winston, its strains and tensions seemed to be increasing with the years. She was approaching forty. Middle age was looming. Had "Time stolen love away," as she had once predicted, leaving only friendship in its place?

For Clementine it seems as if it had. Hers was a passionate, romantic nature, and from the moment she first fell in love with Churchill, she had given him all the love she possessed. Yet it must have been a struggle to maintain the great illusion of romantic love with such a total egotist.

For him there was no problem. He had a simple view of marriage: One "married and lived happily ever after." This way of thinking left him free to dedicate himself to countless other things demanding his attention, like politics and journalism.

It had been different in the early years of their marriage, when Clementine sacrificed her friendships and her role as mother to his great career. Now her dream of their shared political adventure was threatened with her husband's return to the Conservatives.

He had beliefs that, as a Liberal, she could not endorse and plutocratic friends she did not like. He also now had the precocious Randolph to confide in, and a bond was forming between them from which she was more or less excluded. She resented this, as she resented much within her family, but there was little to be done about it— except put up with it or angrily explode when things became too much for her.

Selfish and blithely sentimental, "Mr. Pug" continued much as usual. He needed the assurance of her love and her affection, but she must have known that he would never cease to lead the self-absorbing, driven life he wanted. She had her own allotted part in it, rather like Mrs. Everest in Churchill's childhood, for there were still times when he depended on her. "I feel far safer from worry and depression when you are with me and I can confide in your sweet soul," he wrote when trying to convince her of the joys and pleasures of their new home. "You are a rock and I depend on you and rest on you."

He had a gift for words, and what he wrote was true and touching. But to be a husband's "rock" in moments of his depression was neither "stimulating or warming" for a romantic nature. Being needed could be terribly exhausting.

Part of the trouble was the difference in their makeup, which the years had made worse. She was low on energy, tired easily, and worried endlessly, bottling up her worries in herself. He, on the other hand, seemed to have the secret of perpetual energy and had grown more dominant with fresh political success.

The chancellorship had rejuvenated him. So had Chartwell. Here, in this workaholic's playground, "the darling old schoolboy," as Diana Cooper used to call him, had all his hobbies to absorb him: ever more bricks to lay, more lakes to dam, more pictures to be painted. He had his growing court of carefully selected cronies—audience, supporters, intellectual stimulants—and the affection of his fascinated children. He had his fame and his intense activity. Even his life-long driving force—ambition—was requited for the moment, leaving him content with his world around him. It was up to Clementine to accept it, too.

He was firm with her over Chartwell, telling her that he intended it to be their home for many years to come. As Blenheim descended to the Marlboroughs, so Chartwell would be handed on to Randolph and his heirs. That was his intention. "If you set yourself against Chartwell or lose heart or bite your bread and butter or your pig," he told her, "then it only means further instability, recasting of plans and further worry and expense."

So Clementine had accepted, as she had to, giving up all hope of the kind of country home that would have meant a simpler and more ordinary way of life for her and all the children. She took charge of the furnishing and decoration of the house, aiming to make it "charming," as he knew she would.

She had ladylike good taste and could make the house comfortable, with patterned curtains, rush matting on the floors, and color washes on the walls, against which she dutifully hung her husband's pictures. (Despite her efforts, however, several visitors remarked on the strongly masculine character of the house. Churchill's aura was too strong to be subdued. The setup reminded Harold Macmillan of a government department, and for A. L. Rowse, Chartwell possessed "something of a collegiate atmosphere, a hive of masculine activity, mitigated by intervals of family life.")

She did manage to impose a sense of order on the running of the house, which, given Churchill's habits, was no mean achievement. (Having recovered from his appendectomy, he ate as much as ever and weighed around one hundred and eighty pounds by 1926.) His nephew Johnny Spencer-Churchill described Clementine's role at Chartwell as "that of aide-de-camp extraordinary and Super Quartermaster to the greatest Captain General"—and he still waxes eloquent over the Chartwell meals he remembers.

"The hospitality which my uncle and aunt offered at table was quite out of this world. In addition to special dishes to suit the idiosyncracies of the most demanding guests—Professor Lindemann for instance was a vegetarian, which meant arranging two separate menus—there was always champagne, superb port and brandy for lunch, followed by more port, brandy and cigars when the ladies have withdrawn."

But where Clementine's nature really showed itself was in the

Chartwell gardens, where she could plant her roses and wisteria and colorful herbaceous borders—calming activity for a highly strung and frequently neglected politician's wife.

She could always be relied on to cope with tribal gatherings of the family, particularly at Christmastime, which, according to the childhood recollections of daughter Mary, was "always a glorious feast" at prewar Chartwell.

With Sunny married to the disapproving Gladys, the shared Blenheim Christmases of the past were over, and Chartwell became the place where the Churchills gathered for their celebrations. Only close family were invited.

First on the list would always be faithful brother Jack with Lady Goonie, their two boys, Johnny and Peregrine, and their precocious baby daughter, Clarissa, born in 1920. There would also usually be Clementine's scatty sister, Nellie Romilly, with her two "little lambs," the tiny monsters Esmond and Giles. The only regular outsider at these Chartwell Christmases was the indispensable Lindemann, who, Eddie Marsh apart, was the only member of Churchill's inner circle whom Clementine could tolerate for any length of time. (He had the additional advantage of being both single and extremely rich, thus providing splendid Christmas presents. Churchill particularly enjoyed opening his Christmas presents, and "the Prof" could be relied upon to provide the very best cigars and a case of the great man's favorite champagne.

Good champagne inevitably played an important role in any Churchill Christmas, and Jack would propose his regular—and somewhat typical—Christmas toast: "Good champagne for our real friends —and real pain for our ex-friends!"

As a nonbeliever, wedded as ever to his unshakable routine, Churchill would stay in bed on Christmas morning while Clementine shepherded the children to the morning service at the Westerham parish church. For the evening she would organize a Christmas tree with real candles, followed by the inevitable amateur dramatics in which all the children had to perform. But Churchill was, as always, at the center of these family affairs, and after Christmas dinner he would tell his stories of the past, recite his favorite poems, and sing the music hall songs that he remembered, word-perfect, from his youth.

During school holidays, Chartwell became a center for all the family, together with their friends and their relations. Churchill felt happy with members of his precious family around him.

The result could be exciting—especially for Randolph, who was soon being treated by his father as honorary crown prince of Chartwell. Remembering his own unhappy time at public school, and the anguish he had suffered from Lord Randolph's anger at his own unsatisfactory school reports, Churchill was determined not to make the same mistake with his son.

Randolph's reports from Eton were not dissimilar from his father's when he was at Harrow: "lack of concentration," "failure to understand the importance of his work." But at Chartwell and in close proximity to his father, a different Randolph seemed to be emerging. Like all the Churchills, he was extraordinarily precocious, already fascinated by politics and politicians, well-informed, and with a fluency in argument that delighted Churchill. Totally without shyness, he could expound his views with a youthful eloquence his father envied.

Randolph, of course, was picking all this up from his father and his circle, just as Churchill himself had done from his father and the politicians around him in his youth. Churchill never saw the dangers for his golden boy. Clementine did, but had little influence over Randolph, who was soon permitted to stay up for dinner with the great man's "great contemporaries." Birkenhead, Lloyd George, Beaverbrook, and Bracken—the great political talkers of the day—would come, and after dinner, when Clementine and the ladies had retired, Randolph would be permitted to stay on to join the conversation.

His father, "like a potentate" at the head of the table, would sometimes raise his large cigar to interrupt the flow of talk, and thus ensure that teen-age Randolph had his say, which Randolph, being Randolph and a Churchill, duly did.

There were never-to-be-forgotten moments during these early years at Chartwell: T. E. Lawrence upstaging everyone (even Churchill) at dinner by appearing in the robes of a desert prince; Lindemann bringing out his slide rule to calculate how much champagne Churchill had drunk in his lifetime (it was enough to fill a railway carriage); and Charlie Chaplin, at dinner, rousing Churchill's wrath by arguing for socialism and then making everybody laugh by slipping into his routine as "Charlot."

It seemed idyllic, and many visitors to Churchill's paradise remembered those golden days, basking in the sunlight of the great man's pleasure. For some, however, it proved a dangerous paradise. Beneath the surface, life at Chartwell was not as carefree or as simple as it seemed. Nephew Johnny can remember driving back to London with Clementine after what had seemed a lively if tempestuous weekend and hearing her wearily exclaim, "I just can't stand it any longer."

Johnny was a carefree soul, and something of a joker in the family. Unambitious and totally uninterested in politics (he would become a painter), he enjoyed Chartwell and his uncle Winston (he learned to imitate him—a useful party trick), but otherwise remained quite unaffected by his contact with the great.

Not so Peregrine, who reacted differently to Uncle Winston and the atmosphere at Chartwell. He was a serious child: When asked by his uncle what he wished to be when he grew up, Peregrine replied, "a retired banker." (In fact, he became an engineer.) Churchill's world was not the place for retiring natures. "I found Chartwell living hell," Peregrine said, "disordered, crazy, inconvenient. My uncle was a great man but a frightful bully. So was my cousin Randolph. All those overpowering egos! All that endless talk on politics! After a certain age, I felt the need to get away from all those Churchills. Otherwise they would have squashed me."

His cousin Diana, now in her late teens, seems to have felt the same, and would soon gratefully depart for the peace and freedom of a family in Paris, to learn French, before returning for the London season. Her parents and the society around them seem to have overwhelmed her, and the memories people have of her at Chartwell are of a self-conscious little figure, worried about her plumpness, and easily upset. She would sometimes walk off alone, singing tunelessly.

Patterns formed in childhood persist, and for much of her life Diana would be a lonely figure in a world in which she tried to find her private happiness.

Another member of the family on whom Churchill and the Chartwell dream would have a permanent effect was his favorite daughter, Sarah. Unlike Diana, Sarah enjoyed the rough and tumble of discussion; she had charm and wit, and although something of a tomboy was at ease with her father's famous friends. At heart, though, she said she was "a father's girl," dominated by him, half in love with him, and fascinated by the fame and power around him. Throughout her life Sarah would be ruled by an unceasing quest for fame—and for other father figures.

But among those who were affected by the spell of Chartwell, the most unusual fate of all concerns the elegant fifteen-year-old blonde with whom Randolph became enamored during his final year at Eton. This was his cousin Diana Mitford, daughter of the second Lord Redesdale (who, in turn, was a cousin once removed of Lady Blanche) and sister of an extraordinary group of female siblings, of whom Nancy Mitford would become the famous novelist. The others were Jessica, the left-wing journalist; Unity, the devotee and friend of Adolf Hitler; and Deborah, the Duchess of Devonshire. Diana's brother Tom was at school with Randolph, hence the introduction, and Randolph invited her to Chartwell during the summer holidays of 1928. She had seen nothing like Chartwell in her somewhat sheltered life and immediately fell in love with it.

Coming from a spartan section of the aristocracy, Diana found in Chartwell something of a revelation of the earthly pleasures life could offer: a bathroom of her own, delicious food, and château-bottled claret. She was dazzled by clever Professor Lindemann and fascinated by Eddie Marsh's stories of the famous writers and artists he knew. She was also captivated by Clementine's kindness and good taste. "I used to think that if I could grow up to be as beautiful and elegant as Cousin Clementine and Lady Goonie, I should be totally happy."

But her favorite experience was to listen to Cousin Winston, who struck her instantly as "the cleverest, and most original and most forceful person I had ever met. To sit next to Winston was my *ideal*, even if he paid little attention to me. He would hold forth, always about politics, and I drank in his words."

He was the first live politician she had ever met, and he clearly overwhelmed her.

"If Winston doesn't talk to you, just pull his sleeve and start him off," said Cousin Clementine. Diana never dared to, but her hero worship of great men and power figures seems to have started at the Chartwell dinner table. It would dominate her life—and involve her with Cousin Winston in a very different guise during the years ahead.

# twenty-one

# Wilderness

As the 1920s drew to a close, life for Churchill changed abruptly. In the general election in the spring of 1929, Churchill's electoral campaign was markedly different from that of his chief, the unaggressive Prime Minister, Stanley Baldwin. Baldwin wooed the country with the slogan "Safety First," but Churchill campaigned full-bloodedly against a Labour government, claiming that Labour, "the Party of Plunder," having once condoned the "constitutional outrage" of a general strike, was utterly unfit to govern.

The votes were cast on May 30, and that night Churchill was at 10 Downing Street, whisky glass in hand, to watch the results arrive by ticker tape. He had kept his seat at Woodford, but it was soon clear that there had been a Labour landslide. As the news grew worse, his face grew redder. Shoulders hunched, fury in his face, he looked like a bull about to charge the ticker-tape machine. One of the civil servants feared that if any more Labour gains came in "he would smash the whole apparatus." Apparently his language was unprintable.

As Churchill feared, the result of the election was Ramsay MacDonald's disastrous second Labour government. For Churchill it was also a disaster. Not merely was he out of office, but his actions as Chancellor were strongly held against him; he had made himself appear an out-of-date reactionary, a figure from the past, who was himself unfit for power. Two years later, when Baldwin joined the faltering Ramsay MacDonald in a National government, Churchill would not be included. The night of May 30, 1929, at Downing Street was thus the beginning of a grim decade in which Churchill, although still in Parliament, would stay unheeded and alone in what he called the wilderness of politics.

To take his mind off political defeat and the prospect of a Labour government, in the summer of 1929, Churchill visited North America as guest of the Canadian Pacific Railway. The invitation included as many of his family as he wished to bring, but since Clementine was not enthusiastic—and needed another therapeutic break from her husband and her family—he decided it would be a good occasion to take Randolph, brother Jack, and nephew Johnny.

The party sailed first-class from Southampton on August 3. "What fun it is to get away from England and feel one has no responsibility for her exceedingly tiresome and embarrassing affairs," he wrote to Beaverbrook.

The fun continued throughout the whirlwind tour across Canada and the United States. In contrast with his reputation back in England, in North America he found himself a great celebrity. The CPR had placed a luxurious rail car—he described it as "a land yacht"—at the Churchill's disposal, and his speeches, emphasizing "the mighty ties, incomprehensible to Europeans" linking the Empire and the English-speaking nations, were received with acclamation. This was the first time he had really witnessed the full potential of the land of his maternal ancestors, and he was mightily impressed.

He was also thrilled with Randolph, who seemed to be justifying the hopes he had for him. "I think he has made a good impression on everybody," he wrote to Clementine. "He is taking a most intelligent interest in everything, and is a remarkable critic and appreciator of the speeches I make and the people we meet."

Randolph was also being treated as a celebrity, and with members of the press was showing signs of the bumptiousness that would bring such trouble in the future. (A woman reporter from the *Toronto Star* reported him saying that he thought women "simply did not fit in" with British parliamentary life, and caused a lamentable "lack of dignity.")

But for Churchill, gaffes like this were of little importance compared with the growing admiration he was feeling for his son. Johnny Churchill still recalls an evening when the party had camped by the shores of Lake Louise. Twilight was falling; touched by the beauty of the scene, Churchill fondly said, "Randolph, recite us something." Randolph responded with a passage that he must have memorized at Eton from Lecky's *History of European Morals*. It was on prostitution.

Randolph, an actor like his father, made the most of this long dramatic passage. By the end of it, Churchill was in tears of admiration.

These feelings seem to have survived their journey on to Hollywood, where Churchill was feted as something of a star himself. They were also lavishly entertained by William Randolph Hearst at his legendary castle at San Simeon. Always thoroughly at home with press proprietors, Churchill made something of a hit with the megalomaniac publisher, and agreed to write for him. Randolph took advantage of San Simeon to lose his virginity with some rapidly forgotten female guest of Hearst's.

If Churchill was aware of Randolph's escapades, he tactfully ignored them, and so, up to this point, the trip had been a great success. For Churchill, however, this visit to America had a gloomy ending. Throughout the summer he had played the stock market, confident that he would come back with a fortune. Gambler that he was, he was speculating on tips from one of his millionaire admirers, the financier Bernard Baruch, and ignoring the advice of brother Jack to play it safe. After Hollywood, he also enjoyed himself visiting battlefields of the Civil War (on which he was something of an expert), but he reached New York in time to witness a ruined speculator throwing himself from a window on Wall Street.

The Crash of 1929 had come, and Churchill's savings and his rash investments vanished overnight. He returned to England not in triumph but on the edge of ruin. He was to keep himself afloat only by prodigious efforts as an author and journalist, living over the next few years, "from mouth to hand."

Following the loss of office, the loss of so much money was a bitter blow. The optimistic years were over, and Churchill was badly hit by a midlife crisis. Harold Nicolson was shocked when he saw him in January 1930—"very changed from when I last saw him. A white round face like a blister. Incredibly aged. . . . His spirits have also declined and he sighs that he has lost his old fighting power." It was now that he first began to think seriously of Randolph as his ultimate political successor. He seems to have genuinely believed that he was all but finished as a politician, and that his mortal end was not far off. It almost was.

At the end of 1931, Churchill returned to New York to begin a lecture tour across America (thirty-nine lectures for a guaranteed fee of £10,000). Crossing Fifth Avenue, he forgot which way the traffic came and was hit by a taxi. Injured on the head and thighs and badly shocked, he still managed to identify himself in no uncertain terms.

"I am Winston Churchill, a British statesman," he told doctors before passing out entirely. Later, he manfully completed his lecture tour, but the accident had proved an unexpected blow to his powerful physique. Six weeks later, he still described himself as "very weak and debilitated," and miserably informed his wife that this was the third blow he had suffered in the last two years: first, the loss of all his money in the Crash; second, the loss of his position in the Conservative party, "and now this terrible physical injury." On the verge of yet another deep depression, he told Clementine that he did not think he could "ever recover completely from the three blows."

Trouble dogged Churchill after his return to England and he talked gloomily of being "finished." Politics, family, and finance were creating deep anxiety, and his old resilience had not returned. The parallel between his own life and his father's was not lost on him. Both had been Colonial Secretary and Chancellor. Both had known great political success, dominating Parliament with their oratory. Then, in both cases, there had come the fall from power, political rejection, and the misery of money troubles. Churchill had already lived longer than Lord Randolph, but time was closing in on him. His premonitions of an early death returned, and he wrote to Clementine that he was "entering what will certainly be the last decade of my existence." The time had come to make his dispositions for the future.

That sacred lamp, the all-important gift of power, could soon be safely handed on to brilliant Randolph, just as he had grasped it thirty years before from the lifeless fingers of his father. It was very much with this in mind that Churchill planned the famous birthday dinner at Claridges to celebrate his son's majority in June of 1932. It was then that Lord Rothermere called Randolph "Britain's Young Man of Destiny," and briefly it seemed as if twenty-one-year-old Randolph was truly set to follow in his father's somewhat massive footsteps.

During the early summer of 1932, Randolph was behaving rather like Churchill at the start of *his* career. He used many of his father's early ploys: the pull of family connections, reliance on the Churchill name, the supercharged ambition, and the flair for picking an occasion that would bring him instantly to public notice. By skillful use of all these tactics, Randolph made a striking debut as a journalist.

True to his father's early adage, inherited from Jennie, about "doing business only at the top," Randolph cashed in on Lord Rothermere's support to get himself appointed special correspondent of the *Sunday Graphic*. His assignment was to report the German general elections in which the rising Nazi party was bidding to control the country's tottering Weimar Republic. It was not lost on young Randolph that both Lord Randolph and his father had written for the old *Daily Graphic* in their time, and he set off for Berlin, at the tender age of twenty-one, with the aura—and expense account—of a top reporter.

To the annoyance and surprise of such less privileged journalists as Bruce Lockhart, the "rollickingly bumptious" Randolph did not blunder as expected. He was a natural journalist. He was also very energetic. Thanks to his father, he was well primed on the resurgent militarism that was to dominate the voting, and he somehow used the Churchill name to get himself aboard the aircraft Hitler himself was using for the campaign trail.

The result was something of a journalistic scoop, with Randolph actually observing the future Führer at close quarters and sending back some of the earliest accounts of Nazi rallies. (He described them as a mixture of an American football game, a boy scout jamboree, and a revivalist meeting "conducted with the discipline of the Brigade of Guards.")

As Randolph predicted, the Nazis failed to win the elections outright, but emerged as the largest single party in the Reichstag.

It is hard to know how taken Randolph was by Hitler's personality. He was certainly impressed by him, and sent him a telegram of congratulation after the elections. But he also understood the danger that he represented, and his final report from Germany contains one of the most prophetic of the early warnings on the Nazis. It also gives some indication of Randolph's political awareness and potential as a journalist.

> Nothing can long delay their arrival in power. Hitler will not betray them. But let us make no mistake about it. The success of the Nazi party sooner or later means war. Nearly all of Hitler's principal lieutenants fought in the last war. Most of them have two or three medals on their breasts. They burn for revenge. They are determined once more to have an army. I am sure that once they have achieved it, they will not hesitate to use it.

Later, Randolph would modestly deny that he had "thought all this out for himself" at twenty-one. As he said, "I had sat for many years at the feet of my father." But the words were his, and thanks to his recent close involvement with the Nazi leadership, he was closer to understanding Hitler's true significance than his father. For at this point in his political career, Churchill was more concerned with a very different enemy, that "seditious Middle Temple lawyer, now posing as a fakir of a type well known in the East," Mahatma Gandhi, the leader of the Indian Civil Disobedience Campaign.

Gandhi had been released from prison by the British authorities in Delhi early in 1931. Labour Prime Minister Ramsay MacDonald was promising India dominion status, and Baldwin, for the Conservative opposition, had given his support. Sensing a sellout of the great King Emperor's Indian possessions, Churchill had been enraged. Gandhi, he told the Secretary for India, Edwin Montagu, "ought to be laid, bound hand and foot, at the gates of Delhi and then trampled on by an enormous elephant with the new viceroy seated on his back."

He was particularly furious with Baldwin for supporting Indian independence, and from this moment, Churchill found himself fatally at odds with his party leaders over India. He was to fight a long and self-destructive battle with them that was to continue after the Conservatives returned to power in 1932. It was a battle that absorbed his energies, confirmed his public status as a double-dyed reactionary, and brought relations with his party leader, Baldwin, virtually to the breaking point. It also deflected his attention for a time from his future enemy, Adolf Hitler.

Anxious to alert his father to the aims and the hypnotic influence of the rising German leader, Randolph stayed on in Germany for some weeks after the elections, knowing that his parents and his sister Sarah were due to arrive for a brief stay at the Hotel Continental at Munich in Bavaria. Churchill, who had started his research for his biography of John, first Duke of Marlborough, was passing through Munich on the way to the battlefield of Blenheim. It was Randolph who decided that, since Hitler would be in Munich at the same time as his father, the two of them should meet.

Randolph had no problem persuading his father to agree to this —Churchill was keen to see this leading Nazi for himself. But persuading Hitler was another matter, and Randolph relied on the good offices of the notorious Putzi Hanfstaengel, the Harvard-educated socialite and close friend of Hitler's, whom he had got to know during the election. Hanfstaengel conveyed the invitation to Herr Hitler to join the Churchill family for dinner at the Hotel Continental.

Hitler's reaction was distinctly odd, almost as if he had some premonition of the role this visitor would play in his terrible career. He seemed of two minds whether to accept. "But what on earth would I talk to him about? And in any case, he is a rabid Francophile," he told his friend. After some arguing, it was Hanfstaengel who went off to dinner with the Churchills in Hitler's place.

Churchill seems to have had an uncomfortable time of it when the conversation turned to the subject of the Jews. "Tell your boss that anti-Semitism may be a good starter, but it's a bad sticker," Churchill told him.

As Hanfstaengel left the restaurant, he was surprised to see Hitler himself talking to someone in the hall outside, and suggested he should meet the Churchills over coffee. Hanfstaengel gives a firm impression that Hitler was not there by chance, but he again refused, this time giving as his excuse that he had not shaved. Then Hitler hurried from the hotel, and Hanfstaengel saw no more of him until Churchill and his party left for Blenheim.

This was the nearest Churchill ever came to meeting Hitler. Later, when he knew more about him, he would adamantly refuse to have anything to do with him, although a meeting could have been arranged. Because of this, Randolph later said how glad he was that Hitler never did accept the invitation. But he had no reason to reproach himself for having so nearly staged, at twenty-one, one of the more intriguing might-have-beens of modern history.

Where Randolph did have reason for reproach was over what happened next. For having achieved a more successful and precocious debut than even his father managed, Randolph cheerfully proceeded to throw almost everything away.

Diana Cooper's fortieth birthday fell at the end of August, and to mark the anniversary, the extremely rich and socially obsessed Conservative M. P. Henry "Chips" Channon had organized a party for a group of fashionable rich friends on the Venetian island of Murano. It was to be the social event of the Venice summer season. Somehow Randolph got himself invited—and Channon never quite got over what ensued.

Randolph arrived from Munich in the best of spirits—in both senses. He knew everybody at the party: Lady Cunard and her lover the conductor Sir Thomas Beecham, Robert Boothby, Lady Castlerosse, Brendan Bracken, the art collector Edward James, and his own adored Diana Mitford, who was now married to the gentle Bryan Guinness, but actually in love with Sir Oswald Mosley, who was also present. Encouraged by so many friendly faces, Randolph drank copiously;

becoming even happier, he intervened in a lovers' argument between the heiress Doris Duke and the baronet Sir Richard Sykes. Randolph's intervention was misunderstood by Sykes, who hit him. Randolph hit him back, Doris Duke joined in, and Diana Cooper's birthday party rapidly became one of the smartest public brawls of the early thirties.

What Randolph started rapidly became a roughhouse with broken bottles, broken jaws, and considerable outrage from the general public—all of which was faithfully reported in the next day's British press.

While this was going on, Churchill, accompanied by Sarah and Clementine and his "military adviser," the military historian Colonel R. P. Pakenham-Walsh, was stumping the far-off battlefield of Blenheim, but even there he managed to maintain his lifelong habit of reading the London morning papers, the more sensational of which graphically recounted Randolph's participation in the fight. More followed, for blithely unperturbed by the scandal he was causing, Randolph had embarked on three weeks of riotous relaxation with half the gossip columnists of Europe in pursuit.

Randolph rarely failed an audience. Drunk, pugnacious, lecherous, and loud he was the scourge of Venice. At the Lido, he called Brendan Bracken "brother" (a tactless reference to the unfounded but persistent rumor that Bracken was Churchill's bastard son). When the myopic Bracken chased him down the beach, Randolph grabbed his glasses and threw them into the water, leaving the half-blind financier "standing in the shallow sea and roaring like a bull."

There were more rows, more drunken evenings, and, more seriously, an affair with the shapely Doris Lady Castlerosse. This was improvident on two accounts. In the first place, the lady's husband, Viscount Castlerosse, a former friend of Randolph's, was a famous gossip columnist himself and a notoriously aggressive enemy. (When Castlerosse rang him up and said, "I hear you're living with my wife," Randolph replied, "Yes I am, and it's more than you have the courtesy to do.") And in the second place, there was another rumor which many happened to believe was true, that several years before, in the Ritz Hotel in Paris, Doris had gone to bed with Winston Churchill.

As with so many rumors of this sort, it is unprovable either way (as is the veracity of the great man's reputed compliment to Lady Castlerosse after the event, "Doris, you could make a corpse come!"). Under such circumstances, it was thoughtless of Randolph to appear to follow where his father trod. Churchill cannot have been amused to read in another London paper that Lady Castlerosse's pet name for his son was "Fuzzy-Wuzzy," and that the two of them were constantly together.

Back in London, Randolph continued to enjoy his princely role, taking a well-paid staff job with the *Sunday Dispatch,* then renting an enormous chauffeur-driven limousine and the best suite in the Mayfair Hotel. He was installed there when his father returned to England after a spell in a sanatorium, having contracted paratyphoid on the continent. Illness had not improved his temper, and that autumn relations between father and son turned sour.

Gone were the inflated hopes with which Churchill had planned Randolph's birthday dinner barely six months earlier; gone, too, was the idea of "handing on the torch" to an inspired successor. Venice had changed all that, and angry rows were starting.

"What are you doing?" Churchill asked him. "When I was your age I was reading five hours a day. You spend most of your time in nightclubs, staving off a vast army of debtors by eking out a precarious living as a hack journalist."

After another bitter row, Randolph stormed from the room (as he would do on numerous occasions in the years ahead), and Churchill turned as he often did to Frederick Lindemann for solace and advice.

"Lindemann," he said, "you are a professor of biology and experimental philosophy. Tell me, am I, as a parent, responsible for all the biological and chemical reactions of my son?"

Lindemann's reply is not recorded, but it was an interesting question. With the exception of his womanizing, all of Randolph's essential weaknesses and vices were shared with his father, having been inherited or learned from him or from his friends and cronies. Indeed, their similarities were rather startling.

A love of gambling, an undiscriminating passion for rich friends and luxury, snobbery and bumptiousness—all were shared by both Churchills. So was gluttony, bullying, an almost pathological self-assurance, and a rarified upper-class sense of distance from the humdrum facts of life. Apart from a touch of snobbery, none of these weaknesses afflicted Clementine. Randolph and his father were both utter egomaniacs who, unlike Clementine, were uncomfortably accustomed to getting their own way over anything they wanted. Both were heavy drinkers with a taste for racy company and very large cigars. Both were nocturnal, obsessed with politics, and great talkers with capacious memories. They were so similar, in fact, that Randolph increasingly appeared a carbon copy—or caricature—of his father.

So what was going wrong with Randolph? Why should those very characteristics, each of which appeared an inherent part of Winston's nature, be proving so disastrous in his son?

Churchill had been driven since his early twenties by the constant need to beat the dreaded possibility of failure. Randolph, however, possessed the inner confidence of effortless success. Churchill had learned to keep "Black Dog" at bay through rigorous self-discipline and concentrated work. Talented Randolph, with a happier temperament, saw the need for neither.

For Randolph, the most disastrous difference between them was a very simple one. Churchill had lost his disapproving father figure in unforgettable circumstances at the age of twenty. Randolph, with his dominating father always present, would never have a hope of taking on his father's role.

Churchill might talk of "handing on the torch," but as long as there was breath in his body, Churchill was not relinquishing his hopes of power to anyone—not even his son.

At the end of 1932, there was excitement from an unexpected quarter. At twenty-three, Diana had found some belated limelight for herself at last: She was the chosen bride of a rich and handsome husband.

She needed it, for life had not been easy for this elfin redhead. Clementine, preoccupied as ever with her husband and her own uncertain health, had less patience than ever with her eldest daughter. Sarah described a painful visit to the dressmaker together with Diana and the "beautiful and elegant" Clementine. During the visit Clementine airily remarked that "Sarah is so easy to dress," not realizing that this was a "near mortal blow to Diana."

Diana's obsession with her mother's disapproval never left her, and would always tend to sap her confidence. Her cousin Anita Leslie remembered finding her in tears at the end of her dreaded first London season, "because Mummy is horrid to me and I haven't been a success."

Anita asked her why she thought she had been a failure.

"Because I have sandy-colored eyelashes," she sobbed.

With Sarah soon due to begin her own London season, Diana felt it a disgrace not to have found herself a husband, and her insecurities increased at the thought of people comparing her unfavorably with her prettier, more popular younger sister.

Her father was kinder to Diana than her mother, but he had neither time nor temperament to understand her problems. Nor could he hide the fact that Sarah was his favorite. The result was predictable: Diana was anxious to escape from home and find her own success, pursuing fame and glamour where they seemed most instantly available—on the stage.

Sarah would do the same a few years later, but unlike her, Diana had little acting talent. Her greatest asset was her name, but even this was not the help it might have been. On joining the Royal Academy of Dramatic Art, she found a talented student there already named Diana Churchill (who would, in fact, enjoy a long and successful theatrical career).

Churchill had taken Diana with him on his disaster-filled lecture tour of the United States, and as a favor to him Warner Bros. offered Diana a screen test. Lord Beaverbrook's *Express* ran an article about Diana with a headline asking the question "Mr. Churchill's daughter a film star?"

"No," came the answer from the tests. Back in England, a disconsolate Diana spent time addressing envelopes in Churchill's constituency office, then took a summer holiday at Chartwell.

Diana would later tell her daughter Celia that it was then that she finally decided to get married "to escape from all the endless talk around the Chartwell dinner table." With autumn came news of her engagement—to thirty-two-year-old John Milner Bailey, son of South African mine owner Sir Abe Bailey.

She was reported to have known him "for several years," and Churchill was said to be delighted. Diana clearly needed to get married, and Abe Bailey, who was something of a character, was an old ally and admirer of Winston Churchill. He was also very rich. Diana seemed to have found herself an ideal husband, and on December 12, at St. Margaret's Westminster, Diana and John were married.

The *Telegraph* reported large crowds of embattled women breaking through police cordons when the bride arrived. The scenes were a reminder of the excitement Churchill's name could still inspire. This must have pleased him, coming as it did at this low point in his political fortune and personal morale. He had been determined that his daughter's wedding would be something of a demonstration of family solidarity and his own political importance.

It was a very grand occasion, with the aristocracy and leading politicians on parade. The present list was headed by the King and Queen (who sent a blue enamel dressing table set). The bride "in shimmering ivory-colored silk" wore pearls and orange blossoms; Churchill gave her away. Cousin Sunny lent his London house at Carlton Terrace for the reception.

There, in a ballroom lit by quantities of candles in the enormous

Marlborough chandelier, several hundred guests toasted Diana with extremely good champagne. All agreed that she had never looked prettier, and her husband was described as "bearing himself manfully" through the considerable ordeal of a full-scale society wedding. Afterward he took Diana off for a peaceful bridal night at the Ritz Hotel and then on to a honeymoon in Venice.

Diana, however, did not know her husband as well as she pretended. In her anxiety to escape from Chartwell and marry someone her parents would approve of, she had accepted his proposal in haste. She did not know, for instance, that he had recently been in love with a young novelist named Barbara Cartland, who had found him "sweet and perfectly charming" but who had also rapidly discovered that he drank so much that he frequently became "utterly impossible."

This was a lesson Diana would be learning for herself on her honeymoon, and after her return to London the lesson would continue.

Lending his cousin Winston his splendid London residence for Diana's wedding was not Sunny's only favor during this fallow period in Churchill's life. For years the two of them had taken it for granted that one day Churchill would commence the great work they had frequently discussed: the monumental life of their greatest ancestor, John, first Duke of Marlborough.

Churchill had always been convinced that their ancestral hero had been unjustly treated by historians, in particular by Lord Macaulay. With his exaggerated feelings for his family, and his habit of identifying with his heroes, Churchill had taken particular offense at Macaulay's accusations of the great Duke's avarice, disloyalty, and greed, seeing them as slurs upon his family and ultimately himself.

As early as 1924 there had been talk about the book that he would write to reinstate his hero's reputation. But with his history of World War I unfinished, and his five-year stint as Chancellor to come, it was a project that had had to be postponed. Then, in 1929, with Churchill out of office, Sunny offered practical assistance for Cousin Winston to begin the book.

A large proportion of the great Duke's papers were at Blenheim, and Sunny had jealously preserved them. (He seems to have taken particular pleasure in denying access to them to the greatest historian of the day, G. M. Trevelyan, who was working on his massive history of Queen Anne: Sunny was not one to overlook the fact that Trevelyan was the great-nephew of Macaulay.)

Thus Sunny had been able to offer Winston what amounted to an authorized exclusive for his book, and the writing of the first Duke's life began as something of a sacred trust, which did nothing to prevent its author from demanding—and receiving—a record advance of £10,000 from his publisher, having promised to complete a full, two-volume life in two years flat.

This would be the one rare occasion when Churchill failed to meet a deadline. Politics and crises in his private life diverted him and his subject matter steadily expanded, so that by the time he finished, his life of Marlborough had taken up four large volumes and nine years of its author's life. Since it rapidly developed wider implications both for Churchill and for those around him than an ordinary biography, it is important to understand the nature of this long, involved, and most unusual book.

Even his way of writing was entirely his own, and as with much that Churchill undertook, the life of Marlborough was seen and planned like a military campaign. "He is happiest with a battle on his hands," H. G. Wells had said of him, and from the start Churchill had an aggressive purpose to inspire him: the championing of his hero, and the destruction of his enemy, Macaulay.

The work was organized accordingly, and he enlisted the support of expert allies for his task. Along with his universal adviser, Lindemann, and his military expert, Colonel Pakenham-Walsh, Churchill also relied upon naval historian and professor Keith Feiling, the leading historian of late-seventeenth-century politics at Oxford. Through Feiling he was also able to enlist the aid of a promising young Oxford graduate student, Maurice Ashley, for the donkey-work of the research.

Ashley, who was middle class, left wing, and serious, has described the extraordinary charm Churchill could always summon up for those he liked or needed, and which rapidly reduced him, like so many others in their time, to the status of devoted slave.

He also described his employer's working habits: how, after an admirable dinner in the Chartwell dining room, they would retire to Churchill's oak-beamed study at around 11:00 P.M., where a secretary would be waiting for dictation and the day's real work would start.

He liked particularly to try out ideas or arguments to see if he could make them work. At about two he would express well-feigned surprise at the time and his secretary would be sent home in a hired car. An hour or so later he would reluctantly allow me to go to bed. Then he himself retired to do some serious reading, going to sleep around four. Next morning he would be reading his newspapers and his correspondence in bed about eight.

Like Napoleon he was able to manage on four hours' sleep. He rarely seemed to be in a hurry.

As a scholar, Ashley was particularly surprised by the fact that Churchill started to dictate the beginning of his book before any of the detailed reading or research had begun. What Ashley did not know was that the Duke had been Churchill's hero for so long that he already knew in detail the case he would be making for him. Churchill would rarely bother with the documents himself, lacking the time and training to decipher them; that was Ashley's task.

"Give me the facts, Ashley," he would mutter, "and I will twist them the way I want to suit my argument."

It was very much the way he worked in politics, and he employed his other experts in a similar fashion, using the facts they provided to create the essential scenery around the character and exploits of the Duke, which he would then recount. The result is a most unusual work of the imagination, and less a conventional biography than the work of a great romantic actor creating and interpreting a favorite role. The Duke who emerges from these pages bears unmistakable resemblance to Winston Churchill.

There were more than sufficient similarities between them now for Churchill to feel totally at home in Marlborough's world and Marlborough's character. They shared the same blood and the same heroic name. Marlborough was fifty-two when fate selected him to be what Churchill called "the Saviour of Europe" with his great campaigns against the French. Like Churchill, he had been opposed by insular and petty politicians, like him he gloried in warlike enterprises upon the broadest stage, and like him was indomitably ambitious in his search for honor.

Churchill's life of Marlborough is romantic history in the grandest manner. Dull Queen Anne becomes "a great Queen championed by a great Constable"; Marlborough's wife, the tetchy Duchess Sarah, emerges as a noble heroine. Marlborough himself, his meannesses and double-dealing barely noticed or flamboyantly overlooked, becomes the noblest of warriors, selflessly defending both his country's honor and the integrity of Europe against the King of France.

This was the story Churchill carefully created with his experts, then related in the small hours of the night to his patient secretaries.

At the beginning of his own political career, Churchill had constructed his own political scenario by telling the story of his father's life. Yet there was something even more prophetic in the way he now described the role of this more distant ancestor, a "warrior-king-statesman" who "was for six years, not only Commander in Chief of the Allies, but, although a subject, virtually master of England."

Work on the life of Marlborough strengthened Churchill's links with Blenheim, and soon after starting on the book, he took Ashley there to meet the Duke and show him around the archives.

The contrast between the two devoted cousins had grown with the years. Even in adversity, Winston remained outgoing, confident, and full of zest for life, but Sunny had become ingrown and bitter with his troubles. Most of whatever charm he once possessed had gone. Ashley disliked him instantly, and described him later as "an inspissated little man"—the Oxford dictionary defines "inspissate" as "condensed, dried up," as in the phrase "inspissate gloom," which seems to have summed him up.

Sunny was clearly suffering from the obsessive malady that afflicts inheritors of great possessions: chronic anxiety to preserve his house and wealth against the constant threat of those around him. The great cause of his life had been to save and enhance what still remained of the first Duke's patrimony, but whereas Winston was romantically inspired by Marlborough's great example, Sunny had been driven to the edge of desperation by his task.

All he could see now was the threat the outside world presented to his mausoleum of a house and the feudal way of life that still survived within it. He was convinced that almost everyone was a potential thief. When Ashley gained access to the archives, the Duke insisted that a servant watch him as he worked to ensure that nothing disappeared. (Apparently, Churchill's friend Hilaire Belloc, unlike Trevelyan, had been let into the archives some years earlier, and Sunny was convinced that he had stolen *something*.)

More obsessive still was Sunny's hatred of the lower orders. Sharing his cousin Winston's pathological dislike of socialists and Communists, he envisioned armies of embattled workers as part of some socialist plot drawn up beyond the gates of Blenheim waiting for the moment to invade it. He became apoplectic when he spotted some unauthorized old woman from the village gathering firewood in his park, and during Ashley's first visit, when Churchill mentioned the current unemployment figures, Sunny said he hoped the figures would reach two million as rapidly as possible. (Afterward, Churchill assured Ashley that Sunny had, of course, been joking.)

As he grew older, Sunny had reverted uncannily to Marlborough type, increasingly resembling those misanthropic late-eighteenth-century hermit Dukes of Marlborough. But although he had come to hate the modern world as a threat to everything he stood for, his greatest enemy was now his wife, Gladys. Blenheim was the perfect setting for their mutual loathing and bizarre hostilities. Slightly mad, her beauty ravaged and her life in ruins, Duchess Gladys had turned to breeding spaniels to satisfy her maternal instincts. She also used them to persecute her husband, encouraging them to foul the carpets. It was war by spaniel.

Anita Leslie offers a frontline account of the progress of hostilities. She was at Blenheim with her cousin Randolph in the early thirties. Randolph knew the form already, for as they were waiting for the Duchess to make her appearance before dinner, he whispered to Anita, "Watch Sunny, he hates her guts. Great sport!"

Shortly afterward, with what Anita calls "the claw-clutter of many little dogs," Gladys made her stately entrance into the great salon surrounded by a "moving carpet" of King Charles spaniels. She was "extraordinary to look at—absolutely hideous and yet exotic, with golden hair swept back in a bun and strange blue eyes staring out of the ruin of the stretched face. She advanced in her dirty old clothes, shook hands and waved us gracefully to chairs."

During dinner, the conversation turned to the subject of marriage, and in her loudest voice the Duchess firmly advised Anita not to marry in a hurry. Then, as if Sunny were not present, she continued, "I didn't marry until I'd been to bed with every prime minister in Europe—and most of the kings."

Everybody laughed, except the Duke, who attempted to remain impassive as his grimy Duchess continued to torment him. But that night in the splendor of the famous Blenheim dining room, Anita thought its owner bore a marked resemblance to a rat caught in a trap.

# twenty-two

# Psychic Dynamite

"My dear Maxine!" Churchill exclaimed, descending from the limousine that had brought him and a mountain of luggage from the station. He smiled at his old friend the vast Miss Elliot, the rich and famous American ex-actress who, despite considerable losses on the stock market, was still maintaining open house at the Château de l'Horizon near Cannes.

It was early August 1933. Parliament was safely in recess, and for a few weeks peace reigned in the increasingly bitter battle Churchill was still waging against change in India despite the hostility of Stanley Baldwin and isolation from his party.

As he began his holiday in this most luxurious of villas, with its scented gardens and its view across the bay, he could also briefly forget the threat of German rearmament, which was concerning him as well. He had brought his paints and the final proofs of the first volume of his life of Marlborough to keep him occupied.

With no ministerial income for the last four years, and having long since spent the Marlborough advance, he was again short of money. But staying with Miss Elliot cost those fortunate enough to be invited very little. Several of his family would soon be joining him, and as a personal sacrifice to their current economy campaign, he had boldly decided not to bring his valet, a hazardous experiment. Rather to his surprise, it seemed to work.

"You have no idea how easy it is to travel without a servant," he told his hostess. "I came away from London alone and it was quite simple."

"Winston, how brave of you," she replied.

Miss Elliot was a lion hunter and a considerable snob. "Always remember dear," she told her niece, "that a Lord is that much better than anybody else"—and that year her house was full of gilded lions, including the Duke of Sutherland, Viscount Ratendone, Lady Castlerosse, and other representatives of the international smart set. Less gilded, but more decorative, was a promising young actor named Peter Willes, whom Miss Elliot had recently befriended.

Willes was just nineteen, and it is interesting that this member of the younger generation who had grown up since the war had little real idea who Churchill was. It is also interesting that, unlike serious young Maurice Ashley, he instantly disliked him. Willes found Churchill "bullying and overbearing" when they met.

"At meals he just banged on and on, regardless of anybody else's interests or desire to talk; and if you weren't deeply involved in politics—and I wasn't—he was really a most dreadful bore. All he seemed to do was smoke cigars, eat, drink, and talk far more than anybody else, and never give a damn what anybody thought about him."

While this was an uncomfortable experience for Willes, it was not the end of contact with the Churchills. Randolph arrived, and Willes found him even more objectionable than he found Winston—particularly when he threw his considerable weight about and attempted—unsuccessfully—to bully Miss Elliot into giving him Willes's bedroom. Then Clementine arrived with Sarah, and Willes was captivated—particularly by Clementine.

"She was enchanting, but you could see at once that she was unhappy in that world of the super-rich which her husband obviously adored and felt at home in."

Clementine hated the French Riviera all her life. "God, it's a ghastly place!" she once remarked, conceding, as an afterthought, "I expect it's all right if you're a flower-shop owner or a waiter." Being neither, Clementine had to suffer the additional discomfort at the Château de l'Horizon of feeling at a personal disadvantage in the fast and glossy company, for, as Willes soon discovered, "the Churchills simply hadn't a bean." Churchill, of course, never let this trouble him in the least, "but Clementine worried dreadfully, and used to feel that the others were laughing at her behind her back because of her clothes, which weren't particularly chic by the standards of the South of France."

A further source of irritation must have been the presence there of Lady Castlerosse, but Clementine had never been particularly concerned with idle gossip, and with his mother present, Randolph was briefly on his best behavior. The trouble came this time from his sister Sarah.

Willes described her at this period as "a Bolshie deb"—not on account of her political beliefs (she had none) but from her undisguised dislike of the pampered "smarts" and the snobbish lives she saw them leading. This attitude, which Sarah seems to have picked up from Clementine, would stay with her for life. But that summer at the Château de l'Horizon its chief manifestation was a deep antipathy toward hospitable, title-worshiping Miss Elliot. Sarah thought her vulgar, old, and ugly, and took so little pains to hide her feelings that her father noticed and reproved her.

"My dear," he muttered when she tried to justify herself, "I feel that you are still too young to appreciate the rich and mellow vintage."

His words made little difference. Few things did when Sarah made up her mind, and she and Clementine departed earlier than expected.

Randolph stayed on, having none of his sister's scruples against the undeserving rich. Like his father, he was always ready "to be satisfied with the best," and perfectly prepared to eat their food and drink their excellent champagne. He had just been back to Oxford, and had made a valiant showing in debate at the Union Society to reverse the now notorious motion that "This House is not prepared to fight for King and Country." He had lost, but Churchill felt that he had acted "bravely and courageously," so good relations were restored with his father, and he could happily enjoy the company of Lady Castlerosse or sample the delights of Monte Carlo.

Churchill, apparently oblivious of both, spent much of his day painting in the hot Riviera sun. After dinner, he labored into the small hours on the page proofs of his favorite ancestor.

The first volume of *Marlborough, His Life and Times* appeared in the autumn of 1933 to long and generally enthusiastic reviews. Granted the author's fame and carefully promoted friendships with so many press proprietors, this was not entirely surprising. Despite his exclusion from the Blenheim archives and the attacks upon his ancestor

Lord Macaulay, G. M. Trevelyan generously hailed it as "a major work upon a major figure of the period." Arnold Bennett in the *Express* said that it was "destined to become one of the great biographies in English literature."

Interestingly, one of the very few dissenting voices came from the great expert on the eighteenth century Sir Lewis Namier, who thought that Churchill's obsession with attacking Macaulay was excessive, and who objected to a key ingredient in the author's literary method—his habit of putting himself in Marlborough's place and then describing what he would have thought or done himself. The result, said Namier, was "too much supposition"—and, he might have added, too much Winston Churchill mixed up with the life and achievements of his ancestor.

Not that this diminished the success or readability of the book, which sold 7,500 copies within a month of publication. But the book was not the money-maker Churchill had hoped for. It had not earned out the large advance his publishers had paid him, yet he was saddled with a mammoth project that would take him years to finish.

Churchill had sent presentation copies to his friends—and several of his enemies—in politics. All were, of course, polite in their replies. The Prince of Wales, who was never known to read a book, wrote that he had been unable to put it down, and Stanley Baldwin said how much he envied Winston his "unrivalled style and command of English."

Baldwin was Prime Minister again, but his admiration for his former Chancellor's literary style did not include rewarding him with the only gift he really wanted: a position in his government.

There was no chance of this with Churchill still angrily adding to his enemies by continuing to fight against reform in India. He would not change his attitude to Gandhi and found it "nauseating" to think of this overeducated Indian "striding half-naked up the steps of the Viceregal palace . . . to parley on equal terms with the representative of the King Emperor."

Since Baldwin was irrevocably set on granting India a measure of self-government, Churchill's fate was sealed. Still, he continued his resolute battle against reform right up to 1935, when even he admitted he was beaten. By then he had, of course, totally destroyed all hopes of Baldwin giving him a post in government. As Lord Salisbury said when asked if he would ever have Lord Randolph Churchill back, "When you have just got rid of one boil on your neck, why get yourself another?"

Thus, 1934 began a dismal period for Churchill. He was out of office, short of money, and increasingly regarded as a played-out figure from the past. That spring he also had a grim reminder of his own mortality. His "oldest dearest friend," his cousin Sunny, was seriously ill.

Gladys and the spaniels had briefly driven him from Blenheim, but she was finally persuaded to depart. Sunny returned and soon Gladys and Sunny both began collecting evidence for their divorce. He set detectives on Gladys, hoping to prove that she was mad and taking drugs. She set detectives on him, hoping to prove that he was habitually committing adultery. Hers was the easier task.

By the beginning of 1934, Gladys and her lawyers had a cast-iron case against the Duke, with evidence of Sunny's various affairs, ranging from weekends with Edith Sitwell's sister-in-law, the actress Bunny Doble, to intercourse with call girls in the backs of taxis. Everything was set for the crowning scandal of poor Sunny's life—a bitter society divorce, with Gladys almost guaranteed to win heavy damages. Then, in the spring of 1934, Sunny discovered he had cancer and only weeks to live.

For those family members who knew of the impending divorce, the illness must have seemed a blessing. Sunny's death was now the only way of warding off a further scandal for the Marlboroughs, but Winston was distraught. When his friend Birkenhead had died in 1930, he had told Clementine, "I feel so lonely." With Sunny gone, he would be lonelier than ever.

Sunny, as expected, died with dignity, spiritually consoled by his confessor Father Martindale, shunning morphine to the last, and holding a bedside party for his closest friends—including Winston—the day before he died. A Catholic funeral at Farm Street Church, Mayfair, followed, with the family, Protestant to a man, attending.

As expected, neither Consuelo nor Gladys came. Consuelo was happily at Eze with husband Jacques, and Gladys, her plans for a highly profitable divorce frustrated, was facing a straitened future as an aging Duchess. Dreading being seen—except by her dogs—she had embarked upon the life of a penurious recluse, which ended forty-three years later in the public ward of an old people's home in Northampton, where Gladys, still a Duchess, died in 1977 at age ninety-six.

After the Mayfair funeral, Sunny was interred at Blenheim. Following the burial, Churchill intoned the formula traditionally used at the death of kings: "Le Duc es mort. Vive le Duc!" he shouted. It was Churchillian, but a touch excessive as a way of welcoming Sunny's successor, the obtuse and elongated Bert, formerly Lord Blandford and suddenly tenth Duke of Marlborough.

With his meanness and general boorishness, the Duke has his place in the social history of the thirties as *noblesse disoblige* incarnate. He also stands as an example of the Spencer-Churchills at their worst: philistine, bullying, and with that extraordinary armadillo skin that could protect them from an everyday awareness of their actions.

In his day, his neighbors vied in collecting "Bert Marlborough stories," most of which convey the stunning rudeness of the Duke, generally to those beneath him. There was, for instance, the occasion when an American female guest at Blenheim innocently lit up a cigarette between courses.

"Why are you doing that," barked His Grace.

"Because I enjoy it," came the not entirely nonsensical reply.

"Madam," Bert replied, "I enjoy fucking, but I don't do it at the dinner table."

In 1920, he had married Lord Cadogan's daughter Mary. A large lady with a pronounced military bearing, she was descended from a Cadogan who had fought with Marlborough at Blenheim, and in World War II, when she commanded the women's army forces, she was once mistaken for a male general.

Despite her mannish looks, Duchess Mary gave her husband five children, including the requisite son and heir, Lord Blandford. (Known confusingly as Sunny, he was born in 1926.) Duchess Mary did her best to make Blenheim a happy home for all the children, but with Bert she had her problems. As with his parents, the marriage had been effectively an arranged one—and was no more satisfactory than theirs had been. Bert bullied his well-meaning Duchess, was openly unfaithful to her, and had nothing of his father's feeling for the palace.

Churchill liked Mary and treated Bert with the respect due the Duke of Marlborough. But when Cousin Sunny died the Blenheim he had known died as well. Churchill was sixty that November, and it must have seemed as if the best of life was over.

If only he had been in government, he might still have been happy. Power was the element in which he flourished. In government he could have acted, but out of government he brooded. "Black Dog" began to trouble him again, and the more he thought about the future, the more he envisioned an appalling fate before humanity.

Since 1932, German rearmament had troubled him acutely, for with resurgent German militarism, he could foresee a repetition of the steps that had brought on World War I. The first time this had happened, he had been at the Admiralty with power to create a modern navy. Now he was all too conscious of his impotence—and the unwillingness of Western governments, especially his own, to halt what he believed to be the march to war. The result for Churchill was a grim, depressive's vision of the future.

As a former Minister of Munitions, no one knew better the awful power of modern mass-destruction, and he foresaw another war as a cataclysm for humanity, with massive civilian casualties, horrendous destruction from the air, and the probable collapse not only of Britain and the Empire but of Western civilization. Such was the nightmare that afflicted Churchill in moments of acute depression in his "wilderness" at Chartwell.

In previous spells of prolonged depression, Churchill had always found relief through action and aggression, and it is not fanciful to see his furious attacks upon proponents of Indian self-government as a form of self-imposed therapy. Certainly there was little logic in his battles over India—or in the grotesque bogeyman he created from the hated Gandhi. Nor could his India campaign bring a solution to his troubles, still less alleviate the nightmares that obsessed him.

Luckily, he still possessed a surer method of escape: the life and times of the great warrior-statesman with whom he consorted every night as he labored on the biography. More than ever, he was obsessed with Marlborough. "I am sick and tired of politics; my heart is in the 18th century," he told his publisher; and one can feel his envy of the Duke in the dedication he penned in the luxuriously bound first volume of the biography that he had sent King George V: "This is the story of how a wise Princess and Queen gave her trust and friendship to an invincible commander, and thereby raised the power and fame of England to a height never before known and never since lost . . . and is submitted in loyal duty to a sovereign, under whom our country has come through perils even more grievous with no less honour."

Had Churchill but possessed the power and position of a modern Marlborough, he was confident that he, too, could conduct his country through its latest "perils." Lacking such power, Churchill was forced to adopt a very different role from that of his ancestor.

Among the countless articles he wrote around this time were a number of profiles of the great men of history who intrigued him. Most were modern statesmen, but among them stood one very different figure: the prophet Moses. Here, like Marlborough, was a warrior-king-statesman who, late in life, became the savior of his nation, leading Judeah to greatness in its hour of need. But the emphasis in Churchill's article was not on Moses's victories. Rather, Churchill concentrated on his afflictions as a prophet.

"Every prophet," Churchill wrote with feeling, "has to come from civilisation, but every prophet has to go to the wilderness. He must have a strong impression of a complex society and all that it has to give, and then he must serve periods of isolation and meditation. This is the process by which psychic dynamite is made."

For the prophet Churchill, it was uphill work to warn the nation of the nightmare that obsessed him. His party was against him—as was his reputation—as he began to preach the dangers of a resurgent Germany, the need for toughness in his nation's foreign policy, and his desperate message of rearmament. This was the "psychic dynamite" that he was brewing, but the prophet's role did not sit easily on Churchill's shoulders.

On the surface, life in the Chartwell "wilderness" could still appear as happy and as enviable as ever. One of the prewar Chartwell secretaries, Grace Hamblin, recalls the deceptively easygoing atmosphere; "the front door was rarely locked, even at night, and in the holidays the house was usually full of animals and children." When feeling particularly relaxed, Churchill would sometimes amble out toward the gates, spot a passerby, and ask him in to see the fish and chat about the world in general.

But as he wrote, "when a politician dwells upon the fact he is rid of public cares and finds serene contentment in private life, it may usually be concluded that he is extremely unhappy." When the holidays were over, Churchill could exhibit very different moods at Chartwell. There were times, Miss Hamblin remembered, when "a black cloud seemed to hover round him, and it was best to keep your distance." In moods like this, he could spend an entire meal sunk in heavy silence.

When visiting Chartwell, his nephew Johnny often found that "lunch was devoted to unrelieved gloom about the international situation. My uncle was convinced that war was inevitable . . . and the depressing conversation used to make William Nicholson [the painter] quite sick. More than once he repeated to me: 'Johnny, I'm going to leave the table on an excuse. I cannot stand it any more.'"

To make his gloomy situation worse, Churchill found little consolation in the closest members of his family. There was the worry over

Diana's marriage, which had finally collapsed. After an unsuccessful spell in an alcoholics' clinic, her husband had agreed to a divorce, with the hearing scheduled for January 1935.

Randolph had become an even greater source of worry, and Churchill finally admitted to his wife that he could no longer control him. Randolph had started losing heavily at gambling, and during 1934, Churchill felt obliged to find £1,500 to pay his gaming debts.

Even his beloved Sarah seemed more the "Bolshie debutante" than ever. She had come out with her cousin Unity Mitford (recently expelled from several girls' schools in succession), and this maverick Mitford had a disturbing influence upon Sarah, who described how she and Unity used to go to debutante dances, "but spent much of the time together in the ladies loo, gossiping and playing cards."

This was emphatically not what Churchill and Clementine had desired for their daughter, but there was little they could do about it, especially with Clementine herself withdrawing more than ever from the family.

Clementine and Winston owed an increasing debt of gratitude to rocklike Moppett Whyte, who continued to perform the practical maternal duties of the family Clementine continued to reject. Thanks to Miss Whyte, Mary was developing quite differently from the older children, a sunny, uncomplicated, well-behaved small girl who loved her pony, learned her lessons, and adored her parents—when she saw them. Thanks also to Miss Whyte, Clementine could spend increasing periods at Morpeth Mansions, the Churchills' London flat, seeing a few close women friends and keeping clear of her demanding and disruptive family for days on end. They exhausted her more than ever now, and family tensions, like Churchill's moods, could so easily spark off another of her nervous crises.

It became established that Clementine would come to Chartwell mainly on weekends, and she and Churchill spent longer periods apart. With her nervous problems aggravated by menopause, and Churchill overworked and burdened with the worries of the world, she needed to ease the pressures Chartwell represented. He did not object. As long as he knew that he could count upon his Kat, he could fill every moment of his day—and a large proportion of the night. Absence from her only seemed to make his sentimental heart grow fonder.

## twenty-three

# Distant Friends

In a number of respects, Winston Churchill and Adolf Hitler were uncomfortably alike. Both were ruthless men, obsessed with military power and a driving sense of private destiny. Both were self-educated, self-absorbed, intensely nationalistic, and powerfully aggressive in the face of opposition. Both, too, were strongly egocentric characters, overwhelming orators, natural actors, and mesmeric talkers more than capable of dominating those who fell beneath their spell.

In contrast with the ranting demagogue of the public speeches, Hitler in private was reportedly something of a mimic who could amuse his guests and arouse undoubted loyalty from those around him by force of personality. Both he and Churchill were obsessive workers who enjoyed luxurious surroundings, finding their relaxation in painting, speculative monologue, and nocturnal screenings of their favorite films in their private cinemas. There was even an uncanny similarity in the way the two men sketched out strongly autobiographical fantasies of their intended paths to power: Churchill in *Savrola*, Hitler in *Mein Kampf*.

Churchill might well have acted as Hitler did had he been a German politician in a similar chaotic situation. Although utterly opposed to fascism in Britain, Churchill was not against dictatorship per se. In 1926 after a visit to Italy, he told Benito Mussolini, "If I had been an Italian I am sure that I would have been wholeheartedly with you from start to finish in your triumphant struggle against the bestial appetites and passions of Leninism"; and in 1933 he was describing him as "the Roman genius" and "the greatest lawgiver among living men." In 1935, in an article he wrote on Hitler, he expressed admiration for "the courage, the perseverance, and the vital force which enabled him to challenge, defy, conciliate, or overcome all the authorities or resistances which barred his path" in what Churchill called Hitler's "long wearing battle for the German heart."

What troubled Churchill when he wrote these words was not the nature of the power that Hitler wielded, nor at this stage did he publicly object to Hitler's anti-Semitism. Both were still matters for the German people.

What concerned Churchill were the Führer's military ambitions, whether, as he put it in his article, Hitler intended to "let loose upon the world another war in which civilisation will irretrievably succumb," or chose instead to restore "the honour and peace of mind of the great Germanic nation" through the ways of peace.

In his role of prophet, Churchill feared the former. Frustrated by his lack of power and periodically depressed, it was natural for him to have been profoundly pessimistic for the future and to have taken the gloomiest of views of a resurgent Germany.

But this alone fails to explain Churchill's uncanny insight into Hitler's motives and the danger he presented in the years ahead. Churchill was not noted as a judge of character. On the contrary, he was easily impressed by bogus or flamboyant personalities, and often blundered in his personal assessment of those around him.

But about Hitler, he was unerringly perceptive. Without sharing Hitler's capacity for evil, Churchill had enough in common with him to appreciate the nature of his power and the scale of his ambitions. Almost alone among major Western politicians, Churchill seemed to understand that, if unchecked, Hitler would lead this new aggressive Germany to war.

He also must have realized the way his own career was rapidly becoming linked with Hitler's. War, or the threat of war, was almost certainly the only issue likely to bring him back to a place in government.

Even before his anger over Gandhi and India had subsided, Churchill's private information service was reporting what was happening in Nazi Germany. This secret information came from various sympathetic sources, including highly placed officials in the Foreign Office, such as the young Ralph Wigram and Col. Desmond Morton, head of the government's industrial information service. The mysterious colonel—an unmarried, former Guards officer, and spy—lived in a cottage close to Chartwell and provided his distinguished neighbor with much of his inside knowledge of Germany's industrial potential and growing power in the air.

But there were other links between Chartwell and Berlin, as relations between certain members of the Churchill family and the higher reaches of the Nazi establishment, Hitler included, suddenly became extremely close.

In 1932, Sarah's cousin and reluctant fellow debutante, Unity Mitford, decided that the London social scene was not for her and made a passionate conversion to Sir Oswald Mosley's recently founded British Union of Fascists. This led her, the following year, to attend the Nazi rally at Nuremburg as a dedicated British fascist, and her fate was sealed.

There was a family precedent for Unity's infatuation with all things German. Her grandfather Lord Redesdale (Lady Blanche's brother-in-law and lover) was a great admirer of Wagner and the racial theories of the anti-Semitic Stewart Houston Chamberlain, whose collected works he edited.

Unity, who was barely literate and slightly mad, was not influenced by Lord Redesdale's theories as much as she was by the whole exciting counterculture offered by the Nazis. A large, blond, overgrown schoolgirl, she managed to combine deep hatred for the Jews with a late-adolescent crush on Adolf Hitler. What particularly distinguished Unity was the deep, dewy-eyed devotion she felt for the Nazis; it was a fanaticism most English maidens traditionally lavish on their ponies or their labradors. When, at the end of 1933, she rented a small flat in Munich to be near "the darling Führer," the most hardened Nazis were impressed, for none had seen anything quite like this hoydenish relation of Winston Churchill, with her gushing dedication to the cause.

She set her heart on meeting Hitler, and sat for days on end in his favorite restaurant, the Osteria Bavaria, at around the time the vegetarian dictator usually arrived for lunch. With long legs and intent blue eyes, framed by impeccably Aryan blond hair, Unity was not a presence to be missed. Interest aroused, the Führer asked who she was and, being told that she was the daughter of a member of the House of Lords, the founder of the Reich invited her for lunch and conversation.

It is unlikely that (as it was widely rumored) the Führer ever slept with her. He generally steered clear of physical relationships with the women around him, but he enjoyed her company and found her sufficiently amusing to provoke the jealousy of his one accredited mistress, Eva Braun.

On her side, Unity remained devoted to "the darling leader," religiously wearing the gold Nazi badge engraved with his signature that he had given her, loyally proclaiming her hatred of the Jews wherever possible, and as some believed, even dreaming of the day when she might marry Hitler and become empress of a newer, greater Germany.

Churchill had no direct contact at this time with Unity, and seems to have regarded her much as one more embarrassing member of his wife's family, of whom the less said the better. (What he would have done had Unity become Frau Hitler remains one of the quainter might-have-beens of history.)

But Unity's close connections with Hitler and the Nazi court helped promote a more serious relationship between the Nazi hierarchy and a frequent habitué of Chartwell, which would bring considerable embarrassment in later years; she was accompanied on many of her early trips to Munich by Churchill's favorite Mitford and object of his son Randolph's Etonian infatuation, her glamorous sister Diana.

Since the unforgotten days at Chartwell, when she had hung devotedly on the words of Cousin Winston holding forth across the dining table, Diana had developed a growing passion for politics—in particular, a vulnerability for men of power. Her love affair with Oswald Mosley, the most dominating British politician after Churchill, had ended her marriage to the rich and gentle Bryan Guinness.

Her involvement with Mosley coincided with the fateful period of her lover's life when, impatient with parliamentary politics and strongly influenced by Mussolini and Italian fascism, the former Labour Cabinet minister staked his future on the leadership of the British Union of Fascists.

For Diana, love for Mosley naturally involved acceptance of the fascist cause, which in turn had brought her closer to Unity. (At the same time it started a lifelong alienation from her sister Jessica, who had now decided, with the Mitford taste for passionate extremes, that she was a dedicated Communist.)

In Germany, Diana's situation was different from Unity's. She was older than her sister, more intelligent, financially independent, and a well-known figure in society on her own account. She did not live with

Mosley until well after the death of his first wife, Cimmie, in 1933; and thus, on her visits to Unity in Munich, she was independent, encountering her sister's friends and the excitements of the Nazi scene on her own terms.

Had she not been who she was it is unlikely that Hitler would have troubled with Diana as he did. But well-connected twenty-four-year-old aristocratic English beauties sympathetic to the Nazi cause were not exactly common in Munich in 1935, and her links with Churchill and with the influential leader of the British Union of Fascists gave her a status that clearly made it worth the Führer's while to cultivate her friendship.

The friendship also flourished because Diana found in Hitler something rather similar to what had so impressed her while listening to Cousin Winston—much the same mesmerizing flow of talk, the same concern with power, and what she described as "that surprising frankness often found in men at the top in contrast with mystery-making nonentities."

It is hard to tell how much she was being consciously outrageous, and how much she secretly enjoyed the dangerous notoriety around the Nazi leader. Hitler could offer those he liked some of the flattering and very tempting benefits of power—select luncheon parties in his flat in Munich, places of honor at the Nazi rallies, and invitations to his private box at gala performances of Wagner at Bayreuth. (When Diana told Hitler that *Parsifal* was her least favorite of all the Wagner operas, he paternally assured her, "You will find as you get older that you love *Parsifal* more and more.")

When she visited Berlin she would make sure to inform the Führer's secretariat in advance, and soon after her arrival an evening call would follow from Hitler's adjutant, Bruckner. "Gnädige Frau, wollen Sie zu uns hieruber kommen?" At this, she would stroll from the Kaiserhof Hotel across the Wilhemplatz to the Reichkanzelei, where she would find Hitler waiting for her by an open fire. She had taught herself fluent German, and she enjoyed listening to him, much as she enjoyed listening to Churchill. She insists that Hitler could be every bit as charming, and sometimes they would end the evening watching a film together in his private cinema.

It was very much the off-duty Hitler she was seeing, and however improbable, she insists she found him solicitous, knowledgeable about painting and architecture, and an accomplished raconteur who made her laugh.

She was impressed by his peculiarly mesmeric blue eyes and had no difficulty closing her own to other elements in Nazi Germany. The horrors of World War II lay in the future. The treatment of the Jews, the early labor camps, Hitler's slaughter of his various opponents on the path to power—these were German problems it would have been impolite for a favored foreign guest to mention, particularly when so many leading Nazis were so exceedingly polite and kind to her. Herr Doctor Joseph Goebbels was particularly hospitable, and she found a close friend in his homely and much put-upon wife, Magda.

Befriended by these leading Nazis, Diana felt so confident among them that in the autumn of 1936 she asked a favor that would ultimately appear the crowning blunder of the German adventures of this Mitford cousin of the Churchills.

By now she had set up home with Mosley and they wished to marry. But with the threats he was receiving from the Communists, Mosley feared for Diana's safety if it were known she was his wife. A secret marriage was impossible in Britain, and even in an embassy abroad, news of the ceremony was bound to reach the press. So Diana asked her friend the Führer for assistance.

On October 5, Sir Oswald Mosley led his Blackshirt followers through the East End of London to be confronted by the antifascists in what is still remembered as "the battle of Cable Street." In romantic contrast, he traveled that same night to Germany, and the next day was secretly married to Diana by the Berlin Registrar. Hitler had personally ensured that no news of the ceremony leaked out to the press. (Even energetic Randolph, who suspected what had happened, proved unable to uncover any facts.)

Magda Goebbels gave the wedding lunch in her home close to the Reichkanzelei. The bride wore yellow silk, and her sister Unity was the only family member present. Dr. Goebbels gave the happy couple a twenty-four volume set of the works of Goethe. That evening, at a private dinner, Hitler also gave them a wedding gift: a signed portrait of himself.

This was the second and the last occasion Hitler and Mosley met, and on the following day the groom returned to London. According to Mosley's son Nicholas, Diana, much later, admitted that it had been this contact with Hitler that had ruined his life. In later years, Mosley himself was known to refer to Hitler as "that dreadful little man."

But what is so extraordinary about Diana's friendship with the Führer is that it continued right to the outbreak of the war and in no way seems to have affected her friendship and admiration for Cousin Winston and his family. They remained on close terms; Randolph was still extremely fond of her, and shortly before her marriage, Churchill had had her to lunch at his flat in Morpeth Mansions.

The food was simpler than at the luncheon parties she was used to in the Führer's flat in Munich, but the guests were people she knew and whose company she enjoyed. Apart from Clementine, there was Lord Ivor Churchill and her cousin Sarah, who "dashed in from a dancing lesson."

One might have thought Diana's fascism and her friendship with Hitler and the leading Nazis would have been a subject that was totally taboo among them all. Instead, as lunch proceeded, she soon discovered that "simply everyone, from Winston down, longed to hear any detail I could give them about Hitler."

From Churchill there was no suggestion that it might be ill-considered, let alone dangerous, to have Hitler as a friend. On the contrary, "Winston only wanted to hear about Hitler," recalls Diana, but while telling him all she knew, she says she had a strong impression that he was "already looking on him as a personal rival."

Finally, she told him that they should meet. She could easily arrange it. "You would be captivated by him if you knew him," she assured him. But Churchill's attitude to Hitler had hardened since that night in Munich back in 1931 when Randolph so nearly brought the two of them together around the dinner table.

"Oh, no. NO!" the great man growled.

For Churchill, Hitler's rise to power marked a time of growing tension in politics and in his private life, and the bull-like figure and the brooding features seemed to reflect his powerful preoccupations.

He was increasingly concerned with danger from the air. Most experts, Lindemann included, believed that "the bomber would get through." Studying what proved to be exaggerated estimates of German airpower from Colonel Morton, Churchill was convinced that war with Germany would spell the death of at least a million civilians in London alone from aerial bombardment.

It was Armageddon once again, and for him this grim belief produced alternating moods of fury at a supine government, hope for his own return to power as war drew closer, and a terrible Churchillian despair at the bleak scenario his undiminished powers of imagination created.

At the same time, lacking a ministerial salary, and with the costs of Chartwell to be met, he was working as even he had never worked before to make ends meet. On top of his weekly journalism, there was his never-ending life of Marlborough, which had now expanded into its third volume with no appreciable end in sight.

His best hope of solving his financial problems seemed to lie in the cinema. The film magnate Alexander Korda had offered him £10,000 to prepare a film biography of George V to be shown at his Jubilee in 1935. Churchill had gratefully accepted.

One might have thought a man with such a load of work and worry was a man who needed all the support and sympathy of a devoted spouse, particularly one like Clementine, who once formed her life around his. But this was not entirely the case.

In the first place, there was that enviable psychology that lay behind Churchill's vast capacity for work. As he explained in a passage he wrote in an article on "Painting as a Pastime" two years earlier, he had come to regard himself as one of that rare breed of what he called "Fortune's favoured children" for whom "work and pleasure are one. . . . For them the working hours are never long enough. Each day is a holiday, and ordinary holidays when they come are grudged as enforced interruptions in an absorbing vocation."

Despite a touch of wishful thinking—as in much of what he wrote about himself—there was an element of truth in this. Instead of prostrating him, prolonged periods of work seemed to make him more resilient. As he also explained, he had evolved what he believed to be the perfect method of avoiding mental strain and psychological fatigue. The secret lay in giving the brain fresh interest and activities through constant change. The more variety the better for the weary cerebellum, a private recipe he increasingly adhered to as his work load grew. With his determined powers of concentration, Churchill could fill his days —and much of his nights—with obsessive and obsessional activity: writing, talking, painting, building the interminable wall around his garden, and planning more drastic alterations to the Chartwell landscape.

All were pursued with total self-absorption, keeping him happy and productive. They also made him largely self-reliant—and very boring to his wife. The ministrations of a valet and the close attention of a stenographer were all he really needed (apart from the regular productions of his cook) for days on end.

That left Clementine in a superfluous position, like the wives of many chronic workaholics. He undoubtedly loved her, as he always sentimentally assured her in the letters he wrote when they were apart. But much of her life with him was unromantic and distinctly unrewarding.

Whatever he might have written about each day being like a holiday, it was very much a solitary vacation; and he often used work as a cure for his depressions. His painting was a private pleasure, as were his enthusiastic plans for Chartwell. Clementine continued to dislike the house, and besides, she was not the sort of wife with whom one could share the joys of laying bricks.

Nor were politics the absorbing interest they had shared in the past. She was growing tired of the ceaseless battles that unfailingly aroused her husband's energies. Still a liberal at heart, she showed little solidarity for his last-ditch stand on India, nor did she want to get deeply involved with Germany or the unthinkable prospect of another war in Europe.

Despite his glaring faults, Randolph remained his father's faithful ally in politics, sharing his angriest or most reactionary beliefs and always desperate to be his public champion. Clementine was not.

In 1934, Clementine was forty-nine, an attractive woman with a distinctly limited interest in her family and a sense that youth was running out. To keep her happy, an overburdened Churchill agreed to the "enforced interruption" of a month's holiday with her aboard Lord Moyne's luxurious motor-yacht *Rosaura* in the Eastern Mediterranean, visiting the beauty spots of Syria and Egypt.

This holiday proved a considerable success—not least because Churchill was able to start work on the script for Alexander Korda— and Clementine conceived a sudden taste for foreign travel. This owed a great deal to the amenities of the *Rosaura* and also to the charm and interests of their extremely wealthy host.

Moyne was an old friend of Churchill's. Chips Channon described him as "an extraordinary man, colossally rich, well meaning, intelligent, scrupulous, yet a *viveur,* and the only modern Guinness to play a social or political role."

He was a generous if eccentric host who spent large amounts of money on long sea voyages and was planning a four-month winter voyage to the Pacific to bring back specimens of the Sumatran giant lizard for the London zoo. The Churchills were invited.

A four-month absence from work and politics was unthinkable for Churchill, but Clementine was keen to go. According to Sarah, she had been ill again but was well enough to travel. Solicitous as ever, Churchill agreed, and two days after Christmas the family waved her off aboard the boat train from Victoria. En route to Messina, where she was to embark aboard *Rosaura,* she wrote tenderly to Churchill, saying how much she loved her "sweet and darling Winston," and telling him not to be vexed with his vagabond Kat. "She has gone off to the jungle with her tail in the air, but she will return presently to her basket and curl down comfortably."

Busy as ever, Churchill was a more devoted correspondent than his wife during the five months they were apart. Lengthy news bulletins were conscientiously dictated and dispatched from Chartwell, giving a detailed picture both of Mr. Pug's activities and what was happening to members of the family—particularly Randolph.

But as she read them on the deck of Lord Moyne's yacht as it made its way through warm seas and enchanted islands, the "vagabond Kat," all signs of illness gone, must have felt great relief at being so far away from the turmoil of her distant family. Her own replies were sparse—on several occasions, Churchill felt obliged to cable her for news—and when she did write, they were very much the letters of a wayward wife: hurried, detached, and with those flashes of solicitude guilty wives so often use with absent husbands. For as we know from her biographer, Clementine had found another interest on her voyage, apart from the temples of Bali and the Sumatran giant lizard.

Moyne's current mistress was with them on the voyage, as was his son Kenelm and his wife. Moyne, the perfect host, also provided Clementine with a companion for the journey, a forty-two-year-old bachelor named Terence Philip, who was the director of the London branch of Knoedlers, the New York art dealers. Born in Russia, Philip was handsome, cosmopolitan, charming, and witty, and a friend of Lord Ivor Churchill. Living in the close familiarity of the ship, the inevitable happened, as it often does on lengthy cruises. Clementine fell romantically in love.

This was not entirely surprising, for Clementine always had a strong romantic streak, and she had reached what Balzac called "that dangerous time of life when women realise that it is possible to grow old."

It must have been reassuring to receive the close attentions of a handsome, younger man, particularly one like Philip, who could offer her the very things Winston had so little time for: trivia and gossip and some light relief from the doom that hung so heavily upon mankind.

She would have been less than human had she not hankered after a simpler, happier way of life, freed from the tensions and the constant worries of an aging, super-human husband and a largely unrewarding family.

What she cannot have known is that her love for the attractive Terence Philip posed no danger to her marriage. For the charming Terence Philip was what was known in prewar social parlance as a "society tame cat." Rumored to be discreetly homosexual, he enjoyed the company of women, particularly of slightly older women, and like many of his sort fulfilled a most important social function. Very much the gentleman, he could be invited anywhere as the spare man—and safely entrusted with anybody's wife or daughter. Women might fall in love with him, but he would never fall in love with them. This seems to have occurred with Clementine during this brief, romantic interlude.

Interestingly, in his letters, Churchill showed no sign of jealousy or concern at the presence of the handsome Mr. Philip on the *Rosaura,* suggesting that the worldly Moyne had made the situation clear to Churchill in advance, as one would with a friend in such circumstances. On the other hand, Mr. Pug was missing her. He had been, he told her, "sometimes a little depressed about politics and would have liked to have been comforted by you." He did not begrudge her her "long excursion," as he called it, "but now I do want you back," he wrote her at the beginning of April 1935.

She responded as she knew she had to, telling him how much she loved him, "and that I long to be folded in your arms." And doubtless by now she did, for there must have been a sense of comfortable relief to be returning to the familiar if turbulent world of Mr. Pug.

# twenty-four

# Two Love Affairs

Despite the behavior of his various relations, one might have thought that Churchill could find harmony and peace within his own family. Sadly this was not the case. However much he needed a united family at this time of setback and frustration, on the whole he failed to get it.

After her long cruise and unsatisfactory romance with Terence Philip, Clementine had no alternative but to return to Churchill. Yet she was soon longing to get away again. "It's very nice being back, but, oh dear, I want to start out again very badly," she told a friend. She would never manage another four-month foreign voyage, but with Moppett Whyte still looking after Chartwell and fourteen-year-old Mary, she could at least resume her independent life in London.

Diana was also of little help to her father. Finally divorced from her alcoholic husband, she was left feeling guilty and unsettled. And Randolph, who still worshiped Churchill, never seemed to stop causing him anxiety and acute embarrassment.

Even before Clementine returned from Indonesia, early in 1935, Randolph was embroiled in another typical adventure, which had only added to his father's problems. He had been sent to report a by-election in the Liverpool constituency of Wavertree, the safest of Tory seats. The official candidate seemed certain to defeat his Labour challenger.

Randolph changed all that. Profoundly disagreeing with the official Conservative, he instantly decided to stand against him as a rival Tory. Randolph enjoyed himself immensely, trumpeting his father's policies, winning the press support of Beaverbrook and Rothermere, and splitting the right-wing vote so neatly that Conservative Wavertree returned a Labour member for the first time in its history.

Randolph remained undaunted, but the Conservative high command in London was enraged, blaming Churchill for his son's behavior. This was hardly fair, since Churchill had attempted to dissuade his son from standing—later supporting him only from paternal loyalty. But few believed this, and Randolph had seriously added to his father's problems with his party at a time when he was not in need of further troubles.

But Randolph was now in his stride politically. Undeterred—and unrepentant—he proceeded to sponsor another independent Tory candidate in another safe Conservative constituency: Norwood in Surrey. This proved even more ill-judged than Wavertree, with Randolph's candidate a notorious ex-fascist. Churchill was so infuriated with his son's behavior that he temporarily banned him from the house—and Randolph's candidate, despite support from rich, eccentric Lady Houston, was soundly defeated.

For the Churchill family, however, the Norwood by-election did bring one unexpected bonus. Randolph had taken Diana to help with the campaign, and although his candidate lost, Diana found herself a husband—none other than the winner, a tall, redheaded young ex-diplomat named Duncan Sandys. They married late that summer, and Churchill was particularly pleased. Not only had he got a son-in-law, but he had found what he had hoped to find in Randolph, a young and vigorous supporter in the House of Commons. Then, as Diana's life seemed sorted out at last, came trouble from an unexpected quarter: Sarah.

Despite her debut as a "Bolshie debutante" and the influence of Cousin Unity, Sarah, now aged twenty-one, had given every sign of contentedly accepting life with her parents' blessing. She once described herself as "stagestruck since I was in socks," and her parents, indulging her passion for the theater, had allowed her to start professional dancing lessons in London with her friend Jenny Nicholson.

Miss Nicholson was the granddaughter of Churchill's friend, the painter Sir William Nicholson, a frequent visitor to Chartwell who had given Churchill painting lessons. Sir William was not just an artist, he was a gentleman, and if he felt it safe for Jenny to study dancing, it must be safe for Sarah, too, particularly as Jenny said that she could share her flat and had promised to keep an eye on her in London.

Churchill was in certain ways the most innocent of men, particularly where his beloved family was involved. Great events concerned him, but he was always bored by the small change of the social scene.

In contrast to the "rollickingly bumptious" Randolph, Sarah had always seemed predictable. She had escaped the awkwardness and shyness of Diana, and was exuberant and full of fun. With bright red hair and fine complexion, she was almost beautiful. She was very conscious that her nose, inherited from Clementine, was just a shade too long, but this had done nothing to scare off a succession of extremely nice young men who fell in love with her.

One of the nicest was the young Harry Llewellyn, who had just graduated from Cambridge. Son of a landowning Welsh baronet, he was already a splendid horseman. (As Sir Harry Llewellyn he would become an Olympic gold medalist and the most celebrated showjumper of his generation.)

Sarah visited the Llewellyn home in Wales, and Sir Harry still has sentimental memories of her. "With her beautiful red hair tied up in a bun under a bowler hat, she was a nice horsewoman, and she would really have a go out hunting."

Sarah's life was totally conventional, in the manner of the upper classes of the day. In May 1933, she had made her curtsy to Queen Mary at the Palace, presented by her mother.

Sarah appeared virginal, safely unintellectual, and devoted to her famous father. There seemed every reason to believe that in a year or two she would behave as a gently born young ex-debutante was expected to behave—that is, to marry, if not young Llewellyn, then some other suitable young man, preferably with a title and certainly with money. In the meantime, those simple dancing lessons with Miss Nicholson kept her occupied and out of trouble.

But Sarah was not as placid or as predictable as she seemed and beneath her agreeable exterior lurked the teenager who was so put out by rich old Maxine Elliot at her villa in the South of France. Like her father, Sarah was something of a rebel, and from Clementine she seemed to have acquired a permanent dislike of the smart set and the super-rich society that Churchill felt so happy with. Sarah preferred the unconventional, the free, and the artistic. Above all, she loved the theater people she was now meeting through Jenny Nicholson and her dancing teacher.

In a sense, it was Churchill's fault that things turned out the way they did—although, to be fair, he had weightier matters on his mind than Sarah's future when, in October 1935, she applied for an audition with West End impresario C. B. Cochran. Sarah hoped for a part in his current theatrical revue, *Follow the Sun.*

Mussolini's war in Abyssinia was threatening to spread to Europe. German rearmament, particularly in the air, was obsessing Churchill, and in less than three weeks' time there would be a British general election. There was always the chance that if the Conservatives won their expected victory, Stanley Baldwin might decide to offer Winston office (they did, but he did not).

Had Churchill been a little less preoccupied and a little more informed about theatrical society, he might have sensed the possible effect Cochran and the world around him was having on his daughter.

Sarah, it seems, was secretly quite ambitious. Like Randolph, she longed for a success that would impress her father. She was fame-struck from an early age, and the stage appeared the shortest route to stardom.

Cochran was an old-style theatrical survivor, a producer-impresario who had tried everything from rodeo and roller-skating to representing the queen of the French music-hall, Mistinguett, and producing Noël Coward. Coward's musicals had saved him from bankruptcy, since then he had been shrewd enough to spot the potential of a certain social cachet in his shows.

A thoroughgoing snob, he had invented a new style of chorus girl, one with class and breeding, and renamed his chorus line "Mr. Cochran's Young Ladies." Some were, some emphatically were not, but Sarah wished to join them.

To have Winston Churchill's daughter in his show would be a coup, but Cochran was a realist who knew the dangers that ensue when nice young ladies come in contact with the manifold temptations of the stage. Cochran also knew Churchill rather well, having been general manager of a show of Jennie's at Earls Court, called *Shakespeare's England,* just before the war. (The show had flopped, but Cochran's friendship with the great man's mother had continued until her death.) So he wrote to Churchill, saying that Sarah had asked for an audition, and requesting his consent.

"I pointed out to her that she can only learn the necessary experience to become a star by learning her job in the smallest capacity, which, as she fancies light musical shows rather than straight plays without music, means chorus, with perhaps a tiny part or so."

Churchill replied with equal courtesy, saying—somewhat surprisingly—that he had no objection to his daughter pursuing a career as a professional dancer "at this period of her life." But there were two interesting discrepancies in the correspondence. Churchill made a definite point of saying that Sarah should "play under a stage name." Cochran never mentioned this, and in fact she never did; her theatrical career would always have the full publicity that went with being Winston Churchill's daughter. More important was Cochran's reference to Sarah's ambition to become a star. This was very different from her father's view of her dancing as something that would simply occupy her for a while.

Sarah had her audition, and Cochran offered her the tiny part he promised. *Follow the Sun* included a short up-market ballet sequence choreographed by Frederick Ashton and based on Osbert Sitwell's parody of an Edwardian shooting party "The First Shoot." The music was by William Walton, the scenery and costumes by Cecil Beaton, and Sarah, suitably attired by Beaton, had to imitate a wounded pheasant.

*Follow the Sun* was an uncertain step on Sarah's road to stardom, but the true star of the show was the comedian Vic Oliver, for whom it proved a most successful London debut. Born in Vienna thirty-eight years before, the son of Baron von Samek, a Jewish clothing manufacturer from Brunn, young von Samek had trained at the Vienna Conservatoire of Music under Gustav Mahler before leaving for the States to seek his fortune as a concert pianist. He dropped the "von" while touring the States with dance bands, but it was not until he renamed himself Vic Oliver that he found success in the last role he really wanted: stand-up comedian cracking jokes in fractured Brooklyn-Viennese at the Old Palace Theatre in New York.

Vic Oliver was profoundly serious, a workaholic, and like many professional comedians, entirely devoid of humor. He was also something of a womanizer, twice married with a relinquished but still legal second wife in Austria and a devoted mistress in New York.

But his taste in women was unusual. Seeing himself as something of a theatrical Svengali, he was attracted to beautiful but serious young women whose potential he alone could spot, and whose career as artists he alone could foster. When he met Sarah the outcome was inevitable: a suave Svengali had met an all too eager Trilby.

Sarah described herself at this point as "a father-girl" (which, with Churchill's influence, is not surprising) and confessed to a taste for older, wiser men. Vic Oliver, eighteen years her senior, was a father figure, a star, and an elegant Central European with the sophisticated knowledge of the world that Sarah lacked. He was also undoubtedly impressed by everything that Churchill represented and always held him in the highest respect. Whether the social and professional advantages of marrying the great man's daughter attracted him as well is debatable. If they did, the illusion cannot have lasted long.

It was a swift, passionate romance, with Sarah showing all the ardor of a young girl in her first real love affair. *Follow the Sun* opened in London in November, and by December she and Vic were sufficiently in love to talk of marriage. By now they were together all the time, and within the world of the theater, their secret could not stay concealed for long.

The actress Ellen Pollock remembered lunching with Vic Oliver at the Carlton Grill, where he confided that he "could be marrying into a most unusual family before too long." Pollock had already heard rumors about Sarah, so she asked him outright if Sarah was the girl. When he said yes, she asked if he was in love with her. "I *think* I am," he said. When Sarah joined them later, Miss Pollock knew that nothing would keep Sarah from marrying the man she loved—not even Winston Churchill.

At the start of 1936, Churchill was under increasing pressure from almost every quarter. Hitler, now firmly in power in Germany, had reoccupied the Rhineland. Churchill was totally convinced that a European war was inevitable, and started stepping up his own campaign to tell the nation of the Nazi danger and the need for serious rearmament. A majority of his fellow Conservatives distrusted and disliked him, but his influence was growing. Impressive as ever in Parliament, he still hoped that Baldwin, who had invited him to join a secret official committee on defense, would appoint him to the one post in the government he wanted, that of Minister for Overall Defense Coordination.

In addition to keeping up with his parliamentary duties, speeches, meetings, and committees, Churchill was working almost every night until two or three in the morning on his biography of Marlborough—this on top of his weekly journalism, by which he "laid the golden eggs" that paid the bills for Chartwell more or less.

It was a work load to floor any man, but Churchill seemed to thrive on it. ("The well flows freely," he told Clementine. "Only the time is needed to draw water from it.") Those around him, however, tended to collapse—that summer, his secretary Violet Pearman suffered a stroke brought on by years of overwork. The work load did not help the Churchill marriage either. Clementine was once more feeling the urge to get away from the tensions of her married life, and that February found her enjoying an extended holiday in Austria, with Mary and Jack and Goonie's daughter, Clarissa. Clementine enjoyed skiing, and after years of opting out of her maternal role discovered a closeness with her youngest daughter that she had never had with any of her other children.

Clementine's absence meant that when Sarah broached the news that she was in love with Vic Oliver and wished to marry him, Churchill had to cope with it alone. Even today there cannot be that many overburdened politicians who would respond with sympathy to the news that their favorite daughter wished to wed a twice-married foreign comedian eighteen years her senior. For Churchill it was quite unthinkable, and he responded as he always did when anything he loved was threatened. His aggression roused, he fought with every means that lay within his power.

There was more bullying than subtlety from him in the days that followed. Vic Oliver was summoned to Morpeth Mansions—Churchill refused to shake hands with him. That evening he wrote to Clementine that Oliver was "common as dirt," with a "horrible mouth and foul Austro-Yankee drawl." Churchill had treated him accordingly, telling him that should he dare persist with the engagement he would issue "an immediate public statement which would be painful to them both."

Vic Oliver seems to have acted rather well in this awkward situation. Summoning what dignity he could, he agreed to Churchill's terms: a year away from Sarah, after which there would be no further family opposition to the marriage if both parties still wanted it.

A man of honor, the son of Baron Samek gave his word. And as a man unusually accustomed to getting his way where *his* honor was concerned, the grandson of the Duke of Marlborough must have felt the worst was over.

But Churchill still had to deal with Sarah, which he did a few days later in his study at Chartwell. He tried to bully her as he did her lover. According to her own account, she was "addressed like a public meeting" on the perils of marriage with this "itinerant vagabond." Then, with a fine dramatic touch, he produced his British passport. "In three or four years," he said prophetically, "you may be married to the enemy, and I shall not be able to protect you once you have lost this."

Sarah saw his point, and the interview ended with her promising that she would not marry Vic Oliver until he had American citizenship. Churchill thought that he had won.

"I think I have put her off," he said afterward, smiling at Diana.

"On the contrary," his eldest daughter said. "I think you have chased her away."

Not for nothing was Sarah known in the family as "the Mule," having inherited all the Churchill obstinacy behind her carefree manner. She was in no way party to the gentlemanly agreement between her father and her lover, and she had not the faintest intention of abiding by it—even though Vic Oliver, keeping to his word, swiftly departed for a new theatrical engagement in New York.

By now, Clementine, refreshed and rested from her winter holiday, was on the scene and able to take over the problems with Sarah. Her tactics were subtler than her husband's.

Both Sarah and her mother were early risers, and they often breakfasted together, enjoying the view across the Chartwell gardens to the woods beyond. Clementine had always found it hard to break through her emotional reserve with Sarah and Diana, and since her return, had kept off any serious discussion of Vic Oliver. But finally, at breakfast, Clementine brought herself to make what Sarah later called "an extraordinary suggestion." After saying that the marriage was bound to end in disaster, Clementine proposed that if Sarah promised not to see her lover, she could have the total freedom her strong personality needed—her own flat in London, no questions asked, provided she would abandon Vic forever.

Sarah was deeply shocked by what struck her as the immorality of what her straitlaced mother was suggesting, and refused to discuss the subject any further.

During the weeks that followed, Clementine invited to Chartwell several presentable young men as weekend guests, but Sarah made it clear she was not interested, and the subject of her love for Vic was no longer mentioned in the family. By August, when Churchill departed for his painting holiday in France, he and Clementine believed their daughter's infatuation was forgotten.

Had it been left to Vic Oliver, it probably would have been. His career in vaudeville was booming in the States, and he was now rehearsing for the starring role in a new revue, opening in Boston and then moving on to Loew's State Theatre on Broadway. He was deeply preoccupied, as he always was before a show, and although his previous affair ended when he met Sarah, there was no shortage of pretty girls in Boston.

But Churchill's daughter was not a girl to be discarded. Throughout that summer she had been in constant touch with Vic Oliver in the States, begging him to let her join him in New York. As she pointed out, she had made no promises not to see *him,* and he finally relented, sending her a ticket to New York aboard the S.S. *Bremen.*

Had Churchill been at Chartwell that September day in 1936, events would have been different. Sarah found it hard to lie to him, and he would have guessed what she was up to. But he was on holiday, away from Clementine and the family in the South of France, painting, enjoying an occasional flutter on the tables at Monte Carlo, and basking in the familiar comforts of the Château de l'Horizon. He was then heading north, as guest of the French High Command, for a brisk tour of inspection around the Maginot Line at Metz.

Clementine, who remained at Chartwell, was less perceptive than her husband over Sarah and did not realize that she had visited the bank and withdrawn all her worldly wealth, which amounted to a little over £4. When Sarah told her mother that she would be spending the night in London at the flat in Morpeth Mansions and visiting her hairdresser the next morning, Clementine suspected nothing.

Sarah caught an evening train from Westerham to London, and indeed spent the night at Morpeth Mansions, but the next morning, instead of going to the hairdresser, she took a cab to Waterloo. Photographs taken of her later that morning show her looking very young and pretty and distinctly flustered as she tried to cope with suitcase, passport, and the enormity of what she was about to do.

At Waterloo station she was met by Jenny Nicholson, who was now in the cabaret at the Dorchester Hotel. They had little time together, as the boat train for Southampton was about to leave. As she bid her friend good-bye, Sarah handed her a letter.

"Be sure to give this to my mother."

"Certainly," said Miss Nicholson.

However, as the train pulled out Miss Nicholson decided otherwise. Instead of facing Clementine in person, she had Sarah's letter sent by train to Westerham, then telephoned a reporter friend on the *Daily Express.* This explains the presence of a press photographer by the gang plank of the S.S. *Bremen* at Southampton later that morning, as Sarah embarked aboard the German liner for New York. It also explains how the *Express* for Wednesday, September 16, carried an exclusive interview with Miss Nicholson about Sarah's love affair under the front-page headline: "Miss Sarah Churchill Elopes to the USA."

It was romantic and exciting, but the lovers underestimated Churchill's wrath. Things might have turned out differently had it not been for Jenny Nicholson's passion for publicity.

The letter Sarah had written Clementine had been carefully worded to appeal to her heart. "Please don't be worried—please don't be sad. I will keep you fully informed of my whereabouts and plans. . . . My love to you, darling Mummy." She even added a P.S. begging Clementine to use her calming influence upon her husband. "Please make Papa understand."

However, once the elopement was splashed across the papers, there was no chance of Churchill understanding. The battle was joined.

Events now took a fascinating turn, revealing just how contradictory Churchill could be in a human crisis. By a strange coincidence, these autumn weeks of 1936 saw him suddenly involved with two romantic muddles, both concerning people he was deeply fond of.

Just as Sarah was steaming off aboard the S.S. *Bremen* with the scandal in the daily papers, a far greater scandal was about to burst. King George V had died in January 1936, and had been succeeded by his son Edward, who was King but had yet to be crowned. That fall the love affair between Edward VIII of England and his married mistress Mrs. Wallis Simpson of Baltimore, Maryland, was on the point of turning from an open society secret into the gravest crisis to afflict the monarchy since the far-off days of George IV. The foreign press, particularly in the United States, was full of it, and although the proprietors of the British press had been loyally shielding the British public from the dreadful news, Churchill had known from early 1936 that his monarch, like his daughter, was passionately in love.

Churchill had long been an admirer and friend of Edward's. During his years as Prince of Wales, the King's youthful glamour and apparent deep concern for his Empire had convinced the statesman that in his future monarch he had something of a fellow spirit. They often met, and earlier that year Churchill had been introduced to Mrs. Simpson at Fort Belvedere, the King's own private residence. He had subsequently had several opportunities of observing them together.

There were in fact some striking similarities between the royal love affair and Sarah's: both involved unmarried adults bent on union with twice-married foreigners who themselves were in the throes of divorce; both marriages, in different ways, appeared unsuitable; and in both, Churchill felt impelled to intervene. What is fascinating is the extraordinary difference in his behavior toward his daughter and his King.

With Sarah he reacted like the heaviest of high Victorian fathers; as she complained bitterly in a letter to her mother, no allowances at all were made for her feelings or for the man she loved, who was simply "treated as a low adventurer."

When the story broke in the *Express*, Churchill was still in France, but he promptly ordered Randolph, of all people, to Southampton in his place, sent him a first-class ticket on the *Queen Mary*, and told him to bring his sister to her senses and safely home. Churchill, the man of action, was in fact creating a new drama, which Randolph and the press would make the most of.

The *Queen Mary* was twenty-two hours behind the *Bremen,* and with Randolph now in hot pursuit, the elopement instantly became a front-page story as well as a patriotic race between the German and the British transatlantic liners. A mid-Atlantic hurricane heightened the suspense, but the *Bremen* kept its lead and by the time she docked, more than fifty newsmen were in readiness to interview "Winston Churchill's daughter, the runaway debutante" in person.

It was a good example of how to turn a private crisis into a very public spectacle, which Churchill, with a lifetime's experience in dealing with the press, should have avoided. Sarah, actress that she was, handled the reporters rather well. On the unlikely advice of one of her fellow passengers, Randolph's bête noire, Lady Astor, she called an impromptu press conference aboard the ship. Flustered but very pretty with her red hair and pale blue dress, she dispensed much English charm but little in the way of her intentions.

Nor did Vic Oliver, who had already been given the full treatment by the press. He had been most correct, denying any plans of instant marriage, which was true, since his previous marriage was still in the final stage of its dissolution. Randolph, however, showed up rather badly as usual when confronted by reporters. As the *Queen Mary* docked, he was met by his anxious-looking sister and half the press corps of New York.

"I'm here to take Sarah home. It simply won't do," he blustered.

"But does she want to go?" somebody asked.

"*That* makes no difference. Sarah's too young to know her own mind."

But Sarah emphatically did know her mind—and Randolph returned to England empty-handed. This did little to affect the resolution of his father, who had now returned to Chartwell from the fortresses of France; the light of battle in his eye, Churchill was set to fight this homegrown skirmish to its bitter end.

Through his old New York friend the financier Bernard Baruch, who had been in touch with Sarah, highly paid lawyers were secretly engaged to set legal barriers against the marriage, and private detectives started dredging up anything unpleasant they could find in Vic Oliver's past. Sarah's appeals by telephone to Clementine—and to her father's deeply sentimental nature—made no difference.

But Churchill *could* be sentimental and extraordinarily romantic over a love affair in different circumstances, and those circumstances were rapidly approaching in the relationship between his King and Mrs. Simpson. From the beginning, Churchill had seen the dangers of Edward marrying his mistress, and when informally consulted by Walter Monckton, the royal lawyer, in July 1936, Churchill had firmly advised against Mrs. Simpson's plans to seek freedom by divorcing her husband. By the end of October, Mrs. Simpson had her divorce, and when discussion of the royal romance was finally permitted in the British press, it was clear that the King was bent on marriage. To those in the know, it was also clear that the Prime Minister, stolid Stanley Baldwin, and his obedient supporters were never going to permit the King, who was also head of the established Church of England, to commit the scandal of marrying a divorcée.

On December 2, Baldwin clearly spelled this out to the King; Edward answered that he was set irrevocably on marriage. Impasse ensued and the King requested leave to seek advice from his friend Winston Churchill. Baldwin raised no objection, and Churchill was invited for dinner at Fort Belvedere two evenings later.

Had Churchill been consistent and taken the same stern attitude toward his King's romance as he was taking with his daughter's, he would have saved himself a lot of trouble—and one of the most humiliating setbacks of his political career. His political antennae should have warned him that down-to-earth public feeling was hardening against this royal marriage. (As Edith Sitwell put it, "She has been divorced twice too often for a Queen, and I don't think 'Queen Wally' would sound well.") He should have seen that his King's romance was far more unsuitable than Sarah's, and that the issue was a dangerous diversion from his mission to persuade a lethargic government to rearm against the growing might of Germany. But rarely was Churchill particularly consistent once an issue truly stirred the depths of his imagination, and few things in life could stir it more dramatically than royalty.

Clementine knew all the symptoms in advance. She once described Churchill as "the last believer in the divine right of kings," and warned him against becoming irretrievably involved. She might as well have advised him not to have joined the charge at Omdurman.

Once in the presence of his still-to-be-anointed King, a lifetime of devotion to his sovereign made the decision for him. His monarch was in love and was personally appealing for assistance. How could Churchill not become his champion?

This dinner between Churchill and King Edward must have been an emotional occasion. Haggard from the strains of love and statecraft, Edward apparently "blacked out" twice at the table, and Churchill solicitously suggested he retire to Windsor Castle to recover his composure while two royal doctors manned the gates against the politicians.

It was, in fact, too late for such absurd delaying tactics, as Baldwin, coolly judging the hostility the nation felt for Mrs. Simpson, pressed the King to choose between his mistress and his crown. As events would prove, unromantic Stanley Baldwin was for once completely right; while royalist, romantic Churchill made one of the worst blunders of his whole political career.

Immersed in his trusted role in this royalist scenario, on the King's behalf Churchill pleaded in Parliament for "time and patience" so as to devise a way for Edward to keep his crown and the woman he loved. As so often in Churchill's life, it was another scene from the pages of *Savrola,* with Churchill the romantic novelist taking over from Churchill the realist and man of destiny. The result was deep humiliation, as on two occasions he attempted to plead the King's case in the House of Commons only to be howled down from all sides. Everyone but Churchill knew that, faced with an unprecedented constitutional crisis, the time had come for the King to make an irrevocable decision, which he did by his official act of abdication in December. Churchill was shocked and deeply shaken by the reception he had received in the Commons, muttering darkly (as he did after the Dardanelles) that he was "finished."

His own supporters were bitterly disappointed, feeling that he had sacrificed his growing reputation as the prophet of rearmament for the sake of an ill-judged royal fiasco. Not so Churchill. Devoted to Edward to the last, he lunched with him on the very day he made his

abdication broadcast and apparently wrote every word of it for him, as
the King was all but incoherent.

It was one of Churchill's finest efforts, straight from the pages of
a romantic novel (Savrola, too, once gave up power for the woman he
loved), and full of phrases that would catch the heartstrings of the
nation. Most effective was the line in which the King expressed his
deep regret at not possessing "one matchless blessing, enjoyed by so
many of you and not bestowed on me—a happy home with wife and
children." According to Edward's own account, when he said good-
bye Churchill paused on the steps of Fort Belvedere, "hat in one hand,
stick in the other," with tears in his eyes.

Later, at Chartwell, when he listened to the broadcast he had
written, Churchill wept copiously. Afterward he dictated a personal
memorandum, which remained unpublished until his death, revealing
the full extent to which the romantic novelist had taken charge of his
emotions at the climax of this deeply sentimental business.

He began by speaking of King Edward's "deep attachment for
Mrs. Simpson."

> He delighted in her company, and found in her qualities as necessary to
> his happiness as the air he breathed. Those who knew him well and
> watched him closely noticed that many little tricks and fidgetings of
> nervousness fell away from him. He was a completed being instead of a
> sick and harassed soul. This experience, which happens to a great many
> people in the flower of their youth, came late in life for him, and was all
> the more precious and compulsive for that fact. The association was
> psychical rather than sexual, and certainly not sensual except inciden-
> tally. Although branded with the stigma of a guilty love, no companion-
> ship could have appeared more natural. . . . One must have something
> real somewhere. Otherwise far better [to] die.

Most of these deeply sentimental words applied equally to his
daughter Sarah, but even while dictating them at Chartwell, Churchill
was still refusing to concede an inch in his opposition. Meanwhile,
unhappy and rejected by her family, Sarah naturally relied increasingly
upon her lover—growing more and more attached to him.

There was always a side of her that craved publicity, and now she
was getting it—by dancing in Vic Oliver's show on tour in Boston.
When *Follow the Stars* reached Broadway, Sarah had what any stagestruck girl would dream of: her name in lights on Broadway, and a

billing as "Britain's runaway dancing debutante in person, the guest of Vic Oliver."

Through detectives, Churchill kept in touch with what was happening, and even now tried desperately to stop the marriage. His lawyers had discovered there was still a period to go before Vic Oliver's Austrian divorce was finalized. Fighting to the end, Churchill tried everything he knew to persuade the lady in Vienna to delay things further. She refused.

On Christmas Eve, at New York's City Hall, not even the wrath and ingenuity of Winston Churchill could prevent Vic Oliver from making Sarah his wife.

It was a simple, unromantic ceremony, with only a lawyer and a cleaning lady as witnesses. *Follow the Stars* was over, and shortly afterward they sailed for England on the *Aquitania*. Then and only then did Churchill see the necessity for simultaneous surrender—over the love affairs of both his daughter and his former King.

Stanley Baldwin's reputation had been strengthened, the case for Britain's rearmament was weakened, and the former King of England was in exile. Churchill's own far from satisfactory marriage had suffered, too. Exhausted by the tensions and the drama of these frantic weeks, and upset by her husband's behavior toward Sarah, Clementine had had enough. Peregrine Churchill remembers his mother telling him of Aunt Clemmie visiting their house in Regent's Park and saying that she wanted a divorce from Winston. Goonie advised a period apart, and a weary Clementine left for Austria to think things over.

It was then that Churchill understood the full extent of his defeat, and that as a result of these disastrous weeks, he might well lose Clementine as well as Sarah.

He knew he had to make the best of things even if this meant forgiving Sarah and accepting his new son-in-law. Sarah was invited to a reconciliation lunch at Chartwell—with her husband. "I suppose we must call him Vic," Churchill wrote to Clementine. All he could bring himself to tell her about their new son-in-law was that he was making £200 a week in his current show. Sarah he found "serious and gentle." "Like the ill-starred Duke of Windsor," he concluded, "she has done what she liked, and now has to like what she has done."

# twenty-five

# The Return of
# the Prophet

Early in July 1939, on the eve of
what Cyril Connolly called "closing time in the gardens of the West,"
Winston Churchill came to Blenheim for the last and most spectacular
prewar party ever witnessed in his great ancestral home.

The sense of an impending war made this a vintage year for balls
and parties, and money-conscious Bert decided just for once to spare
no expense in this celebration of his daughter Lady Sarah Spencer-
Churchill's coming out.

A thousand guests had been invited, including the handsome
Duke of Kent, the daughter of the U.S. ambassador, Eunice Kennedy,
and the Duke's distinguished-looking mother—now plain Mme.
Jacques Balsan—making a rare return to the scene of so much former
misery and splendor.

The terraces lovingly created by Sunny with the Vanderbilt
money were festooned with colored lights and Chinese lanterns, and
the footmen, as well as putting on the Marlborough livery, had powdered their hair for the occasion. (This was the last time they would
do so, as they complained that the powder made their scalps itch and
their hair fall out.) Searchlights lit up the trees across the lake, and an
orchestra played the waltzes of Vienna in the Duke's Long Library.

Not everyone, however, was impressed. Randolph, who disliked his cousin Bert and hated Blenheim, had come only to be near the woman he was now in love with—Laura, the beautiful and discontented wife of Lord Long. Formerly Laura Charteris, a granddaughter of the Earl of Wemys and younger sister of the future wife of Ian Fleming, this willful beauty had a taste for Randolph's company but was not in love with him. Randolph, however, as obstinate in love as over politics, refused to be deterred.

"Randolph, you've been drinking," she accused him (hardly an original remark).

"Who hasn't," he replied. "Anyhow, the food is ghastly and the whole performance at a time like this is a disgrace."

He left her, and shortly afterward was engaged in one of his all-too-frequent heated arguments with a fellow guest. Most of his arguments now were about his father, who was still detested by many loyal Tories as well as by fascists, pacifists, and pro-German members of the aristocracy. There was something of a scene, and according to Laura's recollection, someone had to take him home.

Churchill, oblivious, for once, of his son's behavior, was dining quietly beneath the Chinese lanterns with his old friend Consuelo and Anthony Eden, the handsome, youthful-looking former Foreign Secretary. At forty-two, Eden was almost fourteen years older than Randolph, but he did not look it. This may explain why Randolph, who had put on weight and was looking old beyond his years, felt such animosity toward him. He may also have been jealous of his father's closeness with Eden. The men had been allies ever since Eden's resignation from the Chamberlain government early in 1938 in protest against its weakness over Mussolini's seizure of Abyssinia. Churchill would describe Eden then as "one strong young figure standing up against the long, dismal drawling tides of drift and surrender."

Churchill and Eden had drawn closer still in opposition to Neville Chamberlain's disastrous attempt to appease Hitler over Czechoslovakia by meeting him in Munich in September 1938. Afterward, step by step, the European war, which Churchill had so long and so unpopularly predicted, had advanced toward its beginning.

Despite his promises at Munich, Hitler had marched his armies into Prague. He was threatening the port of Danzig, and his emissaries would soon arrive in Moscow to arrange a pact with Stalin that would include the dismemberment of Poland. The war would start in nine weeks' time, sweeping away so much of the world Blenheim represented.

The novelist Daphne Fielding, who was present at the party, compared it with the great ball thrown by the Duchess of Richmond on the eve of Waterloo. It was the last fling of a social order that war would change forever. It was also the end of the old Blenheim Churchill knew and loved. But for all the Churchills, the Blenheim ball marked the end of something else—ten long years of isolation and frustration in the wilderness of politics.

That very week, as the crisis deepened on the continent, the newspaper placards were proclaiming: "Churchill must come back!" But Neville Chamberlain, obstinate as ever, still believed that by including the anti-German Churchill in his government, he would be making war with Germany inevitable. In truth, with Hitler and his newfound Russian allies planning to dismember Poland, nothing Chamberlain could do would make the slightest difference.

Most of the Churchills were in London when war with Germany was officially declared on September 3, 1939. Sarah and Vic Oliver heard Chamberlain's solemn radio announcement at eleven in the morning in their flat in Westminster Gardens; Randolph nursing a hangover in his apartment in the same block, did not.

It was a somber moment, with Chamberlain admitting that this war meant that "everything that I have worked for, everything that I have hoped for, everything that I have believed in during my public life has crashed into ruins!" For Churchill, war meant something very different.

It was the vindication of all the warnings he had been making for so many years. It also brought a personal and long-awaited triumph. Earlier that day, before he broadcast to the nation, Chamberlain had ended Churchill's ten-year exile by offering him his old position at the Admiralty and a seat in the Cabinet.

As First Lord of the Admiralty, Churchill was back where he had been that August day, a quarter of a century before, when war began with Kaiser William's Germany. "It was a strange experience," he wrote, "like suddenly assuming a previous incarnation."

Over lunch, the family discussed their plans. Churchill and Clementine would be moving to the Admiralty, which would soon mean closing Chartwell. As a territorial officer attached to the artillery, Diana's husband, Duncan Sandys, would be joining his antiaircraft regiment; not to be outdone, Diana planned to enlist in the Women's Royal Naval Service as soon as someone could be found to look after their three-year-old son, Julian, and newborn baby, Edwina. (Since seventeen-year-old Mary was now in London with her parents, the invaluable Moppett Whyte again obliged, making a temporary home for Diana's children in one of the Chartwell cottages, although the house itself would close.)

Sarah was just as eager as Diana to go to war, but there was a problem no one liked to mention: Vic Oliver's new U.S. citizenship, which, in theory, made it his duty to return to America. Sarah emphatically refused to join him if he did. War placed a question mark over the couple's future.

The one member of the family for whom war appeared to pose no problems was Randolph. He had already enrolled as a reserve officer with his father's regiment—the 4th Hussars—and was keen to fight the enemy. So was Churchill as he raised his glass and made a toast.

"To victory!"

"To victory!" they all repeated.

From the beginning, Churchill's return to the Admiralty placed him in a unique position for a politician. The prophet's prophecies had come to pass, the seer so long rejected was recalled to power. If he was required to wait to lead the nation while sick, discredited Neville Chamberlain tottered on as Prime Minister, he was clearly the dominating presence in the wartime government.

Here was the vindication of his lifetime, the granting of the role his destiny appointed him to play. There could be no more thought of failure and rejection, no further struggles with "Black Dog." Gone were those recurrent fears of being doomed to follow his father's fate in politics.

Instead, approaching sixty-five, Churchill had won the greatest gamble of his life. When he proposed the toast to victory, it could have been his own.

The first message to the fleet upon his appointment was "Winston is back!"—and he was soon displaying much the same energy with which he transformed the Royal Navy in his youth. Though these months back at the Admiralty coincided with the strange lull of the so-called phony war, before Hitler launched his big offensive against Western Europe, Churchill wasted no time, and swiftly put his imprint on the naval high command. He was soon feuding with his admirals, planning harebrained expeditions, and generally invigorating everything he touched and working wonders for morale. Both in Parliament and from his seat in the Cabinet, he was once again establishing credentials for what he was: the nation's greatest and unrivaled man of war. This was in painful contrast with Neville Chamberlain, whose days as Prime Minister were clearly numbered.

Throughout these first months at the Admiralty, Churchill's staunchest ally and admirer was his son. Unlike Clementine, Randolph's faith in Churchill had never wavered through the thirties. Nor had their fights and disappointments touched the bonds that linked them.

"Randolph's adoration of his father is truly touching," wrote Harold Nicolson, and while Churchill's love of Randolph stopped somewhat short of adoration, his son was still of deep importance to him. As his precious heir, Randolph was his lifeline to the future, the bearer of "the lamp," and the extension of his destiny.

Now that this destiny had brought his father back to office, Randolph was in a situation that few outside the family quite appreciated. As Churchill's son, he now had privileges and responsibilities for which he was painfully unfit. But his worship of his father knew no bounds, and like some overeager schoolboy, he would do anything to please him. He showed this in no uncertain manner a few weeks after war broke out and he found himself in London on a weekend's leave.

He was sleeping, when he could, with the vaudeville star Clare Luce and still romantically in love with Laura, but that Saturday neither was available. Miss Luce was out of town, and Laura had decided she was suddenly in love with an older man, forty-five-year-old Eric, Earl of Dudley.

Meeting his old friend Lady Mary Dunn in the doorway of the Ritz, Randolph asked her out to dine. She, too, was unable to oblige, but suggested that he telephone her home and invite instead a friend who was staying with her. This was a pretty girl named Pamela, the nineteen-year-old daughter of the country-loving Dorset peer, Lord Digby (a former president of the Royal Horticultural Society, known to his intimates as "Carnation Digby").

Randolph took the number.

"What do you look like?" he is said to have asked with customary bluntness when Miss Digby answered. Legend has it she replied, "Redheaded and rather fat, but Mummy says the puppy fat will disappear." No sylph himself, Randolph accordingly asked her to dinner.

One of the most unlikely characters to enter the orbit of the

Churchills thus made her debut—and few were to be more totally transformed by contact with the Churchills than this friendly, pony-loving virgin from the shires.

Randolph's intentions were, for once, impetuously honorable, and nothing as frivolous as love was serving to distort his judgment. As he told American journalist John Gunther shortly afterward, he was determined to embark on active service, and believed he would probably be killed. As heir apparent to the Churchills, it was duty to his line—and more important, to his father—to ensure a legitimate successor lest this happened. Pamela was obviously healthy, and as a family the Digbys were perfectly acceptable, even to a Churchill. Three days after meeting her, Randolph proposed and was accepted.

Clementine disapproved, but as she disapproved of almost everything that Randolph did, this carried little weight. Churchill himself was delighted. He had married swiftly himself and, practical as ever, told his son, "All you need to be married are champagne, a box of cigars and a double bed!"

He also approved of Randolph's motives. As he wrote to his multimarried friend Bend'or Westminster, "I expect he will be in action in the early spring, and therefore I am very glad that he should be married before he goes. She is a charming girl and they both seemed very pleased about it."

The ceremony took place three weeks later at St. John's, Smith Square, with Churchill present. The bride wore blue, and Randolph donned his sword and full cavalryman's regalia.

However unromantic Randolph's overall approach, Pamela at least believed herself decidedly in love. As she explains, "I had had no experience of life or men, and was entirely unformed. I had been to Paris and to Germany to learn the languages, but I had certainly never met anyone like Randolph. What most appealed to me about him was his absolute certainty about everything—particularly about the war, which he believed was going to be extremely long and bloody, and that we should therefore enjoy life to the last bottle of champagne." As she soon discovered, Randolph had a dangerous knack of always finding one more bottle.

Almost everything in Randolph's nature made him unfit him for matrimony. He was wayward, spoiled, pigheaded, drunken, lecherous, and touchingly naive. Thus the matrimonial scales were weighted heavily against him from the start. What weighted them still further was the way his family, while all too well aware of his failings, warmed to his unspoiled, charming bride. Churchill was particularly enthusiastic.

As one of Randolph's friends remembers, "Pam was not particularly beautiful or witty, but she already had an extraordinary talent for making gentlemen of all ages happy." This very much included Churchill. She played bezique with him, called him Papa, laughed at his jokes, and listened to his stories.

Randolph meanwhile was off to join his regiment. But instead of being sent abroad, he stayed in camp in Northern England, where Pamela joined him. Life as Randolph's wife on a captain's pay soon proved a sobering experience. Still, Randolph did his duty to the dynasty, and when Pamela found that she was pregnant everyone was thrilled, Churchill especially. This was the precious grandchild who would bear the Churchill name—and during the months before its birth, Churchill would seize this final chance, for which he had waited all his life, to inscribe the Churchill name in history.

Britain's failure to keep Hitler from invading Norway early in May 1940 sealed the political fate of Neville Chamberlain. Churchill attempted to defend him in debate, but it was Leo Amery (once Churchill's victim in the school swimming pool at Harrow) who repeated Cromwell's dramatic words against their leader in the House of Commons: "In the name of God, go!"

Knowing he had lost all credibility, Chamberlain took Amery's advice and resigned, recommending that the King appoint Churchill his successor. On the morning of May 10, Hitler's armies invaded France and Belgium. That same evening, Churchill was Prime Minister and began to form the coalition government which he would lead until war with Germany was over.

What did it mean to this power-haunted, doom-obsessed orator —who, for ten long years, had nursed his dreadful vision of his nation's fate—to be summoned by events to that "supreme office of State" of which he had dreamed all his adult life?

He made no bones about the sense of exaltation that swept over him despite the gloom and grimness of the situation. This was the position that his father failed to achieve, the culmination of a lifetime's unyielding ambition. As he put it, "I felt as if I were walking with destiny and that all my past life had been a preparation for this hour and this trial."

As so often in the past, the prospect of waging full-scale war aroused his remarkable powers of aggression, and banished any lingering anxieties.

Savrola was now in his middle sixties, but Churchill had changed little from the romantic hero of the novel he wrote at twenty-five. He had always relished awesome situations where he could play the war-like savior. At Antwerp, he had thrust himself into the role of defender of the stricken city; at Gallipoli, his master plan was meant to alleviate the hideous bloodshed of the Somme; and almost single-handed he had tried to overturn the Russian Revolution. All had failed, and he had sought consolation in history. Napoleon's bust was still before him on his desk, but it was Marlborough who offered him his greatest inspiration.

Now, as France was falling and Britain stood alone against another European tyrant, Churchill, like Marlborough, was presented with the greatest role within the repertoire.

Even his age was in his favor now, making him seem a father of the people as he made his famous wartime speeches to the nation. Here he was in his element, offering beleaguered Britain a nostalgic vision of itself from his own embattled view of history. At the climax of his greatest speech as France was falling, as he offered the population "blood sweat toil and tears," he was in fact echoing the rallying cry of one of his military heroes, the indomitable nationalist and general, Giuseppe Garibaldi, who, in the battles to unite Italy, had told the gallant remnants of his own defeated army, "I offer neither pay nor quarters nor provisions; I offer hunger, thirst, forced marches, battles, death."

"To move his people the orator must first be moved himself," the youthful Churchill wrote in his "Scaffolding of Rhetoric." Now, on the edge of national disaster, he had assumed a role like Garibaldi's, and, by rhetoric, was trying to inspire the people with the call of battle.

Not everyone responded. "Rallied the nation indeed!" wrote Evelyn Waugh. "I was a serving soldier in 1940. How we despised his orations!"

Yet for the majority, particularly for those at home, Churchill's heroic vision of the moment worked magnificently. As France's defenses crumbled, the remnants of Britain's army limped back from Dunkirk. In the air, the Battle of Britain started and invasion threatened. Britain was weak and isolated now against an overwhelming enemy. But throughout these awful weeks Churchill's was the voice that offered courage to the people, refusing Hitler's overtures of peace and making a national disaster appear as one of the great heroic moments in the nation's history.

Thus did an eccentric aristocrat/historian, who never traveled on a bus and who was lost without the daily ministrations of his valet, briefly unite all classes against an evil enemy. Thus did he also make himself the symbol and expression of their will to fight.

But Churchill's wartime leadership did not rest entirely on speeches and the projection of his personality. It was his human limitations almost as much as his superhuman strengths that had conspired to outfit him for the warlike power he wielded.

The strengths were obvious: great physical endurance, sustained capacity of will, and powers of total concentration that even in his late sixties made him unique among the politicians of his day. So did his less admirable qualities. There was that driving egotism, for instance; it endowed him with a massive certainty about himself and a refusal to endure any who opposed him. As he put it, "All I wanted was compliance with my wishes after reasonable discussion." There was the aggression in his makeup, which would emerge whenever he was "up" or thwarted. There was the simple schoolboy's love of battle. And there remained the iron in his soul, forged to withstand those periods of despair when misery and deep depression had assailed him.

He was perfectly prepared to charm or bully all those around him to maintain her ascendancy. He could even arouse great loyalty from those he treated badly. Yet when necessary, he could still out-argue anyone who dared to go against him.

It was Lady Goonie who had first described him as "a pasha" for the way he imposed his will upon his underlings. "A secretary is as essential to him as a fountain pen," one of his former private secretaries remarked, and he treated them accordingly. More than ever, he was both a workaholic and intensely organized. Only with such qualities was he able to assume the role of effortless dictator.

But there would always be one crucial difference between Churchill and all the Marlboroughs, Napoleons, and Nelsons who inspired him: They were commanders in the field whose power and fame had come, in the words of Chairman Mao, "through the barrel of a gun." Churchill's had not. However powerfully he roused himself to the dreadful drama of the clash of arms, his power resided in the written and the spoken word.

He was, essentially, an amateur of battle. Yet such was the force with which he acted the role of great war leader, such was the conviction he conveyed, that he virtually became the role he created, and he was swiftly in an unassailable position. His leadership appeared the only credible alternative to domination by "that doom-laden, haunted, evil man," Adolf Hitler. No general or politician could gainsay him the ultimate authority for waging war.

In theory, Churchill was the loyalest, most deferential of King George VI's subjects, "the last believer in the Divine Right of Kings," as Clementine had called him during the abdication crisis. He knew that both the King and Queen would have preferred tame Lord Halifax as premier and once in power, he deployed his impressive battery of charm and courtliness to woo the royal couple and finally efface their lingering distrust of the former champion and ally of the Duke of Windsor.

This task brought out all his reverence for the monarchy; few Prime Ministers had ever been more scrupulous than Churchill in attendance on the sovereign. Yet the truth was that it was Churchill, and not the uninspiring, nervous George VI, who became the essential royal presence during this time of war. George did his duty, but Churchill ruled—with the unself-conscious power of a medieval monarch, directing armies, dismissing and promoting generals, relying on a carefully selected group of favorites to do his bidding, and jealously preventing any overmighty subject from eclipsing him.

He had the presence and the dignity of royalty in his person. While the King, paradoxically, exhibited all the sober virtues of a conscientious citizen, "doing his bit" for the war effort with his middle-class family around him, Churchill was increasingly displaying the age-old habits and activities of an autocratic monarch.

George tried to make himself and his family subsist on the food rations of an ordinary subject, but Churchill had no time for such pretense. "This war will be won by carnivores," he growled, and thanks to extra "diplomatic" rations, Clementine was able to ensure that her cook, Mrs. Landemare, always provided the leader of the nation with the provender he needed.

George personally painted a line around the inside of the royal bathtub at Windsor to ensure that precious fuel was saved by using only a mere five inches of hot water. Churchill was so insistent on his daily bath that according to his nephew, Peregrine, Lindemann spent much time and energy designing a system of heavy-duty batteries so as to ensure that even in a power-outage Churchill could have his full hot evening bath at *Chequers,* the Prime Minister's official country residence in Buckinghamshire.

Churchill's appetite for food and drink were regal—so was his love of uniforms and fancy headgear. His journeys through the kingdom in his special train could become like royal progression, his foreign trips had many of the trappings of the voyages of potentates, and even his everyday routines had echoes of the way great kings had once conducted the affairs of state.

As a subaltern in India, one of the seminal books he studied, along with Gibbon and Macaulay, was the Duc de St. Simon's memoirs of life at the court of Louis XIV.

Now, like the King of France, he had developed the habit of dispatching much of the day's business by dictating every morning to his secretaries as he sat in bed. Like Louis, he would arise around midday, then meet generals, ministers, and visiting celebrities at meals with members of his family. He also used, to great effect, the haughty technique of making those of whom he disapproved wait upon his favor, often to very late at night.

When Clementine referred to Churchill's belief in the divine right of kings, she spoke truer than she probably suspected. Effectively the wartime king of England, Churchill certainly believed that he possessed some supernatural backing to the power he wielded.

This lay in the strange philosophy of life that this agnostic pessimist had carefully constructed to convince himself that he was "chosen" for the exercise of power—the one abiding satisfaction of his driven nature. Natural gambler that he was, he based this belief upon the enormous odds that had always seemed so firmly stacked against him. In the past, whenever he survived a bullet or a bomb, this faith was strengthened. Now that he had also managed to survive the even greater odds of political disaster to be called upon to lead the nation at its greatest crisis, what further proof was needed?

"There has to be a purpose to it all," he told his secretary Jock Colville. And when the war was almost over, he assured Lord Moran, "I believe that I was chosen for a purpose far beyond our simple reasoning."

A regal sense of power with a supernatural sanction is a potent combination, and Churchill as a warlike leader was formidable—to friends and allies almost as much as to his enemies.

## twenty-six

# Family at War

In the autumn of 1940, *Picture Post* commissioned Cecil Beaton to take some photographs of Clementine to accompany an article, and shortly after taking them he also photographed the Prime Minister himself, enthroned in solitary majesty in the Cabinet Room, looking "immaculately distinguishedly porcine, with pink bladder wax complexion and a vast cigar freshly affixed to his chin."

Beaton promised to let Churchill see the proofs for his approval, and by the time he brought them back to Downing Street, *Picture Post* had published the photographs of Clementine. They were not particularly flattering, and a candid friend had told her that they made her look "like a hard-bitten virago who takes drugs."

Clementine was painfully upset, and no sooner was the favorite photographer of royalty inside Number Ten than he found himself assailed by the wife of the Prime Minister at the epicenter of one of her celebrated rages. Accusing Beaton of all manner of deception and betrayal, she was soon in a state of near hysteria, face flushed and eyes awash with tears.

But her rage went as swiftly as it came, and Beaton was left with a pathetic, middle-aged woman on his hands.

"Really it's too damnable," she wailed. "It isn't as if my life has been too easy. It hasn't—but when I married Winston, he loved me."

Beaton took her hand, insisting, "But he *still* does. We all know that!" She wept more uncontrollably than ever. The photographer, unaccustomed to consoling great men's wives, felt obliged to kiss her on the forehead and held grimly to her hand. This still had no effect, and instead of "coming round," she proceeded to sob out an extraordinary confession.

"I don't know why it is, but I suppose my friends are not exactly jealous, but they think that other people could do the job better and that I shouldn't have been married to Winston. After all, he is one of the most important people in the world. In fact, he and Hitler and President Roosevelt are the most important people in the world today."

Beaton felt the situation getting out of hand, and that the time had come to make Churchill's wife "behave with more dignity" rather than offer any more disclosures. So he swiftly changed the subject to his pictures of her husband. She recovered her composure, said she liked them, and Beaton managed to effect his exit.

Tactfully, Beaton sent a bouquet of orchids and roses to Downing Street, and received an "affectionate telegram" from Clementine in return. His pictures of Churchill were published in the press in time for Christmas and proved a considerable success.

But Beaton's strange encounter with Clementine lingers in the mind like a candid photograph of one of the few occasions when the public image slipped, revealing the anxieties that afflicted her in her relations with her husband in his "finest hour."

With his attention focused on the war, Churchill could not have had much time to demonstrate affection, but one wonders if he was ever seriously interested in the sort of deep romantic love Clementine evidently wanted. He had consistently written her romantic, sentimental letters when they were apart, but letters, like speeches, were his stock in trade, and literary love is not necessarily the real thing. Nor was the loving dependence he had always shown for Clementine in times when he was "down"—he had shown the same for Mrs. Everest and Jennie.

He had been frequently "down" throughout the thirties, and Clementine had not always given him the support and constancy he needed. There had been her nervous absences, her separate life in London, her love for Terence Philip, and her permanent dislike of Chartwell. Unlike Randolph, she had not maintained blind faith that Churchill's hour would come. On the contrary, she had often tried to make him face reality, dispose of Chartwell, accept the fact that he would almost certainly not return to power so late in life, and settle for writing books in benign old age instead.

Now this had changed abruptly. History—and Hitler—had dramatically disproved all Clementine's sensible advice and wifely doubts. Her husband, against all odds, had scaled the "great and commanding position in this country" that she had once predicted for him. But much had happened to their marriage in the interim. Now that he was challenged by his "walk with destiny," there was much loneliness in Clementine's position.

Having achieved the greatness he had always dreamed of, Churchill had little need of wifely consolation. What he required was a semi-regal consort, someone able to act a public role beside his own and ensure that his private life proceeded with the pashalike efficiency he wanted. Neither task was easy for Clementine. Nervous and insecure as ever, she was haunted by those feelings of inadequacy and guilt that she had blurted out to Beaton.

Apart from Mary, she still had little closeness with her children. Earnest and overwhelmed by a realization of her husband's extraordinary importance, this lonely woman did her best to act the great man's wife—and did it with immense determination.

There were some bumpy moments at the beginning, for she could be rough with underlings when she felt her dignity impugned. For example, Churchill's private secretary, Jock Colville, found her "abusive" when he took the liberty of giving instructions to her secretary, the admirable Grace Hamblin, brought over from Chartwell.

"Mrs. C. considers it one of her missions in life to put people in their place and prides herself on being outspoken," he recorded grimly in his diary. (Later, it is only fair to add, he became one of her great admirers.)

Nor was it only private secretaries she put in their place. Her daughter Mary described a luncheon party at 10 Downing Street shortly after the collapse of France, when Clementine turned upon no less a figure than Gen. Charles de Gaulle: The British, acting on Churchill's orders, feared that the large French battle fleet in North Africa might be taken over by the Germans. On July 3, the British fleet, having failed to persuade the French fleet in the harbor of Oran to join them, had opened fire, sinking three French battleships and killing more than a thousand Frenchmen. During the lunch that took place at Downing Street shortly after, someone tactlessly asked de Gaulle whether the remainder of the French fleet would join the Allies, bringing the swift rejoinder from the general that what the French navy would probably like to do would be to turn their guns upon the British.

It was a remark to be diplomatically ignored, which Churchill did, but Clementine turned on de Gaulle; in the schoolgirl French she picked up in Dieppe—and liked to show off when she had the chance—Clementine treated him much as she treated Colville, saying that his words "ill became either an ally or a guest."

The general must have realized he had met his match in Clementine. He apologized profusely, and the next morning Clementine received a bunch of flowers even larger than those she had had from Beaton.

Around this time she also felt obliged to lecture Churchill in writing on what she called his "rough, sarcastic and overbearing manner" to colleagues and subordinates. She suggested that with "the terrific power" he possessed, he should "combine urbanity, kindness and if possible Olympic [sic] calm." This was valuable advice, which only Clementine could give her husband—how much effect it had on Churchill is another matter. It is an interesting reflection on the marriage that even such wifely counsel could only be entrusted to a letter.

What all this makes clear is that, whatever fears she may have had about her husband's love and her own abilities, this vulnerable woman was learning to adopt a role to match his own.

Despite Beaton's photographs, her looks were perfect for the part, and so was her manner. Unlike Churchill, she maintained genuine rapport with ordinary people, taking much trouble to visit working-class Londoners when German air raids started at the end of 1940. (It was partly thanks to her visits to Londoners sheltering nightly from the blitz in extreme discomfort in the London Underground that their crowded conditions were improved.) She launched aircraft carriers, sponsored homes for nursing mothers, acted as patron for important wartime charities, and performed her self-imposed duties with dedication.

Pursuing what she saw to be her duty, she was the most selfless of patriotic figureheads; yet the same could not be said of the other members of her family. Since she felt a moral obligation to correct them, this caused problems.

The most glaring case of all was one that not even Clementine could do anything about. Within weeks of taking power, Churchill himself had had to face an uncomfortable conundrum: What to do about Clementine's fascist relatives, the Mosleys.

"A modern prince, taking his inheritance for granted." The twenty-first birthday portrait of Randolph Churchill by Sir Philip Laszlo.

Diana with her first husband, John Bailey. Later she told her daughter that she married chiefly to escape the endless talk at the Chartwell dinner table. The marriage lasted barely a year.

"A woman like you could be a whole world to a man," said Trotsky of Churchill's romantic cousin, Clare Sheridan. Here she is seen with her children.

15

16

Churchill's least favorite son-in-law—the Austro-American comedian Vic Oliver, with his wife Sarah (right) and Phyllis Luckett, the young actress the Svengali-like comedian wished them to adopt.

The Cecil Beaton picture that brought Clementine to a state of "near hysteria" when a friend told her that it made her look "like a hard-bitten virago who takes drugs."

18

Pamela Churchill with Winston Churchill junior
in 1943 when her marriage was already under
strain. When she reminded Randolph that
Winston was her son, her husband bellowed,
"No! My son. I'm a Churchill."

19

The U.S. President's personal representative, Averell Harriman, the British
Foreign Secretary, Anthony Eden, and the U.S. Ambassador to Britain, John
"Gil" Winant. All three would be romantically involved with members of the
Churchill family.

20

Churchill and Clementine may have been hoping that their daughter Mary would wed a prince, but her marriage to Captain Christopher Soames in 1947 brought a key new personality into the family.

Sarah with her second husband, Anthony Beauchamp, shortly after their marriage at Sea Island, Georgia, in 1949. "If you think that by insulting him you can change by one jot the opinion I hold of him—you are most sorely mistaken," she had told her father.

21

Churchill, "at peace within his habitation," in the Chartwell garden surrounded by three generations of his family. (From left to right) Duncan Sandys with his wife, Diana, and their son, Julian; the two eldest Soames children, Emma and Nicholas; then Winston Churchill, Jr., and Clementine with his sister, Arabella, and their father, Randolph.

23

Onassis drives Sir Winston. The Greek multimillionaire became Churchill's favorite host in his eighties, and for Onassis, Churchill was "the big fish" who added immensely to his prestige.

"I'm not an alcoholic. I'm a dipsomaniac. I love the stuff," said Sarah, seen here outside her favorite bar in Rome in the 1960s.

In adversity the dynasty continues. Shortly before his dismissal from his post as Opposition spokesman on defence in 1979, young Winston Churchill and his wife, Minnie, stand with their son, Randolph, before the Parliament Square statue of Sir Winston.

In strictly practical terms, it was hard to think that Diana Mosley or her husband posed a real threat to the safety of the realm. Diana was nursing a four-week-old baby and was preoccupied with her sister Unity.

When war broke out, conflict between Britain and her beloved Gemany was more than Unity could bear. She had tried to kill herself but bungled the attempt. On Hitler's orders, she was returned to Britain, via Switzerland, and was now surviving, brain-damaged, with nothing left to live for. She had become a pathetic victim of the man she had worshiped. Diana helped look after her.

Oswald Mosley was even less of a menace than his wife. Once a close associate of Churchill and member of the Other Club, he had been a guest at Randolph's famous twenty-first birthday dinner at Claridges and had supported Churchill's calls for British rearmament. His true hero had been Mussolini—"the most interesting man in Europe," he once called him. His brief involvement with Hitler was solely through his wife, and he seems to have genuinely disliked him. Now in his late forties, and in uncertain health, Mosley had attempted, unsuccessfully but with total seriousness, to reenlist in his old regiment in order to defend the Empire.

All of this, however, was totally beside the point—particularly for a new Prime Minister rallying his country in a struggle for existence. As Mosley's biographer writes, "an extraordinary and typically British feature of the situation was that the Mosleys, Churchills, and other leading personalities in this drama, all came from a tiny social and political class [who] knew each other well, had stayed in each others' houses and shared the same life-style."

This could have made Churchill—and "this tiny social and political class"—highly vulnerable had there been a hint of favored treatment for his relatives and friends. There was also the uncomfortable fact that, at that very moment, the swift collapse of Western Europe to the Germans was being helped by a Fifth Column of fascist and pro-German elements within each country.

The Mosleys might profess their patriotism—fascists like Pierre Laval and Vidkun Quisling did the same in France and Norway, respectively—to excuse their collaboration with the Nazis. But the fact remained that Sir Oswald Mosley was the leader of the principal fascist organization in Britain, and his wife was known not merely as an old admirer of Nazi Germany but as a close and valued friend of the archfiend Adolf Hitler. She had actually met with him for the last time at Bayreuth on the very eve of war in August 1939, when he told her he was perfectly convinced that Britain would honor its treaty obligations and go to war if he invaded Poland.

But there did remain a human problem for the Churchills. Whatever motives lay behind her close relationship with many of the leading Nazis, Diana Mosley had been perfectly within her rights to visit Hitler in Berlin in time of peace—just as Churchill's cousin Clare Sheridan had been when she got to know the leading Bolsheviks in Moscow back in 1922. And as with Cousin Clare, Churchill had had a particularly soft spot for his adoring "Dynamite," as he called Diana in the days when she had been a favored guest at Chartwell. Indeed, her fatal path to Munich and Berlin may well have started at the Churchill dinner table, when she had first picked up her taste for dominating statesmen and expensive claret.

Her shadowy portrait, in a large, half-finished painting by Churchill himself of the family at dinner, was still at Chartwell. Randolph had never ceased to love her, even after she married Mosley. And Churchill, though perfectly aware of the full extent of her contacts with the leading Nazis, had felt no need to warn her of the potential consequences. (Indeed, as we have seen, he used her as a source of information on the Führer when she lunched with the Churchill family in 1936.)

But if Churchill felt pity or responsibility for someone who had been so close to him and to his family, he could not show it; for the Mosleys were passionately hated, not only among the parties of the Left, on whom Churchill was relying for the unity of his coalition government, but also by many on the Right, who had envied them their looks and wealth and past success in Germany and Italy and saw them as useful scapegoats for their own pro-Nazi or pro-fascist sympathies. In Diana's own words, she and her husband had become "untouchable," and within a month of Churchill taking power, both were arrested on his ultimate authority.

No charges could be brought against them, for they had done nothing illegal. Despite this, both were imprisoned under the Emergency Regulations in conditions of considerable hardship and among convicted criminals—Mosley at Brixton and Diana in a lice-infested and unsanitary basement cell in the women's jail at Holloway. She was also parted from her four-week-old son, Alexander.

The treatment of the Mosleys brought something of a split within the family. According to Colville's diaries, news of their plight produced "much merriment" between Sarah and her sister Diana, who presumably felt their fascist relatives had received their just deserts. But faithful Randolph almost instantly attempted to obtain improved conditions for them. According to Colville, family-loving Winston was "piqued" to hear of the state that they were in, but paradoxically, it was the very closeness of their relationship that made it difficult for him to help them. Any change was certain to be picked up in the press, and favoritism to friends of Hitler who were relations of the Churchills could have been politically disastrous.

With hindsight, Lady Mosley herself makes an interesting point about her situation at the time with her cousin Winston, "Of course, it was extremely difficult for him," she says, "and without trying to be at all conceited, the closest parallel I can think of was with the way that George V felt obliged to cut off totally from Lord Mountbatten's father, the German Prince Louis of Battenburg, because of the anti-German outcry at the beginning of the first world war."

There was one concession Randolph was able to obtain for Diana through his father. The one thing that thoroughly disturbed him was the news that a female member of the upper classes was unable to take her daily bath, and an order came to Holloway that Lady Mosley was to have this privilege. It was, she says, "a kindly thought of Winston's," but as there was insufficient water and only two "degraded bathrooms" in the entire prison wing, this was one wartime order Churchill issued that could not be observed.

Clementine seems to have remained implacable about the Mosleys' fate—even as late as 1943 when her cousin Lady Redesdale (who had been her bridesmaid when she married Churchill) asked her help in securing the release of her daughter and her son-in-law, whose health was causing some anxiety. Lady Redesdale was the original of the eccentric "Muv" in her daughter Nancy Mitford's novels, and the meeting of the two extremely strong-willed cousins was distinctly frosty, with Clementine apparently "irritating" Muv "beyond measure" by assuring her that "Winston has always been so fond of Diana" and adding that the Mosleys were probably better off in prison than they would have been facing anti-German patriots outside.

In 1940, there could have been some truth in this, but by 1943, feeling against the Mosleys had subsided, along with the threat of enemy invasion, and in fact, the Mosleys were released shortly after. Whether or not Clementine played any part in this remains unclear but is most improbable.

The Mosleys spent the rest of the war quietly in the country, then departed for a house they bought not far from Paris called La Temple de la Gloire. Neither Clementine nor Churchill saw either of them again, but Randolph and Lady Mosley, picked up their friendship when the war was over.

The best example of Clementine's sharp concern that her family set a good example—not to speak of the queenly way with which she managed to enforce it—came at the beginning of an invasion scare in 1940. Many children were already being sent to Canada in an attempt to save them from the war. Someone suggested that the two princesses, Elizabeth and Margaret Rose, should go as well, bringing the swift retort from Queen Elizabeth that, whatever the danger, her place was always with the King, and that she would not be parted from her daughters.

Simultaneously came the news that, despite the royal example, a Churchill child—nephew Johnny's five-year-old daughter Sally—was on the point of being shipped to friends in Canada. This would never do. With the royal children bravely staying put how could a Churchill, even a five-year-old, think of quitting?

Through Clementine's direct intervention with the Foreign Office, Sally's passport was canceled and, as the child was just about to leave, an official was dispatched, on Clementine's authority, to stop her boarding the boat train to Southampton. There were tears and inevitable publicity—the gist of which was that the Churchill children, like the royal family, were staying put before the enemy.

There was a curious postscript to this incident. Churchill had emphatically agreed with Clementine and was deeply touched by the publication in the *Times* of an anonymous letter from an eleven-year-old schoolboy, begging his parents not to send him off to Canada. The patriotic child insisted he would rather run the risk of death in Britain than miss the chance of witnessing his country's finest hour.

Here was a true Churchillian, and so moved was Churchill that an eleven-year-old should pen such noble sentiments that he insisted the child be found. After considerable efforts by his secretariat, he was, and Churchill personally inscribed one of his own books and sent it by special messenger to David Wedgwood Benn, brother of the future Labour Cabinet minister and left-wing activist, Tony Benn.

Happily for Churchill, his own son and heir was just as patriotic. Despite their bitter fights and Randolph's drunkenness, gambling debts, sexual escapades, social and electoral disasters, arrogance, and sloth, he had remained the loyalest of sons to his embattled father.

A devoted heir is a boon to any monarch, especially one with a sense of dynasty as strong as Churchill's, so when the old man came into his kingdom in 1940, Randolph was in a strong position. From the beginning this caused problems.

Clementine, for one, could not abide her son's influence upon her husband—a feeling shared by many in Churchill's entourage. The difficulties Jock Colville first encountered with Clementine were nothing compared with the outright shock and horror he experienced on coming face to face with her son.

"One of the most objectionable people I have ever met; noisy, self-assertive, whining, and frankly unpleasant" was what Colville wrote in his diary after his first encounter with Randolph. There was more to follow during the heroic summer months of 1940, including a celebrated dinner held at 10 Downing Street in June for members of the general staff. Randolph shared his father's visceral contempt for the generals of World War I, and well primed with parental whisky, he was soon holding forth on the inefficiency, complacency, and lack of warlike spirit in high places. During another uproar with the military, this newly enlisted young officer was heard bellowing: "But general, I was not accusing you *personally* of cowardice. . . . "

Such incidents explain why Randolph never had a hope of playing Pitt the Younger to the great wartime Prime Minister—or of even enjoying the preferment his father could so easily have given him. Churchill had nothing against nepotism. (Quite the contrary; old allies like Lindemann and Brendan Bracken would be promoted to the House of Lords.) And, indeed, Randolph continued in his strange position near the throne—unemployable and unpromotable but somehow necessary to his father's peace of mind.

One thing that Churchill's vast new reputation won for Randolph was the seat in Parliament that he had struggled to secure on his merits. A vacancy occurred for the constituency of Preston, and since elections had been discontinued with the war, Randolph was nominated by the local Tories. This was done solely as a loyal tribute to his father, and he took his seat for Preston unopposed in September 1940.

This was an emotional moment for them both—and particularly for Churchill. He had once dreamed of taking his seat in Parliament beside Lord Randolph; now the succession was continuing in the flesh. When Randolph made his maiden speech, Churchill made a point of being present, but he kept his back to him throughout for fear of showing his emotion.

Soon afterward, Churchill was able to enjoy an even more important moment for his precious dynasty for which Randolph *was* responsible. At Chequers, on October 10, 1940, Pamela was safely delivered of a boy.

During her pregnancy, as bearer of the great white hope of the Churchills, Pamela finally had been confirmed as a sort of favored daughter and accepted as a total member of the family—as neither Duncan Sandys nor the unfortunate Vic Oliver had ever been. While Randolph was training with his regiment, Pamela lived with the family at Downing Street, was often included in official dinner parties, and became a real favorite of her new "Papa." When the air raids started, she even slept in the bunk bed beneath him in the former wine cellar in nearby Storeys Gate, which had been converted into a shelter for the Churchill family.

Clementine, as always, had insisted on an adjacent, single-bedded room. This meant that poor Pamela was regularly awakened by her father-in-law when he rolled into his bunk around 1:30—and was kept awake by his heavy snoring through the night.

Pamela makes the point that, during this period before her child was born, she still regarded Churchill not as a great world figure but as a very busy but devoted paterfamilias. "As far as I was concerned," she said, "he was primarily someone who loved his family, and who was very kind to me, so that it seemed quite natural to be living in his house. It was only gradually I realised I was also living in the presence of history."

One thing she had seen, during the invasion scare that autumn, was Churchill's aggressiveness and private relish for the threat of battle. In Clementine's presence she asked him what they could do if the Germans came.

"Well, you can both take one dead German with you," he replied.

"But how could we do that without a gun?" said Pamela.

"My dear," said Churchill with complete seriousness, "you would both go into the kitchen and arm yourselves with carving knives." (At this very moment, Churchill had just devised the motto "Take one with you!" to inspire the defenders.)

Almost simultaneously Pamela also received her first hint of the importance Churchill was now giving to his place in history—and to the continuation of his name within the Churchill dynasty.

Somewhat late in life, Bert Marlborough's long-suffering wife,

Duchess Mary, had just produced a second son. With grown-up children (Lady Sarah was working in a factory in Oxford, and the heir, Lord Blandford, was at Eton), Bert professed to be both shocked and baffled by this late-in-life pregnancy, but the Duchess was delighted. And despite the fact that the Battle of Britain was occurring in the skies of southern Britain, she was determined this latest child should have a traditional christening at Blenheim.

One of the guests, Diana Cooper, wrote in her diary of "champagne and tenantry on the lawns and nannies and cousins and healths drunk, all to the deafening accompaniment of aeroplanes skirmishing, diving, looping and spinning" in the sky above. She also described the baby as being "godmothered by Clemmie Churchill looking most radiant and gay." But the most interesting entry in her diary is the name this "Ducal Marlborough baby" was given at its christening. To go with the splendid christening, the Duchess had proudly picked the name of the most celebrated member of the family: Winston Spencer-Churchill.

It must have caused a fearful upset when Clementine relayed the news to her husband on her return to Downing Street.

According to Pamela, Churchill had already set his heart on passing on his name to her unborn baby. He had been taking it for granted that his grandchild would be a boy and was determined it should bear the name of Winston Churchill. So was Pamela, who was apparently in tears of disappointment, not anticipating the strain she might be placing on her son to live up to the greatest name in Britain. (Had she realized, she says that she would almost certainly not have given her assent.)

As it was, Churchill was incensed at the thwarting of his plans, and was instantly on the telephone to Blenheim. The name Winston Churchill, he insisted to the Duchess, belonged to him, and he was determined to pass it on to his grandson.

"But how does Pamela know that hers will be a boy?" the Duchess asked.

"Of course it will be. And if it isn't there'll be others."

Only Churchill could have made a duchess change her child's name after it had been officially registered and christened. But it was obviously so important to him at this historic moment that the Duchess finally agreed. The child became Lord Charles Spencer-Churchill (a name which he insists he is very happy with), and when Pamela duly produced the son the family was counting on, the greatest name in British politics was awaiting it.

The christening, held in the nearby church at Chequers, made clear the depth of feeling Churchill was attaching to the dynasty, the family, and to this child who would bear his name after he was dead. He sat throughout the ceremony with tears streaming down his cheeks.

"Poor infant," he said finally, "to have been born into such a world as this."

# twenty-seven

# Poor Randolph

For eighteen-year-old Mary Churchill, 1940 ended with what she recorded in her diary as "One of the happiest Christmases I can remember."

She had recently left school, and her tomboy, pony-loving phase was over, leaving her a credit to the secure and straightforward upbringing given her by Cousin Moppett Whyte. She was fresh-faced, blue-eyed, serious, and good, with none of those hang-ups for one or the other of her parents that plagued her siblings. She loved them both with total and uncomplicated dedication. "She has," wrote Colville of her now, "a naive and rather charming adoration for everything connected with her family"—"except Randolph," he added in discreet parenthesis.

In this Mary was evidently echoing her mother's feelings about Randolph as a source of worry and disruption to the family. But that Christmas even Randolph was basking in the family's approval as he brought his pretty wife and eight-week-old son to Chequers for the Christmastide reunion.

This was a family occasion like the Chartwell Christmases of years past, the only outsiders being the duty clerk, John Martin, and that sere Chartwell regular Professor Lindemann. (He was the only one of the Churchill cronies Clementine would have asked to the festivities:

He neither drank nor gambled, and even in the middle of the war he managed to bring his usual expensive Christmas presents.)

Sarah brought her husband, suave Vic Oliver who had decided to stay on in England and who was finding fame and fortune as a highly popular wartime stage comedian. ("Much the most courteous member of the family," Lady Goonie once remarked about him, "and the only one you could count on always to open a door for a lady.")

Diana, still working in London with the W.R.N.S., came with her two young children, Julian and Edwina, and her husband, Duncan Sandys, who, in addition to remaining an M.P., was now on active service with the Royal Artillery. Moppett Whyte, the linchpin of the family, was also present.

But the happiness that marked the second Christmas of the war came from the very center of the family. During the years before the war, Christmas had always brought brief moments of relief from the frustration and bitterness that never ceased tormenting Churchill while he was out of office. But now, unchallenged in supreme authority, with a great war on his hands, Churchill was a happy man. During the summer of 1940, when he had been one of those who knew how little stood between invasion and defeat, he had awakened every morning with a sense of imminent disaster. But Britain had survived, and so had he.

His only cares now were heroic ones, and he greeted each morning feeling, as he said, "as if he had a bottle of champagne inside him and was glad that another day had come." With an official salary of £10,750, and both 10 Downing Street and Chequers staffed and provided by the state, he had no money worries, no problems with the servants, no sense of the encroaching doom he was powerless to fight.

He possessed power and was in the great position he had dreamed of all his life. None could contradict him, the country was united around him, and he was fully in command against the evil powers that he felt were threatening the nation.

In the air, the Battle of Britain had been fought and won. Hitler had missed his opportunity to invade across the English Channel, and the first stage of war in North Africa had ended with the Italian army in mass surrender.

Although the German blitz against London was reaching its crescendo, Churchill's prewar nightmare of widespread panic and more than a million casualties from German bombs had not occurred. "London could take it," and already the R.A.F. was beginning to retaliate against German cities, but neither side had sent its bombers out on Christmas Eve. Before leaving London, Churchill had chosen and dispatched his personal presents to King George VI and Queen Elizabeth. The King received one of the famous "siren suits" (ideal to slip on when the air-raid siren sounded) that Churchill had devised himself— a sort of one-piece romper suit for adults in dark blue velvet. For Elizabeth he chose that invaluable guide to sound English, Fowler's *English Usage*. His staff made do with his greetings for "a busy Christmas and a frantic new year" and a suggestion that they go to church on Christmas day.

He did not go himself, but worked all morning. In the evening, the Churchills dined off a gigantic turkey, sent on behalf of his old benefactor Lord Rothermere, who had died a few weeks earlier. He had asked from his deathbed for this gift to go to Churchill. There were also Cox's Orange Pippins, an offering from another leader in an earlier war, the ailing Lloyd George, who sent them from his home at Churt.

Dinner over, it was time for the traditional Churchill Christmas sing-along. The Christmas truce extended to Vic Oliver, who accompanied on the piano. According to John Martin, "the P.M. sang lustily, if not always in tune, and when Vic played Viennese waltzes, he danced a remarkably frisky measure in the middle of the room."

"I have never seen the family look so happy or so united," wrote Mary at the end of that day's diary entry.

But the war that united them would soon be driving them apart. All three married Churchill children would be hit by it, and the first to suffer was the couple who should have been the happiest of all.

Proud of having done his duty by continuing the Churchill line, Randolph sailed off to war in February 1941 with the small 8th Commando group he had joined some months earlier. His destination was Cairo, and he was keen to fight. But for Randolph, war, like peace, had to be conducted like a party. The 8th Commando, a distinctive group of flamboyant misfits, alcoholics, and idle rich, including Evelyn Waugh, a novelist of genius, was the sort of party he enjoyed. He felt very much at home among them.

Pamela, meanwhile, was equally at home with baby Winston in a rented rectory in the country that they had found for £30 a week.

"Oh Randy . . . oh my darling, isn't it rather thrilling. Our home, yours and mine and baby Winston's—our own family life—no more living in other people's houses," she had written.

But as his ship continued around the coast of Africa, Randolph's memories of family togetherness faded. The gambling gene that Clementine believed had helped destroy her mother and her brother Bill was doing much the same for Randolph. It certainly brought him little profit. Aboard ship, Waugh recorded in his diary: "there was very high gambling, poker, roulette, chemin de fer every night. Randolph lost £850 in two evenings."

By the time the ship reached Cape Town he was seriously broke, and after lunching with the South African Prime Minister, his father's old friend Gen. Jan Christian Smuts, he was obliged to cable home for money.

Despite increasing evidence to the contrary, Pamela had been able to convince herself that life with "Randy" could turn out to have a happy ending. Now this conviction left her. In a flash she saw that "if there was going to be any security for baby Winston and me it was going to be on our own."

Some jewelry was sold, and the rectory closed up. Baby Winston was parked with a most unlikely baby-sitter, his godfather and Randolph's erstwhile employer Lord Beaverbrook (who was continuing to pay Randolph his prewar journalist's salary). Pamela, undaunted and alone, set out for wartime London and a £12-a-week job in a ministry. The sheltered English rosebud was about to flower.

Early in 1941, with Britain still beleaguered and America considering joining in the war, the President of the United States dispatched two envoys who would both play crucial roles in the Grand Alliance Churchill had set his heart on forging between Britain and the United States. They would also have an intimate effect upon his family.

One was the former Democratic Governor of Massachusetts, the bushy-browed and idealistic, Lincolnesque look-alike, John "Gil" Winant. The other was a very different character whom Roosevelt had appointed his personal representative in order to expedite the flow of arms to Britain and her Allies, including Russia. This was his old friend and political associate, the coolly patrician Averell Harriman, son of the immensely wealthy railway king E. H. Harriman, creator of the Union Pacific.

"I want you to go over to London and recommend everything that we can do, short of war, to keep the British Isles afloat," Roosevelt had told him.

At fifty, and with all the money and possessions even a very rich

American could want, this twice-married, power-loving sportsman saw in the task the sort of challenge he was looking for.

Naturally, both Americans were received by Churchill and his entourage with open arms. Withdrawn Gil Winant, who, as Churchill's President of the Board of Trade, the socialist Hugh Dalton soon discovered, "improved considerably after a shot or two of good Scotch whisky," swiftly made himself a close and trusted member of the family. He got on particularly well with Clementine, who warmed to the manner and beliefs of this shy and idealistic American Liberal. Unhappily married, and with a wife deposited in far-off Concord, Massachusetts, Winant was soon discovering among the Churchills the sort of surrogate wartime family he needed. Scarcely a week went by without the trusty Gil being invited as a weekend guest to Chequers or to Ditchley Park in Oxfordshire, a perfect eighteenth-century house belonging to the rich Anglo-Americans Ronald and Marietta Tree. Churchill used Ditchley Park as a retreat from the periodic threat of German bombers. Like some eighteenth-century grandee, the Prime Minister always spent his weekends in the country, continuing his work far from the pressures and destruction of the capital.

Harriman was also feted by the family, and particularly by Churchill, who was doing everything he could to woo America. Here was a sympathetic presence who was in close and trusted contact with the U.S. President. Much of the detail and extent of U.S. aid for Britain depended on what Harriman said, but in his case there was neither time nor inclination to develop the same sort of friendship that Winant had with the Churchills. Harriman was far too rich and smart to arouse much sympathy in Clementine, which made the friendship he did strike up with one family member particularly important.

On April 7, 1941, just a few weeks after Harriman's arrival, Jock Colville was up early and, strolling after breakfast in the morning sun down Horse Guards Parade, was intrigued to see "Pamela Churchill and Averell Harriman also examining the devastation."

Harriman was more than old enough to be twenty-year-old Pamela's father, and she would soon be sharing a flat with his daughter Kathleen, who was studying in London. The girls were of an age and got on famously. Despite this, tall, dark Averell was really interested in "the auburn, alluring Pam Churchill," as people were beginning to call her.

"He was the most beautiful man I ever met," she would say nearly forty years later when recalling that far-off London springtime.

"He was marvelous, absolutely marvelous-looking with his raven-black hair. He was really stunning." And according to the opera-loving newspaper proprietor Lord Drogheda, Averell, too, "was mightily smitten by Randolph Churchill's glamorous young wife."

After the *sturm und drang* of life with Randolph, who could blame Pamela enjoying the company of a handsome and devoted older man? Certainly Churchill and senior members of his government, like Lord Beaverbrook and Brendan Bracken, were delighted that the influential Harriman and his daughter Kathleen were so well looked after by this charming member of the Churchill family. When Harriman departed on a brisk, fact-finding visit to the Middle East, it was natural to suggest that good old Randolph entertain this distinguished American just as his little wife was doing back in London.

Since arriving in Cairo, Randolph had failed to find the heroic military life he had set his heart on since the outbreak of the war. Once, in the Oxford Union, he had gallantly proclaimed his eagerness to "Fight for King and Country," but nobody would let him.

Precious Randolph had to be protected—for Churchill felt himself unequal to the sacrifice he was asking of the families of every serviceman and woman in the country. According to Colville, "when Randolph had asked to be allowed some more active part in the war," Churchill remarked that "if Randolph were killed he would not be able to carry on his work."

So it was that, despite his genuine eagerness to fight, something always kept Randolph from the battle zone. Commanding officers were shy of using him, and in early May, when most of his former comrades from the 8th Commando were dispatched to Crete after Greece surrendered, something mysteriously stopped him from going. It was just as well, since most of them were either killed or captured.

Instead, Randolph was promoted to the rank of major and placed in charge of press relations as Staff Officer at G.H.Q., where he swiftly made himself unpopular. Deprived of his chance to prove himself in battle, Randolph returned to his customary diversions of gambling, drunken rows, and fornication. His unpopularity increased with the knowledge that he regularly exploited his privileged contacts with his father.

His criticisms of the commander in chief (which he sent to Churchill in the diplomatic bag) seem to have played a part in Gen. Archibald Wavell's swift departure to become Viceroy of India after the Germans captured Crete in April 1941. Similarly, Randolph's suggestions for a resident British Minister in the Middle East led to Churchill sending out Oliver Lyttleton to the post he created. When Harriman arrived in Cairo to look into how American supplies could be increased, Randolph joined the mission on his father's orders.

The mission was a marked success, and Randolph was soon sharing the enthusiasm of his wife and his father for the handsome East Coast millionaire.

"I have been tremendously impressed by Harriman," he told his father. "In ten very fully and active days he has definitely become my favourite American."

"I found him absolutely charming, & it was lovely to be able to hear so much news of you & all my friends," he wrote in a letter to Pamela at the same time. "He spoke delightfully about you and I fear that I have a serious rival!"

Just as Harriman was leaving for the Middle East, Churchill had been upset to hear that his son-in-law Duncan Sandys had had "a frightful accident." By now he was a colonel, working as Liaison Officer between the Defence Secretariat and Anti-aircraft Command. His driver had fallen asleep while at the wheel during a nighttime drive to Wales, his staff car hit a bridge, and Sandys, who had been sleeping with his shoes off, had both feet crushed and suffered injuries to his back.

Diana, still working with the W.R.N.S., arrived from London just in time to stop the surgeons from amputating both her husband's feet. The accident left him badly crippled and marked the end of his military career—as it did Diana's naval one. From now on he required looking after, and it pleased the devoted Diana to have her husband dependent on her for a change. The marriage improved, and a third child, Celia, was conceived. As for the broken military career of Colonel Sandys, there was, as Churchill wrote to Randolph, "always the House of Commons."

Churchill was powerful enough to indulge in more regal nepotism now. Since Randolph had his unearned seat in Parliament, and Lindemann was basking in the splendor of the peerage as Lord Cherwell, why not make his deserving son-in-law a minister? As soon as Sandys was able to hobble around Westminster with a walking stick, his father-in-law appointed him Under-secretary at the Ministry of Defence, thus starting an important political career for Duncan Sandys.

"What about Vic Oliver for Minister of Information?" somebody shouted in the House when the appointment was announced. But that ministry was occupied already by another of Churchill's faithful friends, Duff Cooper. Besides, the comedian's days within the Churchill family were numbered.

On the surface, Sarah's marriage was a success. She and Vic had bought a large house in the country, and both had been appearing on the London stage. The problems of her husband's nationality had been sorted out, and with his stage appearances, he had become an extremely popular radio celebrity. With success and prosperity around her, Sarah's marriage and career seemed unaffected by the war. Then, in October 1941, during a weekend at Chequers with her parents, Sarah asked her father a most unexpected favor. (It was, she always claimed, the only occasion when she asked him to use his influence on her behalf.)

It must have come as a surprise to Churchill when she suddenly announced that relations with her husband had reached a "breaking point." But far from being particularly upset, Churchill's first concern seemed to be with keeping up appearances.

"I hope he is going to be a gentleman and give you a divorce."

"Of course not, Papa," she said. "I'm leaving him."

This amused him.

"Cheeky bitch!" he said to her. "I wouldn't let you leave me."

"And I'm not asking you for your advice. But you can do me a favour."

It was then that Sarah asked her father to arrange for her to join the ranks of the Women's Auxiliary Air Force as soon as possible. Within twenty-four hours all was settled, and Sarah was Aircraftwoman Second Class Oliver, with her marriage and her stage career effectively behind her.

For the time being there was no question of divorce, as there was no one else she wished to marry, and her relations with Vic were amicable. The rest of the family professed to be puzzled and upset to hear the news—romantic Mary was actually in tears. Sarah later liked to claim that even her father "had become rather fond of Vic by now."

This was, however, not the case; far from being fond of this son-in-law, Churchill himself bore part of the responsibility for the sudden breakup of Sarah's most unusual marriage.

Churchills can be magnanimous to those they defeat, but not to those who have defied them. Churchill never really forgave Oliver for stealing his beloved Sarah. This apart, there was also much about this son-in-law that grated on his nerves—his looks, his particular brand of wise-cracking humor, the outrage he inflicted on the sacred English language, and even his success, which was bringing him more than twice Churchill's salary as Prime Minister.

Churchill's dislike of Oliver clearly did not help the marriage, and although its breakdown had much deeper roots than this, most of them traced back to his influence within the family, particularly over Sarah.

She was always said to be the child who was most like him. She was certainly the only one to have inherited enough of his spirit to have stood up to him and marry the man she loved against his wishes. But despite this, she had firmly remained what she used to call "a father-girl," a woman who had obviously attempted to exchange one father figure for another when she opted for her middle-aged comedian. As a dominating father, Churchill had undoubtedly influenced her choice of husband in another way as well.

Like Randolph—and to a point, Diana, too—Sarah had always been obsessed with fame and with achieving some glittering success that would impress her father. Success on her own terms would also let her face him without being either swamped or bullied. Hence her obsessional longing to become a star even before going on the stage. Oliver had genuinely done his best to make her one. She had come to love the theater; she also loved her fellow actors and would clearly never want for work. But at twenty-seven she was not a star, and it was becoming all too obvious she never would be.

It was this, more than anything, that broke the marriage. She and Vic had both failed—she to become a great actress, he to make her one. Then came the ultimate indignity. Oliver found himself another protégée with whom to play Svengali. Her name was Phyllis Lucket, she was barely twenty, and she looked like Sarah when she married. There was no question of Vic Oliver having an affair with her. He was simply and straightforwardly obsessed with the hidden passion of his life: the creation of a great star from an unknown actress. So single-minded was he that he failed to see why Sarah was upset when he suggested that, since they had no children of their own, they should jointly adopt Phyllis.

It was shortly after this that Sarah decided that her marriage—like her quest for stardom—had no future. She was in something of a vacuum now, with little idea of what could take their place. As she told her father, she was in no hurry for a divorce, and by joining the

W.A.A.F. she intended to postpone making a decision until the war was over.

She seemed lighthearted but Churchill worried over her, as he did with all the family.

When Sarah and Randolph weren't arousing Churchill's parental anxieties, trouble came from the farthest reaches of his extended family. In early 1940, Clementine's nephew, the erratic Giles Romilly, had been captured in Norway while working as a war correspondent for the *Express*.

The Germans failed at first to realize who he was, but when they discovered that he was Churchill's nephew, he was put in isolation as a potential hostage, and then transferred to the top-security camp for very special prisoners of war in the notorious castle of Colditz, where he spent the remainder of the war.

Meanwhile, Giles's brother, Esmond, since fighting with the International Brigade in the Spanish Civil War had migrated to the United States, married his cousin Jessica Mitford, and settled in Washington, D.C. As a dedicated anti-fascist he decided to enlist. Esmond saw no other way to go about this than to go directly to the British Ambassador in Washington to volunteer for flying service with the Canadian Air Force.

"Are you a Communist?" the Ambassador, Lord Lothian, asked Churchill's notorious "Red Nephew."

"Are you?" he responded, one member of the British upper class to another.

By summer 1941, Esmond was on active duty as a navigator with a light bomber squadron stationed in Lincolnshire; at the end of November, his aircraft failed to return from a raid on Hamburg. Jessica was still in the United States, but just about to bring their daughter, Constancia, back to join Esmond in England, when she heard that he was missing.

With Malaya threatened by the Japanese and Singapore about to fall, Churchill had greater claims on his attention than the fate of a nephew who had aroused his deepest disapproval in the past. In Russia, Stalin's armies were fighting for survival, and in just a few days' time, on December 7, 1941, Japanese aircraft were to launch their surprise attack on the U.S. base at Pearl Harbor, which would finally bring the United States into the war.

It was a crucial moment for the Western alliance. Churchill decided that the time had come to confer with his most important ally on the joint conduct of the war, and he sailed aboard the flagship *Duke of York* through the submarine infested North Atlantic to meet the President in Washington.

Jessica was away from Washington when he arrived. Returning shortly after, she was told a secret service detail had come to take her to a service at Arlington church—where Churchill and Roosevelt, comrades in arms at last, would be singing their favorite martial hymns together—so that she could see her famous relative.

"I told them it would have taken more than a carload of cops to get Decca into a church, even with the Prime Minister and the President of the United States," her host remarked. But Jessica was desperate for any news of Esmond. She telephoned the White House, was put through to Mrs. Roosevelt, and fixed an appointment to see Churchill there the next morning.

Clutching eight-month-old Constancia, swaddled in a white wool suit, she was conducted into the great man's presence; as usual, he was doing his morning's work in bed, "and looking absolutely marvelous, like some extravagant peacock in his bright silk dressing gown," embroidered in blue and red with golden dragons.

The troubles of the past forgotten, he greeted her affectionately.

"He was extremely sympathetic from the start, and it turned out that he had made his own inquiries about Esmond. But the worst had happened. He had to tell me that there was not the slightest chance that Esmond had been taken prisoner. His aircraft had come down in the North Sea and there were no survivors. Winston seemed deeply moved."

So moved, in fact, that to cover his emotions he changed the subject and proceeded to give Jessica news of other members of her family, including her sister Diana, who was still in prison but had recently been united with her husband.

Completely unaware of Jessica's feelings on the subject, he assured her that he was doing all he could to make the Mosleys comfortable, even arranging for some of the other prisoners to do their prison chores for them.

"I went into a total rage at this," said Jessica, "servants for the Mosleys when Esmond had just been killed by my sister's precious friends! I told him they should both be put against a wall and shot."

If Churchill was startled by her reaction, he did not show it; instead, he returned to the subject of Esmond Romilly and spoke of his admiration for his hero's death. As she was leaving, his secretary discreetly handed Jessica an envelope. Inside were five hundred dollars.

"Later the rumor went around London that I threw the money back at him," Jessica recalled. "Of course I didn't. Five hundred dollars was a small fortune in those days. But I did feel there was a flavor of blood-money about it, although I'm sure that it was kindly meant. So I gave some of it to my host's daughter to buy a horse, and the rest went to a political campaign."

Before flying back to England, Churchill had a five-day holiday in Florida with one of his oldest friends, Sunny Marlborough's former duchess, the elegantly aging Consuelo, who, since the loss of her two magnificent French houses to the Germans, was sitting out the war with her husband, Jacques Balsan, in considerable luxury in Palm Beach built by her mother.

Churchill needed the break to recharge his batteries after the strain of his visit to the Roosevelts—so much had been at stake. He was sixty-seven. During this historic visit, he had made his famous address to a joint session of Congress, playing up his own American ancestry, and proudly promising that the two great English-speaking peoples would "walk together side by side in majesty, in justice and in peace." He had addressed the Canadian Parliament and signed both the new Grand Alliance against the Axis powers and the pact that led directly to the United Nations Organization. He had also secretly suffered a minor heart attack, which left him tired and weak.

Churchill flew back to London knowing that he would be called to account for some of the worst disasters of the war: In Malaya, Singapore was just about to fall as Britain's Far Eastern Empire crumbled to the Japanese. Stalin's armies seemed unable to sustain the Germans on the eastern front, and in North Africa, victory had switched abruptly to defeat as Rommel's Afrika Korps was about to retake Benghazi and threaten Cairo. When Churchill arrived in London, Randolph was there to greet him, having flown from Cairo on three weeks' leave.

Happily for one and all, Averell Harriman, after his historic visit to Moscow, had returned to the United States to arrange supplies of American war matériel to his country's latest ally, Joseph Stalin. Baby Winston was still gurgling contentedly with his nanny at Cherkley, kind Lord Beaverbrook's country house in Surrey, and Pamela seemed resigned to temporary reunion with the returning warrior.

She soon had a chance to watch him in action—not in battle but in the House of Commons, in the role that he had always dreamed of: defending his hard-pressed father in a full-scale parliamentary debate on a vote of confidence.

The loss of Singapore produced the first real signs of discontent with Churchill's leadership, and there were criticisms of "the central direction of the war" from both sides of the House. There was a bitter personal attack on Churchill from the socialist Emmanuel Shinwell, who claimed that the Prime Minister was out of touch and had fatally misjudged events. (More effective was a later taunt from his other main parliamentary critic, the socialist Anuerin Bevan, that "the Right Honourable Member wins every debate but loses every battle.")

Randolph, resplendent in his major's uniform, rose to defend his father—and, as always, overdid it.

Misjudging the mood of the House, his florid oratory fell flat as he bitterly attacked the great majority of members who had supported Chamberlain at Munich, then tried to flaunt his military knowledge as a serving soldier.

Predictably, this brought trouble and noisy interjections.

"Will the Honourable and Gallant Member—I call him that because of the uniform he wears—please tell me on what occasion he has been, as a soldier, in a battle where he has been shot at by the enemy at 1500 yards?" asked Commander Archibald Southby from the Conservative back benches.

From his seat nearby, Harold Nicolson saw Churchill "looking embarrassed and shy" at this. Directly after the debate, Southby had the misfortune to encounter Churchill in the corridor. He tried to excuse himself, but Churchill was in a rage.

He shook his fist in Southby's face. "Do not speak to me," he shouted. "You called my son a coward. You are my enemy. Do not speak to me."

Randolph's loyalty to his father had once again backfired, and making an exhibition of himself in Parliament can have done little to enhance him in Pamela's less than star-struck eyes: Nicolson had not missed the sight of "Randolph's little wife squirming in the Gallery throughout his speech."

Once again it was left to Churchill to assert his power in one of his most powerful parliamentary speeches. The next day, January 29, he pulled out all the stops and, tired as he was, convinced the House of his unfailing confidence, "never stronger than at this moment, that we shall bring this conflict to an end in a manner agreeable to the interests of this country, and in a manner agreeable to the future of the world."

In spite of Randolph's ill-judged intermission, Churchill won his vote of confidence by 464 to 1; after the vote was taken, Nicolson observed him "arm in arm and beaming" with Clementine as "they pushed through the crowds in the Central Lobby."

At this grim moment of the war, Clementine was unassailable. Gone were the feelings of inadequacy that she had blurted out to Cecil Beaton two years earlier. Dignified and conscientiously aware of where her duty lay, she had taught herself the queenly role that rather suited her. Gone, too, was the memory of that period before the war when she had doubted Churchill's sense of destiny. Pressed at this crisis of the war, he increasingly relied upon her to ensure the smooth running of the private world that meant so much to him. Nor had she grown averse herself to the pleasurable accompaniments of power—the chauffeurs, secretaries, bodyguards, and the sense of being at the hub of things.

So there was some significance in the fact that it was Clementine rather than her son who was by Churchill's side in the Central Lobby after his successful peroration. It should have been Randolph. After all, he was the precious heir briefly back from active service, and he had done his best to plead his father's cause as he had so often in the past. But he had failed, and it was Clementine who inevitably gained.

Clementine had never made a secret of her original decision to place her husband's career before her children. Then, largely thanks to Randolph, it had seemed that she had failed. The bond between father and son appeared to have displaced her from her position as Churchill's prime supporter. Even the worst excesses of the heir apparent's private life had been unable to dislodge his father's faith in him—and the illogical deep love he bore him.

But now that Clementine had made herself so indispensable, it was Randolph who began to find himself displaced.

"The cause of all the trouble between Randolph and his mother was simple jealousy for Winston's affection and attention," Laura remarked. "Originally she couldn't forgive Randolph for taking Winston from her, but now the boot was on the other foot and it was Randolph who envied Clementine her place beside his father."

In this potentially explosive situation, Randolph, true to form, continued to place himself firmly in the wrong, often from the very best of motives.

One of the greatest sources of contention between Randolph and his parents proved to be his marriage, which was already showing classic signs of being past repair. According to Bruce Lockhart, Pamela soon reached the point where she could hardly bear the sight of Randolph, who physically "repelled her with his spotted face and gross figure." Heavy drinking and the Cairo fleshpots had done little for his personal appeal, and the contrast between this khaki-clad Silenus and the elegant Averell was unfortunate. So was the state of Randolph's temper.

According to reports Bruce Lockhart had from Kathleen Harriman, Randolph attempted much the same pashalike behavior toward his wife that he had seen his father use—but with less success. He objected strongly to the way young Winston was still parked out on Beaverbrook with a nanny.

"I want you to be with my son," he told her.

"He also happens to be *my* son," Pamela replied.

"No!" bellowed Randolph. "My son. I'm a Churchill."

But Pamela now had war work of her own engaging much of her attention. Impressed by the way she made visiting Americans feel at home in wartime London, Brendan Bracken had suggested that her talents be employed more systematically. He proposed the creation of a select club with official backing where top-ranking U.S. servicemen, journalists, and diplomats would find themselves welcome, hear lectures, and generally mingle with the cream of political and polite society.

Thanks to Bracken's influence, money and premises were found. Pamela moved into an apartment in Grosvenor Square, and the club was established in the shadow of Westminster Abbey in the evocative surroundings of Westminster School (the boys having been evacuated).

As head of London's Churchill Club, the younger Mrs. Churchill was a great success. Her credentials as the wife of Churchill's dauphin were impeccable, as were her personality and appearance. Gone forever were the shyness and the puppy-fat.

"She is a very tasty morsel," wrote Evelyn Waugh to Nancy Mitford. Carnation Digby's daughter was becoming an accomplished hostess: svelte, attentive, immaculately dressed, and projecting something of the authentic aura of Churchillian regality on her own account.

This was something she would never lose, and it would launch her on one of the most colorful society careers of her generation. She would be much admired by the American celebrities who visited the

Churchill Club, and several beside Harriman fell in love with her, including another multimillionaire, Jock Whitney, and the famous war-correspondent and hard-bitten broadcaster from wartime London, Ed Murrow, who tried hard to marry her.

Such success inevitably caused jealousy and gossip among the more feline members of society, which did not include Clementine and Churchill, who remained devoted to their daughter-in-law. From her own marital experiences, Clementine could sympathize with Pamela's problems with Randolph, and Churchill, who loved her like a daughter, was impressed by the efforts she was making to improve Anglo-American relations.

"Pamela seems very well, and is a great treasure and blessing to us all," he assured Randolph in a letter he wrote him in May 1942.

But Randolph, back in Cairo after two months of unrewarding leave, was beginning to think otherwise. Always attuned to the gossip that emanated supersonically from the White's Club bar in London, even at the height of war, he had heard talk—probably misleading—of the relationship between Pamela and the man who had once been "definitely my favourite American." He was not jealous. Sexual jealousy was almost unique among the deadly sins in that it was not part of Randolph's nature. But anger was, and he was angry that Harriman had taken advantage of his friendship after being recommended by his father. He was also most upset that his parents—particularly his mother—refused to see the slightest wrong in Pamela but could be so critical of him.

For once again his worthiest intentions had misfired, and there was trouble now from one of his genuine efforts to redeem himself. Sick of his protected life and galled by the jeers he endured in Parliament, he had volunteered for parachute training and was attached to an embryonic unit of the Special Air Service.

It was the sort of military adventure his father would once have been unable to resist, but when Clementine heard about it she was furious. How typical of Randolph to be trying to do something "sensational" again, without a thought of his responsibilities! Not only had he a "very young wife and baby," but his father was carrying the burden of the war. How could he think of adding to his worries?

So incensed was Clementine that she felt impelled to write her husband one of her wifely missives on the subject. Bearing in mind what Colville had written about Churchill's fears of being unable to continue "should anything happen to Randolph," it makes interesting reading. For Clementine, consciously or unconsciously, was clearly undermining Randolph by playing on her husband's fears.

After the scene in the corridor with Commander Southby, Churchill's natural instincts must have been to admire Randolph for disproving the slur of cowardice by his dangerous decision. Not so Clementine; instead of praising their son for his courage, all she could bring herself to say was that "I grieve that he has done this because I know it will cause you harrowing anxiety, indeed, even agony of mind." She ended by suggesting that she should send Randolph an "affectionate" telegram, begging him simply to rejoin his regiment for his father's sake, and give up further thoughts about the S.A.S.

Wisely, she had second thoughts about sending this letter to her husband—and Randolph was permitted to begin his life of long-delayed adventure with his father's blessing. So while he gained with his father, Randolph only made worse his very poor relationship with his mother.

As usual, nothing he could do was right.

"Poor Randolph!" said Clementine's secretary, Grace Hamblin.

# twenty-eight

# Master of Alliances

By the end of 1942, the heroic phase of Churchill's wartime leadership was ending. He was no longer heading an embattled nation in a lonely struggle for survival. The true test of his leadership now lay in Britain's new position between her two great allies, the United States and the Soviet Union, in a worldwide struggle with Japan and Nazi Germany.

The U.S. and U.S.S.R. were infinitely larger and more powerful than Britain, with interests and war aims of their own. But Churchill was determined to maintain his own, and Britain's position. Inspired by history and his dreams of destiny, he would deploy the whole armory of his complex nature to achieve this, and it would be a masterly performance. Marlborough had "ridden to victory with the alliances of Europe in his hand." The time had come to follow his example.

As head of his Grand Coalition against the French, Marlborough's most important ally had been faithful Prince Eugene of Austria, who placed the essential troops and resources of the Austrian empire alongside Britain's at his disposal.

Churchill had inevitably cast the President of the United States in the role of his trusty Prince Eugene. He had courted, lectured, and attempted to inspire the U.S. President like a warrior monarch with a richer, less experienced ally in a common cause.

Thanks largely to the understanding Churchill established with Franklin Roosevelt in their early correspondence, Britain had been able to rely on the United States as the all-important "arsenal of democracy" when Britain fought alone. At this point, Churchill still appeared the dominant partner in their relationship, and when the statesmen met—as meet they did on ten occasions—the Prime Minister never failed to impress the President with the rhetoric and trappings of a great occasion.

The President had gone along with this up to a point—but *only* up to a point. The more the U.S. became involved in the war, and the greater its contribution in matériel and men, the clearer it became that Roosevelt would not accept Churchill's supremacy forever. At the Casablanca conference early in 1943. Churchill was able to persuade Roosevelt to accept his plans to advance through Sicily and Italy, but the President insisted that Gen. Dwight Eisenhower was to command the Allied forces when they invaded northern France. Churchill agreed that the war with Germany would only end with its unconditional surrender. Even then, the United States faced the prospect of a long hard war in Asia, where its interests could be very different from those of Britain and its precious Empire.

Despite these differences, Churchill remained devoted to Franklin Roosevelt. He treated Joseph Stalin much differently. Stalin, after all, had been one of the original "hairy Bolshevik baboons" whose crimes in the 1930s far exceeded those of the "fiendish criminals" Churchill attempted to destroy in 1920.

But with Stalin's armies having just achieved their greatest victory of the war, at Stalingrad, cooperation was essential and Churchill needed to establish a relationship with the Soviet leader that would permit at least an element of trust and understanding for the future.

"If the Germans invaded Hell, I'd put in a good word for the Devil," he remarked, and when he first flew to Moscow, in August 1942, personal contact helped to change his attitude toward the "ogre" and he found Stalin to be less the Bolshevik baboon than a tough, hard-drinking warrior-statesman, something of an actor on his own account.

Churchill had always had a taste for coarse, hard-drinking men of power, and in their late-night sessions in the Kremlin (Roosevelt, an early riser, tended to drop off in the middle of Churchill's late-night perorations), Churchill and Stalin formed a natural, if unlikely, twosome.

This had not stopped them from having bitter disagreements,

with only little Pavlov, the interpreter, in attendance. Churchill did not want to launch the second front in northern France, which Stalin was demanding, until all preparations were complete. There were also arguments about the form and scale of Western aid to Russia. And crucial questions over future Russian spheres of influence, particularly in eastern Europe, stayed unresolved.

But even while arguing, the two superstars seemed to be enjoying each other's company—and the competition of trying to outdo one another before an audience. Playing on Churchill's publicized (but carefully controlled) capacity for alcohol, Stalin had a table set out with an assortment of uncorked bottles for their delectation. To upstage the old warrior's well-known love of meat, Stalin ostentatiously consumed an entire pig's head in front of him.

In return, Stalin was shrewd enough to leave Churchill with the impression that as a Briton he could outdrink him and stay sober.

As far as Churchill was concerned, the result was a sense of considerable rapport that enabled him to overlook the crimes of Stalin's earlier existence.

"Call me Winston. I call you Joe behind your back," said Churchill.

"No, I want to call you my friend," replied the genial mass murderer.

While it could not last, this friendship was important in these early days of the wartime coalition. But the true test of Churchill's role as the Master of Alliances came as Churchill was about to turn sixty-nine, when all three leaders met to confer together for the first time at Tehran in November 1943. Among the issues for discussion was the whole course of the war in Europe, the Anglo-American invasion of the Continent, and the war against Japan.

On the very threshold of old age, the dream of supreme power on the stage of history, which had haunted Churchill all his adult life, had finally achieved remarkable reality. He might have been some great king-emperor, disposing of the future of the world at a gathering of mighty princes.

Two weeks earlier, on November 12, 1943, he had set sail from Southampton, like the great potentate he was, aboard the battleship *Renown,* accompanied by Randolph and Sarah and a retinue of statesmen, generals, ambassadors, and personal advisers. His destination was Cairo to confer once more with the President of the United States.

Churchill had been far from well, with a heavy cold, a bad sore throat—which almost stopped the flow of words—and the aftereffects of various injections. When the ship stopped at Malta he had had to spend two days in bed.

But at Cairo, in the presence of the President, he rapidly revived. "It really is wonderful how they both get on—they really like and understand each other . . . " wrote Sarah to her mother. Even Foreign Secretary Anthony Eden, who was present at their meetings, was amazed at the patience with which Churchill "played the role of courtier" with Roosevelt. (It would have been more amazing had Churchill not treated the President with patience, remembering how much richer, greater, stronger his resources were, and how much victory depended on the United States.)

On November 28, the two leaders traveled separately to meet Stalin at Tehran, the farthest point outside the Soviet Union they could tempt the suspicious Russian leader.

November 30 was Churchill's sixty-ninth birthday, and clearly an emotional occasion. There would be tears in his eyes when he received the presents and congratulations from the British residents of Tehran. That evening, with Sarah and Randolph to support him, he gave a formal birthday dinner in honor of Roosevelt and Stalin at the British Legation. Amid the caviar, the endless toasts, the heavy humor, and the large cigars, neither the historical nor the personal significance of the occasion was lost upon him.

From his earliest days, his one unwavering ambition had concerned the active exercise of power. Now, as he reminded the two other leaders, they jointly represented probably "the greatest concentration of worldly power that had ever been seen in the history of mankind."

There is no mistaking the pride behind his description of that birthday dinner in the Persian capital: "On my right sat the President of the United States, on my left the master of Russia. Together we controlled a large preponderance of the naval and three-quarters of all the air forces of the world, and could direct armies of nearly twenty millions of men in the most terrible of wars that had yet occurred in human history."

At Tehran, Churchill did his best to impose his historical-romantic concept of the war on the principal performers. One of his first acts was to present courageous Marshal Stalin with a sword of chivalry. Stalin, uncomfortably decked out in a mustard yellow Soviet marshal's uniform, received the famous "Sword of Stalingrad"—a symbolic gift from the distant King of England—from Churchill, who was similarly attired in the uniform of a commodore of the R.A.F., complete with pilot's wings. Stalin kissed the hilt, but Roosevelt, unimpressed by Churchill's gestures, laughingly brandished it around him from his position in his wheelchair.

As the conference proceeded, it was Roosevelt who made it clear that his role as Churchill's Prince Eugene was definitely over. Despite their carefully nurtured friendship, Roosevelt was growing tired of Churchill playing Marlborough at their meetings. There were also signs that he was impatient with Churchill's taking him and the massive efforts of the great United States for granted. He was particularly worried that Churchill might be attempting to divert the power of the United States to supporting something no decent Democrat could countenance, the revival of the old, outdated British Empire.

When Churchill was not present, Roosevelt could not resist the chance of making deals direct with Stalin—thereby causing trouble for the future and fueling suspicion that the English-speaking allies were not immutably united.

Despite this, at Tehran at least, Churchill's rhetoric and sense of history offered the conference a unifying theme and even brought a measure of agreement on a concerted strategy in Europe before dealing with Japan. Stalin was reconciled to the delay of the Anglo-American second front until mid-summer 1944; it was agreed that the Soviet Union would enter the Pacific war after victory in the west, and the pattern of the war in Italy and the Mediterranean was broadly if pragmatically decided. The Allies even agreed to Churchill's pet plan for a daring amphibious landing at Anzio eight weeks later. Under the circumstances, it is doubtful whether Marlborough, the master of alliances, could have done much better.

For Churchill, the exalted role that he adopted also served a private purpose. One of the mysteries about this phenomenal old statesman is how he still sustained the energy and passion of his wartime leadership, continuing to dominate his generals and domestic politicians and playing his impressive part at Tehran despite the weakness of his own position.

Ever since his time in India in his early twenties, Churchill had been learning to transform himself, by concentrated will, to act the great dramatic roles his strange imagination would create to overcome his dread of fear and failure. The mechanism rarely failed, and the most effective roles were still the aggressive ones. It was aggression that sparked off the formidable inspirations of Churchill's "up" syndrome, and this potentially depressive, small, fat man was once again transformed by his wartime power.

In this he was unique among the wartime statesmen. His "great talent for show-off exaggeration and make-believe," about which his father once complained, had produced something akin to what can be seen with legendary actors in their greatest roles. Imagination and reality converged as he embraced the part that he created. Power was his theme, history his stage, and in looks, speech, gesture he became the warrior-statesman locked in battle for the future of the world above the dross of commonplace existence.

Even his conversations with his doctor sounded like something out of Shakespeare. "Stupendous issues," he remarked before dropping off to sleep, "are unfolding before our eyes, and we are only specks of dust which have settled for a night on the map of the world."

In the past, this sort of rhetoric had been a source of both inspiration and great disaster. Now, at the very center of "the most terrible of wars in human history," he seemed able to marshal his power within it.

Sarah enjoyed herself at Tehran. She used to say she chose the W.A.A.F. because of the color of the uniform, because air force blue set off her auburn hair and pale complexion. At twenty-six, she still possessed a dancer's figure, animated features, and considerable feminine allure. She certainly remained enough the actress to play the part of her father's favorite princess, using all her charm on the Allied leaders.

Roosevelt, who flirted mildly with her, she "simply loved," and she even acted up to Stalin. Seeing him simply as genial Uncle Joe, she was much taken by the Georgian. He was, she wrote, "a great man, of that there can be no doubt." She said that his sense of humor was every bit "as darting and swift as Papa's."

But her real interests were beginning to turn toward American Ambassador John Gil Winant, who had fallen seriously in love with her. He was very much her type: an older man, assured, good-looking, and something of a loner at the center of the diplomatic world. She was attracted to him, but she was well aware of the trouble her love affair could cause within the family. Winant was married, and she could not risk a scandal. She had seen the trouble Randolph's marital disasters caused. She knew how jealously her father viewed her, and was very cautious.

For all her mulish obstinacy in the past, it was impossible for

Sarah not to fall beneath her father's dominating spell. At his birthday banquet, when all the toasts were being made, it was only her old restraint that stopped her from proposing "Papa's health" and telling everyone that he was not only a great statesman but "a nice father too —and more."

Sarah's natural warmth was working to offset the tensions and the jealousies within her family. She was that rarity in families, a natural peacemaker who genuinely wanted those around her to like each other. During her time at Tehran, she took the time to write her mother long, newsy letters so as to make her feel included in what was happening. In the course of them she even did her best to put in a good word for Randolph.

She described his exemplary behavior at the birthday banquet: no arguments and only a moderate amount to drink. "He is trying you know—there is a big change in him," she added. And it was partly thanks to Sarah that the close relationship between Churchill and his son seemed to have been restored. She was certainly a loyal ally to her brother, but the balance between Churchill and his son was as delicate as before.

Randolph was as important as ever to Churchill. They had so much in common: similarities of character, memories and anecdotes, and shared ambitions from the past. There was no one else in whom Churchill could confide as he did with Randolph, and on the voyage to Cairo, they had been inseparable.

During the conference this trust continued. Randolph scored something of a coup with a long after-dinner tête-à-tête with Stalin. He really was "trying," and in Churchill's eyes this must have made a satisfying contrast to the behavior of Roosevelt's son Elliot, who had infuriated Churchill by taking seriously one of Stalin's "jokes" on the need to exterminate the entire German high command when the war was over. (Churchill stumped from the table in disgust.)

At Tehran, Churchill entrusted Randolph with the sort of task by which he could have made himself indispensable. It had been decided that Turkey should be wooed to the Allied cause, and Randolph was dispatched to the Turkish city of Adana, in his father's personal aircraft, to meet Turkish President Ismet Inönü on his behalf. In fact, he made two visits to Turkey in swift succession, and it was largely thanks to him that a very worried Inönü was persuaded to meet Churchill when he returned to Cairo. (Here the courtship of Turkey ceased as its anxious President, despite kissing Churchill on both cheeks, wisely made it clear how much he cherished his neutrality.) Randolph was excited to have been of use, but then, as so often in his life, success was followed by catastrophe.

When the Tehran conference ended, the elder Churchill's great performance ended with it. The act was over, the willpower that had been sustaining him relaxed, and the next few days spent back in Cairo finishing his discussions with Roosevelt were dogged by diarrhea and a reappearance of his earlier ailments. One of the three most powerful men on earth admitted he was now so weak that he could no longer dry himself after his evening bath, but "lay on the bed wrapped in my towel until I dried naturally"—something he could not remember ever having done before.

His doctor—formerly Dr. Charles Wilson, now ennobled for services to Churchill as Baron Moran—feared that his master had completely exhausted himself at Tehran. He worried about a lack of concentration as the great man spent a lunchtime meeting swatting flies, then rambled on in a disjointed after-dinner monologue without realizing that some of his distinguished guests were fast asleep. But the chief victim of his mood change was his son.

Randolph confided what occurred in a note to his beloved Laura Charteris. All his efforts to the contrary, she was now married to the Earl of Dudley, but Randolph had made a way of life of refusing to acknowledge facts that did not suit him, and firmly refused to think about her as a married woman, or to consider the existence of the Earl. As much in love as ever, he insisted on writing to her as he always had —and unrequited passion played its part in his current troubles with his parents.

It was a letter written on December 8, 1943, that gave the news. After describing the excitement of his trips to Teheran and Turkey, he added gloomily, "my pleasure in all this has been greatly spoiled by the fact that W. and I still don't get on. It is the same old trouble in the back of his mind, reinforced by his belief (so true in political affairs) that he can get his way by bullying and obstinacy."

Another of the rows that battered their relationship had suddenly erupted. After the high of Tehran, Churchill was suffering stomach pains and was far from being in the best of tempers. Randolph had drunk too much as usual, and a reference to his marriage brought an immediate explosion.

Churchill was obsessed about the breakdown of this marriage. "R's marriage is going wonky and W is terribly distressed," Harold

Nicolson had written. "The old boy is tremendously domestic and adores his family." This was what Randolph had referred to in his letter, and the situation between them had become intolerable. Tehran had provided a diversion, but now the subject could not be avoided.

Churchill and Clementine still insisted on regarding Pamela as the harshly treated mother of the scion of the Churchills and had even been helping her with money. (To Randolph's chagrin they were paying Pamela a regular allowance of £500 a year tax-free, and until now no one had discussed the possibility of divorce.)

Churchill had not objected to divorce in Sarah's case, but then, he had thoroughly disliked Vic Oliver. ("I find myself rather envying Il Duce," he supposedly remarked on hearing how Mussolini had executed his son-in-law, Count Ciano.) In contrast, he and Clementine remained fond of Pamela, who treated them with kindness and concern. Besides, young Winston was involved. Churchill doted on his grandson and Clementine frequently reminded him of Randolph's failings as a husband: his extravagance, his irresponsibility, his lack of feeling for his family and for his father.

Randolph saw things differently. He, after all, had rushed into marriage at the start of war, largely to please his father and provide an heir and namesake for the precious dynasty. He had acted from the best of motives and had done his duty. Now he was getting all the blame because the marriage had not worked.

The family had encouraged Pamela's friendship with Harriman, and she had other smart American admirers. What hypocrisy to say that Pamela was wholly innocent and he was totally to blame.

Having just faced Roosevelt and Stalin, it was not surprising that Churchill was in a mood to be "obstinate and bullying" to Randolph on the subject of his marriage. Harsh words were spoken and Randolph stormed off in tears, swearing that everything was finished between them. Relations were still strained when Churchill flew to Tunis three days later.

He had a crowded schedule, for he was planning to confer with American and British leaders in Tunis and Algiers before visiting his favorite general, General Sir Harold Alexander, the victor of Tunisia, in southern Italy. Churchill's excitement was building up for the forthcoming landing at Anzio, south of Rome, despite ominous similarities with the landings at Gallipoli.

Churchill envied Alexander his command in the field, and could not keep away from the action. But by the time his plane touched down at Tunis, the strains of the last few frantic weeks caught up with him. On December 11 he collapsed.

Pneumonia set in. There was a minor heart attack—his second after the undisclosed attack two years earlier in Washington. By December 15, the "Lord Doctor," as Diana Cooper christened Moran, was seriously worried for his patient's life.

Churchill, however, was not. With his star performance at Tehran behind him, he seems to have regarded death with equanimity. Death had never worried him particularly—"an event so natural and indispensable to mankind," as he once called it.

He and his party were occupying a villa outside Tunis, close to the ruins of an empire that had been suddenly destroyed forever. The parallel was not lost upon him. "I suppose it is fitting I should die beside Carthage," he remarked. "If I die, don't worry," he told Sarah, who had remained beside him. "The war is won."

Others regarded his departure less philosophically. News of his illness caused alarm back in England, and Moran, who stayed at his side, prescribed the new wonder-drug, M & B, and organized specialists and nurses for his patient.

While he was sick, Sarah read him *Pride and Prejudice*. Until now, Churchill had never found the time for anything as frivolous as English literature, but he enjoyed Jane Austen, and she seems to have assisted his recovery. So, to a point, did the arrival at the villa of other members of his family—first Randolph, who had departed in agitated circumstances some days earlier, then Clementine, who was rushed from England in considerable discomfort, together with secretaries Grace Hamblin and Jock Colville.

By Christmas day he was back on whisky and cigars, and after conferring with General Eisenhower—newly appointed Anglo-American supreme commander for the forthcoming invasion of northern France—he was able to enjoy what his secretary John Martin called "a soporific Christmas lunch of turkey and plum pudding" with his wife, his daughter, and his son in the winter sunlight of North Africa. It seemed like a united family, with its members offering affection and support around the convalescent statesman. Beneath the surface it was not that simple.

Clementine made an odd remark on her arrival. Welcoming her, Lord Moran spoke of the emotion Churchill showed when told that she was coming. At this she "smiled whimsically," remarking, "Oh yes, he's very glad I've come, but in five minutes he'll forget I'm here."

• • •

Power had come between them. Clementine was no longer his confidante in great affairs, as she had been in World War I. This had left her often lonely in her dignified position. Publicly, she was much admired and regarded with considerable affection. She had developed a public presence, having finally controlled her lifelong shyness, but beneath this she remained as vulnerable as ever.

Her first attempt to accompany her husband to a major wartime conference—to Quebec in 1942—had proved a singular ordeal. Eleanor Roosevelt, most fluent and engaged of political wives, with her obvious intellect and awesome self-assurance, made Clementine feel at a disadvantage. This in turn had made her irritable—even when Roosevelt indulged in a bit of lèse-majesté by calling her "Clemmie" to her face. (Only her husband and oldest friends and family were permitted that. As Jock Colville wrote after her death, "Intimately as both my wife and I knew Lady Churchill, we never called her Clemmie to her dying day.")

She had been upset and angry, and then, as so often in the past after one of her nervous outbursts, prostration had followed. When she recovered, it was decided she would not accompany her husband on any future major trips abroad. Instead, Sarah and Mary would take turns in acting as what they called "family ADCs" to give their father familiar support upon these great occasions.

This left Clementine with the role of queen in residence at 10 Downing Street and Chequers, consort and consolation in his moments of infrequent relaxation, and gracious hostess when the need arose. Yet she was far from idle. She took the charities she ran extremely seriously, especially the chairmanship of the Y.W.C.A. and of the nationwide Red Cross Aid to Russia campaign she headed after 1941.

But despite so much activity, there remained an element of discontent in her position, which could erupt with unexpected passion, particularly when jealousy became involved.

She was not given to forgiveness and could be as venomous as ever against any she believed to have usurped her rightful place in her husband's confidence. Lord Beaverbrook, one of Churchill's oldest surviving friends, had also been one of the very few he trusted in the bleakest days of 1940. By February 1942, when Beaverbrook had just finished his heroic stint as Minister of Aircraft Production—and also providing a home for several months to baby Winston—Clementine wrote about him to her husband: "My Darling—Try ridding yourself of this microbe which some people fear is in your blood—Exorcise this bottle imp and see if the air is not clearer & purer."

Within the family she could act rather similarly. Diana got on particularly well with her father, who enjoyed her sense of humor. (During a period when she worked as a volunteer in a West End hospital, Diana made a point of collecting remarks people made about him that she thought would amuse him. They invariably did.) But Clementine's relations with her eldest daughter were as difficult as ever. Diana was dotingly in love with her cold and dominating husband, and fully occupied with her three young children and her house in Chester Square. Clementine seemed to resent this, and her relations with this segment of the family were not improved by the fact that she found her son-in-law an ambitious bore.

But within the family circle of the most powerful man in Britain, the firepower of its presiding matriarch tended to be drawn most frequently to the son and heir. The cartoonist Osbert Lancaster, a friend of Randolph's, exaggerated somewhat when he said, "The truth was that they hated one another's guts." But it was fair to say that the old antipathy between mother and son found further aggravation from the war and from the jealousies and strains that came from Churchill's position. Once these strains were eased—as they were with Churchill's illness—relations between Randolph and his mother temporarily improved.

Although he was rapidly recovering, Churchill accepted Lord Moran's firm advice that he should go someplace warm to convalesce—and not join General Alexander's troops in Italy. So, Christmas over, and cheered by the news of the sinking of the German warship *Scharnhorst*, Churchill and his rapidly expanding court flew on to take possession of a spot that he would always love: the glamorous Villa Taylor in the French Moroccan holiday resort of Marrakesh.

Although it was January, there was sunlight and luxury amid what Clementine described as a "mixture of the Arabian nights and Hollywood." And there to greet him was one of the few women from the past whose company he genuinely enjoyed: the still beautiful Lady Diana Cooper, whose husband, Churchill's old friend and ally, the Conservative M. P. Duff Cooper, was now his personal representative with the Free French in Algiers.

The warlord of Tehran was suddenly transformed—as he always could be when his aggression was switched off—into something gentler and touchingly eccentric, which Diana Cooper recognized from the Chartwell of before the war.

"There was our old baby in his rompers, ten-gallon cowboy hat and very ragged oriental dressing-gown," she wrote; and for the next two weeks, the convalescent "schoolboy" cheerfully enjoyed his unexpected holiday in "a millionairess's pleasure dome, all marble and orange-trees, fountains and tiles in the richest Mohamedan style." The potentate was at his ease. Neither the war nor a visit from de Gaulle could mar his pleasure.

He slept, he drank, he picnicked, and he painted. Even Clementine's enemy, Lord Beaverbrook, turned up to keep her husband happy; since Churchill obviously loved his company, there was little Clementine could do but graciously accept him.

Gracious acceptance was the order of the day, and with Sarah still present to keep an eye on her father, Clementine could gratefully depart for bed each night at 9:30, leaving her husband talking the night away as usual.

Diana Cooper described how Churchill finished a picnic by insisting on clambering up a massive boulder, and how members of his entourage hauled him up, puffing like a grampus, with a tablecloth around his middle. In the Moroccan heat and after a recent heart attack, this must have been alarming, but according to Diana, "Clemmie said nothing, but watched him like a lenient mother who does not wish to spoil her child's fun, nor yet his daring."

The person who particularly benefited from this happy atmosphere was Randolph, whose defects as a husband and son were temporarily forgiven, if not entirely forgotten. Since seeing action briefly with the S.A.S. in Sicily and southern Italy, he had been pushing hard to get more active service. Thanks to one of the decisions made by the Western powers at Tehran, he seemed to have succeeded.

At Tehran, it was agreed to give full support to the Yugoslav partisan leader, Tito, in his fight against the Germans; and a British military mission, headed by the Tory M. P. Brigadier Fitzroy Maclean, was being sent to his assistance. Maclean was still in Cairo. Randolph knew him, and the courageous brigadier did something few commanding officers would have contemplated. He said he was perfectly prepared to take Randolph with him.

(Explaining his decision, Maclean insisted that not only was Randolph "thoroughly dependable, possessing both endurance and determination," but that he "felt he would get on well with the Yugoslavs, for his enthusiastic and at times explosive attitude to life was not unlike their own.")

Randolph was genuinely overjoyed. After four long years of waiting, this was the sort of important active service mission he had always wanted—and which his father might have undertaken in his own heroic youth. But first it was essential to obtain Papa's consent and arrange the final details with him. With the sort of princely gesture he could still summon when the need arose, Randolph personally conducted Brigadier Maclean from Cairo to Marrakesh aboard the aircraft that had been consigned for General Alexander.

An author and man of action, Maclean was the sort of man to appeal to Churchill. "No gentler pirate ever cut a throat or robbed a ship," he wrote about him later, quoting Byron's description of a character in *Don Juan*. In the happy atmosphere of Marrakesh, Maclean's plans and optimistic attitude to Randolph proved contagious. Not only was Churchill totally convinced of the need to back the Communist Tito against his royalist partisan opponent, Draža Mihajlović; he also seemed genuinely excited by the prospect of his son Randolph joining the military mission.

Although it would clearly be hazardous to join the partisans behind the German lines, no more was heard about the dire effect on Churchill should anything happen to his son. Great kings traditionally entrusted their sons to their allies as a sign of earnest intent in time of war. And so Major Randolph Churchill flew off to Yugoslavia with his father's blessing. Maclean bore a fulsome letter from Churchill to Tito, promising him "all the aid in human power," and setting out Maclean's credentials. "With him at your headquarters," Churchill proudly added, "will be serving my son, Major Randolph Churchill, who is also a Member of Parliament."

Since Churchill had sanctioned Randolph's mission, Clementine could only go along with it. In a letter to Mary she said she thought the work would suit him.

# twenty-nine

# The Shadows of Victory

Clementine's most revealing remark about what the war meant to her husband came in a conversation with Diana Cooper shortly after Randolph's departure for Yugoslavia. With victory in Europe now in sight, Diana drew the inevitable parallel between Churchill and Marlborough, but suggested that "when the war was over, instead of building Winston another Blenheim," his grateful country ought to give him "an endowed manor house with acres for a farm and gardens to build and paint in." Clementine shook her head. "I never think of after the war," she said. "I think Winston will die when it's over. You see, he's seventy and I'm sixty and we're putting all we've got into this and it will take all we've got."

When she said this, Winston and Clementine were in fact in their seventieth and sixtieth years respectively, but there were several times, during the last eighteen months of the war in Europe, when it looked as if Clementine would be proved right. Nevertheless this final chapter of the war was a triumph for Churchill's powers of survival, as age and circumstances turned increasingly against him. Despite them, he was able to sustain the legend he had created, and it is fascinating to see the legend growing as both his health and his grasp upon the world-wide conduct of the war began to fail him.

His great plan for an amphibious attack on Anzio to the north of Naples was a grievous disappointment, like so many of his flights of strategy. Strongly resisted by the Germans, the landing was not that sudden, wildcat blow that he believed would lead to the rapid liberation of the whole Italian peninsula. Italy became the scene of a bitter war of slow attrition, and not that lightning strike at what he called "the armpit" of the Reich by which he had hoped to bring a swift conclusion to the conflict.

This ended Churchill's dream of forestalling the Soviet advance through eastern Europe and striking a crucial blow against the Germans in the Mediterranean and the Balkans before the second front began in northern France. It also underlined the way that overall direction of the war was passing to the United States and the Soviet Union. Nothing could disguise his subordinate position to the American command, once the Allies finally invaded northern France in Operation Overlord in June 1944, and with the Red Army rolling back the enemy in eastern Europe, it was clear that Stalin would impose his will on all he conquered.

As Clementine feared, pneumonia and the heart attack in North Africa had hit her husband harder than generally appreciated, and at times he felt weakened and depressed.

"I'm through," he had told Beaverbrook in the spring of 1944. "I just can't carry the burdens any longer."

Having said this, and being Churchill, he almost instantly revived, but the strains were showing, and not only on him but also on those around him. His official—and largely ignored—Deputy Prime Minister, Labour leader Clement Attlee, was driven to complain by letter of the unbusinesslike conduct of affairs in Cabinet. Churchill reacted like an insulted monarch, took to his bed, and then decided to ignore the letter. More serious, his acknowledged successor in the party, the deeply diplomatic Anthony Eden, while continuing his courtierlike submission to his master, secretly agreed with the complaints.

But such was the P.M.'s prestige and power that none of these difficulties seriously affected his authority. Objections and murmurs of revolt within the House of Commons made little difference either. He knew how to handle *them*—just as he also knew from long experience how to keep his generals on the tightest rein.

In the process, he almost drove his Chief of Imperial General Staff, the down-to-earth Ulsterman Gen. Alan Brooke, insane with his late night outbursts and the frequency with which he changed his mind. Only the force of Churchill's personality—and Brooke's loyalty —kept this essential general at his post.

As if to offset what was happening within his government, Churchill seemed more immersed than ever in his public role as great war leader. A common reaction from those meeting him for the first time was that he appeared not only more formidable but physically larger than expected. Remarks about his regality were frequent. "No one dared pursue a topic of conversation that did not meet with his approval," wrote a friend of Randolph's after lunching at 10 Downing Street. "Many guests would have found royalty easier to deal with."

What few noticed—or if they did, felt it politic not to mention—was the way contact with the war could still revive him. Conflict had never failed to excite him, and once excited, his energy was unabating.

To witness the fighting at first hand, and to keep himself occupied with fresh activities, Churchill was traveling more than ever. Flying was still a personal adventure, and as the war expanded, he was continually on the move, with the accoutrements of earthly power around him. Roosevelt's gift of a luxurious four-engined Skymaster aircraft for his personal use made this possible. The large aircraft was equipped with a dining room, a private bathroom, a bedroom with a comfortable single bed from which he could work as usual, and an office for his staff and secretaries.

In June 1944, however, the King personally deprived him of the great event he had been anticipating: his presence at the D-Day landings. This was one occasion when gentle King George VI was known to have overruled the wishes of his mighty subject, arguing with what appears suspiciously like pique that if the King of England was not permitted to be present, neither was his irreplaceable Prime Minister. It was a test of Churchill's loyalty toward his monarch—and a dreadful disappointment.

Churchill's Parliamentary Private Secretary Sir Leslie Rowan told Colville that it was at this point he detected that his chief began "losing interest in the war, because he no longer has control of military affairs. Up till Overlord he saw himself as Marlborough, the supreme authority to whom all military decisions were referred. Now, in all but questions of wide or long-term strategy, he is by force of circumstances, little more than a spectator."

Churchill's spectator status did not keep him out of France for long, and a few weeks later, he was being photographed giving his famous V for Victory sign to the troops in Normandy. Then he was off to Italy, in the uniform of a colonel of the 4th Hussars, visiting his frontline troops and telling General Alexander, "I envy you your command of armies in the field. That's what I should have liked." It was his old ambition to be a fighting general. Instead, he was a statesman and an international celebrity, vastly famous, universally respected, but with little real power to affect the final outcome of the war.

Despite this, war remained "man's natural occupation"—for him at any rate—and he refused to be concerned with any other while it lasted, certainly not with growing aspirations in his own country for better education, health, and housing and a fairer social order when the war was over. Concern with such things struck him as irrelevant and probably unpatriotic, for he was an autocratic ruler and growing more reactionary with little tolerance of criticism. There was in fact surprisingly little sign of discontent in Britain, and the media was under strict control. But Churchill was absurdly touchy over the occasional criticism of his government that did reach the press—and touchier still about his personal reputation.

The satirical treatment of aged leadership in the film *The Life and Times of Colonel Blimp* seriously upset him. On the other hand, he could never have enough of the romantic patriotic film *Lady Hamilton,* with Laurence Olivier starring as his hero, Adm. Horatio Nelson. He is said to have seen it in his private cinema on seventeen occasions, always with extreme emotion.

After his return from Italy, Churchill was once again stricken with pneumonia. "If you go on playing the fool like this you're certain to die," said Brendan Bracken. But instead of dying, willpower and Lord Moran helped Churchill recover so as to attend in August 1944 another mammoth conference—his second at Quebec—with the President of the United States.

This involved the most impressive voyage of Churchill's whole career: a larger retinue than ever, both Mary and Clementine in attendance, and Britain's greatest liner, the *Queen Mary,* to accommodate his party in extraordinary luxury. Colville described the meals aboard as "gargantuan in scale and epicurean in quality, rather shamingly so."

Here was the grand opera of wartime leadership that Churchill loved—the infinite accompaniments of power, advisers, press photographers, the drama of the meetings—and the long discussions with the President upon the progress of the war, conducted "in a blaze of friendship." It was a blaze that now included Clementine, who was finally permitting Roosevelt to call her "Clemmie."

But friendship, however heartfelt, failed to convince Roosevelt of the growing threat Stalin's armies posed to a future Europe, nor did it make him sympathetic to Churchill's fears for his cherished British

Empire. Still less was Churchill able to convince Roosevelt and his military advisers of his latest great strategic plan to preempt the Soviet advance in Europe by a sudden strike toward Vienna (reminiscent yet again of the strategy Marlborough followed in the great campaign that led to Blenheim).

But whatever limitations on his power were revealed at Quebec, Churchill himself had rarely seemed more comfortably majestic as he stood before the newsreel cameras like the god of battles in a sailor's hat. Nor did he permit news of the annihilation of the 1st Airborne Division at Arnhem with seven thousand casualties to oppress him unduly. "I have not sustained any feeling of disappointment over this, and am glad our commanders are capable of running these sort of risks," he cabled Field Marshal Smuts, who had sent commiserations.

Back in London, other great events were calling him to fresh adventures—first by airplane to Moscow. Since Roosevelt was refusing to stand up to Stalin over Polish independence—the forgotten reason Britain went to war—Churchill would go himself to plead the cause of Polish liberation.

This flying visit was another personal triumph: banquets, a hero's welcome, and an unprecedented public appearance with Stalin at his side at a tumultuous state performance of *Giselle* at the Bolshoi Ballet. (Churchill preferred the singing of the Red Army choir that followed.) No one questioned his extraordinary prestige, although the visit made no difference to the lost cause of the Polish nation.

There was another demonstration of his international prestige a few weeks later, when he flew with Clementine and Mary to newly liberated Paris. According to General Brooke, enthusiastic crowds along the Champs Elysées "went quite mad over him," chanting "Churcheel! Churcheel!" as he drove to the Arc de Triomphe with his ancient sparring partner, General de Gaulle, now head of the provisional French government. (How things had changed since those days in 1941 when Churchill remarked apropos of the general, that the heaviest cross he had to bear "was the Cross of Lorraine.")

Just before Christmas 1944 he was even able to enjoy one final old-style personal adventure, which Harold Macmillan rightly called "a sort of super Sydney Street."

One concession that he had obtained from Stalin in Moscow was an understanding that postwar Greece should stay within the British sphere of influence. This, however, was not preventing Greek Communist guerrillas from seizing power in the wake of the retreating

Germans. Since the Communists had fought gallantly against the Third Reich it was a delicate situation, which Foreign Secretary Eden was prepared to settle with his well-known diplomatic caution. Churchill wanted other methods.

That Christmas eve at Chequers, he strapped on his large revolver and, leaving a tearful Clementine behind him, boarded his Skymaster for Athens and personally took charge of operations.

He was a very old Savrola as he drove through Athens with his generals in an armored car, calling up air support to blast what he called "the rebels," conferring with the different factions, and personally urging the discredited King of Greece to surrender power to a regency. Flying home a few days later, Churchill, a happy man, could congratulate himself that, thanks to his decisive action, the red tide had been halted in one European country—and Greece was safe for Greek democracy. (Others did not see it quite that way, and Churchill was strongly criticized, particularly in the U.S., for interfering in the internal politics of Greece, and for attacking Greek patriots who fought the Nazis.)

His trip marked a brief resurgence of the sort of high adventure he had longed for in his twenties—and virtually his last effective exercise of power as an international war leader. When the German counterattack in the Ardennes had been defeated, his urgent pleas to Washington failed to result in Anglo-American forces taking Berlin before the Russians reached it. Similarly, the "Big Three" conference at Yalta in the Crimea on February 4–11, 1945, confirmed his fears that the Soviets would swamp postwar eastern Europe, but he found himself unable to prevent Stalin from outmaneuvering Roosevelt.

Roosevelt, in fact, was dying. At Yalta, Colville described him as looking "old and ill . . . a hopelessly incompetent chairman," having lost all powers of concentration. Despite Churchill's presence, Stalin had little difficulty getting what he wanted. On the point of victory, the Grand Coalition that Churchill had romantically believed in effectively collapsed.

On April 12, he heard Roosevelt was dead. Churchill mourned Roosevelt in Parliament as "the greatest champion of freedom who has ever brought help and comfort from the new world to the old," but he did not attend the funeral on the grounds of pressure of events in Europe. (He was represented by his Foreign Secretary, Anthony Eden, and later said how much he regretted not going to the funeral and meeting the new U.S. president, Harry Truman, at the ceremony.) On the following day the Red Army entered Vienna. It was a solemn moment, leaving Churchill with what he called "the shadows of victory" on the edge of the greatest triumph of his life as German opposition crumbled. But victory, as sweet as it was, was to bring a crisis to his private life that was as unforeseen as he was unprepared to meet it.

The same applied to all the members of his family, Clementine included. During this final chapter of the war in Europe, Clementine had been sharing in her husband's fame, and it was working wonders for her brittle confidence.

Since recovering from the nervous crisis that had prostrated her in 1943, she had made something of a comeback as hostess both at 10 Downing Street and Chequers. When roused, she could be as formidable as ever. Colville remarked upon her caustic interjections in the conversation, and she was quick to put down any signs of disrespect toward her husband. (She was particularly hard on the victor of Alamein, Field Marshall Bernard Montgomery; she thought him bumptious and was quick to slap him down for signs of impertinence. Churchill never seemed to notice. Later she got to like him.)

Her appearance beside Churchill at the second Quebec conference in August 1944 had formed a striking contrast with her miserable time in Canada in 1942. (She had even followed a public speech of Eleanor Roosevelt's with a short one of her own.)

It was quite a transformation from the unhappy woman she had been three years earlier. But more than her awareness of her popularity, there was a subtler reason for this growth of confidence.

As often happens in such situations, she was becoming stronger in relation to a considerably older husband whose powers she felt to be declining. When she had confided to Diana Cooper that she thought Churchill would not survive the war, she was not exaggerating. Lord Moran thought the same. He wrote in his diary "Churchill was not the man he had been" after he nearly died at Carthage at the end of 1943, adding that "he could easily go at any moment."

Knowing this, Clementine saw it as her duty to protect and comfort him as much as possible. Not that this was easy, with the manic rate of his activities as the European war was ending. She could not make him take things easier, although she had done her tearful best that Christmas eve before he flew to Athens. Nor could she make him change the habits of a lifetime. He was still eating and drinking on a scale few men of his age could equal, still taking his sacrosanct siesta in the afternoon, conferring until 2:00 and 3:00 in the morning and, after a substantial solitary breakfast, working through the morning from his bed.

Sleeping apart as they had done for years, this meant that her actual contact with him was largely confined to mealtimes, almost invariably in the presence of official guests. (According to her appointments diary, the two of them dined à deux on weekdays on only four occasions during the whole of 1944).

All she could really do was offer him her presence and support, be there when needed, and conscientiously perform her own activities aided by Miss Hamblin. (In April 1945, Clementine was in Russia with Miss Hamblin on a six-week visit in her role as official head of the Red Cross Aid to Russia campaign. She was there when Germany surrendered.)

Yet there remained one self-appointed task that increasingly obsessed her: guardian of her husband's greatness. Throughout the tribulations of their marriage, she had always been concerned with this, and now it was of great importance. Nothing must be permitted to detract from the aura that surrounded him—neither troubles in the family nor weaknesses or failings of his own. This was no easy task, but she was lucky to possess one single-minded ally in the family: her youngest daughter, the devoted Mary.

More than ever now, Clementine had reason to be grateful for the work of Cousin Moppett Whyte. Thanks to her influence on Mary, there was one Churchill offspring who was modest, dutiful, and undemanding—and whose love for both her parents was simple and unfeigned. So was Mary's love of God, of country, and the common cause behind the fighting. Still in her early twenties, she worshiped Churchill, both as the hero of the nation and as an aged father-figure bearing the burdens of the war upon his sturdy shoulders.

She was intensely proud of him, but unlike brother Randolph did not exploit this pride to personal advantage. She had enjoyed no favors as an antiaircraft battery commander in the London blitz—apart from occasional informal visits from her beaming father to her Hyde Park gunsite—and had risen, very much on merit, to the equivalent rank of captain. When Hitler's final secret weapon, the V1 flying bomb, was launched at southern England, her battery was moved to Kent in the first line of defense.

Most of her weekend leaves were spent at Chequers with her parents, but she was unaffected by the presence of the mighty. In his diaries, Colville frequently remarked upon her gaiety and energy. Laura

Charteris remembered Mary as "extraordinarily wholesome, and always so beautifully turned out in her uniform that she would have made a perfect model for a women's armed forces recruiting poster."

Mary was inclined to fall in love impulsively. For a few days she was unofficially engaged to Lord Duncannon, and throughout the Quebec Conference was nursing a hopeless passion for a handsome young French parachutist. But unlike the equally impulsive Sarah, love did not lead her to rebel against her parents. The Lord and the parachutist were both discarded on Clementine's advice, and she turned her attention to more serious matters. As her mother's favorite, she shared Clementine's sense of personal responsibility toward her father; when Clementine departed on her six-week tour of Russia, it was to Mary that she entrusted him.

"Darling," she wrote, "supposing anything happened to me (e.g., air crash) do you think you could be released from the A.T.S. on compassionate grounds to look after Papa? Because he would need it. . . ."

There could be no question of entrusting such a task to Diana. Quite apart from Clementine's antipathy toward her eldest daughter, Diana had her own life to live with three young children, a large house in London, and an ambitious and demanding husband whose political career was flourishing on its own account.

Sandys himself was not overanxious for too much contact with his parents-in-law, being sensitive to suggestions that he had married for the sake of his career and owed his position entirely to Churchill. In fact, as Minister for Works, with responsibility for a large department, he succeeded less from family connections than from a driving energy that earned him more admirers than friends. (Brendan Bracken had recently accused him of "relying too much on the *führerprinzip*.")

Although strongly influenced by Churchill as a young M.P., Sandys had little of the bonhomie and gusto Churchill liked from those around him. A son-in-law whose company he enjoyed might have drawn Diana back into the family, but Sandys had a tendency to do the opposite. "There is good stuff in this fellow—great industry and guts—and it makes me sad that Winston is only bored with his son-in-law," wrote Moran.

But Diana was devoted to him, and photographs reveal a worried-looking wife whose looks were going and a debonair politician entering his prime. He was handsome and attractive to other women, who offered him a certain independence from a demanding wife and her overwhelming family. Diana was becoming insecure and jealous. Her husband was learning to remain aloof from her unhappiness. And Clementine was not the sort of mother Diana could confide in, any more than she could bother her great father with her problems.

There were also complications in Sarah's relationship with her father that, just as with Diana, would have prevented Clementine envisioning her as his guardian angel in her absence.

On the surface, Sarah had simplified her life when she left Vic Oliver and joined the W.A.A.F. Friends insist there really was no bitterness between them, and in Oliver's extraordinarily discreet short book of memoirs there is not a hint of the indignities he suffered from Churchill; he describes the breakup of his marriage as "a case of two people who had loved each other and had grown apart."

He remained a highly popular radio comedian, and apparently continued to be the old Svengali, soon discovering another young actress to adopt and career to mastermind.

Sarah, meanwhile, possessed a small income of her own and a bachelor apartment in a modern block in Park Lane. According to Paul Medlicott, who helped write her autobiography, the two important trips she made as "family A.D.C." to Churchill at Tehran and Yalta "brought her closer to her father than she had ever been before, leaving her almost stagestruck with her love and admiration."

Therein lay the problem that was to afflict Sarah for years to come. The more she fell beneath her father's spell, the more wary she became of forfeiting her precious independence, for she had learned how ruthless he could be at asserting his dominion over those he loved. It was because of this that she refused his offer to influence Air Chief Marshal Sholto Douglas to get her a comfortable job in the operations room of R.A.F. Fighter Command—which would have meant a promotion and "being stationed half way between Chequers and London." Instead, she opted for a course in aerial photographic interpretation, then spent the rest of the war at Medmenham in Berkshire, working on reconnaissance pictures taken by the R.A.F. over Germany.

This was high-pressure work requiring precision and long hours. She was popular, proud of her skill, and the job provided something of the precious independence she required. But it also meant she had to live two separate lives—one on weekends in the all-important world around her father, the other in her working life at Medmenham.

One of her fellow W.A.A.F.s, Pauline Bretherton, remembers "how careful Sarah always was to keep these two existences apart." She came to understand the strain this put upon her. "Sarah was desperately conscientious and determined not to ask for favours, but she was very much aware of being the P.M.'s daughter, and of having to live up to her position."

"You've no idea how tough it is, having a famous husband and a famous father," Sarah once remarked, and Mrs. Bretherton remembers her acute anxiety about "letting Papa down." "For Sarah, it was crucial to maintain face at whatever cost, which made her a terrible bottler-up of the emotions.

"She was always very nice about her mother. 'Poor Mummy,' she would say.'It really gets too much for her at times.' But she was totally and utterly obsessed with her father, going to Chequers most weekends to see him, and telephoning him whenever she had the opportunity."

Mrs. Bretherton believes this double life placed an extraordinary strain on Sarah. "She could be almost hyperactive, and I've seen her too exhausted when she went to bed to take her face off."

She also had a feeling that Sarah was somehow disappointed in herself. "It was as if she'd set herself such aims to live by, and blamed herself for failing to achieve them."

Against this background Sarah's love affair with the now besotted American Ambassador Gil Winant only added to her problems. Had he not been already married, he would have been ideal for her—another older man, idealistic, handsome, lonely, and clearly needing her. Clementine had grown extremely fond of him as well, and in wartime Britain, in close proximity to the Churchills, Winant had found something he had never known before: intimacy with supreme power, a sense of belonging at the center of great events, and the undoubted spell of Churchill's presence.

"Gil was in love with all the Churchills," said a diplomat who knew him well—and at the center of this most glamorous of families was the enchanted, vulnerable princess, the great man's daughter. Sarah would meet Winant during his regular weekend visits to Chequers, as well as at the two major conferences they attended. Her Park Lane apartment was five minutes' walk from the U.S. embassy in Grosvenor Square.

She found that Winant's love was all-involving. According to Mrs. Bretherton, "Sarah showed not the slightest interest in any of the men around throughout her time at Medmenham." But she and Winant had to be painfully discreet. Had news leaked out that the United States Ambassador was conducting a liaison with Winston Churchill's daughter in the middle of the war, the scandal would have broken John Gil Winant. It would probably have broken Sarah, too.

The agony that followed her elopement with Vic Oliver eight years earlier had been hideous enough. It was impossible to contemplate the effect another scandal would have on her father, especially at a time when he was bearing such responsibilities.

The result, like so many of Sarah's love affairs, was a doomed, unhappy, tense relationship. Despite heroic efforts at discretion, it proved impossible to keep it absolutely secret. Colville for one knew all about it, and Sarah was convinced her father knew as well. Many years later she would wistfully refer to this "old love affair which my father suspected but about which we did not speak."

Now with the war moving to its close Winant sensed the pressures there would be from his wife and family in Massachusetts, and an air of tragedy started to infect his love for Sarah Churchill.

Randolph meanwhile had been fully occupied with his private war in Yugoslavia, but even this had proved another anticlimax. Despite his father's fulsome letter, Tito had virtually ignored him, leaving Randolph to soldier on as part of a British military mission to the Communist partisans.

His contribution to the partisans is hard to gauge—he spoke no Serbo-Croat, hated communism, and had little interest in the country. He was brave when harried by the Germans, and uncomplaining when injured in an air crash, but there is a firm impression that the true reason Randolph stayed so long in Yugoslavia was to keep him out of trouble and prevent him from bothering his father back in Britain. During one short leave in London there was a dinner at Downing Street that ended with Randolph shouting down his father, striking Sarah, and being ejected by the marines. It was after this that, as something of an incentive to remain in Yugoslavia, Randolph was actually allowed to pick some friends to keep him company; these included Evelyn Waugh and Freddie Birkenhead. But neither man could cope with weeks on end of undiluted Randolph in the mountain villages of Croatia.

Life there with Randolph soon became so tense—and boring—that, to keep him occupied, Waugh bet him £10 that he couldn't read right through the Bible. Randolph gave up after the Old Testament, with the verdict, "God! Wasn't God a shit!"

By October 1944, Randolph and Evelyn Waugh had ceased to be on speaking terms. "He is not a good companion for a long period," wrote Waugh in his diary, "but the conclusion is always the same—that no one else would have chosen me, nor would anyone else have accepted him. We are both at the end of the tether as far as work is concerned and must make what we can of it."

Waugh had in fact spent part of the time with Randolph correcting the proofs of his most successful novel, *Brideshead Revisited,* which he had just completed, but Randolph had accomplished nothing. Even the military glory he hoped for had eluded him; his recommendation for the Military Cross was downgraded to the humbler Member of the British Empire medal to avoid suggestions of favoring Churchill's son. Waugh left Yugoslavia in November at his own request. Birkenhead followed him a few weeks later.

By the new year the mission to Yugoslavia was over and Randolph was in Rome where he underwent surgery for a damaged leg. He was back in London late that spring as the war in Europe drew to a close. By mid-April 1945, the Allies reached northern Italy, the American and Russian armies met in Germany, Mussolini perished in Turin, and as April ended the Red Army took Berlin.

On the evening of May 1, Churchill was dining with Lord Beaverbrook when Colville brought a report from Hamburg radio announcing Hitler's death. "He died," according to the German broadcast, "fighting with his last breath against Bolshevism." "Well, I must say I think he was perfectly right to die like that," said Churchill. Beaverbrook remarked that he obviously hadn't died like that—and later news confirmed that Hitler had committed suicide in his bunker in Berlin. The war against Germany and Italy was over.

Churchill had a brief period to savor victory. Hostilities in Europe officially ceased on May 8, Victory in Europe Day. Clementine was still in Moscow with Miss Hamblin. "All my thoughts are with you on this supreme day my darling," she cabled him from Moscow. "It could not have happened without you."

At three o'clock he spoke to the nation over the radio, after which he visited the King. That evening, in his siren suit, he was on a balcony above Whitehall addressing the vast crowd beneath, "This is your victory," he told them. "No, yours!" they roared back and he led them singing "Land of Hope and Glory."

It was a time of triumph and extraordinary emotion and few suspected how rapidly his reign would end. He had promised a general election as soon as the European war was over. It took place on July 8, but because of delays in counting the votes of servicemen abroad, the result was not known until July 26.

# thirty

# Opposition

There are few more potent demon-strations of the fickleness of political power than a change of govern-ment after a British general election. Few such changes have been more dramatic than that which summarily dismissed Winston Churchill from the premiership on July 26, 1945, some seven weeks after the greatest triumph of his life.

The day before the election, Churchill had been the victorious war leader, conferring with Stalin and the new U.S. President, Harry Truman, in Potsdam, in defeated Germany. There he had discussed the terms to be imposed on Germany, American plans for waging war against Japan, and the President's decision to drop the atom bomb on Nagasaki on August 6. But after his party's overwhelming electoral defeat, he was Prime Minister no longer, and although he had kept his parliamentary seat for Epping, he was now effectively a private citizen.

The Labour party, previously the minority partner in his wartime coalition in the Commons, had won 393 seats, an overall majority of 146 over all other parties in the House. The 585 Conservative seats (relics from the last general election of 1935) were now reduced to 213. Clement Attlee, the self-effacing socialist who had been Chur-chill's official (but largely ignored) Deputy Prime Minister throughout the war, now held the "great position" that had been Churchill's during five of the most exciting years in Britain's history. (In the debacle, both Randolph and Duncan Sandys had lost their seats.)

Churchill did his best to treat this earthquake philosophically. "It's absolutely monstrous how ungrateful the nation has been," Leslie Rowan's wife told him when she heard the news, but Rowan only smiled at her and shook his head. "That's politics, my dear. That's politics," he said.

In fact, the election results came as an appalling shock. Mary describes lunching with Churchill on the day they were announced. They sat "in Stygian gloom [as] Papa struggled to accept this terrible blow."

There was much discussion among the Conservative faithful over whom to blame. For Lord Beaverbrook, the culprit was the Conservative party—and for a large part of the Conservative party it was Lord Beaverbrook. For others, it was Churchill—largely on account of a notorious preelection speech he had made equating the Labour party with the Gestapo. Some blamed defeat on the armed forces' vote, others on the women's vote. But the fact was that the war had brought an overwhelming shift of social aspiration that was reflecting through the whole of British society. Churchill and the Conservatives were tending to be seen as figures from the past. Attlee and the Labour party were seen as part of a brave tomorrow. A sea change in British politics was occurring. But for Churchill, this very personal defeat hit him more profoundly than all but his closest friends appreciated.

A few days after the results, Churchill had an early-morning caller in the shape of good Lord Moran. The tradition of British politics that a defeated P.M. instantly vacate his official residence had deprived the Churchills of their home at 10 Downing Street, and he was making do in the penthouse suite at Claridges.

As usual at this hour, Churchill was sitting up in bed with the newspapers. It was a sunny morning and he appeared quite cheerful, but when Moran happened to remark upon the room's amenities, Churchill replied "I don't like sleeping near a precipice like that," he said, pointing to the balcony, and added, "I've no desire to quit the world, but thoughts, desperate thoughts come into the head."

This extraordinary comment has lain unremarked upon in the pages of Lord Moran's bulky diaries. But if Churchill was serious—and there is little reason to imagine he was joking—it helps explain much that is otherwise inexplicable in his behavior at this time and throughout what remained of his extraordinary political career.

The words echo the description, which he also gave to Moran, of the way that deep depression hit him in his late thirties, when he was Home Secretary in Asquith's government, and "the light had faded from the picture." When those earlier attacks of "Black Dog" were at their worst, he had felt a similar urge to violent self-destruction. This political defeat had evidently caused a bout of harrowing depression as bad as any in the past.

This in itself was strange. Churchill was nearly seventy-one, and logically he should have felt at least some relief at being freed at last from all those burdens he had frequently complained of in the war. Logically, too, he must have known his place in history was secure. He had surpassed even his extraordinary ambitions, and all the honors his once honor-hungry spirit could desire were there for the asking. He still had his "earthly paradise" at Chartwell to look forward to. There were his wartime memoirs to compose, the four volumes of his *History of the English-Speaking Peoples* waiting to be finished. He had his favorite friends to entertain, warm climes to visit, his growing family to enjoy.

Churchill often liked to quote from Maeterlinck's "Life of the Bee," on the way one tiny grub, when fed the magical royal jelly in the hive, became transformed into a queen. It was the same, he said, with power, which was another sort of royal jelly, and he would quote the story to account for the success that Clement Attlee was enjoying as Prime Minister.

In fact, the parable applied equally to Churchill, whose entire life had been a glowing testimonial to the transforming qualities of power. Power and the feeling of omnipotence that goes with it, had enabled him to overcome those hidden fears of failure that Lord Randolph had cruelly predicted. With his ascension, his deepest cravings for success had been satisfied, and for the last five years he had played the most exalted role of all, matching the exploits of his greatest heroes.

Now, suddenly deprived of this power, he was a monarch toppled from his throne. He who had slept soundly through the grimmest crises of the war found himself needing sleeping pills. "What is there to stay up for after midnight?" he asked sadly. Potentate no longer, he was at the mercy of the "unabsorbed residuum of pure emptiness" that had threatened him and driven him since adolescence.

There were simpler deprivations that also rankled: the loss of official cars and residences, the departure of the ministerial secretaries, and the abrupt ending of the special "diplomatic" rations that so richly sustained him through the darkest moments of the war. He was genuinely shocked when confronted with the weekly rations a normal citizen received in 1945; this lifelong carnivore was suddenly hating his food with its largely meatless content.

The abrupt change in life-style hit Clementine, too, for however wearying at times, the war had given her an unequaled role to play and undoubtedly revived her marriage. Lonely she may have been, with a husband so preoccupied, but she had been admired and respected on her own account; and she was always there to help him when required. This, too, had gone, and suddenly it must have seemed as if her life and her marriage were collapsing around her.

Her presence now only seemed to make her husband's humor worse. Exhausted and depressed herself, she craved the peace and quiet of retirement, the very thought of which filled Churchill with unmitigated gloom. She was wretchedly unhappy, and there seemed no alleviation. "In our misery," she wrote to Mary, "we seem, instead of clinging to each other, to be always having scenes."

At this sudden crisis in their parents' marriage, all three daughters rallied in support. Diana and Duncan lent their apartment in Westminster Gardens. Mary secured a compassionate posting back to London. And since it was clear that her parents needed a period apart, Sarah decided to accompany Papa on a painting holiday to a villa on Lake Como being used by his favorite soldier, Field Marshal Alexander. With Churchill out of power, even this was complicated. During the war, Churchill had simply ordered Sarah or Mary to accompany him on foreign journeys without a moment's hesitation, but now Sarah needed Winant's intercession to obtain leave of absence from the W.A.A.F.

Once at his easel and away from London, the change in the fallen leader was spectacular. A few weeks earlier, Moran had been witnessing "constant outbursts of childish petulance," but suddenly it seemed as if nothing could upset "the even serenity of these autumnal days beside the lake."

As usual, Churchill enjoyed Sarah's company. He also suddenly enjoyed his food, the perfect autumn weather, and the marble and gilt-mirrored luxury of the villa. In fact, as he told Moran, he was finding "the solution to his troubles in his paintbox," just as he had thirty years before when thrown out over the Dardanelles. Even the sudden appearance of a hernia failed to shake his equanimity. (Moran dispatched an emissary to Milan with the unlikely task of buying a surgical truss for Churchill.)

What everyone was witnessing was a recurrence of that crucial Churchillian phenomenon that Beaverbrook had noticed in World War I: the baffling switch between the two quite separate personalities that lay at the heart of Churchill's complex nature.

"When successful," Moran wrote, "Churchill's arrogance, intolerance and cocksureness assume alarming proportions." But in adversity he found him "gentle, patient and brave."

As usual, absence also made him sentimental over Clementine. The diplomatic Sarah, trying to repair the rift between her parents, was careful to report this to her mother. "We never see a lovely sight that he doesn't say—'I wish your mother were here.' "

But he also said, gazing out across the lake, "I'm damned glad to be out of it. I shall paint for the rest of my days. I've never painted so well before."

In fact, he needed to decide about his future. Those who felt he should retire from politics for good included not only Clementine but his deputy within the party, his "Princess Elizabeth" as he called forty-eight-year-old Anthony Eden. Eden was deeply in awe of Churchill, but privately he "couldn't wait for the old boy to go," leaving him free to lead the party. And Clementine, according to Grace Hamblin, was still nourishing her prewar dream of that graceful Georgian country house set in its lawns in perfect English countryside.

But now that Churchill's spirits were reviving, he was thinking otherwise. His brush with "Black Dog" must have reminded him how much he still required the "royal jelly" of politics and power to keep depression at bay, and he returned from Lake Como with his mind made up. Not only would he lead the party, but he would efface the stigma of defeat and win the next election.

One of the first signs of Churchill's resolution was his decision to purchase an extensive new headquarters in the heart of London. With this in mind he bought two adjacent houses, close to the park at Hyde Park Gate. These would provide offices for his secretariat and would be the Churchills' London residence for the remainder of Winston's life.

A further sign of his recovery was the speech he gave in January 1946 at Fulton, Missouri, during an early winter visit to the United States. A few days of preparatory painting and extremely hearty eating with Consuelo Balsan in Palm Beach had added to his strength, and his grim prediction of the growing threat of the Soviet Union was a clear return to his prewar role of embattled prophet preaching his testament of the doom that once more hung above humanity.

When he warned that an "Iron Curtain" had descended across

Europe "from Stettin in the Baltic to Trieste in the Adriatic," he was speaking words few in his audience were prepared for. When he reached Washington, President Truman avoided any reference to his speech.

But this time around the seer was not to languish in the wilderness for long. With his former friend and ally, Stalin, rapidly fulfilling Churchill's prophecies, Churchill's reputation for omniscience increased—as did his appetite for life and politics.

Back in London, a Conservative M.P. who lunched with him was surprised to see his aged leader down a dozen oysters, two good helpings of roast beef, steamed pudding, and the statutory bottle of champagne.

With Churchill's appetite restored, Eden would have a long wait to succeed him, but many in the party seemed convinced that Churchill could still be tactfully deposed. Instead, the excitement of the House of Commons was reviving Churchill's formidable powers of aggression—and the adrenaline was rising.

"I get the impression that the Tory party are most embarrassed by Winston's presence," wrote Harold Nicolson in May 1946. "They cannot edge him aside. They can only throw him out and that they do not wish to do."

Churchill was still too important to be thrown out, and Attlee's government had become the latest enemy he was itching to attack. R. A. Butler described him now as "gloomy, grouchy, sullen in his retirement, bursting with vigour and vengeance." "A short time ago I was ready to retire and die gracefully," he muttered. "Now I'm going to stay and have them out. I'll tear their bleeding entrails out of them."

During 1946, as Churchill was girding himself for battle at Westminster, he also had to face the unpleasantness of two divorces in the family. The first was Sarah's, which occurred, practically unnoticed, early that spring.

Although he generally disapproved of divorce—"why can't they forget their troubles and just get on with it?" was his usual attitude to marital problems, his own included—he was clearly delighted to be rid of Oliver as his son-in-law.

In a letter to her father, Sarah later reminded him of how, when he "knew it was all finished finally and legally with Vic, you called me across the room and whispered in my ear: 'Free!' "

She added that she had not really been free at all, as she had been in love. What she did not tell her father was that her lover had been Winant. The ending of the war now brought a crisis to this love affair by making Winant and Sarah come to a decision for the future. It was clear that Winant was depending more on her than she on him, and both were petrified of scandal—Sarah in particular. Deeply concerned as to the effect this could have on relations with her father, and fearful of "letting the side down," she was still as tense as ever.

From the beginning, the affair had been curiously unreal. There had been too much secrecy and guilt, and too little time for everyday love to grow between them. Now she felt the need to reassert her independence in the only way she knew: by pursuing stardom and success upon the stage. Acting was her one escape from what she called the "cage of affection" in which she felt herself imprisoned.

As for Winant, since Roosevelt's death, he had felt himself increasingly out of touch and out of favor with the new administration in Washington. Unhappy with what was happening in the world, he became hopeless and depressed and begged Sarah to wait for him to get divorced and marry him.

But there were twenty years between them, and this vulnerable man had all the problems of a wife and family in Massachusetts, while Sarah was ambitious for the future. One friend of Sarah's who occasionally saw the two of them together says they reminded him of the old obsessed Emil Jannings and the young Marlene Dietrich in the film *The Blue Angel*.

Their unhappiness increased throughout the summer of 1946. She was still fond of him and very sorry for him, but she refused to talk of marriage. He could talk of little else.

For Sarah, what seemed like a solution came when her agent, Al Parker, found her a part as the heroine of a film version of Antonio Fogazzaro's melancholy classic, *Daniele Cortis,* being shot in Rome. Here was her starring role at last—and a perfect excuse to make a break with Winant. The film's director, Mario Soldati—better known today as a distinguished novelist—had chosen Sarah from screen tests she had made in London.

"She was absolutely perfect for the part of the unhappy Elena," he said. "I wanted a tortured woman, a tragic woman, a desperate, aristocratic foreign woman—and here she was."

Acting opposite the Italian matinee idol Vittorio Gassman, Sarah could believe herself a star at last—and she was to find Rome a place of refuge for the years ahead.

But Winant refused to accept the end of the affair. He had by now resigned his ambassadorship, but instead of returning to the United States he had rented a house in Mayfair, close to his old embassy, to wait for Sarah. He was miserable and lonely. When Colville called, he found him "only happy talking about old times." A few months later, with Sarah still in Rome and still refusing to marry him, he finally returned to Concord, Massachusetts, with what friends describe as a broken heart.

By coincidence, Randolph's marriage had ended almost simultaneously with Sarah's—and with just as little fuss. Even Churchill had finally accepted that the marriage was beyond repair, and Randolph was anxious to pick up the threads of the bachelor existence he had so happily led before the war.

Lunatic optimism, personal extravagance, social outrage, and the thickest skin in London were helping him not only to survive but prosper. His greatest asset was the Churchill name. Coupled with the fact that, like his father, he possessed an instant opinion on every subject, he was guaranteed a lucrative career in journalism. He was always on the move, often to the States, where his exploits kept him firmly in the news.

Early in 1946, Evelyn Waugh encountered Randolph in Hollywood and described him as "Britishly drunk all the time, soliciting respectable women at luncheon parties etc." But although Waugh pretended to be shocked, there was something about Randolph, even at his most outrageous, that made him irresistible—particularly to Americans.

He was becoming that old-world specialty, a character, and, as Churchill's son, was something of a draw on the small-town lecture circuits.

"Do you think that I should use *The Name?*" his friend Alastair Forbes remembers Randolph asking him at a Washington party, as if it were some secret weapon. He could be boorish but he was rarely malicious, and there was a certain democratic gusto even to his famous rudeness. As the television journalist and traveler Alan Whicker put it, "at least Randolph was always as offensive to ambassadors as he was to waiters."

"Dear Randolph, utterly unspoiled by failure!" exclaimed Noël Coward as the unmistakable bulk of Churchill's princeling made its majestic entry into the Ivy Restaurant at about this time—a remark that had more truth than Coward probably intended. For Randolph was still convinced of his predestined status as his father's son and heir. Secretly he still believed that he would magically inherit the seamless mantle of paternal power and one day become Prime Minister himself.

Setbacks ignored, his confidence remained mysteriously unshaken. He still assumed a style he could ill afford and rented a house in Belgravia. Blackballed from the Beefsteak Club, he unashamedly applied again and was elected. Even relations with his father were stronger than their rows suggested. Before delivering his Fulton speech, Churchill checked it first with Randolph.

Divorce from Pamela actually improved relations between Randolph and his parents by ending their temptation to take sides against him. Pamela had also made things easier by leaving London for the South of France when war in Europe ended. She felt that once the Churchill Club had closed its doors, there was little to keep her tied to London. The rich and powerful Americans she loved had also flown. Averell Harriman had made it clear he could not marry her; nor could Ed Murrow, whose wife had just had his baby.

She says she found English women at this time "insipid and rather silly," but she was not a woman's woman, and the social skills that made her such a draw in wartime London had their uses in peacetime France. So did the Churchill name, and in Paris lay a new society for her to conquer.

She found herself a spectacular apartment beside the Seine, at 4, Avenue de New York, and with considerable style began to do what best became her, forming a fresh circle of rich admirers around her. Explaining Pamela's success, Diana Cooper—whose husband, Duff, was now Ambassador in Paris—used to call her "The Universal Aunt" because of the trouble that she took with people.

These included such deserving cases as Aly Khan and Elie Rothschild, who became devoted to her. During this period, little Winston spent a lot of time in England with the Digbys and the Churchills, who loved him dearly. He saw little of his father.

Meanwhile, Sarah had arrived in Rome but almost immediately fell ill with a suspected kidney infection. Fortunately, the shooting of the film had not begun, but the illness was serious enough to worry Clementine, who dispatched Mary "to keep Sarah company and to see that she was taking proper care of herself."

Mary went off on this errand of mercy in what she described as "a state of high emotion with a good-looking young man in tow." This was twenty-six-year-old Captain Christopher Soames, a very tall young man who was currently Assistant Military Attaché with the British embassy in Paris. The news of his surprise arrival in Rome with Mary caused much consternation back at Chartwell.

It was not simply their daughter's unexplained and headlong conduct that upset Winston and Clementine. (She, after all, was twenty-six herself, and it was high time she thought of marriage.) But Clementine liked to think that she and her daughter had no secrets from each other and, at bottom, the Churchills had considerably higher hopes for Mary than an unknown captain in the Guards.

During a recent visit to Brussels, they had been warmly entertained by Prince Charles of Belgium, newly elected Belgian Regent in place of his disgraced brother, Leopold, who had been accused of collaboration with the Germans. Mary accompanied her parents on the trip, and Churchill's profound reverence for royalty was aroused by this unassuming, patriotic Prince. Churchill had several late-night conversations in the palace, during which Charles evidently bared his soul to the aged monarchist, who now responded with considerable emotion.

"I was painfully affected by all you told me about your brother's singular attitude and behaviour to you in those long tragic years," Churchill wrote the Prince later. "I have a brother who is five years younger than me and whom I dearly love and have always cherished. I grieve indeed that you have never found the same kindness and protection which Nature decrees."

It was not entirely surprising that the Churchills felt that they possessed the answer to this lonely Prince's problems. Who better than their daughter Mary to help alleviate his heavy heart. Who better than Mary to help him in his hour of need?

According to Diana Cooper, this was very much what both the Churchill parents had in mind when they arrived with Mary at the Paris embassy en route home after visiting the Belgian Regent. And it was then that, unbeknown to them, their daughter rapidly forgot the forty-three-year-old royal bachelor for the more robust attractions of Captain Soames.

Soames was not the man to miss the opportunity of a lifetime, nor did he waste the few romantic days he spent with Mary by the bedside of her convalescent sister. Before returning to his duties back in Paris, he and Mary had become engaged.

Soames must have seemed a most unlikely candidate for the hand of the Churchills' treasured daughter. Descended from a family of brewers and known at Eton by the nickname "Soapy Soames," he was not a popular young officer, and had emerged from wartime service with the Guards with a somewhat patchy reputation. But brash and pushy though he may have been, Christopher was the man Mary loved. And although Clementine was less than pleased to hear of the engagement—having presumably been envisaging herself the mother of a princess—the Churchills had found in Captain Soames the son-in-law they needed.

Almost from the start he got on famously with Churchill. "The great thing about Christopher," says Randolph's friend, the politician Julian Amery, "is that he wasn't in the least frightened by the old gentleman."

The fact was, he was too much of a bully himself to let Churchill bully him. Unlike Duncan Sandys, who, as Moran says, "couldn't follow Churchill's moods," Soames had a natural instinct for the things that pleased him. He would play cards with him, drink with him, listen to his reminiscences, and make him laugh. By the time of the marriage, in February 1947, Soames was firmly and irreplaceably ensconced within the Churchill family. Backed with the power and influence of Churchill's name, another important political career was just beginning.

Mary's marriage to "the Chimp," as Clementine had christened Soames, took place at St. Margaret's Westminster and was a happy family event. Churchill by now had totally recovered from the shock of his defeat in 1945. He had reestablished undisputed power over his party and, despite his age, was proving an effective leader of the opposition in the House of Commons. Far from declining gracefully into that impotent old age he dreaded, he seemed to be defying time itself, and remained the most active of political volcanoes, spewing the fire of rhetoric upon the Attlee government in some of the most effective speeches of his whole career.

In the meantime, life in opposition seemed to suit him. During the worst of the London winter, he was able to depart for the warmth of Marrakesh or the South of France. He was revered throughout the world, his words commanded vast respect, and he was even freed at last from worries over Chartwell. Knowing his problems of maintaining the estate, a group of rich businessmen had bought it from him and presented it to the National Trust as a future Churchill shrine with the stipulation that he lived there undisturbed until he died.

Clementine had also come to terms with her husband's firm refusal to retire, and here Mary's marriage proved an unexpected blessing. Shortly before the wedding, Christopher developed symptoms of
a duodenal ulcer, which meant he had to leave the army. Since the
newlyweds had nowhere to live, the Churchills offered them the farm
at Chartwell, which Christopher could manage.

This started a new era for the house and the estate, with the
Soameses taking over from the aged and increasingly cantankerous
Moppett Whyte, running the place efficiently and taking care of the
frequently exhausted Clementine. This left Churchill free to immerse
himself again in all his old activities and the wartime memoirs he was
now beginning.

But just as it seemed that everything was comfortably arranged,
Churchill's equilibrium received another jolt, followed by a most disturbing episode.

Three weeks after Mary's marriage, Churchill was abruptly summoned to his brother's deathbed. After Goonie's death in 1942, Jack
had made his home at 10 Downing Street with the Churchills. He had
his own small room at the top of the house, and everybody loved the
Prime Minister's gentlemanly, unassuming brother. He was immensely
proud of Winston, and his daughter Clarissa believes that this was
probably the happiest time of his life. But recently Jack had been ailing
with a weakened heart. This had not kept him from enjoying his status
as Winston Churchill's brother and it was a distinction that, not long
before he died, had helped him to achieve his final great ambition:
election to Lord Randolph's favorite London club, the Turf.

Thus Jack died a happy man, but his deathbed was an emotional
occasion, with his children—Johnny, Peregrine, and Clarissa—present. Churchill was in tears when his brother said farewell, and Johnny
said that "when my father began the death agony we left my uncle
alone with him in meditation." According to Winston, Jack "had no
fear & little pain. . . . The only thing Jack worried about was England.
I told him it would be all right."

Jack's peaceful, patriotic death seems to have sent Winston into a
bout of deep depression. "Do you think we shall be allowed to sleep a
long time? I hope so," Churchill wrote when replying to a letter of
condolence from his old friend Lord Hugh Cecil. He also told Cecil
how lonely he was feeling, "after 67 years of brotherly love," and how
he still remembered "my father coming in to my bedroom at the Viceregal Lodge in Dublin and telling me (aged 5) 'You have a little
brother.' "

However, it was not so much memories of Jack as of Lord Randolph that seem to have now struck Churchill with unusual force. At around this time, Sarah told Peregrine that her father was complaining of recurrent nightmares of Lord Randolph; and Johnny describes an emotional meeting with his uncle at the time of the funeral in which Winston, self-obsessed as ever, talked not of Jack but of his own "prostration" when Lord Randolph died. In an extraordinary scene, Churchill finally mastered his emotions by taking a copy of his book *The River War* from the bookshelf and reading aloud from it for half an hour. "That's pretty good writing, you know," he told his somewhat puzzled nephew. "I wish I could write like that today."

Some months later, during a weekend at Chartwell, Churchill read Sarah and Randolph something else that he had written. Entitled simply "Private Article," it was a factual, down-to-earth account of how he had recently met his father's ghost.

The piece was emphatically not some piece of old man's whimsy but a serious treatment calmly describing how Lord Randolph suddenly appeared in the studio at Chartwell "looking just as I had seen him in his prime. . . . A small slim jaunty figure with a large moustache." He was "filling his amber cigarette holder with a little pad of cotton-wool before putting in a cigarette," just as Churchill remembered him doing.

During the ensuing conversation, Churchill proceeded to fill his father in on some of the key events since his death—two horrifying European wars, the decline of the Empire, and Europe threatened by a Marxist Russia. The ghost said how glad he was not to have had to witness such disasters, and then and only then did Lord Randolph show any genuine emotion toward Winston, but it was not benevolent emotion. Suddenly Lord Randolph was repeating all those bitter and dismissive accusations that had haunted Churchill all his life.

Winston remarked to Lord Randolph how he had been brought up "in the tradition of democracy," producing the stinging rejoinder "I never brought you up to anything." Lord Randolph then proceeded to enumerate all his son's bitterly remembered failings. "Bottom of the school! Never passed any examination, except into the cavalry. Wrote me stilted letters. I could not see how you would make your living on the little I could leave you and Jack, and that only after your mother. I once thought of the bar for you, but you were not clever enough."

Here, in black and white at last, was Winston's version of Lord Randolph's condemnation, which had been hanging over him for fifty years. Here was one source of those anxieties that had fueled his intense ambition and brought him to the verge of suicide and bleak despair. And here was that grim prediction of failure, which Churchill's whole career had sought to alter.

What is amazing is that, at seventy-two, the most famous man in Britain was still haunted by such judgments from a sick and long-dead father—and that he felt obliged to write them out in detail, then read them to his family.

But Churchill had his reasons. The "Private Article" was presumably based upon the recurrent nightmares he had been having of his father, and shows all the signs of careful and attentive composition. It is in fact a very skillful piece of writing whose deadpan style conceals its author's all-important purpose, which is partially revealed at the end. Throughout the account of what has happened to Britain since Lord Randolph's death, it is noticeable that Churchill ventures nothing of his own achievements; when he finishes, it is Lord Randolph who rather condescendingly compliments him on the knowledge he has been displaying.

"Of course you are too old now to think about such things, but when I hear you talk I really wonder you didn't go into politics. You might have done a lot to help. You might even have made a name for yourself." With which Lord Randolph gives his son a "benignant" smile, and with "a tiny flash" vanishes for good.

It is, of course, Churchill himself who is really having the last laugh on his father, and the whole story, far from being the sentimental old man's reminiscence of a much-loved father, is really nothing of the kind. Its author is doing what he must have longed to do on countless occasions since his father died: meet Lord Randolph's ghost on equal terms and prove his predictions wrong.

It is very cleverly and neatly done. There is no argument and no recrimination from Churchill. Instead, very lightly and wittily he lets Lord Randolph demonstrate that the dead can be completely wrong about the living, and that the judgments that he passed on twenty-year-old Winston have been utterly negated. Winston has won. He has become a greater figure than his father ever was, and the fact that his father is so ignorant about his son's achievements actually provides the punch line of the story.

Churchill was evidently satisfied once he had written out this curious account and had read it to his children. He made no attempt to publish it. Instead, he locked it in a box and never referred to it again. Randolph discovered it after his father's death and published it.

He called it "The Dream." A better title might have been "The Exorcism," for by writing it Churchill appears to have disarmed Lord Randolph's ghost. With that tiny flash he described, his father took his leave of him and seems to have troubled him no further.

Churchill was now free to devote his energies to his wartime memoirs, which were his real answer to Lord Randolph's indifference to his achievements. For although he relied as usual on assistants and advisers—principally Bill Deakin, the Oxford don who first helped him on his life of Marlborough—this massive work was essentially his personal version of the war, and represented the version of himself as the great war leader that he wished posterity to remember.

Failures are very much glossed over as are such controversial events as the disastrous commando raid on Dieppe in 1942 or the mass destruction of the German city of Dresden by British bombers with vast civilian casualties in January 1945. For as with all his major works, *The Second World War* appears to have one fundamental purpose: to establish that in everything that matters, Churchill had been absolutely right from the beginning.

In his customary manner, Churchill dictated the book in its entirety to his secretaries, with the result that one hears his voice on almost every page.

Translated and serialized throughout the world, the memoirs, the first volume of which appeared in June 1948, were a great success, leading to the Nobel Prize for Literature in 1953.

While writing *The Second World War,* Churchill appears to have enjoyed reliving the great events he describes. Certainly he spent more time on writing than on politics. Completely cured of the gloom following his brother's death, he began enjoying all his postwar splendor and prosperity, for the memoirs also made him rich, and while to minimize taxation much of the royalties were placed in trust to benefit his children, Churchill was able to enjoy a proportion of his money.

Chartwell was flourishing with the Soameses living there, and a new generation was appearing on the premises. Along with the goldfish and the butterflies, the chickens and the geese, there would soon be two Soames grandchildren for Churchill to enjoy—Nicholas, born in 1948, and Emma, born in 1949 (three more, Jeremy, Charlotte, and Rupert would arrive in the 1950s). Mary could look after Clementine, and while Soames continued to get on so splendidly with Churchill, the former captain had much to learn from the former lieutenant of Hussars, not least of all how to turn from soldiering to politics.

While the Soameses basked in the sunlight of the great man's favor, some of his other children were less fortunate. Sarah in particular had been having a miserable few months toward the end of 1947.

Since his return to Concord, Winant had been suffering acute depression. Short of money and out of favor in Washington, he was convinced he had no future. His marriage had not recovered from the war, and he still missed Sarah. He had telephoned her frequently in Italy, begging her to have him back. "If you won't, I'll shoot myself," he told her. On the night of October 10, 1947, in an upstairs room of his home in Massachusetts, he carried out his threat.

Sarah was not mentioned in the press or at the inquest. But Winant had been talking to her shortly before he killed himself, and according to Soldati the effect his suicide had on her was shattering. She had no reason to blame herself for what occurred—their affair had long been over and Winant had been a congenital depressive. But she inevitably reproached herself, feeling that she brought nothing but unhappiness to those who loved her. To make things worse, *Daniele Cortis* was a flop and the critics had panned her. As Soldati put it, "Her talents as an actress were not equal to the star she wished to be—and the Churchill name was too big for her to live with." It was then that friends noticed she was drinking heavily.

Clementine made a point of insisting that they attend Winant's memorial service in London. And Churchill, who must have known what Winant meant to her, took Sarah with him when he went to Marrakesh that winter to finish the first volume of his memoirs, expenses paid by his U.S. publisher.

During this period, Randolph was also more troubled than he appeared to be, and as usual, relations with his father lay at the root of his unhappiness. Churchill was getting bored with his son. "We have a deep animal love for one another," he admitted, "but every time we meet we seem to have a bloody row." Worse still, Randolph's role as Churchill's heir seemed threatened. Chartwell had been intended as his patrimony, but it would now pass to the National Trust on Churchill's death.

Mary said that with age, Churchill could no longer bear the strain of the endless arguments with his son, but a more probable reason for Randolph's dropping out of favor was probably her husband, Christopher, who, as Colville put it, "without malice or intrigue or any ostentation on his own part, stepped into the shoes so long predestined for Randolph."

One source of jealousy he no longer needed to contend with was his ex-wife, Pamela. Since she had gone to Paris, his parents saw little of her, and it was now that Churchill was heard remarking, "What's this I hear about Pamela taking up with an Italian motor mechanic?"

This improbable remark was a reference to one of the richest men in Italy, the playboy, sportsman, and heir to the Fiat Motor Company of Turin, Gianni Agnelli, who, in his early forties and still unmarried, was enjoying wine, women, and Ferraris in the South of France before shouldering his great inheritance.

Having spent the war at the court of Winston Churchill, Pamela was inevitably attracted to this future uncrowned king of Italy. And adaptable as ever, she was soon holidaying at Agnelli's villa in the South of France, talking with a noticeable Italian accent, and even considering converting to Catholicism. She also thought of having her marriage to Randolph annulled by the Vatican. Marriage to Agnelli would complement her life with the Churchills—and provide young Winston with the settled background he needed. For although he would soon be attending smart Le Rosay School in Switzerland, Pamela was worried at his tendency to eczema and asthma.

Like Pamela, Randolph also felt the urge to settle down, and once more did his best to marry Laura. Since her marriage to Lord Dudley had collapsed—"insane jealousy, hideous temper, quite impossible"—Randolph tried to take his place. Laura's reasons for refusing him are interesting: "Fond as I was of Randolph I was never in love with him. Perhaps his father's influence stopped him ever growing up, so that as a lover one could never take him seriously."

Someone Laura did take seriously was the youthful publisher Michael Canfield, who as well as being handsome, rich, and charming was reputedly the secret offspring of the late Duke of Kent. (His adoptive father was Cass Canfield, head of the New York publishers, Harper and Row). When he became Laura's third husband in 1948, Randolph ignored the marriage, as he had her others, and remained in love with her—but this did not keep him from looking for a wife.

Randolph already knew the beautiful June Osborne. A colonel's daughter, she was nearly thirty, dressed well, and spoke impeccably, yet she remained unmarried—having gravitated to the upper reaches of literary bohemia where husbands were difficult to find. For a time she had been the mistress of Randolph's handsome friend the journalist Alastair Forbes, while she shared a house with the biographer Peter Quennell. And in 1947, the talk in the White's Club bar was that Cyril Connolly was in love with her and contemplating marriage.

Ever since they were boys together at Eton, Randolph had treated this distinguished man of letters as a joke, and it was possibly to annoy him that he proposed to June himself. To his surprise, June accepted.

Neurotic, vulnerable, and deeply conventional at heart, June was even more unsuited to the role of Mrs. Randolph Churchill than Pamela had been. But Randolph was that awkward phenomenon: an unmarriageable man who wanted a wife. And once accepted, he was not letting go.

Evelyn Waugh, who understood this, assured June, in what must have been a tongue-in-cheek letter of congratulation, that Randolph was "essentially a domestic and home-loving character who has never had a home." Waugh also spoke of Randolph's "unique natural capacity for happiness which, one way or other, has never been fully developed. I am sure," he added hopefully, "that you will be able to do this for him."

The Churchills met the Osbornes for lunch at the Savoy, and a three-month-long engagement followed. This included never-ending arguments, a suicide attempt by June, and a fight between the lovers on the Thames embankment after which June seriously considered charging Randolph with assault.

The engagement would have scared almost anyone but Randolph from the altar. "You can't seriously think of going through with it, " said Laura.

"Of course I am," Randolph told her. "It's a scientific fact that couples who fight before marriage live happily ever after."

This was just another of Randolph's optimistic fallacies, but, undeterred, he married June in the presence of the Churchill family at Caxton Hall on November 2, 1948. His father, anxious to see him settled and to compensate him for losing the inheritance to Chartwell, had arranged for the trust fund to buy him a house in Westminster for £14,000. And although the marriage was even stormier than Laura predicted, June rapidly produced a daughter. She was a pretty baby, and to placate his father, in November 1949, Randolph had her christened Arabella, after the Duke of Marlborough's sister Arabella Churchill, who had been mistress to King James II.

Churchill was delighted, and the birth of Arabella seemed to coincide with the revival of his fortunes. Attlee's Labour government had outlived its popularity, surviving the general election of February 1950 by a mere six votes.

Churchill could afford to wait. He had his memoirs to complete before taking his revenge against the socialists. By the summer of 1951 they were all but finished, and that August saw him at the Annecy in the French Savoie, working on the final volume. He had traveled to Annecy from London on the grandest scale, with French Railways transporting fifty-five trunks and sixty-five smaller articles out for him —but finding the weather in France disappointing, he decided to go on to Venice.

His secretary told him that the train did not stop at Annecy and they would have to drive to Geneva to catch it.

"Kindly remember I am Winston Churchill," he told her. "Tell the station master to stop the train."

The train duly stopped, and Churchill and his luggage got to Venice.

A month later he was back in England fighting another general election, which the Conservatives won outright with a majority of seventeen. The result was declared on October 26 so that, a month short of his seventy-seventh birthday, he was returned to power. Not only had he reversed the defeat of 1945. His appointment as Prime Minister in 1940 had rested on the vote of the House of Commons. Now for the first time he had become Prime Minister by the vote of the British people.

# thirty-one

# The Secret Battle

Had Churchill not become Prime Minister again in October 1951, it is hard to think of any other position in the country that could have been safely entrusted to this ailing, elderly Englishman. He was going deaf and losing his once formidable powers of memory and concentration. He smoked and ate and drank too much. The arteries that fed the brain were closing up, the nerves in his back had been affected, and according to Lord Moran, he had never fully recovered from a stroke he had sustained some eighteen months earlier while staying with Lord Beaverbrook in the South of France. As with most of Churchill's illnesses, the stroke had been effectively hushed up, but Moran thought a recurrence virtually inevitable.

"Very, very old, tragically old," replied Bob Boothby when Harold Nicolson asked how he found the new Prime Minister the day after taking office. And Oliver Lyttleton described him as possessing "the tired look of a trawler captain who had reached harbour after a buffeting." Not even Clementine believed this storm-tossed skipper of the ship of state could stay much longer on the bridge.

Not that she wished him to. She understood how desperately he had wanted this final spell in office to efface the humiliation of defeat in 1945. But now that he had it, she urged him to retire gracefully before too long, and he agreed to do so, certainly within a year. This was greeted with relief by his colleagues, in particular by his P.M.-in-waiting, Anthony Eden. Back in his old job of Foreign Secretary, this diplomat's diplomat had been happy to return to his allies and admirers in the Foreign Office, but he was happier still at the prospect of becoming Prime Minister after all those years in Churchill's shadow.

But no one quite appreciated the effect the return to power had on Churchill, and his final ministry provides a signal demonstration of how "the great elixir," that "mystical royal jelly" could revive almost all the qualities that once made him great. Rhetoric, aggressiveness, courage, rocklike obstinacy—all were marshaled in one grand endeavor to fight off age and stay in office. Like some ancient general on a long retreat, he soon relied on every subterfuge he knew to dodge the moment of surrender.

To begin with, almost everybody wished him well. "You and I derive great pleasure from the fact that the old boy is back in power which he revels in, and that the last lustre of his life should be spent in place and power which is health to him," wrote Lord Bracken to Lord Beaverbrook. Bracken also wrote to Churchill urging him to "be a lazy premier."

This seemed sound advice even if there was, as someone said, a strong whiff of "Old Lang Syne in the corridors of power," as he assembled his "cronies Cabinet" around him. Although Bracken and Beaverbrook declined to reenlist, he had R. A. Butler at the Treasury and Harold Macmillan in charge of housing. His son-in-law Duncan Sandys became his Minister for Air, Field Marshal Alexander his Minister for Defense, and the newly elected member for Bedford, his other son-in-law, Captain Soames, was his all-important Parliamentary Private Secretary. Churchill's policy, he said, was simple: "houses and meat and not getting scuppered." In fact, he changed little of Attlee's legislation, and it was still generally assumed that he would "soon be handing on to Anthony" when the first of an unexpected series of events offered him a chance to play things very differently.

Early in February 1952, Grace Hamblin was working on letters with Clementine in her room in 10 Downing Street when a grim-faced Churchill entered. "Go!" he shouted at Miss Hamblin. "Go!"

Miss Hamblin went; when Clementine later apologized for her husband's behavior, she explained that he had just received the news that King George VI had died in the night at Sandringham. Churchill was deeply, indeed painfully, affected, and all the romantic feeling in his nature was aroused as usual at a poignant royal occasion. He spent a whole day locked in composition of the epitaph that he would broadcast to the nation—one that, in terms of rhetoric, rivaled the abdication speech he wrote for George's predecessor back in 1936. "The king walked with death as if death were a companion, an acquaintance, whom he recognised and did not fear. In the end death came as a friend," he said.

Churchill did this sort of thing so well that nobody remarked that this simply was not true. Far from treating death as a companion, George VI's doctors had kept the King in ignorance of the seriousness of his illness; he had died quite suddenly in his sleep after a day's shooting, completely unaware that he was suffering from lung cancer.

Churchill was profoundly stirred, but his sorrow at King George's death was sweetened by the succession of Elizabeth II. "I whose youth was passed in the august, unchallenged and tranquil glare of the Victorian era, may feel a thrill in invoking once again the prayer and anthem, 'God Save the Queen!,' " his epitaph had ended.

Well might he feel a thrill, for as he knew quite well, it would take at least a year to complete the arrangements for the coronation (finally set for June 3, 1953), and as Moran wrote, Churchill instantly "set his heart on seeing the young Queen crowned before he gave up office." Nothing would keep him from being present as Prime Minister —not even the scare he had a few weeks later when a cerebral disturbance affected his powers of speech, making him fear the onset of another stroke.

There was no stroke, and relations between this aged P.M. and his impatient Foreign Secretary began to fray as Eden became increasingly exasperated by Churchill's presence and by the way he ran the government. Then, in August 1952, harmony was suddenly restored thanks to an unexpected member of the Churchill family. Early that August, the engagement of Churchill's niece Clarissa to Anthony Eden was announced.

Clarissa was a most untypical Churchill. From the moment her mother had chosen her name from the heroine of Samuel Richardson's novel *Clarissa Harlow,* this precious daughter had seemed destined for a world different from the political and international affairs that so obsessed the Churchills. Clarissa was as bright as she was pretty, and although she got on well with her famous aunt and uncle, politics bored her. After a year at the Sorbonne, just before the war, she settled in Oxford, making friends with such Oxford luminaries as Maurice

Bowra, Isaiah Berlin, and David Cecil. During the war she did factory work; afterward, she did publicity for Alexander Korda and the publisher George Weidenfeld.

Eden, whose first marriage had ended in divorce some five years earlier, had met Clarissa outside the orbit of the Churchills at a London dinner party in 1947. Until then, she had not known him, for despite his close political association with his leader, Eden and the Churchill family had little social contact, and news of the engagement caught the Churchills rather by surprise.

Churchill himself appeared delighted, giving Clarissa £500 as an engagement present and telling Colville that he "felt avuncular towards his orphaned niece." He added that he thought she had "a most unusual personality." Colville himself wondered how much marriage would change this "strange and bewildering" young woman, and whether she would "help to calm the vain and occasionally hysterical Eden."

For a while it looked as if she might. After a register office wedding at the end of August, Churchill gave the reception at 10 Downing Street—and seemed untroubled by the thought that before too long he and Clementine would be surrendering this home of theirs to the bridal couple. It was generally assumed that the marriage would make Churchill's resignation less painful by keeping the succession within the family. Indeed, now that his political heir-apparent had married the daughter of his beloved brother, this should have been the moment for the family to become more united. But with the Churchills, things rarely happened as one might expect, and the strains within the family, particularly among the elder children, were actually increasing.

This was most evident with Randolph, who reacted very strangely to his cousin's marriage. They were, in fact, good friends, and when Evelyn Waugh greeted news of the engagement by publicly criticizing Clarissa, as a natal Catholic, for marrying a divorcé, Randolph had promptly put his former comrade firmly in his place. "What business is it of yours? You are not the Cardinal Archbishop or the editor of *The Tablet* or even like me, a cousin."

But Randolph, in fact, disliked the marriage even more than Waugh did—not on religious grounds but because of his almost pathological resentment of Eden. In Randolph's eyes, by marrying "Jerk" Eden, as he always called him now, Clarissa was aiding and abetting the principal usurper of his own predestined place beside his father. For Churchill's victory had left Randolph in a miserable situation. While Soames and Sandys, by their reelection to Parliament, had both been able to enjoy the great man's governmental bounty, Randolph had once more ignominiously failed to get elected, having been firmly beaten at Devonport by his fellow Beaverbrook journalist, the Labour politician Michael Foot.

Randolph's old ambition to become Prime Minister was, amazingly, unshaken, but he felt that his father's return to office had spoiled his chances. "I can do nothing while he is there," he used to say, and instead of being able to count on Churchill's political support, he watched jealously as it became diverted, first to Soames and Duncan Sandys, and now, through Clarissa's marriage, to his enemy Eden.

Randolph's misery boiled up a few weeks later when Churchill failed to take him along on his special train, as he did Soames and Clementine, to the Tory party conference at Scarborough. Churchill seems to have wanted nothing more sinister than a peaceful journey, but Randolph reacted like a jilted lover. In a long and anguished letter to his father, he complained of the agony of being "repeatedly disregarded, rejected & snubbed by the person one loves most in the world." Churchill did his best to reassure Randolph, but as Prime Minister he had more important matters with which to deal than a forty-year-old son who drank too much, embarrassed him in public, and whose second marriage was already showing signs of collapsing just as his first had done. For not even the birth of Arabella had made Randolph change his habits, and he and June were feuding more than ever.

During this early period back in power, Churchill was not enjoying particularly close relations with his daughter Sarah either. After the unhappy period following Winant's suicide, Sarah had pulled herself together and, cashing in on the Churchill name, had started getting parts as a celebrity actress on American television. Then she fell in love again, this time with Anthony Beauchamp, a British society photographer then working in the United States. Early in 1949, while holidaying in the South of France, Sarah had taken Beauchamp to meet her parents at Monte Carlo. The visit started well enough, with Beauchamp even spending an evening with Churchill in the casino, where he introduced the great man to his special system at roulette. Then something went embarrassingly wrong. Beauchamp, though handsome, smooth, and very charming, did not measure up to Churchillian concepts of a gentleman. (Born Entwhistle, he had changed his name to Beauchamp for professional and social reasons.) And Churchill began treating him as he had Vic Oliver, whom he had also thought "common as dirt," at their first meeting. Hurt and insulted, Beauchamp left abruptly. Sarah was very angry, and expressed her feelings in the sharpest letter she ever wrote her father, making it all too plain whose side she was on. "If you think that by insulting him you can change by one jot the opinion I hold of him—you are most sorely mistaken. . . . I love you very much—nothing can ever change that—but I see now how right I have been to build a life for myself, and arm myself with four good hoofs & a crusty carapace, for the slings & arrows of family life are sharp indeed."

Never again, she swore, would she subject any of her friends to Churchill's contempt, and as good as her word, she did not inform her parents when she married Beauchamp at Sea Island, Georgia, in October 1949. Once she heard about the marriage, Clementine did her best to restore relations with her daughter, but as far as Churchill was concerned, Sarah's second marriage was a repetition of her first and brought yet another son-in-law he could not tolerate. Largely because of this, the Beauchamps continued to live in the States.

Sarah could cope with life, and was perfectly capable of creating a separate existence away from the family as she said she would, but her sister Diana was less resilient against the pressures crowding in on her. During this period, Diana caused Churchill and the family increasing concern. Most of her troubles lay with feelings of inadequacy, particularly now that her husband was a successful minister in her father's government. Sandys was reasonably discreet about his affairs with other women, and she still loved him dearly, but less than ever was he the sort of husband a dependent and insecure wife like Diana needed. Nor was Clementine much help to this neurotic daughter for whom she had so little understanding and felt so little sympathy. Much of Diana's neurosis originated in Clementine's lack of love for her in childhood, and her misery and absence of self-esteem were still bound up with feelings that her mother had no time for her and disapproved of her.

Early in 1953, Diana had a severe nervous breakdown. Although its immediate cause was marital unhappiness, it was not her husband who bore the brunt of her neurotic anger, but Clementine. When Diana lost control and ran hysterically out of her London house, it was Randolph who was called to find her. He finally discovered her close to home, hiding in some bushes and armed with a carving knife. Later he told Laura that Diana was threatening to kill Clementine. He calmed her down and brought her home, but said that she was so pathetic that taking the knife away was "like disarming a butterfly."

Diana's breakdown was the start of a wretched period spent in clinics undergoing treatment, none of which could change her underlying problems. Her husband maintained the appearances of the marriage, and her mother tried to get on better terms with her—without great success. While Diana's relations with her mother would fluctuate, the one member of the family who always had a calming influence on her was her father. It was now that he told her of his own near nervous breakdown, when "the light faded from the picture" during his time as Home Secretary. Mary writes that Churchill always found "psychological troubles and their explanation quite beyond his ken," but the fact that they shared a similar depressive tendency must have helped him understand Diana. Certainly, Churchill was always gentle and supportive of Diana, but during this Coronation Year of 1953 he had other family problems with which to contend, in particular his own relations with his political heir-apparent, now married to his niece.

Eden's marriage was apparently extremely happy, but by the beginning of 1953 this handsome, highly strung politician was becoming nervous and depressed about his future. "He doesn't think the Old Man will ever go," wrote his principal private secretary Evelyn Shuckburgh, adding that he was so disheartened that he was listening to Clarissa's advice to quit politics for good at the coronation, and opt for the House of Lords with the title of Lord Baltimore ("after an ancestor of A.E.'s who was Governor of Baltimore.").

This defeatist mood was partly due to Eden's sensitivity to the sniping going on against him, particularly from Beaverbrook's *Express,* and partly to his health. Even before his marriage he had been suffering recurrent bouts of jaundice that were traced to a gallbladder infection, and in April 1953 he was persuaded to undergo routine gallbladder surgery.

This operation was to have far-reaching implications, not only for Eden but also for British politics and the whole extraordinary conclusion of Churchill's time in office.

Had the operation been successful, Churchill could hardly have avoided retiring at the coronation. On the edge of his ninth decade, even he would have found it hard not to honor his long-term understanding with his successor and relinquish power to Eden as Stanley Baldwin did to Neville Chamberlain after George VI's coronation in 1937.

But there were complications during the operation. The surgeon's knife slipped, partially severing the bile duct, and although a second operation did save Eden's life, he was left dangerously ill, with his system being slowly poisoned from the leaking bile duct. His only hope lay in a new and risky operation to install an artificial bile duct that was being pioneered at the Lahey Clinic in Boston, Massachusetts. The doctors gave mid-June—well after the coronation—as the earliest possible date for this third surgery.

With Eden far too sick to act as Foreign Secretary, Churchill insisted on shouldering those responsibilities in addition to his own. Far from being worried by the extra work, he seemed all too eager at the prospect. For suddenly it seemed as if destiny was extending him a golden opportunity to achieve a grand finale to his whole career.

Just a few weeks earlier, on March 15, Stalin had died, and he was succeeded by his virtually unknown fifty-year-old Deputy-Premier, Georgi Malenkov. With Stalin gone, and Eisenhower just elected President of the United States, there seemed an opportunity at last for a fresh start in the West's relations with the Soviets. By making a direct appeal to Malenkov for an informal summit conference with himself and Eisenhower, Churchill might well be instrumental in "unfreezing" the cold war, settling the dangerous disagreements between East and West, and banishing the threat of nuclear annihilation from the world forever. As he put it to Parliament, the leaders of the world "might feel that they might do something better than tear the human race, including themselves, to bits. At worst they might have established more intimate contacts. At best we might have a generation of peace."

Knowing Churchill, one can see the way his mind was working. Here was another great dramatic opportunity on the stage of history, and a summit meeting might provide a repetition of his tripartite meeting with Stalin and Roosevelt at Tehran in 1943. Then he had been a god of war; now he could make a final contribution to the human race as prince of peace.

This was particularly appropriate in this year of the young Queen's coronation, and after a historic breakthrough in the cause of peace, Churchill could then stand proudly with his sovereign at her crowning, before departing, like the Duke of Marlborough in Rysbrack's altarpiece at Blenheim, on a cloud of universal gratitude and glory.

Impotently watching from his sickbed, Eden hated the whole idea of Churchill's summit on the grounds that such idealistic interventions rarely worked (he vividly remembered Chamberlain's attempt to bring "Peace in our time" through a summit meeting with Hitler in Munich in 1938). But there was little he could do; his leader was thoroughly aroused and had an enthusiastic press behind him. Although the mutual suspicion between the Soviet Union and the United States would soon abort the old man's dreams of a hopeful summit, this coronation springtime was an optimistic period for Churchill. In April, he accepted the Order of the Garter from the Queen—the highest personal honor in the royal gift. He had glumly turned it down when it had been offered after his electoral defeat in 1945, but as *Sir* Winston Churchill he was now at one with history and envisioning the coronation as the signal for a national revival to equal the renaissance of the young Queen's predecessor, Elizabeth I.

Such was his enthusiasm for the youthful Queen that Colville believed that although "he was an old man whose passions were spent," Churchill genuinely fell in love with her. The palace audiences lengthened, he placed the Queen's photograph by his bedside, and was soon reverently hailing her as "wife and mother . . . heir to all our traditions and all our glories."

Churchill's enthusiasm for the coronation as a source of national revival may have aroused the feelings of the country, but they did not extend to permitting ordinary people to watch the ceremony on television. When BBC-TV approached the government for permission to place their cameras in Westminster Abbey, Churchill the aristocrat was indignantly against the idea, believing it a vulgar intrusion that would place too big a burden on the Queen. (Privately, he said, "I don't see why the BBC should have a better view of my monarch being crowned than me.") It was only the insistence of the Queen herself, following angry comments in the press, that permitted television coverage of her coronation.

Despite this, his arrival at the coronation—complete with decorations, bottle-green Trinity House uniform, and dark blue Garter robes and hat—was one of the great appearances of his career. All three generations of male Churchills were in the ceremony. Young Winston was a page ("Boy, tell your mother to get your hair cut," barked Field Marshal Montgomery at the dress rehearsal); Randolph had the Alice-in-Wonderland title of Gold Staff Officer. And for Cecil Beaton one of the supreme moments of the coronation came when, descending from his carriage to the acclamation of the crowd outside the abbey, "that great old relic, Winston Churchill, lurches forward on unsteady feet, a fluttering mass of white ribbons at his shoulder and white feathers in the hat in his hand."

A few days later Churchill and Clementine saw Eden and Clarissa off at Heathrow Airport as they headed for the crucial operation in Boston.

It was successfully performed on the morning of Tuesday, June 20; that same evening, Churchill, with blue garter sash worn proudly across his chest, seemed in better form than ever as he welcomed the Premier of Italy to dinner at Downing Street. He gave a witty speech about the British visit of an earlier Roman statesman, Julius Caesar, but as the meal ended, found himself incapable of rising from his chair. Some thought him drunk, but others, like Soames and Colville, realized the truth. This was the stroke Moran had predicted. One of the most singular episodes in postwar British politics had started.

At first, the effect of Churchill's stroke seemed slight. Tough as ever, he insisted on chairing Wednesday morning's Cabinet, and only Macmillan seemed to notice his unusual silence. But the stroke was what doctors call "a slow leak," which gradually affected his speech and then paralyzed his whole left side. He could barely stand when he left for Chartwell on Wednesday afternoon; by Thursday morning Moran was telling Colville that Churchill was unlikely to survive the weekend.

With her father on the verge of death, Sarah was summoned from New York. Reaching Chartwell, she was shocked by what she saw, and when she gave her father her old greeting—"Darling, Wow!"—he feebly squeezed her hand but could not answer. Her arrival seemed to have helped him, because although he remained weak and paralyzed over the weekend, he showed little sign of dying. Slowly his speech returned and he managed to complain to Moran, "I am a hulk—only breathing and excreting." Grateful for even this evidence of life, Clementine began to vehemently assert that whatever else he did, he must definitely retire.

Yet even now Churchill was determined not to go, and as on so many earlier occasions, his strength of will seemed capable of conquering his ailing body. What Moran called his "Secret Battle" to survive had started.

"There are moments," Moran wrote, "when he does not want to do anything, when a dreadful apathy settles on him, and he nearly loses heart. But he always sets his jaw and hangs on."

What was remarkable—and typical—of Churchill was his instinctive grasp of power even in extremis. Even as the effects of the stroke grew worse on the drive to Chartwell that Wednesday afternoon, he had already been instructing Moran that on no account should the press be informed of his condition. And during the days that followed, he insisted on a total news blackout of the truth.

Just as he had with Moran, Churchill gave Colville "strict orders not to let it be known that he was temporarily incapacitated and to continue to ensure that the administration continued to function as if he were in full control." This involved considerable deception of Parliament and the media, but his orders were faithfully observed by all around him. Not since the bizarre conspiracy that kept the moribund Woodrow Wilson on as President of the United States had there been anything quite like it.

When the Queen heard that he was ill, and thoughtfully suggested visiting him at Chartwell, she was hurriedly put off on the grounds that "people would think that he was dying and he was not." A more compelling reason was that the Queen, with her sense of constitutional propriety, would certainly have been alarmed to see her Prime Minister, like his deputy, completely incapacitated and would have had to insist on a legitimate substitute. "Tell her we'll meet at the St. Leger," Her Majesty was told.

More of a problem was what Colville cheerfully described as gagging the British press. This proved all too easy. Three press lords, all close friends of Churchill—Beaverbrook, Bracken, and Camrose— were summoned to Chartwell, where Colville explained the situation. He described them as "pacing the lawn in earnest conversation," the upshot of which was that, out of respect for Churchill's wishes, the three peers used their influence with their editors and other press proprietors to ensure a total news blackout over Churchill's illness. To flatter and placate a sick old man, neither Queen nor Parliament nor people was allowed to know that Britain was without an effective, legally constituted leader.

During this crucial period much depended on the family at Chartwell. Instead of returning to the United States, Sarah stayed on and played her part in his recovery by reading to him, as she had after his wartime heart attack at Carthage. (This time it was Anthony Trollope, not Jane Austen.) Randolph, on the other hand, was hardly the calming influence his father needed, and Diana had barely recovered from her breakdown. There was, however, one member of the family more than capable of doing what was needed: son-in-law Christopher Soames. Aided by the ever-tactful Colville, he effectively took over. It was now that this surrogate son and heir assumed the role of which Randolph might have dreamed.

Colville was possibly overstating things when he wrote that Soames "now held the place in Churchill's heart so long reserved for Randolph, who had been incapable of filling it," but certainly Randolph could not possibly have done what Soames did during Churchill's five long weeks of incapacity following his stroke.

During this period, R. A. Butler continued to chair meetings of the Cabinet. Like all the ministers, he knew Churchill was not well. (How much more he knew will always be debatable.) But the official line was simply that the P.M. was suffering from overwork and resting at Chartwell. Immediately after the stroke, Lord Moran had issued a deliberately misleading bulletin to this effect. It was a fiction that Soames played a crucial part in loyally maintaining.

For government business to continue, ministers and heads of department needed regular decisions that only the Prime Minister could give. According to Colville, these ministers "were entirely ignorant of the Prime Minister's incapacity," but as Churchill from the beginning of his stroke refused to delegate his powers to anyone, someone had to deal with these papers, and that someone was Christopher Soames.

Theoretically, he was forbidden to see Cabinet papers or secret documents, but clearly he had to; and since he was considered closer to Churchill's thoughts than anyone else, it was left to his discretion how to deal with the Prime Minister's business until the P.M. could deal with it himself. For Churchill, this was "lazy premiership" with a vengeance, and it was largely thanks to his large, bluff, very canny son-in-law that his absence seemed to make so little difference.

Soon a race for recovery was developing between the seventy-eight-year-old Prime Minister and his fifty-four-year-old successor— with Churchill pulling ahead. After a stroke of such severity, his improvement began to be spectacular. His friend and American publisher Walter Graebner of Time-Life, Inc., seeing him in late July, told Churchill he was looking much as he remembered him before the stroke. Churchill was delighted. "This decaying carcass can still bring fame to anything, so long as it is not overworked," he told him.

A convalescent Anthony Eden returned from Boston with Clarissa, then departed on a cruise around the Mediterranean. "Circumstances," muttered Churchill to his doctor, "convince me of my indispensability."

By August, he was well enough to resume his governmental business, but although Eden was now restored to health, there was no talk from Churchill of retiring. Instead, he was carefully conserving all his energies for the crucial test that lay ahead if he was to stay in office: the leader's speech to the party conference in October.

With Eden waiting in the wings, Churchill knew that should he fail or blunder, he would have to yield. But Churchill did not fail or blunder. Less than four months after a major stroke he delivered a prime ministerial speech to the conference that brought a great ovation from the hall and guaranteed his future. A sun-tanned Eden seated prominently on the platform had no alternative but to smile and applaud the leader. After the conference there was no more speculation as to the Prime Minister's retirement.

For Eden, the situation was becoming ludicrous and rather painful, but although his wife was a member of the family, there was little Clarissa could do to help him or to break the deadlock. Under her uncle's premiership, the government was quietly successful, and feelings in the family had changed. At the time of his stroke, most of the family agreed with Clementine that he should definitely retire. But now, even Clementine believed that for his own sake he should be left to enjoy his position as long as possible. To be forced from office now, she thought, would kill him. Even if it didn't, it would spell the start of what she called his "life in death, his death in life."

So as the months went by, there was always some compelling reason for Churchill to stay on in power. During 1954, it was the fact that this was the year of his eightieth birthday, and that in November the House of Commons was planning a full-scale presentation in Westminster Hall. Graham Sutherland had been specially commissioned to paint his portrait, and Churchill was determined to enjoy his birthday as Prime Minister. In November, both the birthday and the presentation came and went—with still no mention of retirement.

By early 1955, Eden, never the most phlegmatic of men, was close to desperation. For over four years this eighty-year-old Prime Minister had excluded him from power. But the fact was that even now Churchill could rise to a great occasion like no one else in Parliament —as he did with his last great speech on March 1 announcing the British production of the hydrogen bomb. Age had not changed his voice or dimmed his rhetoric: "It may well be that we shall, by a process of sublime irony, have reached a stage where safety will be the sturdy shield of terror, and survival the twin brother of annihilation," he had concluded.

Yet there were times when lethargy descended and "more time was given to bezique and less to public business." At one of these moments, Churchill agreed to hand over to Eden in early April.

Having said this, all his old man's bitterness and rage erupted at the thought of what he would be losing. Cornered and unhappy, he began to convince himself—and others—that he was being hounded out of office, and Colville writes of the "cold hatred" he began to feel for Eden.

Back in his father's favor, Randolph did nothing to discourage such emotions, and there were signs of Churchill's final days in office ending with the bitterest of battles. That they did not was largely due again to Soames, who persuaded Churchill to depart with dignity. It was one of the most important services he did him.

Colville was present when the Churchills gave a farewell dinner at 10 Downing Street on April 4. It was a great political occasion, attended by political grandees, all the family, the Edens, Prince Philip and the Queen. Randolph, true to form, got drunk, "and insisted on pursuing Clarissa with a derogatory article about Anthony Eden." It was otherwise an elegiac evening.

Churchill seemed reconciled at last to his surrender, and on the following day planned to drive to the palace where he would give the Queen his resignation. (He would also refuse the formal offer of a dukedom, thinking that it would do no good to Randolph and "might ruin little Winston's political career.")

When the dinner ended, Colville helped him upstairs to his bedroom, and for a while he sat silently on the bed, still wearing his knee breeches, Order of Merit, and Order of the Garter. Colville imagined he was having thoughts of fond regret at leaving Downing Street, but that was not what was on his mind.

In a final letter to the Queen, Churchill had told her, "I feel that yr. Majesty is right to put complete confidence in Anthony Eden, who has given proof of his character and capacity over so many years."

But now Churchill turned to Colville, stared at him, then said with vehemence, "I don't believe Anthony can do it."

# thirty-two

# Pausaland

Back in 1928, when Churchill was enjoying the Riviera sunshine at Maxine Elliot's villa in the South of France, the mistress of his great friend Bend'or, Duke of Westminster, was building a villa of her own a few miles away on a pretty hillside overlooking Menton.

Bend'or's mistress was Chanel, the most influential French couturier of her day. The Duke never make her Duchess of Westminster, as she had dreamed of being, but throughout the thirties, Coco Chanel had continued to regard her villa, which she called La Pausa, as a place of secret refuge and delight. By a coincidence, La Pausa came to serve much the same purpose for Churchill some twenty-five years later, during his early eighties.

Churchill had begun the new year of 1956 in a state of all-too-familiar misery. Hating the English winter, he was unoccupied and bored and more or less intolerable to all around him. He detested being old. "I feel like an aeroplane at the end of its flight, in the dusk, with petrol running out, in search of a safe landing," he told R. A. Butler. Even Lord Moran was writing in his diary of Churchill's wish to die, since "he no longer finds any fun in life."

The family had no idea how to cope with him as he talked gloomily of "waiting about for death." Clementine, worn out and miserable herself, began the year in the hospital being treated for neuritis, a painful inflammation of the nerves. Then she departed, as she had often done before, on a convalescent cruise to faraway Sri Lanka with her old friend Sylvia Henley.

In earlier days, Churchill would probably have spent a month or two in Morocco during Clementine's absence or, failing that, with Max Beaverbrook at Cap d'Ail. But he was now too old and too demanding to entrust himself to a North African hotel, however splendid, and Beaverbrook was old and ailing, too—certainly too old to offer him the attention and amenities he needed.

None of his other rich Riviera friends could help him either. Miss Elliot was dead, and Somerset Maugham, in his famous Villa Mauresque at Cap Jean St. Ferrat, was more or less insane. (When Maugham had suggested that Churchill share the rejuvenating therapy of the famous Swiss longevitist, Professor Paul Niehans, Churchill had refused on the grounds that giving up whisky for six months was a bad exchange for prolonging one's existence.)

The one enticing invitation Churchill did receive came from the very rich Hungarian who had managed his prewar foreign literary affairs, the Jewish millionaire connoisseur and businessman Emery Reves, who was living in the south of France at La Pausa, which he had bought in 1953 from Chanel.

In 1946 Reves had enriched himself—and Churchill—still further by selling the foreign rights to the leader's wartime memoirs to great advantage. (The deals Reves made for Churchill had included $1,150,000 from Henry Luce for first U.S. serial rights for the memoirs on behalf of *Life* magazine.) With Churchill now engaged in finishing his *History of the English-Speaking Peoples,* agent and author had further business to discuss.

His current secretary, Miss Doreen Pugh, and his daughter Diana were more than willing to accompany him on a winter break, and what began as something of a business trip for Churchill almost instantly became considerably more.

There was much at La Pausa to appeal to him. The villa was one of Chanel's most stylish creations, a place of light and elegance and casual luxury set amid olives on a hillside high above the sea. Since buying it, Reves had steadily embellished it with his choicest treasures, including nine Renoirs, four Cézannes, three Degases, and his mistress, a lavender-eyed former model from New York named Wendy Russell. There was also a dedicated staff and a cellar few could equal in the South of France.

For Churchill, it was the perfect house in his favorite spot on earth, and he was treated like the great celebrity he was. The staff included one of the finest chefs in France. Emery was a fluent cosmopolitan who could talk on anything, and Wendy was not only very pretty but had learned the knack of flattering the elderly and great.

Visitors to La Pausa were requested to put on slippers to protect the highly polished floors. Churchill was given slippers of his own, and scarcely had he put them on his elegant small feet than he felt remarkably at home. England, with its miseries, was forgotten, and so was his oft expressed desire for easeful death. Miss Pugh told Moran that "he had seemed twenty years younger" with the Reveses. His idyll in what he came to call "Pausaland" had started.

For some time, much to Clementine's dismay, Churchill had been talking of purchasing his own abode in the South of France. She refused to have anything to do with it, but a few months after he returned from Pausaland, he was back again determinedly looking for a house.

But where could he find a home as comfortable and perfect as La Pausa? Where else a couple as devoted to his every whim as Emery and Wendy? To this old Victorian "the charm and seclusion of 'private life' in private houses, with private service, was very powerful," said Mary.

Honored and delighted by his presence (who else on the Côte d'Azur could boast a guest of such enviable distinction?), the Reveses insisted that he treat La Pausa as his own. Churchill did exactly that.

His visits lengthened, and over his next four years at least twelve months would be spent at La Pausa. According to Wendy, "I'd have a message through from London saying he was coming, and often adding he was in a deep depression. But from the moment he arrived there'd be no sign of it. He was always happy here. He loved the weather and the views which he could paint, and he'd say, 'in England when I look out of the window it's usually raining and it's really *bloody*.' "

"The sun is Churchill's greatest life-maintainer," said Brendan Bracken; and as well as the winter sunlight of the South of France, there were other things in Pausaland that England and rainswept Chartwell could not guarantee: a chance to work in peace and freedom from the outside world.

"He was so *soft*, so very sweet and charming, like a baby. He was no longer leader of the government, or fighting a war, and he could relax and be himself with those who loved him," Wendy recalled.

The Reveses played records of Mozart for him, which he never listened to before, and Emery lectured him about Cézanne. They also spoiled him unashamedly. When he finished the last volume of his *History of the English-Speaking Peoples* there was an engraved gold cigar case from Van Cleef & Arpels, and on his eighty-second birthday there were eighty-two magnums of Dom Perignon champagne.

An additional pleasure of Pausaland was that everything was free, and that all the members of the family were welcome, too. During the next few years almost all of them descended and enjoyed its splendid hospitality. Sarah and Mary and Diana, and their children, all came, so that at times it seemed as if the Churchills actually owned the place.

Almost the only Churchill who failed to enjoy herself in Pausaland was Clementine. Her ancient phobia against the rich life of the South of France was as strong as ever. She found life at La Pausa claustrophobic. While Churchill thoroughly enjoyed the pashalike treatment as he always had, Mary tells us "he was not companionable" to his equally demanding wife.

Clementine abruptly found she had very little in common with her hosts, and was less than entranced by the devotion Churchill was arousing in a younger, very pretty woman. Clearly embarrassed by Clementine's behavior to Wendy, he did his best to smooth things over. After one uncomfortable joint visit, he even wrote to Wendy in an attempt to put her mind at rest. "Clemmie was astonished that you thought her manner to you had hardened during the last few days of her visit. She was concerned that you should have imagined this. Do put it out of your mind, my dear."

But whatever Churchill wrote to the contrary, his wife's attitude was clear. She was determined to have as little as possible to do with the adoring Reveses, and he was equally determined to enjoy their company and the pampered life of Pausaland.

Thus it was that, even in his eighties, much of Churchill's married life continued to be lived apart from Clementine. Outwardly they seemed the most devoted ancient couple in the country, living "happily ever after," as Churchill had insisted they should. But their devotion could not bear too much proximity, and thanks to the Reveses and La Pausa, their discreetly separated lives continued.

As Colville put it, "Clementine thought her husband's least admirable characteristic was a yearning for luxury so pronounced that he would accept hospitality from anyone able to offer the surroundings and amenities he enjoyed."

Selfishly—or wisely—he refused to change his habits, but like

the practiced journalist he was would write her loving letters of conciliation "in his own paw" when they were apart.

But if Clementine liked to keep away when Churchill was in
residence at La Pausa, others visited him there in splendor, including
President Réne Coty of France, Konrad Adenauer, de Gaulle, Prince
Rainier of Monaco and his wife, the former Grace Kelly, and even his
one-time king, the Duke of Windsor, and his wife. (The old monarchist, who knew of the Duke's Nazi contacts during the war, nevertheless
greeted him with the respect due to his former sovereign. It was noticeable, however, that he avoided calling the Duchess "Royal Highness.")

At La Pausa, Churchill was treated much like royalty himself. The
Reveses dressed for dinner in his honor, and the great man's guests,
however numerous or grand, were welcome at a moment's notice.

On Churchill's arrival, Emery would meet him at the airport in
his Rolls, and Wendy, combining great respect with girlish adoration,
addressed him as "Darling Sir" or "Pumpkin Pie," depending on his
mood or the occasion.

Churchill glowed visibly in her affection, prompting Noël Coward's sour observation that "this great man, historically one of the
greatest our country has produced, and domestically one of the silliest,
is absolutely obsessed with a senile passion for Wendy Russell."

Perhaps he was, although it seems unlikely; Wendy describes
Coward's remark as "hogwash." While a willingness to make the most
of the pleasures of La Pausa is hardly evidence of silliness, still less is
it galloping senility.

For in his way, Churchill was as resolute during these years of
his decline as he had been during the years of his ascendancy. His
enjoyment of La Pausa is only one example of his strength of willpower
and remarkable physique. There is no question that he was failing. The
arteries to the brain were closing up; in 1956 alone, there were two
small strokes, producing a condition that Moran called progressive
"bleaching of the seat of reason." But none of this prevented him from
staging constant Sarah Bernhardt—like comebacks from the very jaws
of death. Seeing him now, Cecil Beaton noted that at eighty-one Churchill actually looked very fit, "like a very healthy baby."

In fact, he had more to enjoy than a reading of Moran's diaries
suggests, and even in London, there were certain treats that never failed
to cheer him up.

He still enjoyed his visits to the House of Commons where, although he spoke no longer, he was still treated as its most distinguished member. Much as he had hated Harrow, his old school had now attained a golden glow in ancient memory. Every year he loved to go there for the annual "Songs," joining in the tunes that he assured the school "have inspired my actions and my life." (Not, alas, his favorite Edwardian music-hall songs he used to sing in moments of elation.)

Another source of swift rejuvenation was the bonhomie and conversation of the Other Club. Here he could still hold forth in convivial male company—and still stay up as late as ever with his friends and cronies. This was one of many London clubs of which Randolph was emphatically not a member. When Beaverbrook proposed him, Churchill swiftly blackballed the suggestion.

The death of several of his oldest friends left gaps in the membership and nothing could repair them—Lindemann, "the Prof," had died in 1957, followed by Bracken a year later.

It was some measure of what Malcolm Muggeridge once called "the vast wash of Churchillian influence" that both these strange outsiders also died as members of the House of Lords. Bracken was only fifty-eight, young enough to once have been rumored to be Churchill's son. "Poor dear Brendan," Churchill murmured when he heard the news, and when he arrived for Lindemann's funeral at Christ Church Oxford, the congregation to a man had risen in his honor. Churchill was, as ever, vain enough to relish all such regal gestures and was delighted when a woman in the Hotel de Paris in Monte Carlo, curtsied as he passed.

He also had more serviceable admirers, such as Antonio Giraudier, a rich Cuban living in New York, who sent him free cigars and brandy; and Mme. Pol Roger, who, learning of his deep affection for her eponymous champagne, ensured that he would be unfailingly provided with as much of it as he could manage to consume.

During this period, Churchill was finishing History of the English-Speaking Peoples, which he had been writing when interrupted by the outbreak of the war. This kept him occupied. "I still like work," he told A. L. Rowse, who was one of several professional historians helping him complete his labors.

Although extremely well preserved and barely seventy, Clementine was not enjoying life with anything close to the relish of her aging husband; but then, he had been able to arrange his life entirely to suit himself. She had not.

She was the one who would have to bear the brunt of Churchill's moods of boredom, mounting irritation with the world, and blank despair when he left La Pausa to return to cold, gray England. Chartwell had ceased to be his playground. He could no longer lay his bricks, philosophize about his pigs, or swim in his patent outdoor swimming pool. The farm was sold, and paradoxically, now that Chartwell itself belonged to the National Trust and was destined to become his personal memorial, he was losing interest in it. Clementine, on the other hand, appeared delighted at the thought of Chartwell, which she had hated, ending as their mutual monument. She began to plan accordingly, but in the meantime, there was the living Churchill to be taken care of.

Luckily, his most detailed personal requirements—from putting on his socks to drying himself after his bath—were taken care of by the saintly Sawyers, his eccentric but devoted valet (on duty fourteen hours a day, seven days a week). Walter Graebner describes how he "woke him, brought him his breakfast, handed him his newspapers, let his dog in, took his dog out for a walk, ran his bath, dried him, took out his clothes, inserted cuff-links, helped dress him, tied his tie, handed him his hair brushes, helped him on with his shoes, tied his laces. . . . " There was also a new private secretary, a former diplomat named Anthony Montague Browne—a pillar of discretion and resourcefulness. He would be increasingly relied on by the family—and Churchill—during the difficult years that lay ahead.

But no one could take the place of Clementine entirely, and there were times when the burdens of the marriage were intolerable. One of her friends wrote that "Clementine's almost pitiful perfectionism and qualms of conscience would always have made happiness less accessible to her than to other people."

Nervous stress was at the root of the neuritis that plagued her, along with fresh attacks of lethargy and periods of deep prostration. But at the heart of all her problems lay the situation that had dogged her married life from the beginning.

However difficult Churchill was to live with, Clementine had rarely doubted her husband's greatness. This had been the surest bond between them, and she had seen her faith confirmed in his great role as his country's savior. Now in the evening of their days, she believed it was her mission to maintain his dignity and the legend of his greatness that had inspired them both and given point and purpose to her married life for nearly half a century.

One sees this most dramatically in Clementine's behavior over Sutherland's notorious eightieth birthday portrait of Churchill that had been formally presented to him by the House of Commons.

Great men are always at the mercy of the portrait painter, which is why dictators keep official artists under the tightest possible control. During the war, Churchill, too, had taken pains to see that his official portrait photographs expressed the qualities he needed to project: toughness, resolution, and the famous bulldog look that matched his speeches.

But as Sutherland was commissioned by Parliament. Churchill had no say over the result. One cannot have a veto on one's birthday present, and Sutherland was far too famous to accept censorship of anything he painted. His portraits of such celebrities as Helena Rubinstein, Lord Beaverbrook, and Somerset Maugham had made this former abstract painter the most talked-about—and controversial—British portrait painter of the fifties.

In person, he was the least bohemian of artists—conservatively dressed, a natural charmer, and a very handsome man. "Mr. Sutherland is a wow!" was Clementine's first reaction when she met him, and Churchill had responded rather similarly to dark-haired Mrs. Sutherland on the occasions when the painter and his wife came to Chartwell.

Knowing how sitters can react, Sutherland had taken care not to allow Churchill to see the finished painting until shortly before the presentation in Westminster Hall. And Churchill, moved and flattered by the great occasion, had been careful to control his feelings, briefly thanking his fellow parliamentarians for "this remarkable example of modern art, which combines force with candour."

Although Churchill was not depicted as the bulldog who defied the Nazis but as a powerful yet haunted elder statesman, most of the audience felt that the great man had accepted the unflattering but striking portrait of his aged self with typical good humor. Those who knew him, however, understood his true feelings from his reference to "modern art." As a highly traditional amateur painter, Churchill held strong views on that controversial subject. "Alfred," he once remarked to his friend Sir Alfred Munnings, the president of the Royal Academy, as they strolled down Piccadilly, "If I saw Picasso walking down the street ahead of us, do you know what I would do? I'd kick him up the arse."

Since Picasso never came to London, there was no danger of this curious assault occurring, but stuck with this public portrait that he hated, Churchill felt similarly inclined toward its painter. According to Mary, the portrait had "quite ruined" his birthday. "Filthy," he spluttered to Lord Moran. "I think it is malignant." Cecil Beaton overheard him talking angrily with Diana Cooper: "These modern chaps. You're in their power. They make some drawings, then they go away and do their damnedest. They like to make a fool of you."

Since then, Churchill had been brooding on about the portrait, which had been consigned to the shameful depths of the cellar of his house at Hyde Park Gate. His feelings about it were somewhat different from an old man's brief, offended vanity. After all, for almost sixty years he had been the butt of political cartoonists taking the most extraordinary liberties with his appearance, so why was he so mortified by Graham Sutherland?

Moran gives an interesting explanation. "Since the end of the war," he writes, Churchill had spend much time and effort "arranging and editing the part he will play in history," and would not submit to anything that undermined it. His whole life, of course, had been a sustained attempt to gain a place beside Marlborough and Napoleon where his father's criticisms could no longer reach him. He had succeeded phenomenally, but as Moran noticed, he was now intent upon enhancing and preserving the legendary afflatus around his person. (The historian Piers Brendon points out that even his final work, *The History of the English-Speaking Peoples,* is one long heroic epic "whose unwritten climax and conclusion is his own career.")

Churchill's physical appearance, too, was part and parcel of the legacy intended for the history books, and once more Moran was intrigued by the old man's satisfaction when a bust by a sculptor he approved of—the flattering but fifth-rate Oscar Nemmon—was placed between the Guildhall statues of Nelson and the Duke of Wellington.

Churchill the embattled bulldog, Churchill in his siren suit, or Churchill resplendent in his Garter robes—these were the images by which he intended to be remembered. Graham Sutherland's was not. The fact that the unfortunate artist had genuinely attempted to express his own deep admiration for the ancient statesman, and had produced a work of great originality, hardly mattered. This was not how Churchill saw himself—or intended eternity to see him either.

Outraged at the personal betrayal by a painter he and Clementine had befriended, Churchill had no intention of permitting Sutherland's subversive image to survive. "I shouldn't be surprised if no one got the opportunity of looking at it after my day," he told Diana Cooper.

But much as he loathed the painting, it is hard to think of Churchill destroying it himself. As a painter, he had a respect for any work of art, and the Sutherland had been the unanimous gift of that all-but-sacred gathering, the British House of Commons.

Clementine, however, was immune to all such qualms. She was not a member of the House of Commons, and some twenty years before had shown her mettle by putting her foot through a Sickert drawing of her husband that she felt had done him less than justice. It is not difficult to kill a painting, and there is no reason to believe that anybody helped her. The canvas can easily be cut out of the frame and burned; and this, it seems, is what she did sometime in 1956, probably while her husband was abroad.

Ironically, it seems that she had originally liked the picture—certainly she did when given a special preview of it by Sutherland's friend and patron the courtly Kenneth Clark. But since Churchill hated it and it offended the enduring legend of his greatness, she felt she had no alternative—and did her duty. (Later, when she told Mary and her son-in-law what had happened, she was puzzled by their shocked reaction, and agreed to keep the picture's fate a secret.)

During the last fraught period of Churchill's life, there was a more dangerous threat to his legend—and his equanimity—one with which Clementine could never cope. Like some aged monarch at the sad conclusion of his reign, Churchill found that the citadel of his heart, his precious family, had started to collapse around him.

This entry in Evelyn Waugh's diary for July 1955 (based on a letter from June herself) gives some idea of what the greatest man in Britain was having to put up with in the bosom of his family:

> . . . a gruesome evening at Chartwell. Randolph getting drunk and calling Soames a shit, enraging Winston with diatribes against Jerk Eden. Winston so shaken with fury that June and Clemmie feared another seizure. Randolph stormed up saying he would never see his father again, June already in bed, forced to dress and start packing. Then at 1 a.m. Sir Winston padding down the passage in pyjamas, saying, "I am going to die soon. I cannot go to bed without composing a quarrel," and kissing them both. Randolph next day sober and obsequious at luncheon.

Hardly surprisingly, Randolph's marriage to his amiable, neurotic, and much put-upon second wife ended soon afterward, with

June departing with their infant daughter Arabella. Her departure did not produce the dramas that had followed Pamela's. Churchill was not devoted to June as he had been to Pamela, nor was the precious grandson, heir and namesake, now involved. But as with the previous divorce, Clementine unwisely took the side of Randolph's injured wife, thus aggravating her customary tense relations with her son.

Most reports of Randolph at this time read like dispatches from a battlefield. Not long after the row at Chartwell he was pouring a pot of coffee over Ian Fleming's wife (Laura Charteris's sister, Ann), then heaving R. A. Butler into his own fire. (Quite an achievement this, considering Butler's bulk and Randolph's unathleticism. The singed statesman was extracted by Randolph's old friend, Julian Amery, who retained patrician calm throughout the fracas.)

He also brought a stunned conclusion to a West End dinner party after quarreling loudly with the stately Lady Pamela Berry, wife of Michael Berry (later Lord Hartfield), proprietor of the *Daily Telegraph*. A dark and hirsute beauty, daughter of Lord Birkenhead, Lady Pamela had known Randolph since childhood, giving him what he felt to be the right to the last word in the argument. "Look here my girl," he shouted out as he departed, "you'd better go home and have a shave. You've not been using that electric razor given you for Christmas." (Later he was puzzled that the Berrys banned him from their home. "Don't come if you value your life," Lady Pamela replied, when he suggested himself for dinner.)

The catalogue of Randolph's victims at this time included politicians, press lords, television interviewers, and society hostesses. And each occasion is distinguished, if not entirely excused, by the fact that most recipients of Randolph's misbehavior, faintly—if not so painfully —deserved it.

For a lapsed puritan like Malcolm Muggeridge, Randolph was a necessary social scourge, Mayfair's own privileged purveyor of the wrath of God to the repellent rich. "Like the sirens in the blitz, his arrival at any social gathering sends everybody scampering for cover," Muggeridge wrote.

Randolph the morning after was less indulgent to his own behavior. "I should never be let out in private," he admitted in a rare moment of repentance.

Some thought Randolph was unhinged, others saw him as a coarse, insensitive, and drunken boor—but there were many who, despite his failings, stayed surprisingly devoted. (These included

Laura, happily married, at last, to Michael Canfield and still the object of Randolph's unrequited love.) He had finally made peace with Pamela: They lunched occasionally and found they got on surprisingly well together. "All he really needed now," said Pamela, "was a spot of genuine success to give him something to be proud of," but this was something that continued to elude him.

As a political journalist, he was lively and had all the right connections, but his social reputation made him far too many enemies. His bold attempt at war reporting in Korea ended with an early flesh wound in the leg. His short book on an ancient enemy—*The Rise and Fall of Sir Anthony Eden*—was too embittered to be taken very seriously (except by his parents, who were said to be deeply embarrassed). His greatest triumphs came in court, on the two occasions when he sued successfully for the sort of libel he was inevitably attracting. (One involved £5,000 damages from the Sunday *People* newspaper which had described him as "a paid hack . . . the slightly comic son of our greatest statesman, who poses as a political expert but whose offer to serve as an M.P. was rejected time and again."

Randolph's wit and flow of words made him a notable litigant, and revealed the memorable barrister he might have been. But there were too many might-have-beens about him now, and friends were worried that the habits of a misused lifetime had finally caught up with him.

According to author and journalist Alan Brien, who in his youth was one of the faithful young gentlemen who worked for Randolph as research assistants, he "always drank treble whiskies in a tumbler topped to the brim with water—a mixture guaranteed to mainline direct into the bloodstream." (Randolph believed that neat whisky acted slower.) From shortly after breakfast, this was his lifeline, but although drink was blamed for his excesses, some suspected that the causes ran much deeper.

It was Cecil Beaton who suggested that at heart Randolph was "emotionally upset, and carrying on a feud against the world. One's heart went out to him in his suffering," Beaton added. And always, the deepest cause of Randolph's sufferings seems to have lain with his father, and relations between them remained as ambivalent and uncomfortable as ever.

"Winston was the only person Randolph truly loved," insisted Laura. Like most of Randolph's friends, she could never satisfactorily account for the battles that ensued between them. "Drink," she use to say. "Randolph always fought when he was drunk. But he could never tell me why."

Perhaps it was simpler than she suspected, and Randolph understood the problems that his father's influence had brought him. "Beneath the mighty oak no saplings grow," he used to say when asked why he was as he was. But how exactly had "the mighty oak" destroyed him?

It is now that one discerns Randolph's fate in all its strange complexity, and how the pattern of his life completes the tortuous relationship between Winston and his father, Lord Randolph. Randolph's infancy had been ruled by Churchill's obvious desire to create an ideal childhood in his close relations with his son. Not only did he spoil him, but he seems to have identified with him as well, casting the golden Randolph in the part of the perfect son he wished that he had been himself.

Father and son became inseparable in mutual hero-worship. From childhood, Randolph modeled himself upon his father; Churchill had encouraged this, determined that this eager, powerful small boy became endowed with all the qualities for political success: brilliance, skill with words, and knowledge of the powerful and rich and worldly.

In his obsession to placate Lord Randolph's ghost, Churchill's own early life had been ruled by guilt and a passion to succeed his father. Now he was passing on to his son the same exaggerated passion.

After the trauma of Lord Randolph's death, Churchill and Randolph would jointly re-create the grand succession of the Churchills. Randolph would enter Parliament at his side, as Churchill had dreamed of entering it beside Lord Randolph. And with this child, so lavishly endowed with all the gifts that he could offer, Churchill could finally rebuild the dream of the perfect father-son relationship he lost forever at Lord Randolph's death. When his own death came, Randolph would be there to carry on.

Out of this perilous—and curious—relationship, two things had happened: one predictable, the other almost inconceivable. Predictably, Randolph had remained emotionally a spoiled child, with all his father's virtues and vices melded into a sort of complex caricature of Winston Churchill. But while precociously possessed of all the skills of politics, society, and journalism, Randolph lacked the one essential that had brought his father triumph and success: his unrelenting drive to self-redemption, goaded forward by the memory of a demented and disapproving father.

What had been unpredictable in Randolph's situation was what had happened, late in life, to Churchill. Winston had once believed that, like Lord Randolph, he would "burn out young," leaving his precious son to take his place. Instead, at the age of seventy, Churchill had started to achieve such greatness as to make an heir superfluous, and particularly an heir like Randolph. Since then, it was interesting to see how Churchill had been effectively disinheriting his son. When he first refused a dukedom, one of his reasons was the absurdity of making Randolph "Marquess of Toodle-do"—and finally successor to the title Duke of Chartwell. Then, the ownership of Chartwell, which he had once regarded as Randolph's birthright, was to be passed to the National Trust. And finally, came the painful lesion from his son: the constant arguments, the patronage that went to others, and the undisguised preference for Soames's company.

Much of this, of course, was Randolph's fault. But equally, one can see how bitter Randolph must have been, and how, in a sense, Churchill was to blame. Randolph was his creation; Churchill, more than anyone, had made the boy what he was. Not only had he spoiled and encouraged him, but he had also thoroughly imbued him with those dreams of the ideal father-son relationship that he had longed for with Lord Randolph.

Now, in his eighties, Churchill had all but solved the strange conundrum of his life. By making himself the savior of the nation, like Savrola, he had settled accounts with his father—and himself. He had achieved the place in history he had dreamed of, and had no need of dynasties to keep alive his name. Too great for a successor, he was the culmination of the line; and myth would guarantee him immortality. Randolph, once the precious "Chumbolly," the only son and heir, was now unnecessary, and the true cause of Randolph's "feud against the world" and so much drunken suffering was that Randolph knew it too.

Randolph was not the only member of the family to whom the Churchill legacy was bringing problems. On January 12, 1958, while he was in the final stages of his divorce from June, a woman calling herself Jane Doe was arrested for drunken and abusive behavior outside a seaside bungalow at Malibu Beach near Los Angeles. The police had been summoned to the house by a telephone operator reporting obscene and abusive language on the line. Miss Doe was even more abusive to the law, and it took several burly policemen to hold her down and drag her into a police car. At the police station the petite Miss Doe proved so violent that a straitjacket was required, and she was left to cool off overnight in custody.

The next day, charged with being drunk in a public place, Miss

Doe admitted that her real name was Sarah Churchill. This was an occasion Sarah found the Churchill name a disadvantage, for the case attracted maximum publicity. After paying a $50 fine, she was reported suffering "exhaustion and emotional strain," but two days later managed to appear in a live television play called "Love Out of Town."

On sobering up, her first thought was her father's reaction, assuming he would see one of the many press reports. Luckily, Churchill was mellowly installed at La Pausa (for once with Clementine), and Wendy was a calming influence on both, insisting that Sarah come as soon as possible to join them all in Pausaland. Randolph was dispatched to Malibu to arrange for her return to Europe.

It was his second mission of this sort involving Sarah, and he was more successful than he had been in his attempt to free her from the clutches of Vic Oliver twenty years before. But once again he behaved badly when confronted by journalists. Interviewed by John Wingate on WABC's "Night Beat," an affronted—and well-fueled—Randolph gave his most famous public exhibition of the Churchill wrath in action. Questioned about Sarah's antics, he suddenly erupted. "I never discuss matters affecting members of my family with total strangers. . . . I wouldn't think of asking you about your sisters . . . or your father. I don't even know if you had a father or if you know who your father was." Wingate kept his cool, but the ensuing uproar was considerable, raising additional questions of exactly what was going wrong with Churchill's children.

Clementine was secretly convinced that Sarah, like Randolph, had inherited—probably from Lady Blanche—the "drink gene" that had helped to destroy her mother and her brother, Bill. But Churchill was more positive. He, after all, was a lifelong heavy drinker who had always rigorously controlled his intake ("I've never seen anyone make a double brandy last as long as Sir Winston," wrote a young observer.)

"Alcohol," Churchill apparently told Sarah, "must be your servant, never your master." He might have reminded her of one of his mother's favorite remarks. "No one with Jerome blood should ever touch spirits. We're born intoxicated." But Churchill, with his love of liquor, had always set a bad example for his offspring, who lacked his massive self-control—and equally massive capacity. But as with Randolph, Sarah's tendencies had roots that went much deeper into real unhappiness than most suspected.

The immediate cause of her collapse was yet another private tragedy, which had left her lonelier and more vulnerable than ever.

Since marrying her handsome Beauchamp, Sarah had known little contentment. Obsessed as ever with the stage, she had continued her regular appearances on American television, where the Churchill name had proved a substitute for stardom. But her second marriage worked no better than her first.

Once again both parents had actively disliked her husband. He was too glib, too handsome, and no more a gentleman than Vic Oliver had been. (A further similarity between them was that Beauchamp had also changed his name.) Just as Sarah had fallen in love with Oliver because she thought he possessed the magic key to stardom, so she had genuinely thought Beauchamp's photographs of her could repeat the process.

"She absolutely *loved* to be photographed," said her theatrical agent Maggie Parker. "I wished she wouldn't bother so much with looking at her photographs and concentrated on her acting, but she adored seeing pictures of herself as a star." When Beauchamp, tired of photographing Sarah, turned to television production back in England, the marriage more or less expired. He became involved with drink and drugs and had several disastrous affairs; then, early in July 1957, Beauchamp resolved his troubles by consuming a massive overdose of sleeping pills.

The residue of suicide is always guilt, but this was worse than when Winant killed himself. This was the second suicide of someone she had loved—and this time it was very public.

Recriminations started—with rumors, accusations from relatives and girlfriends, and considerable press publicity concentrating on the fact that Beauchamp was Churchill's son-in-law.

Childless and menopausal, Sarah was haunted by a sense of failure—first her marriage to Vic Oliver, then Winant's suicide, and now "my Tony," as she called him, dead as well. She was convinced she brought misery to all who loved her, but according to several friends who knew her, Sarah's greatest fear was still her father's disapproval.

"She was still a 'father-girl,'" said her old friend actress Judy Campbell. "He remained the only man who really counted in her life, but she was petrified before his greatness, and felt she had to keep her independence. That was why she longed to be a star, and when she failed, everything collapsed around her."

Maggie Parker said the same. "She had been so dedicated, so all-absorbingly ambitious, but she had never accepted the fact that she lacked the qualities that make a great actress. She was forced to accept it now, and a light went out for her. It was then that Sarah really started drinking."

After two weeks at La Pausa, Churchill paid for her to spend several months drying out in a clinic near Zurich. This was the first of many cures and clinics Sarah would endure, but they all had one thing in common: They made no difference to her drinking. Like Randolph, Sarah was now hooked on alcohol for life. "I'm not an alcoholic," she use to say. "I'm a dipsomaniac. I love the stuff."

Gamely, she struggled on with her career. Early 1959 saw her in the role of a neurotic spinster with Anthony Quayle and Cliff Richard in a Terence Young film called *Serious Charge*. It was a part that rather suited her, for she was soon facing a serious charge in real life.

She was arrested, drunk, in Liverpool, where she was playing Peter Pan, and four policemen were needed to get her into court. "Like many real drunks," said the devoted Ellen Pollock, "Sarah was two quite separate people. Sober, she was a golden girl, but drunk she was a fiend, and very very strong."

On conviction—a £2 fine and a year's probation—it was once again her father she was most concerned about. He was in Pausaland, as usual. "Love, love, love. Don't bite me," she cabled him pathetically. But he could be more understanding with Sarah than with Randolph, and he wrote to Clementine urging her support. "I think they treated her very roughly at Liverpool & aroused her fiery spirit. I hope she will convince you that her affliction is part of the periodic difficulties which are common to women at the change of life, & above all that she will persevere at her profession."

Persevere she did, with Churchillian resolution; if she had finally accepted that she would never be a star, she needed more than ever the sense of purpose and security the stage could offer. Its members, with their gossip and their friendship, had become her family.

The one member of her actual family on whom Sarah did rely now was Diana. The two sisters were as much opposites as ever— Sarah the extrovert, Diana the anxious introvert—but they had more in common than in the past: disappointment, loneliness, and the shared strains of being Churchill's daughters. It was Diana, more than anyone, who saw Sarah through the aftermath of Beauchamp's suicide. Diana, with her private sense of humor, could always make her sister laugh and seemed to understand her perfectly. Despite this, in her own withdrawn, self-effacing way, it was Diana rather than Sarah who was most at risk.

According to her daughter Celia, "she never really recovered from her nervous breakdown." She was in her early fifties now; "a white-faced, tense, little woman, worried about her looks" is how a neighbor described her. She had had several periods of electric shock therapy, but it was doubtful how much good they did.

One of her few close friends, Nuala Allason, said that in addition to being "desperately shy, Diana was completely lacking in self-esteem. She would occasionally arrange small dinner parties, and take enormous trouble. Like Clementine's, her food was always excellent. 'This is how things were done at Chartwell,' she would say. But then she would add, 'But do you think anyone will want to come?' "

She drank, but on nothing near the scale of Sarah and Randolph, and during spells of deep depression, she sometimes said that she would kill herself. The breakup of her marriage troubled her acutely. "She loved my father to the day she died," Celia said, and apart from loving him, she missed the strength and the protection he once offered her against the world outside. For as Diana Mosley says, being "quite unlike Randolph and her sisters," Diana "lacked robustness."

This was something Duncan Sandys possessed. Efficient, ruthless, debonair, he had continued his ascent up the ladder of political success. Churchill had launched him, but he was continuing unaided, first as Minister for Overseas Development, and then as Commonwealth Secretary. "A cold fish, but a mightily determined one" was how one journalist described him. As attractive as ever to women, loneliness was never his problem.

Nuala Allason discovered that "one thing never to discuss with Diana was religion. It was somehow mixed up with her breakdown, and she became terribly distressed." In fact, she was deeply religious, and part of her lack of self-esteem was the feeling that even God was rejecting her.

In a very different way, Churchill's favorite niece, Clarissa, also became a victim of the fate that seemed to strike the younger members of the family. By marrying her uncle's political heir-apparent, she seemed guaranteed a glittering future. And despite her husband's endless wait to succeed her uncle as Prime Minister, it was as if the Edens were inheriting the family business once they took up residence at 10 Downing Street.

But there would be not great succession, and in November of 1956 her husband's position as Prime Minister was threatened by a sudden crisis over the Suez Canal. Defying existing treaties, the Egyptian nationalist leader General Nasser took over the canal. Supported by France and Israel, Eden replied by sending troops to Egypt, but when widespread international condemnation followed, he withdrew them. Bitter controversy ensued at home and Anthony Eden, by now in failing health, resigned the premiership in January 1957, to be succeeded by Harold Macmillan.

From retirement, Churchill gave his attitude toward the Suez Campaign in answer to a question from his grandson Winston. "I do not know that I would have had the courage to start it in the first place —I certainly would never have dared to stop halfway!"

In retrospect, the whole forlorn campaign against the seizure of the canal seems like a final curtain call for Churchill's Empire. With it also vanished the career of Churchill's chosen political heir forever.

Before her marriage, Clarissa had had a deep antipathy to politics. With a sick and deeply disappointed husband on her hands, she felt increasingly that it was "a beastly profession." Now they were effectively freed from it for good. He was made Earl of Avon, and they settled at their farm in Wiltshire, where Clarissa saw him through further bouts of illness, and gratefully resumed the country life she loved. She had no regrets for Downing Street, nor finally had he. But in the words of his biographer, Robert Rhodes-James, "Anthony Eden's greatest source of ill-luck had been Winston Churchill."

The real winners in the family were now the Soameses, who, apart from Duncan Sandys, were its only members seriously benefiting from the influence Churchill had dispensed around him.

Marriage to Mary had transformed the captain and while the love of this Churchillian princess had not exactly turned the frog into a prince, Soames was rapidly becoming a successful, old-style, high Tory politician.

Soames was, in fact, far smarter than he seemed, and possibly the key to his remarkable success was summed up in a brief note by a diplomat who knew him well: "Plays bridge with a lot of flair, and makes money out of it at White's by staying sober."

It was this shrewdness that gave Soames his remarkable advantage in the Churchill circle. He had continued to get on splendidly with his father-in-law, and when Churchill was particularly miserable or bored or lonely, Soames was invariably around to cheer him up. "Be careful not to seem to be stepping too quickly into Randolph's shoes," the courtly Colville warned him. Of course he had, but unlike Randolph, he had been smart enough to make the most of his startling opportunities. There was the Churchill name, the Churchill contacts, and all the lessons to be picked up from the master. Instead of Randolph or Anthony Eden, it was Soames who finally became the major beneficiary of Churchill's power and reputation.

As a member of the holy family of British politics, Soames had the all-important aura that would guarantee his almost automatic rise from Churchill's Parliamentary Private Secretary, to a junior ministry in Eden's government, then his appointment to Minister of Agriculture at the age of thirty-nine.

If the Reveses offered Churchill his greatest happiness abroad, the Soameses did the same in England. At the center of a happy marriage, Mary stayed the ideal daughter to her parents in adversity—and, in contrast with all her siblings, had remained the optimistic, balanced human being Moppett Whyte had brought her up to be.

There would finally be five Soames grandchildren, and even after the family moved from the farm at Chartwell to a larger house in Kent, they continued to come to Chartwell whenever Churchill was in residence.

"The older he got, the more he seemed to like young people around him," said Emma Soames. "For us he was simply Grandpapa, an extremely sweet old man at the center of the universe, who used to watch us children in the pool at Chartwell or sit in the garden in a sort of reverie. He seemed to glow with a sort of wonderful old age."

One of Soames's most successful moves with Churchill was to encourage him to become a race horse owner. (His horse Colonist II, carrying Lord Randolph's racing colors, delighted Churchill with various successes, including winning the Winston Churchill Stakes.) But for Randolph, even this was unforgivable. "You mean the Master of the Horse," he would scathingly answer anyone unwise enough to mention Soames.

Randolph's relations with his own two children were predictably stormy. One result of the two divorces was that both children made their homes with their respective mothers, which was just as well since Randolph could be a most alarming and erratic father, particularly on the occasions when he saw his son.

He was jealously devoted to his pretty daughter, Arabella, and as if to contrast her with the Soames children, did his best to present her as a sort of Churchillian crown-princess. "Arabella will not come out; she will emerge, like a flower," he said proudly. In fact, she had a most disordered childhood, torn between her mother's straitened circumstances (June had not remarried) and the chaos and excitement that was Randolph's element. Sometimes there would be holidays at Chartwell or brief stays in the South of France with Grandpapa. The result, as Arabella puts it, was that "I grew up to adore my father, but Grandpapa was God."

Her brother, Winston, was in a different situation. He was still theoretically the favorite grandchild, the natural heir and bearer of the greatest name in British politics. But by now there was little sign of the great succession Churchill once attempted to create.

Randolph must have been the most undesirable of fathers for the sensitive and conventional small boy. There was much bullying and embarrassment for young Winston, who has memories of waiting endlessly at Whites while Randolph finished yet another drink.

On the other hand, young Winston hero-worshiped his grandpapa and says, "I still honestly believe he was the greatest Englishman who ever lived."

Unlike Randolph, Pamela tended to indulge young Winston, and for the boy, his mother would always represent the world of rich, cosmopolitan society, which she inhabited. As for Pamela herself, she was at the center of the international social set—still glamorous, still with the splendid apartment beside the Seine, and still as popular as ever with the superrich with whom she felt increasingly at ease. Agnelli had gone to take control of the family car business, the Fiat empire in Turin, and marry the bride his family desired for him—the beautiful and very grand Neapolitan Princess Marella Caracciolo di Castagneto. But there were others—Elie Rothschild, Jock Hay Whitney, even Frank Sinatra—whose names would regularly appear with hers in the social columns along with the inevitable speculation.

Socially, the name Churchill meant much the same to Pamela as it did politically to Soames. It was the password to the superrich, an international certificate of total social approval, which had brought her almost everything she wanted out of life—except a husband.

As for more distant relations, Sunny's son Bert was still bad-tempered and still installed as the tenth Duke of Marlborough. Like Churchill, Bert had become a legend—but not a particularly appealing one. (For Evelyn Waugh's son Auberon, for instance, Bert was, "One of the stupidest and most richly absurd characters the English aristocracy has ever produced"; he was famous for his "appalling rudeness, amazing tactlessness, and quite extraordinary greed."

Many anecdotes support this. One tells of Bert throwing away his toothbrush shouting, "Bloody thing doesn't work!," when his valet had simply forgotten to put toothpaste on it for him in advance. Another describes Bert arriving in New York during a snowstorm and trying to argue with the recorded message on his daughter's answering machine: "You stupid woman, don't you realize I'm the Duke of Marlborough?" And there was the time when Bert, an expert shot, went shooting with filmstar David Niven and downed a carrier pigeon by mistake. "Anything for me, Bert?" asked Niven, who later claimed it took the Duke a week to see the joke.

None of this influenced Churchill's affectionate attitude to Bert, whom he treated with the deference due to the head of his distinguished family. Randolph, on the other hand, despised his cousin unreservedly. Perhaps the most unattractive of Bert's many unattractive failings was the bullying and public ridicule of his large and longsuffering wife, Duchess Mary, who more than anyone made Blenheim actually work. He is said, however, to have been good with children—his own loved him—and when talking to the working classes was rarely at a loss for an appropriate dirty joke. Just before the war, he had a short affair with Laura, which was probably the origin of Randolph's hatred.

According to Laura, the Duchess herself used to urge her to go out with her husband. "She used to say 'it kept him happy.' " Since she and Bert had remained good friends, Laura discovered that the Duke possessed a closet passion for horticulture, together with an unexpected skill at naming plants, which appealed to her.

But according to Laura, Blenheim itself depressed him. (A lot of things depressed him; he had inherited the Churchill melancholy in full measure.) She believed he would have willingly given over his palace, and its worries to the National Trust but for a superstitious dread of being known as the Duke who sold his birthright.

One of the many ironies about the Marlborough saga is the fact that now, although nearly sixty years had passed since Sunny had married Consuelo, the Vanderbilt inheritance remained as crucial to the family as ever. Consuelo, a great survivor, and the grandest dame of all, was in her eighties, but her fortune continued to be regarded as the one great hope of "enriching the noble family" (as Sunny's lawyers had put it when drawing up the marriage contract back in 1896).

"That must wait until Mummy dies," was Bert's habitual answer to any major problem in the palace. But true Vanderbilt that she was, that powerful old lady with the swanlike neck was hanging on to her enormous fortune. There were, however, hopeful signs that the bounty of the Vanderbilts would still work wonders for the Dukes of Marlborough. Although attached to the United States and her houses in Palm Beach and on Long Island, Consuelo in old age seemed increasingly attracted to the house—and to the family—that had caused her so much trouble in the past.

On her frequent trips to visit Bert at Blenheim, Consuelo was increasingly regarding the mansion as her own ancestral home. She had started to restore parts of the palace at her own expense, and had bequeathed several favorite portraits of herself to hang there. More important still, she had decided to be buried at Bladon churchyard close to Blenheim where Sunny was entombed. In life she had loathed him and found happiness as Mme. Jacques Balsan, but death was different.

For Bert, now pinning all his hopes on the Vanderbilt inheritance, this boded well, but there had been a blow to his testamentary expectations. His brother Ivor—"the Mannikin," that *"Créature de Limoges,"* and Consuelo's favorite son—had for years been continuing his bachelor existence, playing competition-standard bridge at the Portland Club, seeing his analyst each week, and searching for perfection.

Buying a farm in Hampshire, he had spent some happy years trying to produce the perfect eating apple. As a cattlebreeder, he had raised an unsurpassed dairy herd, and for a period he bred splendid horses. Then at age forty-nine, he married. His young wife, Elizabeth, of course, was very beautiful. Then in 1956, Lord Ivor died.

Unfortunately (for Bert), Ivor did this shortly after having fathered the perfect heir, a most appealing child named Robert. Worse still, Grannie Consuelo had become devoted to her favorite son's offspring, who was now destined to inherit Lord Ivor's portion of the great inheritance. Bert took this badly, as his seeming stupidity did not extend to money. Nevertheless, determined to save Blenheim from the tax man on his death, and guided by his indispensable accountant, he had made over all his great possessions (apart from the casual million) to his eldest son and heir, John George Vanderbilt Henry, who had inherited the title of Lord Blandford and who was also known as Sunny.

Sunny Blandford was a tall and nervous youth who was overshadowed by his dominating father, but he was a successful peacetime soldier. In 1951, instead of marrying Princess Margaret, as his mother hoped, he had married Susan Hornby, the spirited daughter of the chairman of W. H. Smiths, the newsagents. But the new Lady Bland-ford, having presented Sunny with a son named James and a daughter, Henrietta, had, after many dramas, left him for another.

So pretty Lady Blandford was not at Blenheim that September day in 1958 when the Marlboroughs gave a special dinner for Clemen-tine and Winston to commemorate their engagement by the lake at Blenheim half a century before. Other than the family, the guests included the historian A. L. Rowse, who described Clementine as "all billowing gown and broadened out with age," but he was shocked to see how much Churchill had aged in the three years since he last saw him: "much more feeble . . . unsteady on his feet . . . the embers of a great fire, all the force gone" and with advancing deafness, "rather impenetrable." At first, said Rowse, "we were reduced, as with the very old, to treating him like a child." Rowse found it touching to see Churchill now, after another minor stroke, "all contentment and old-world courtesy," and he described how the great man sat through much of dinner with the Duchess's miniature dachshund on his lap, trying, to the animal's disgust, to feed it delicious lobster mousse.

But Churchill was not as senile as he seemed. After dinner he won £21 off the Duchess at bezique, and when someone asked the old agnostic if he would be attending church in the morning, he offered up the perfect answer. "At my age I think my devotions may be at-tended in private." Even more private were the old man's secret reasons for making this sentimental return to Blenheim more significant than any of those weekend guests appreciated.

# thirty-three

# The Dark Angel Beckons

"To die in the sunlight and be spaded under before the dark"—this was how Churchill once described the perfect way to meet one's maker. He had long been taking it for granted that he would be buried in the ground of Chartwell, preferably in a spot with a view across the Weald.

But just as he had schooled himself against the threat of death, so he pretended not to be at all concerned about his funeral. During discussions on the disposal of Chartwell to the National Trust, he had casually offered to "Throw in the corpse as well for £50,000." But this was probably bravado.

Now, with his demise approaching, the subject of his funeral and burial had become a matter of concern, especially after his latest brush with death at La Pausa early in 1958. (A late lunch, much to drink, and chemin de fer until 7:00 P.M. had brought on bronchopneumonia. Summoned from England, Lord Moran once again rescued him.)

Churchill had been only faintly grateful. It was, he told Moran, "a comfort to know that I shall not lurch into the next world without warning."

Others—Her Majesty the Queen included—took the warning more seriously. On hearing of her greatest subject's latest illness, Moran says that "it entered her head that he was very old and frail and might die." Royalty must be professionally concerned about such matters, and with regal common sense the Queen decided that "her people" would clearly wish Sir Winston to be awarded the supreme postmortuary honor of a royal-style lying-in-state in Westminster Hall.

Yet when she questioned Prime Minister Macmillan, she learned that nothing had been arranged. A decision was needed in a hurry, but the P.M., unflappable as ever, reacted with his own distinctly casual brand of old-style practicality.

A few days later, Lord Moran was invited down to Birch Grove, the Macmillan country mansion, and as the two men strolled together through the daffodils, the Prime Minister asked, "How d'you think Winston is? What's likely to happen?"

The doctor was not rating his patient's chances highly, and Macmillan answered with a touch of that weariness he tended to assume when puzzled. "One doesn't like to talk about it, but I suppose we should do something." Moran offering no suggestions; the Prime Minister continued, "I wonder what *he* would like done? Wellington was buried in St. Paul's. Yes, and Nelson, too. Winston likes bands—I think." With that the conversation ended.

Macmillan's attitude that a gentleman had a duty to consult a friend about his funeral resulted in a telephone call to that effect soon after. It was, as Montague Browne admitted, somewhat macabre, but Churchill was delighted. Nelson and Wellington apart, the only commoner given a state funeral in the last century and a half had been Gladstone; and for someone as concerned as Churchill with his place in history, this was the final accolade, the greatest of concluding ceremonies, in which he would effortlessly play the central role.

The rarity of such honors meant that there were few precedents to follow. "What actually is a state funeral?" Randolph inquired of the Royal Master of Ceremonies, the Duke of Norfolk. "A funeral paid for by the state," the Duke, practical as ever, answered.

Churchill needed to be practical as well. The first decision to be made was where he wanted to be buried—a question that was on his mind during the weekend spent with Clementine at Blenheim. Apparently, it was then that he decided not to spend eternity in the grounds of Chartwell after all.

Since Chartwell would pass to the National Trust on his death, and be managed by strangers and visited by tourists in their thousands, it would no longer be the seat of the dynasty he had once intended it to be. Blenheim, however, would always be the tribal center of the family. It was his birthplace, haven of his youth, and it remained an incomparable setting for a hero. In nearby Bladon churchyard lay his parents, and after his sentimental journey back to Blenheim, he decided he would join them there forever.

Once he had settled on Bladon churchyard for the burial, Churchill's imagination became inevitably hooked on questions of logistics. He approved of matching Wellington's funeral with the full-scale service in St. Paul's, but how was "the Body," as he now referred to it, to be conveyed from Central London to far-off Bladon churchyard?

With his perpetual landsman's fascination with water, Churchill hit on a solution. Since the Thames was navigable as far as Oxford, it should be feasible to take the bier upstream by barge. Detachments of the fighting services, together with their bands, could line the banks; the population could join them to salute his passing on the bosom of the great historic river.

It was a splendid notion, but, alas, as someone pointed out, the barge would need to pass through countless river locks en route to Oxford, making the journey impossible in under two whole days. A further problem was that military service cutbacks had left insufficient personnel in Britain for even the skimpiest attempt to line the river. Churchill was disappointed.

As Macmillan had guessed, Churchill requested "as many brass bands as possible," but otherwise he appeared content to leave his funeral details to a small committee code named "Operation Hope Not." However, the invaluable Montague Browne, who was a member of the committee, kept him informed of what was being planned to honor him.

Meanwhile, Clementine, watching her eighty-five-year-old husband's health fluctuate from day to day, was convinced that his death was imminent. During a car journey from Chartwell up to London, there had been a seizure that had robbed him of all power of speech. Although his speech returned, it left him in the depths of a hideous depression. Even Clementine had never seen him so bereft. "It was never like this in the past," she told Lord Moran. In the past, he had always had a hundred things to do; now all he had was reading, "but he does not enjoy what he reads. He cannot paint. . . . He simply wants to stay in bed."

Moran diagnosed another minor stroke, but, knowing Churchill's strength of will and powers of recovery, believed his patient would probably survive. Sure enough, within a week, Churchill was on his feet and determined to deliver a promised speech to his constituents at Woodford, where he was still M.P.

As usual, Churchill got his way. Mary and Christopher Soames were there to give support, and Clementine was beside him on the platform. Those who saw this all but final public speech witnessed an unforgettable performance. He appeared immensely old and utterly exhausted, and during the introductory speeches he remained slumped and lifeless, bald head nodding, pale gray suit appearing overlarge for his old man's body. But when the moment came for him to speak, there was a transformation. It was as if breath had suddenly been pumped into him. As he slowly staggered to his feet, the skills of the old orator he was sustained him.

He spoke for twenty minutes, somewhat shaky at the beginning, then gathering momentum as if that extraordinary voice were somehow emerging out of history. He urged courage in the face of all the perils currently confronting "this beloved island race," and finished quite abruptly, when whatever strength had been supporting him appeared to vanish. Once more he seemed immensely weary, and only the practiced strength of his son-in-law beside him got him safely from the platform.

What one was seeing was the famous willpower once again in action. For periods it could still be summoned up, as it was, a few weeks later, for one final trip to Washington, which he had had his heart set on, and where President Eisenhower somehow entertained him. Then that summer, accompanied by his secretary but not by Clementine, it was time once more for Pausaland.

Once again, the Reveses' hospitality and the Riviera sunlight did their work, and despite the heat of August, he was briefly rejuvenated, relishing the food and the attention, painting once again, and staying up at night as late as ever.

In fact, it was his host who was under strain. Late that August, Churchill decided on a brief return to London to attend an official banquet for the U.S. President. Emery Reves saw him safely off from the Nice airport, planning to meet him back there in a few days' time. But returning home, Reves suffered a heart attack. So instead of rapidly returning to La Pausa as intended, Churchill was compelled to spend the remainder of that summer with Clementine at Chartwell.

He did not know it, but he had seen the last of happy Pausaland, for although Reves soon recovered from his heart attack, and he and Wendy were both anxious to have Churchill stay with them again, they were up against an unbeatable opponent. Aristotle Socrates Onassis had now joined battle to play host to the world's most famous house-guest.

It was in 1956 that Randolph first brought Onassis to dinner at La Pausa to meet his father. One of the richest men in the world, Onassis had set his heart on meeting Churchill, and had been courting Randolph, hoping for an introduction. Randolph was actually a guest aboard the Onassis yacht, *Christina,* on the night of the dinner.

It was an uncomfortable evening. Reves, as a highly cultured Jew, looked down on Onassis as a serious vulgarian anxious to exploit their treasured guest for publicity or something worse. Onassis, who was clearly nervous, did behave a little oddly, sweating profusely, talking compulsively, and treating Churchill like some sort of Eastern potentate.

Wendy felt embarrassed by the whole performance, but Churchill was clearly taken with Onassis. "He made a good impression on me," he wrote afterward to Clementine. "He is a vy able and masterful man & told me a lot about whales. He kissed my hand."

Churchill had always had a taste for flamboyant buccaneers, particularly very rich ones, and even more so if they possessed large, luxuriously appointed, motor-yachts. Sir Ernest Cassel, Lord Moyne, the Duke of Westminster—those golden ghosts from Churchill's past —had all owned sumptuous vessels that he had unashamedly enjoyed, but none could have equaled what Churchill called "the monster-yacht" belonging to the Reveses' dinner guest.

Moored in the harbor at Monaco—much of which Onassis also owned—the *Christina,* a converted former naval frigate, was the most luxurious example of the genus in existence. (Impressive El Greco in the stateroom, two-thousand-year-old Cretan mosaic as a dance floor, bar stools covered with the foreskins of whales his whaling fleet had slaughtered. Only Reves noticed the El Greco was a fake.)

"Oh, my dear, dear friend, welcome, welcome aboard!" said the beaming multimillionaire while mysteriously invited press photographers snapped the statesman as he staggered up *Christina*'s gangplank. Churchill seemed delighted with the yacht, ignored the photographers, and made himself agreeable as its nervous owner knelt at his feet to spoon-feed him caviar. Churchill's last—and most unlikely—friendship had started.

For Onassis, Churchill was "the big fish" for whom nothing in the world was too much trouble. And for Churchill, Onassis was a rich man with a very large yacht that he seemed perfectly prepared to place at his disposal. (Later, when asked why he deserted old friends for this dubious Greek, Churchill answered, "Which of my old friends offers me his yacht?") At times, Onassis undoubtedly bored him, but almost everybody bored him by now, and he could always turn his hearing aid off when he was bored. He was, however, perfectly prepared to invite Onassis back for lunch at Hyde Park Gate, and even propose him as a member of the Other Club.

In return, Onassis was immensely generous, not just in terms of money (which presumably means little to a multimillionaire) but with the care and time he personally lavished on Churchill and on almost every member of the family. In all, he acted as Churchill's host on eight extended cruises, including the West Indies, the Canary Islands, and the eastern Mediterranean, where the *Christina* tactfully sailed through the Dardanelles at dead of night to avoid reminding Churchill of Gallipoli. One of the rules aboard the *Christina* was that anyone playing cards with Sir Winston lost.

Onassis treated him like royalty, and like royalty, Churchill and the family took his hospitality more or less for granted. "What would you like to be in another existence, Sir Winston?" Onassis asked him. "A tiger," said Churchill, "and what about you, Ari?" "Your budgerigar Toby," said Onassis.

Why he was so obsessed with Churchill is debatable. Onassis was not a sentimental man, but with his wealth he seems to have indulged a passion for acquiring worldly greatness. He had the greatest opera singer in the world as his mistress, would one day have a U.S. President's widow as his wife, and was happy to boast of having the world's greatest living statesman as his friend. Less romantically, friendship with Churchill would certainly impress the smartest international society and, more important still, impress Onassis's elegant and socially sophisticated wife, Athina. Although the daughter of another Greek shipping magnate, Livanos, "Tina," as she was known, had been educated and raised in England. While Ari was the father of her two children, she could still treat him as an uncouth peasant.

Also, as Emery Reves had long discovered, friendship with the Churchills was extremely good for business. In the aftermath of Suez, when the canal was blocked, Onassis had the opportunity to make vast profits with his supertankers bringing oil to the West around the coast of Africa. But according to his public relations adviser, Nigel Neilson, Onassis required acceptance from the still suspicious British oil establishment. Once he was known as the friend and host of Winston Churchill, Onassis had the entrée he needed—and was quick to use it. During the period of his friendship with Churchill, Onassis impressively increased his fortune.

In return, Onassis carefully watched over his guest, and would risk interfering with the family if he felt it necessary. Even aboard the *Christina* trouble could still erupt with Randolph. On one occasion there was such an argument between Randolph and his father that Onassis decided Randolph had to leave. Easier said than done, as the ship was somewhere off the coast of Greece. However, arrangements were made, via radio-telephone to Athens, for an invitation to be sent to Mr. Randolph Churchill to interview the King of Greece. It was a scoop that, as a journalist, Randolph could not ignore, but how to get to Athens? For Ari, nothing was too much trouble to protect the peace of mind of his treasured guest. *Christina* abruptly changed course for a nearby island where a seaplane from Onassis's Olympic Airways was already waiting in the harbor. Randolph embarked, and a few hours later was in Athens enjoying an exclusive interview with King Constantine, while Churchill was enjoying freedom from the aggravation only Randolph could create.

Thus did Onassis keep the great man happy—and for a period Churchill managed to combine these cruises, on which he was always accompanied by Clementine, with his holidays at La Pausa. But early in 1960, after Reves's heart attack and a voyage with Onassis to Antigua, all this ended.

This time, when the *Christina* docked at Monaco, Churchill made no attempt to contact the Reveses or go for his customary stay at La Pausa. Instead, he and Clementine spent some days as Onassis's guests at his Hotel de Paris in Monte Carlo, then returned to London in his private aircraft.

The Riviera is a small and unforgiving place, and the Reveses had inevitably aroused resentment from the way they had jealously guarded and protected Churchill in the past. (There was, for instance, no love lost between them and the Rainiers of Monaco on the subject.) And so for Churchill to be seen so publicly deserting what for years had been his favorite Riviera family in favor of Onassis, was the sort of snub to set the gossip-mongers busy.

Majesty is fickle, and Churchill was extremely old and tired—certainly too ancient to resist Clementine's dislike of Pausaland any longer—and the Reveses took considerable offense.

He had, of course, used and dropped people whenever it suited him throughout his life—most politicians do. But when later that summer he tried returning to La Pausa, Reves refused him in a bitter letter that began "Dear Sir Winston" and complained of the way he had deserted them.

Wendy was ill from all the intrigues that followed and would soon be returning to the States. Reves was equally upset. "There is a certain way of disregarding other peoples' feelings which drives sensitive human beings to the borders of insanity," he told his former houseguest.

Churchill apologized to Wendy, assuring her that "the months I spent at your charming house were among the brightest in my life." But he had forfeited Pausaland forever, and subsequent visits that he made as Onassis's guest to the Hotel de Paris were no substitute for the comfort and attention he had known with the once devoted Reveses.

A year later, Churchill was back at the Hotel de Paris, and Montague Browne was telling Lord Beaverbrook of Churchill's boredom there with "nobody about at all"; and how for want of somewhere suitable to go, he and Churchill had taken the liberty of sitting in the sun at the deserted garden of Beaverbrook's villa at Cap d'Ail. It was a melancholy picture.

For Clementine, too, the end of her husband's trips to Pausaland was more of a loss than she expected. Without them there was little to alleviate the strain on her as the final stage of Churchill's sad decline began in earnest, and several of the closest members of the family started to decline as well.

Randolph still drank as much as ever, although by now it might have seemed that he had come to terms with the fate life—and his father—had dealt him. He was too old to change his character, but he had at least changed his habitat, having left London and his favorite perch in the White's Club bar for an unassuming pale pink country house at East Bergholt in Suffolk.

As something of a consolation for not inheriting Chartwell, this was paid for from the trust that Churchill had set up for his children; and here, following the recipe for happiness that Voltaire gives at the conclusion of *Candide,* Randolph had settled down to cultivate his garden.

He was proud of the fact that Constable once lived and painted in East Bergholt, and as a sort of motto fixed a plaque on the terrace with a neat quotation from the painter's letters: "I am come to a determination to make no idle visits this summer nor give up any time to commonplace people. I shall return to Bergholt." There were in fact few "idle visits" now, for apart from his garden, which he loved, Randolph had discovered certain consolations that kept him safely anchored to East Bergholt. The first of these was Natalie, the wife of his nearest neighbor, Robert Bevan, an elderly and highly successful advertising executive. Natalie was fair-haired, beautiful, and charming. Randolph, now separated totally from June and lonely in the country, predictably fell in love. They became lovers, but Natalie was wise as well as beautiful. "I was in love with Randolph but I knew we could never possibly survive at too close quarters in that house of his."

She was also very fond of Mr. Bevan. The result was that most hazardous of civilized arrangements, which seems to have suited everybody admirably, Randolph especially. Randolph had always been devoid of sexual jealousy; and while deeply sentimental and susceptible to women, could never cope with all the incidentals of a married situation. Now he had what he had always needed: romance without restrictions, devotion without drudgery, and passion without responsibility. In this one department of his life at least, Randolph appeared a happy and contented human being.

At times he begged Natalie to marry him, but as she said, "he was not really marriageable. He loved his friends, he loved to drink and stay up far too late, so I would simply leave him and go home to bed. In the end he never really minded." At the same time, Natalie looked after him, holidayed with him (including trips to the South of France and on the *Christina*), and seems to have delighted all his friends, including the ever-loved Laura. (She was still happily married to handsome Michael Canfield, and Randolph spent his Christmases with them. "Frankly, I was delighted to see the old boy so happy. Natalie was a saint," said Laura.)

One effect of Randolph's move to Suffolk was that he saw considerably less of both his parents. Time had not eased the mutual antipathy between him and his mother, nor had Clementine's support for poor unhappy June improved the situation. Inflexible as ever, Clementine could see few redeeming features in her son, and according to one friend, "there were times when she could hardly bear to be in the same room with him."

According to Laura, "Even now Randolph blamed his mother for the trouble there had been between him and his father—and with both his wives. And beneath it all he found it hard to forgive her for never having loved him." Hardly surprisingly, he felt that she supported Soames against him. More superficially, he used to say that her stupidity annoyed him, and he became infuriated when he felt that she was showing off her "schoolgirl" skills at foreign languages. "What can you do with a woman who pronounces 'menu' as 'may-nyew'? in English," he exploded.

One of his assistants at East Bergholt has memories of a rare occasion when Clementine actually arrived for lunch. This ended so prematurely that Clementine spent forty minutes at the local station waiting for her train to London rather than endure Randolph a moment longer.

Between Randolph and his father things were different. Emotionally, he was as much bound up with him as ever—even their bitterest rows were never final—and early in 1960, it was Churchill who agreed to the arrangement that, along with the love affair with Natalie, seems to have given Randolph his most lasting happiness. Even before the war, Randolph had been anxious to write the story of his father's life. Churchill was always wary of revelations by those who knew him at close quarters. "You're not *writing* anything?" he regularly asked Grace Hamblin during the days she was working as a Chartwell secretary, and he seems to have been just as wary of anything that Randolph might commit to paper. But while refusing to allow the youthful Randolph to write about him, he did say that he would one day have the chance—and promised that the book would make his fortune.

Since then, the whole subject of Churchill's official biography had been shelved. Throughout his life, Churchill had taken such immense pains to explain and justify himself in print, that his literary memorial clearly had to be exactly as he wanted. In his official "life," the legend he had built around himself had to be enshrined forever—and the literary equivalent of a Graham Sutherland was too terrible to contemplate. Churchill, who never threw a thing away, had hoarded an immense archive for the great biography, but as the years ticked by, he seemed unable to decide upon the great biographer. Randolph stayed in the running, and he had set his heart on doing it.

It would redeem the failure of his life—and guarantee financial resurrection in the process. (Like his father in his heyday, Randolph had a hard time with his cash flow). But Churchill, not surprisingly, still had doubts about his son's fitness for the monumental task. To prove himself to his father, Randolph embarked upon a long political biography of the noble, rich (and, truth be told, tedious), seventeenth

Earl of Derby. Thanks largely to his literate literary assistant, Alan Brien, the book was finished and received polite reviews. Finally, in July 1960, Natalie was greeted at the house by an exultant Randolph waving a telegram. "He's asked me! He's asked me at last!" he shouted.

Randolph's daughter, Arabella, also remembers the excitement. "Millions!" he whispered as she went to bed. "It will make us millions!"

"Dearest Papa," he wrote to Churchill, "your letter has made me proud and happy. Since I first read your life of your father, 35 years ago when I was a boy of 14 at Eton, it has always been my greatest ambition to write your life."

While Randolph was euphoric in his new role as the great biographer, his ex-wife Pamela was also happy. Approaching forty, and with twelve years as a divorcée behind her, she had married the rich, glamorous, and already thrice married New York theatrical producer Leland Hayward. Since the departure of Agnelli, her years in Paris had not been easy. True, she had known the friendship and affection of very rich admirers and had lived in considerable luxury. Her furniture was Louis XVI, her Rolls was ever at the service of her friends, and she was rumored to spend $10,000 annually on flowers. But as Somerset Maugham had once reminded her, it was time she married.

Hayward, famous as the producer of *The Sound of Music* and previously married to the actress Margaret Sullavan, was still very much wedded to his third wife, Nancy, when Pamela met him in New York during a visit to the Whitneys in 1959. Hayward apparently had a prejudice against Englishwomen ("They all have had bad teeth and talk through their noses and they're all amoral."). He also had a formidable young family by Margaret Sullavan, including the budding actress, Brooke. But from those formative years with the Churchill Club in wartime London, Pamela had learned the art of capturing the hearts of high-powered eminent Americans. She also had the aura of Paris and the great brand image of the Churchill name.

Hayward was spellbound. According to Brooke, "It was as if he was entering a kind of golden circle through his association with her," and despite the problems of children and divorce, Pamela became the fourth, and final, Mrs. Leland Hayward in the spring of 1960.

The Churchills sent congratulations and a check, and while Randolph gave the standard ex-husband's reaction—"With that round face and those legs how ever did she manage it?"—Pamela proved the perfect wife for Leland Hayward, taking a close interest in his work, nursing him when he was sick, and adapting with extraordinary success to the world of the theater and smart New York society. "Mama is a chameleon," young Winston is said to have remarked.

Unfortunately, marriage came too late for Pamela to give young Winston what she had long been seeking for him—a reliable stepfather and the settled home she knew he needed—yet there were some compensations. Winston got on well with Leland; there was a base for him in America whenever he required it, and on his twenty-first birthday, Pamela was able to replace his ancient Fiat with a brand new Jaguar and Leland paid for him to take flying lessons. Winston was still at Christ Church, Oxford, at the time, and it is interesting to compare him with his father on the eve of that fateful birthday party at Claridges twenty-nine years earlier. Randolph, at twenty-one, had worshiped Churchill, modeled himself slavishly upon him, and although rebelling hard against authority, believed in his destiny to follow his father to the heights of power and glory.

In 1961, Randolph's twenty-one-year-old son could not have been more different. Far from worshiping his father, Winston was extremely wary of him; instead of seeing Randolph as a model to be copied, Winston on the whole regarded him as a notable example of what should be avoided. (To this day, he is a passionate nonsmoker, virtually a nondrinker, a nongambler, and the least gluttonous of men.)

Photographs reveal a physical resemblance between them at the age of twenty-one, although young Winston lacks the slightly suspect beauty of Randolph's Laszlo portrait. In temperament, however, Winston seemed much closer to his mother, being equable, agreeable, and something of a late bloomer.

What he appeared to lack entirely were those appalling but distinctive qualities that Randolph had absorbed in childhood from his father: the arrogance, the extra layer of skin, the sense of supercharged superiority—all of which had made young Randolph so difficult to cope with but had also marked him as a distinct phenomenon.

Young Winston, to the probable relief of all around him, was not a phenomenon. Nor was he particularly Churchillian. Although brought up mainly by his mother—and his devoted Nanny Martin— he had remained surprisingly unspoiled by the rich society around her, and was not the playboy he might well have been. He was an earnest, active, otherwise unremarkable young man with the unavoidable distinction of having the greatest name in Britain. His problem was what on earth to do with it.

As cherished heir and namesake, he had always held a special place in his grandfather's affections, but although he had often stayed with his Churchill grandparents, there had been nothing of that almost superstitious sense of intimate succession that had dominated Randolph's early manhood.

During young Winston's childhood, Churchill was too busy, and later on too old, to get to know his grandson all that well. On one occasion, he gave him a cigar case and two boxes of cigars, not realizing his grandson's deep dislike of nicotine; on another, when young Winston had driven up from Oxford to lunch with his grandfather, the old Victorian remarked, "You did not drive yourself, did you? I trust you had your man drive you. With the provision I have been able to make you, you should certainly be able to afford that."

It was all extremely touching, and Winston revered Grandpapa Churchill. For him, as he wrote in his autobiography, his grandfather was quite simply "the greatest Briton in the history of our country." But the young Winston's sense of awe before this stupendous predecessor was very different from his father's early role as future "carrier of the lamp."

Although, as a boy at Eton, Winston had sometimes found his name a burden ("Take this for being a shit! Take this for being a bastard! And take this for being Winston-bloody-Churchill!" his schoolmates chanted as they beat his bare behind with rubber-soled slippers), there were some tangible advantages to be derived from "the name."

As Randolph pointed out, his son possessed "the greatest byline in journalism," and after leaving Oxford, young Winston made the most of it. World leaders like de Gaulle, the Kennedys, and King Hussein of Jordan were delighted to be interviewed by Winston Churchill (Hussein actually called him "Sir"), and as he proudly claims, by twenty-three he was already "one of the highest paid journalists in Fleet Street."

For the youthful Winston, however, this was not enough. In 1964 he married Minnie d'Erlanger, daughter of Sir Gerard d'Erlanger, founder of prewar British Airways and a member of an Anglo-French banking family. Churchill gave Winston a generous check, and in his thank-you letter, Winston promised his grandfather to "carry the name Churchill, which you made great, with honour into the future." For young Winston, this meant only one thing: politics. Randolph, speaking from long and sad experience, counseled his son to become an engineer. But Winston had made up his mind.

While young Winston prepared for his political career, Randolph took up his role as Churchill's biographer. One of his earliest tasks was to examine the Blenheim archives. Despite the fact that they disliked each other, Bert had grudgingly invited him over for the night, and he arrived in time for dinner, bringing Winston and a young research assistant with him. Bert was living in the palace on his own, his unhappy Duchess having died in 1961. Dinner was served in a small unheated room that, although devoid of books, was still referred to as "the library." The food was uninviting, and Bert, instead of bothering with his guests, sat watching television at table.

A lesser man than Randolph might not have felt annoyed. After several drinks, his rage exploded. "Bert," shouted Randolph, "your bloody library's not a library, your food's disgusting, and television's not a substitute for conversation over dinner." Bert disagreed just as strongly, at which point Randolph arose, summoned his party, and left Blenheim abruptly.

"Never mind," he said, consoling his research assistant as they drove away. "I'll get everything sent over. Bert is so ignorant he doesn't even know he's got archives."

Bert's problem, unbeknownst to the family, was that, since the Duchess died in 1960, he had started missing her and had increasingly retreated into himself. While she was alive, he had bullied and made fun of her; now he was miserable and bored. One ray of light that did strike Blenheim came from the glamorous remarriage of his son, the heir to the dukedom, which indirectly brought together two quite separate worlds in Cousin Winston Churchill's life.

Onassis's attempt to employ his intimacy with Churchill to win over his Anglophile wife, who was twenty-nine years his junior, could not avert the inevitable divorce in 1958; but it had produced an unexpected sequel. Tina was not particularly impressed by her husband's friendship with Churchill and his family, but she was very taken with a key member of the Churchill circle—the future head of the whole family, Sunny Blandford.

Tina was beautiful, very rich in her own right, and tired of life with Ari. Sunny was vulnerable and lonely—and would one day be a duke. Early in 1961, in a chaotic Greek marriage ceremony in Paris with more journalists than guests, Tina Onassis somewhat improbably became the second Lady Blandford. "So Ari, we are related at last!" Churchill said to Onassis when he heard the news.

But even these Churchill relatives, with title, wealth, and everything that life could offer, seemed cursed with the family unhappiness. The new Lady Blandford was popular at Blenheim, not least for her generosity toward the servants—something few members of the family could be accused of. But she and Sunny were patently unsuited and had no children. They lived increasingly apart, and in 1970 she summoned her servants, offered them double pay to accompany her to Paris, then swept out of Blenheim, taking her impressionist paintings and most valuable possessions, never to return. After an amicable divorce from Sunny in 1971, Tina married her brother-in-law Stavros Niarchos, dying in mysterious circumstances three years later.

In her own way, Sarah was becoming an equally tragic figure, and during 1960 the family had to come to terms with the fact that Churchill's favorite daughter was an incurable alcoholic. She was also a very public one, as her court appearances—and sentences—increased: in February 1960, £2 for assaulting a taxi driver in Lucan Place; in July, £2-10s for being drunk and disorderly in Ebury Street; and in November, a year's probation following a brawl at the Riverside Club, Westminster. A few months later, she broke her probation and spent ten days in Holloway Prison.

Her father's eminence made little difference. He was too old, and too fond of alcohol himself, to have had the remotest influence over what had now become an illness. Clementine was terrified of scandal, and her concern for Sarah must have added to her "nervous fatigue, depression, and anxiety state" that in February 1961 her doctors felt required hospital treatment.

Sarah was concerned about her mother, and had learned to dread her steely disapproval just as she pitied her pathetic states of deep anxiety. But nothing Clementine did could make her daughter change her habits; neither could clinics, psychiatrists, or doctors.

Sarah managed to continue in the role of Peter Pan, thanks to extraordinary powers of recovery and her popularity among other members of the cast. "*Was* there an incident last night?" she would ask her stage director, Ellen Pollock, when arriving late and very hung over for a rehearsal. According to Miss Pollock, Sarah had the usual alcoholic's lack of recollection of her drinking, and refused to think about the consequences.

But by the end of 1961, even Sarah had to realize the trouble she was bringing to the family. It was in order to escape from her psychiatrists, her sense of guilt about her parents, and what she referred to as "the attentions of the boys in blue," that she decided to decamp to a villa in southern Spain. The sun shone and whisky was cheap, and against remarkable odds, Sarah found herself another husband.

Henry, Baron Audley, had ended up in southern Spain after a lifetime of considerable futility. He was drunken, gay, and all but penniless—and had just recovered from a massive stroke. But he was also good company and extremely charming, and these two unlikely, lonely people fell in love. For a while they lived and drank together. Then in April 1962, at the register office in Gibraltar, Henry made Sarah Lady Audley.

Diana, who flew out from England, was the only member of the family at the ceremony. Since Churchill and Clementine were cruising with Onassis at the time, their attitude was not recorded, but Randolph was delighted. His first, entirely predictable, reaction was to look up Henry in Debrett's *Guide to the Peerage,* where, on discovering that Henry was the twenty-third baron of the fourth oldest dynasty in England, he remarked, "Well, *that* puts the Marlboroughs in their place!" But not, alas, for long.

The Audleys remained contentedly in Spain for fourteen months. Then, in July 1963, Lord Audley died—quite suddenly—of a cerebral hemorrhage, while Sarah was with him.

Clementine, still suffering from nervous stress, was too ill and too fatigued to give her freshly widowed daughter much assistance; instead, she gave Diana £1,000 to fly to Spain to comfort her sister. This was a role Diana was adept at, and Sarah was grateful for her help at the funeral at Malaga. When Sarah finally returned to Chartwell, her father met her at the door. "We stared silently at each other; then he took my hand and said simply, 'We must close ranks and march on.' "

Closing ranks became increasingly important for the Churchills during 1963. With Churchill in his late eighties now, Clementine was finding it impossible to cope with him. Just as she had never been maternal with her children, so, as Montague Browne said, "she was not prepared to become a mother to her husband." The acute fatigue and depression that had been plaguing her for months grew worse, and in October she was admitted to Westminster Hospital for the same electrotherapy Diana had endured.

Not that Diana's many courses of psychiatric treatment had been able to resolve her problems and her deep unhappiness. She remained absurdly insecure, and her sense of religious persecution was as bad as ever. There were periods when she and Clementine attempted to forget the past, but the wounds Clementine had inflicted on her daughter went too deep to be entirely ignored.

Diana's greatest source of misery was still the breakup of her marriage and the loss of her beloved husband. In April 1962, Duncan Sandys had married his thirty-three-year-old mistress, French-born Marie-Claire, the recently divorced wife of his former colleague, the Tory Minister of Agriculture Lord Hudson. On the day he married, Diana officially reverted to her maiden name. Typically, she tried to make a joke of it by apologizing to her former friend and namesake from her days at RADA. "I am sure that Diana Churchill, the actress, will agree that there is room for two of a good thing," she told reporters.

Sadly there was little to joke about in Diana's situation. Like Clementine, she remained acutely and dangerously depressed, and sometimes talked of suicide. But she was courageous in the way she fought against her mental misery. By forcing herself to work as a voluntary counselor with the Samaritans, she involved herself in the lives of others as desperate as herself. Her doctor hoped that this would help her face her problems, and for a while it did, but in mid-October 1963, Diana heard that Marie-Claire, the second Mrs. Duncan Sandys, had had a baby.

The following Saturday evening neighbors saw Diana returning to her house in Chester Row, alone. During that afternoon she had been with her daughter Edwina and had told her that on Sunday she would be visiting Clementine in the hospital and then dining with Churchill at the house in Hyde Park Gate. Diana never visited her parents. Instead, she was found the next morning dead on the bedroom floor when her housekeeper came to call her. An inquest a few days later gave a verdict of suicide from an overwhelming dose of sleeping tablets.

Since Sarah had now returned to Spain, Mary had the task of breaking the news to both her parents. Clementine was under deep sedation and it took a while for the news to filter through to her, thus cushioning the shock. With Churchill, age and the blunting of his sensibilities had much the same effect. Mary described how, when he finally understood what had happened, he "withdrew into a great and distant silence." "As he grew older," she added, "he seemed to acquire a degree of insulation from sad or unpleasant news about those he loved."

This was just as well because, to complete the Churchills' load of misery, there were further worries over Randolph, as the accumulated years of manifold indulgence finally caught up with him. Earlier that year, he had proudly visited the United States with young Winston to receive the Honorary Citizenship of the United States that President John Kennedy conferred on Churchill. At eighty-nine, there could be no question of him going in person, and it seemed that Randolph's greatest moment was to stand in as his father's proxy.

He had always been able to imitate Churchill, and at the ceremony in the White House rose garden, he sounded strangely like his father as he read the letter of acceptance that Churchill, with Montague Browne's assistance, had composed for the occasion.

Randolph was greatly enamored of the Kennedys, who represented everything he felt that he had wanted out of life: glamour, youth, vitality, and that greatest prize of all, the political power that had cruelly eluded him. Like the Churchills, the Kennedys appeared as a great political family, but they were still in the ascendant. Randolph was all too well aware by now of his own family's decline—and of the chances he had lost forever.

He was again visiting the Kennedys when Diana died, and soon after his return to England he caught pneumonia. He only partially recovered, and at fifty-two was suddenly looking old beyond his years. The fat rambunctious man had turned thin and anxious. He ate little, drank as heavily as ever, and was smoking eighty cigarettes a day. He was losing weight and when X-rays revealed a patch on his lung, cancer was suspected.

Randolph treated his operation, early in 1964, much as he had always treated waiters, women, and events he disapproved of. As a snob, he had always found something intolerably common about hospitals, and did not allow the medical routines to get him down. He charmed the nurses, bullied the matron, and when the surgeon tried to stop him from going home, Randolph told him, "Doctor, I pay you to cut me up, not to dictate my whereabouts."

Lord Lambton visited with some bottles of very good champagne. "Just put them in a bucket for me, nurse," said Randolph, thinking that they needed chilling. He was upset when the nurse tipped three bottles of vintage Bollinger into his plastic slop-pail.

To everyone's surprise, his own included, the excised portion of his lung was not cancerous, which prompted Evelyn Waugh's celebrated mot: "A typical triumph of modern science to find the only part of Randolph that was not malignant and remove it!"

Randolph relished the remark when someone told it to him, and irreverently cabled back to the Catholic novelist, in time for Easter Sunday, "Have a Happy Resurrection!"

Randolph convalesced with Natalie in Biarritz and Capri, then returned to East Bergholt to continue work on the biography. She remembers him "trying to act as if nothing untoward had happened." But she thought it ominous that he was now drinking beer instead of whisky. "After that operation I am fairly sure he knew his days were numbered."

But Randolph still managed to take Laura to visit his father in his room at Hyde Park Gate in the summer of 1964, not long before the great man died. There was an unsmoked cigar between his lips, and for much of the time they sat in silence, but Laura felt that even now Churchill was battling determinedly against extinction. As she was leaving, he summoned up his energy and smiled. "The Dark Angel beckons—but I still say no!" he muttered.

At the end of Goethe's *Faust,* the Devil renders his account, and as Faust is made to pay him back the price of his ambitions, those he has loved are sacrificed as well. Churchill might well have been the aged Faust, with the contrast between so much worldly glory and the hopelessness and gloom engulfing him and those around him.

Almost since adolescence, he had lived life as an unrelenting war against depression and a primal dread of failure. To defeat these enemies, he had deployed prodigious energies, had never risked the boredom of an idle moment, and had been ruthlessly and unbelievably ambitious. In the process, he had built a legend of indubitable greatness; now that his active life was over, the legend was no defense against the self-destructive gloom so basic to his nature. "My life is over but is not yet ended," he had told Diana just before she killed herself.

As a nonbeliever, he was haunted by the finality of oblivion, which left him no recourse against his old obsessions. Montague Browne, who had the unenviable task of keeping him company through many of his darkest moments, said Churchill was deeply troubled by a bitter sense of failure. "He felt that everything that he had done had ended in disaster. He had won the war but lost the Empire, communism had swallowed up half of Europe, and socialism was threatening the world he loved at home."

Lord Moran, witnessing the same obsession, had told him to forget posterity. But Churchill, in his old man's misery, would not be placated. "I ought not, I must not, be held to account for what has gone wrong," he answered sadly. Medically, Moran believed that the atrophying of the senses would slowly blunt the edge of his anxieties. But as a friend, he pitied him at Chartwell, sitting "there in the great house through the interminable days, often alone, waiting for the end."

Some years before, Churchill, in a somber, after-dinner mood, had been gazing at the fire. "Curious to imagine oneself a log," he remarked. "Reluctant to be consumed, yet obliged *eventually* to give way." Now that the fire of his life was burning low, he was waiting patiently to be consumed.

He found his daughter Sarah his greatest comfort, and she would sit with him for hours, willing the time to pass. "What time is it, Sas?" he would ask. "Twelve o'clock, Papa," she would answer. Five minutes later he would repeat the question. And Sarah would give the answer. In an earlier period of depression, Diana had tried to cheer him up by reminding him of everything that he had done in life.

"I have achieved a great deal to achieve nothing in the end," he muttered, and refused to listen to her efforts to convince him otherwise.

Perhaps it all seemed like a dream to him now. Just as he had made the daydreams of his youth reality and acted out imagined roles in great achievements, were the achievements turning back into a dream?

On November 30, 1964, Churchill turned ninety. He had to spend the day in bed, but he managed to stagger to the window for the small crowd waiting patiently outside; in the evening there was a birthday dinner by candlelight with all the family around him. Four weeks later came the stroke that was to kill him.

Everybody knew that this was one occasion when not even Lord Moran's skills could save him, and even he seemed finally prepared for those "smooth black curtains" he had so long avoided. Throughout his life, as Britain's greatest man of war since Wellington, Churchill had borne responsibility for innumerable violent deaths of others. Now, in extreme old age, in comfort and in peace, he waited for his own. It was a fine, dramatic deathbed, with no pain—Clementine and young Winston by each side of the bed, Sarah drunk, Mary tactfully shepherding grandchildren in to see him. Randolph was there to kiss his hand, and Lord Moran to ease his passing. There was even a priest to give the blessing of a God in whom he never had believed. The Queen was kept informed, and silent crowds attended patiently outside the house. It was in character that his last words were uttered not to Randolph but to Christopher Soames when he tried to offer him champagne. "I'm so bored with it all," he said with a sigh. He then sank into a peaceful coma, so he never knew that as he lay dying, another generation was added to the line. On January 22, Winston's wife, Minnie, had a son. Continuing the tradition of alternate names, they called him Randolph.

"In the midst of death we are in life," the baby's namesake and grandfather wrote to Clementine telling her the news.

It was very different from that other deathbed, seventy years earlier, when Churchill witnessed the agonies of his dying father, with the family assembled in his grandmother's house in Grosvenor Square. The days continued and he lingered on in coma. Jock Colville remembered seeing him one morning early in 1950, and hearing him remark, "Today is the twenty-fourth of January. It is the day my father died. It is the day that I shall die, too."

For nine days after the stroke Churchill lay unconscious as if sleeping gently. Then on January 24 he died.

All followed as he had known it would, and in death the worn-out, sad old figure of his final years was re-created into the sort of legendary being he had dreamed of all his life. For three days he lay like a medieval king in Westminster Hall, and despite the cold, nearly 200,000 people filed past the coffin. Some wept. All passed in silence. His granddaughter Emma Soames, fourteen years old at the time, remembered being "overwhelmed by the beauty and the sheer theatricality of the whole occasion."

The funeral on January 30 was, as one commentator wrote, "one of those rare and memorable occasions when television's multiple insect-eye makes us all partakers in a great ritual of race." It was a unique occasion: the great cathedral filled with presidents and foreign royalty, the one occasion when the Queen herself attended as a mourner at a commoner's funeral.

Even more than with the lying-in, the funeral was inspired theater —with the bands he had wanted, the hymns he had loved, and a great religious celebration for this stalwart nonbeliever. Broadcast on television, with Laurence Olivier reading excerpts from his speeches, each part of this state funeral had enormous impact on the nation—although it was hard to be precise about the essence of this mass emotion.

Some saw it as the funeral of the British Empire, some as a

requiem for the heroism of the war, others as the burial of a mighty subject and the nation's final hero. What is certain is that it could have happened for no one else, and that the legend Churchill built around himself was at the center of an unforgettable media event.

His old enemy Clement Attlee, who would just survive him, nearly fainted and had to be provided with a chair. One of the few who sobbed emotionally throughout the service was Onassis. The family members were dry-eyed and stoic, befitting the occasion. Randolph, as principal mourner, though mortally ill himself, had followed the cortege on foot with his son, Winston, at his side. Clementine, with Sarah and Mary beside her, rode in a carriage lent for the occasion by the Queen. Grandchildren rode in other carriages behind her.

It was only when the service ended and the coffin was embarked at Westminster Pier for the symbolic crossing of the Thames, which Churchill had wanted, that the family's solemn facade was briefly threatened. Sarah had somehow stayed erect throughout the service. She was, however, very drunk, having been barely sober since her father died. Knowing this, Clementine had passed a message to the attendants, asking them to stop her daughter Sarah as she left the cathedral. Because of this, Sarah did not see her father's body cross the river, or the dockside cranes that dipped in homage at his passing. (According to Sarah this was originally one of Churchill's own suggestions.)

Nor did Sarah travel with the family on the special train—pulled by the locomotive named "Sir Winston Churchill"—that took her father on his final journey back to Blenheim and to Bladon churchyard where, after so much misery and so much glory, Churchill was reunited with his father.

# thirty-four

# Aftermath

Clementine was seventy-nine when Churchill died and still had twelve more years to live. The National Trust duly took possession of Chartwell for the nation, the house in Hyde Park Gate was sold, and Clementine moved into a small apartment just around the corner in Princes Gate. Here she could relax at last, cherish her memories, and see her friends and family.

Her classic looks refined with age, and there was a serenity about her now that had not been evident when Churchill was alive. The nervous symptoms that once plagued her ended. So did the troubles with her children.

As Churchill's widow, Clementine was much revered, and although she was made a baroness in her own right by the Queen, within the family she seemed increasingly dependent and endearing. Frailer and deafer with the years, she remained as much the perfectionist as ever, still changing for dinner and insisting on the standards at table that she had maintained when Churchill was alive. Even when her mind was going at the end, there were glimpses of the strength that enabled her to hold her own with Churchill for more than half a century. She survived to the age of ninety-two before joining him in Bladon churchyard in December 1977.

Other close members of the family were less resilient, and Churchill had left an uneasy legacy for some of the members of his precious citadel who survived him.

Randolph was now beyond repair, a sad successor to that "rollickingly bumptious" youth whose father had once seen him as his political successor and proudly given him that twenty-first birthday party at Claridges thirty-three years earlier.

Cecil Beaton met him shortly after his father's funeral and was shocked at his appearance, "old and grey like a haggard hawk." But Randolph, being Randolph, tried to convince him that he was happier than he'd ever been. "At last I'm doing something to justify my life. The biography of my father will be the best thing I've ever done, my contribution to the world," he muttered huskily. Beaton was not convinced. "His eyes looked so abysmally sad," he wrote.

True to his word, Randolph was hard at work upon the great biography as if to snatch the embers of success from the bonfire of a lifetime. Yet, not for the first time, he had underestimated the scale of his father's vast career, which would require eight large volumes—and twenty years hard labor by Randolph's biographical successor, Martin Gilbert, to complete. Randolph saw only the first volume, covering his father's childhood, published in 1966.

He still enjoyed his garden, had Natalie to care for him, and had his research assistants to keep him company. But he ate next to nothing and his body was collapsing. He was fifty-seven, eleven years younger than his father had been when he became Prime Minister in 1940, when he died in his sleep on June 7, 1968. It was one of the few things in his life that he did peacefully.

Like Randolph, Sarah's fate was also inextricably linked with Churchill's. While he was alive, she had loved him deeply and reacted powerfully against him, feeling the need to keep her independence. After he died the pattern continued—and so did her drinking. In her early fifties, Sarah's favorite escape route was into the life of a bohemian semi-intellectual on the fringe of Rome's dolce vita. She painted, wrote poetry, and chose her lovers as if still needing to proclaim her independence from paternal criticism. For some reason, men with aliases attracted her. After Vic Oliver and Anthony Beauchamp, she found another lover who had changed his name. This was Ernest Leroy Jackson, a black painter and entertainer from Philadelphia, Pennsylvania, who called himself Lobo Nocho when he came to Rome. He was a flamboyant, gentle character, and while they lived together, he did his best to cope with Sarah's drinking. For a period in the mid-sixties, they were officially engaged.

But Sarah found it hard to maintain any close relationship for long, and when the affair ended, she returned to her chaotic ground-floor apartment in Belgravia. London was not an easy place for Sarah with her acting career virtually over, but some of her theatrical friends stayed faithful and helped her devise her own one-woman show of song and recitation called *An Evening with Sarah Churchill*. The vision of an aging actress with her memories might be embarrassing, but she enjoyed the sense of being center stage. Among the songs she sang was one her father wrote for his children called "Mr. Puggy Wug."

Her relations, like her friends, were wary of inviting her to stay, and the only member of the family she saw regularly was Clementine. Until well into her eighties, she would arrive once a week at Sarah's apartment in a chauffeur-driven car and take her out for lunch. Sarah's friends discovered that this was one day they could count on Sarah staying sober. When her mother died, Sarah was sixty-three, and her looks had gone. At the memorial service in Westminster Abbey, she seemed a tragic figure as she and Mary together laid a wreath on the slab that bears the words "Remember Winston Churchill."

During her last years, Sarah became notorious in various Chelsea pubs as Duchess Sarah. She sold what jewelry she had and moved from pub to pub according to the credit they would offer. She was frequently alone, and when drunk was sometimes violent. But even now the Churchill name protected her. The neighborhood police, knowing who she was, took care of her and often brought her home at night without asking questions.

Like her father, she was inordinately tough, but by 1982 she knew her days were numbered. "Nothing would induce me to live my life again," she told a journalist not long before she died, but on her deathbed that September she confided to a friend, "I don't mind going, because I know Papa is waiting." She was sixty-seven when she departed.

Mary continued as the one exception to the doom that seemed predestined for all of Churchill's children. She was forty-two when he died, and with Christopher and their five exuberant children living happily in the country, was healthy, balanced, and preeminently sane. According to her daughter Emma, "She firmly slapped us children down if we showed the slightest sign of getting above ourselves as grandchildren of the Greatest Englishman. She also firmly kept all publicity away from us throughout our childhood."

When Soames lost his parliamentary seat at Bedford, after the Labour victory in the 1964 general election, something of the old dynastic element still helped him. He was rich, having inherited his share of the family brewing fortune, and in 1968, Socialist Prime Minister Harold Wilson decided that a wealthy Tory married to a Churchill was the perfect representative for a Labour government in France.

In fact, he made an excellent ambassador, speaking good French, being tall enough not to be overshadowed by President de Gaulle, and appearing every inch the sort of caricature upper-class Englishman that Frenchmen relish. The banquet years of La Famille Soames had started, and during their four years in the magnificent embassy building on the Faubourg St. Honoré, it was as if the afterglow of Churchill's power was surviving in his youngest daughter and son-in-law. It was an important time in Franco-British relations, and Soames played a crucial role in his country's entry into the European Common Market. Mary was extremely popular in France, as, increasingly, was Soames, who was mellowing into the distinguished figure who went on to Brussels as one of the first Commissioners of the Common Market. By his mid-fifties, he had transmuted from party politician into elder statesman, member of the House of Lords, and Conservative grandee. As such, he performed his last important task in government; as Governor of Rhodesia he presided over the changing of this last great British colony into independent Zimbabwe.

He did this while retaining the affection of many African politicians, including the new Prime Minister, Mugabe, who said he ended by "fondly loving him"; but there was something strange in the fact that it was Churchill's favorite son-in-law who was winding up this last great remnant of the British Empire. Returning to England, Soames spent a period as leader of the House of Lords, but there was little real sympathy between this old-style Tory and the very new-style Conservative premier, Mrs. Thatcher. After angry disagreement over her plans for the civil service, he resigned from her government in 1981 and died of cancer six years later.

He had not achieved that central role in politics for which he had once seemed destined as Churchill's son-in-law. Still less has his eldest son, Nicholas, who entered the House of Commons in 1983. A successful businessman and friend and one-time equerry of the Prince of Wales, the young Soames is physically very like his father, but he has lacked the priceless benefit of having Winston Churchill as a father-in-law. His family connections may even have impeded him in the changed political climate of the eighties, and he has not enjoyed even that humblest place in government which members of the Churchill family once almost automatically expected.

Churchill's former son-in-law Duncan Sandys also continued his ascent through the upper echelons of power after 1965. He had seemed unaffected by Diana's tragedy and, like Soames, having lost his parliamentary seat in 1964, continued as a European statesman, founding the so-called European Movement. With his successful second marriage, his peerage (he was created Baron Duncan-Sandys in 1974), and a rich career in business he seemed an enviable figure. The Churchill years had served him well, and it was not until his later years that his reputation faltered. His use of offshore trusts to avoid personal taxation was widely criticized, as was the company of which he was chairman, the massive Lonrho Corporation, which Prime Minister Edward Heath described as "the unacceptable face of capitalism." He died, aged seventy-nine, in 1988. Sandys's personal contact with the Churchills ended even before Diana died, and their children—Julian, Edwina, and Celia—have been even more removed, living determinedly private lives and benefiting little from what remained of the Churchill connection.

Yet this connection still had power to affect the lives of certain members of the family, as one sees in the very different fates of Randolph's two ex-wives, Pamela and June. Pamela had always made the most of the Churchill contacts, and in 1971, when the death of her second husband Leland Hayward left her suddenly alone and rather badly off, the wartime years with Churchill provided her salvation. By chance Pamela met her old admirer Averell Harriman. Once the source of such bitterness between Randolph and his parents, Harriman was now in his early eighties, widowed, richer than ever, and splendidly preserved—so well preserved, in fact, that although he was over eighty, Pamela agreed to marry him. They had ten happy years together, forming a climax to Pamela's extraordinary career and uniting two political families, the Churchills and the Harrimans. He died in 1983 leaving his widow $75 million and the ex officio position of Washington's leading hostess of the Democratic party.

When the Gorbachevs came to Washington in 1989, it was Pamela Churchill Harriman whom Raisa Gorbachev called upon before paying her respects to Nancy Reagan. And had the Democrats won the presidency, Pamela might well have rounded off the career that started in the Churchill Club in wartime London by returning as American Ambassador.

But whereas Pamela owed so much to her contact with the Churchills, June seemed to have been finally defeated by them. Shell-shocked from her years with Randolph, and lacking Pamela's panache and bounce, she wilted. Sad and unsure of herself, she was too proud —or too impractical—to exploit her situation. Clementine kept in touch with her, largely for Arabella's sake, but even this made June fearful that she might be criticized about how she was bringing up her daughter. Short of money, she found life immensely difficult and, after a mastectomy in 1968, decided she could not remarry. Instead, she had a number of devoted gay admirers, none of whom realized that she was terminally ill with cancer. Early in 1980, rather than end her days in the hospital, June, discreet as ever, took a massive overdose of sleeping pills and joined the group of suicides around the Churchill family.

As a very old man, Churchill had always had a soft spot for June's blue-eyed daughter, Arabella. At his golden wedding celebration in Monte Carlo, Arabella had recited Greek poetry (in translation) in his honor; and Nancy Mitford predicted she would marry a duke (conveniently offering to introduce her to her teenage nephew, who was heir to the Duke of Devonshire). But Arabella was afflicted with her mother's insecurity about the Churchills. Grand life depressed her, and instead of marrying her duke, Arabella opted out. She worked for a leper charity for a while, then in a vegetarian restaurant. Later, she became a hippie and joined a Welsh hillside commune, married a schoolteacher, had a son named Jake, divorced, and is now married to a juggler and living happily in a small, extremely simple house in Glastonbury.

The most intriguing fate of all the Churchills was what remained in store for Randolph's other child, Arabella's half-brother, Winston, whose whole future had seemed so assured when his grandfather argued the Duchess of Marlborough into letting him bestow his all-important name on him in 1940.

True to his eve-of-marriage promise to his grandfather to "maintain his name with honour," Winston had duly entered politics, and at twenty-nine had duly won the Labour-held seat of Stretford in Lancashire for the Conservatives. (In 1983 the constituency was redesignated Davyhulme.) He was subsequently appointed opposition spokesman on defense, with the likelihood of holding office when the Conservatives returned to power. But politics can be a bitter business, and ironically Winston's name and great political inheritance helped destroy his chances of political advancement.

First came the fraught question of Rhodesian independence, which had yet to be sorted out by his uncle Christopher Soames. During 1979, policy toward that troubled British colony was giving many Conservatives a genuine crisis of conscience. The leadership, mindful of Third World members of the Commonwealth, decided to abstain over the continued use of sanctions against the traditional (but illegal) white settler regime in Salisbury led by Ian Smith. But Winston absolutely disagreed, and following his conscience, decided he would vote against them. Churchill had never feared to vote against his party, but when young Winston did so, he received little sympathy from the Conservative chief whip and was summarily dismissed as an opposition spokesman as he walked out of the division lobby.

All was not lost, however, it seemed that Winston's lapse might be forgiven. Mrs. Thatcher liked him, and shortly after, when Ronald Reagan called on her in London, one of the few politicians he wished to meet was Winston Churchill. Mrs. T. duly invited Winston for a meeting with the future president in her office. (One story has it that Reagan was surprised that Winston Churchill was so young.) Winston's prospects seemed considerably brighter. Margaret Thatcher was an ardent admirer of his grandfather, and when she became Prime Minister herself soon after, she was said to be warming to the idea of a Winston Churchill in her government.

But then came another blow to Winston's prospects, involving the ultimate political banana skin, a sexual scandal—and here it was undoubtedly his name that made him vulnerable and magnified the whole disaster. Like many happily married men before him, Winston had been having an affair—his was with Soraya, ex-wife of the Arab millionaire arms dealer Adnan Khashoggi. Few knew about it, and it was appalling luck that during an entirely unrelated Old Bailey blackmail case, Soraya was compelled to reveal to the judge the identity of her current lover. The connection between a former spokesman on defense with the ex-wife of a notorious arms dealer was imprudent, to say the least, but it was the name Winston Churchill that guaranteed the story front-page banner headlines in the daily papers. The publicity destroyed forever Winston's fondly nourished hopes of office.

All this may have been a blessing for Winston. He has since become an admirable back-bench constituency M.P., and thanks to his devoted wife, his marriage rapidly recovered and has been happy. He has four children, many friends, a chalet in Switzerland, and a Georgian house near Chartwell.

But the good life and the career of a satisfied back-bencher are different from the great political career his grandfather had envisioned —first for Randolph then, when he failed, for his grandson Winston. For Churchill had not merely loved his family. He had seen it as a dynasty in the sense in which the dictionary defines it: "a line of hereditary rulers." Churchill himself had carried on the line that stretched back through his father to the Dukes of Marlborough. But Randolph had bungled it, and now young Winston had too lost his opportunity.

There is, however, one place where a Churchill dynasty of sorts continues: at Churchill's birthplace close by the spot where he is buried— Blenheim Palace. Winston's cousin, ninth Duke Sunny, and his son Bert may have lived unsatisfactory lives compared with his, but as dynasts they succeeded where he failed. Against considerable odds, the Dukes of Marlborough have maintained their right to rule their palace and inherited possessions with remarkable success.

Bert survived as the tenth Duke of Marlborough until 1972, and just before the end he even scored off his departed Cousin Randolph by persuading Laura, the love of Randolph's life, to marry him. Laura was now a widow, Michael Canfield having died some three years earlier. Bert offered her the family pearls that had belonged to Catherine the Great, and she said that he appeared so lonely, and Blenheim itself was such a challenge, that she finally accepted him. ("Randolph would have turned incandescent had he known what I was doing.")

Laura took her role as Duchess seriously, and was planning to transform and modernize the interior of Blenheim, but she never got the chance. The marriage lasted less than fifty days. In February, after a wet day's shooting, Bert suffered sudden intestinal failure, and on March 11, his previously overshadowed son, Sunny Blandford, entered into his inheritance as the eleventh Duke of Marlborough.

But by the time he died, Bert had not only beaten Randolph over Laura; in terms of the dynasty, he had also done surprisingly well by Blenheim and the dukedom. Like all provident modern British noblemen, he had been paying close attention to his tax accountants and had already passed on to Sunny the bulk of the inheritance more than seven years earlier. This meant that on his death, Blenheim and its land and treasures stayed largely unmolested by the tax man.

The new Duke had also staged an early middle-age recovery himself by finally marrying his ideal modern duchess—Rosita Douglas, a strong-willed former Swedish fashion designer of Scots descent, by whom he had two more children, Edward and Alexandra. He also proved to have inherited enough of the Vanderbilt genes—and Consuelo Vanderbilt's money—to make a fortune out of shrewd investments in the boom years of the seventies and early eighties.

Thus, his new Duchess was able to accomplish what Laura of the Fifty Days had dreamed of doing—redecorating, refurnishing, and generally updating Blenheim. Thanks to her taste and her husband's business acumen, Blenheim was ideally suited to exploit the growing tourist interest in historic houses, rapidly becoming one of the most popular and profitable stately homes on the British tourist circuit. (In 1990 it rated third in popularity, with half a million visitors, adults paying £5.50 a head.)

Sunny proved something of a showman, and his new duchess, unlike almost all her predecessors, actually loved living in the palace with her children. This was a further tourist attraction, but just as it seemed that Sunny had solved the problems that bedeviled Blenheim since long before his grandfather married Consuelo, trouble started at the point at which all dynasties are vulnerable—the heir apparent.

With a chaotic childhood and all those melancholy Marlborough ancestors, it was not entirely surprising that Sunny's eldest son, James Blandford, had problems. His lack of intellect hardly mattered—intelligence is not required to inherit a dukedom. But when, following his Harrow education, the Brigade of Guards refused him a commission, trouble started.

As a titled, rich, trainee insurance-broker in New York, the young Lord Blandford turned as easily to drugs as Randolph and Sarah had to drink. Somebody once described him as "born with a silver spoon under his nose," and he rapidly progressed from marijuana and cocaine to heroin. By the time he returned to England in 1982, the twenty-five-year-old marquess was addicted.

His stepsister, Christina Onassis, was so alarmed at his condition that she tried to save him by having him kidnapped on a trip to France and forcibly detained at the Château Gage clinic outside Paris. He inevitably escaped, and his next three years form a melancholy tale of failed cures and dramatic press reports as the heir to Blenheim spun out of all control. A policeman was assaulted and a chemist shop was ransacked for drugs, and finally a judge sentenced Blandford as a common criminal to three months' imprisonment, two of which he served in Pentonville.

All this was bad publicity for the upper classes. More to the point, Blandford's addiction posed a real threat to Blenheim and the Marlborough dynasty. Nothing could dispossess James Blandford of his title and his rights to the dukedom when his father died, but it was impossible for Sunny to follow Bert's example and turn over the palace and all possessions to an heir who was an addict. For a period, Sunny cut off completely from his son, and Blenheim itself was highly vulnerable. If Sunny had died, the Marlborough estate would have been hit by such heavy death duties that Blenheim would almost certainly have been sold.

With so much at stake, it was particularly important to secure a happy ending to the troubled story of James Blandford. And luckily for him, and for the future of the Marlboroughs at Blenheim, his life as an addict reached a crisis in the summer of 1986 when he was discovered by the police in a cellar off the Edgeware Road in London. He was forty-two pounds underweight, and barely surviving on a mixture of cocaine and vodka. Faced with a choice between life as a marquess and death as a junkie, Lord Blandford chose the former.

A clinic practicing the so-called Minnesota Method helped him kick the habit, and he was reunited with his family. For a while he studied at an agricultural college and lived in a house on the Blenheim estate. Recently, he married twenty-six-year-old Rebecca Few-Brown, an extremely pretty girl who could one day make a charming Duchess. But whether the marriage lasts that long already seems in doubt—as does the nature of Lord Blandford's "reformation."

No former addict ever considers he is cured, and marital troubles, motoring offenses, and a return upon the scene of James Blandford's former friends, have once more placed a question mark over his future and his fitness to inherit Blenheim.

Certainly the Duke, his father, has been taking steps against any eventuality, and although he and the family legally own the palace and the estates, he says he sees himself as "virtually a trustee and custodian of Blenheim—not only for Britain, but for those throughout the world, who cherish the historic and artistic tradition Blenheim represents."

To protect it, he and the trustees have been vesting its future in a heavily endowed Blenheim Foundation to guarantee the palace and the park in perpetuity—whatever the vagaries of any future heir inheriting the title.

It is appropriate that "Blenheim's greatest son" is also helping to maintain the Marlborough dynasty in residence in the house that meant so much to him. For Churchill's legend now forms Blenheim's principal attraction for the tourists, who flock to see the room where he was born, the palace and the grounds he had enjoyed with his cousin Sunny, and the family plot where he is buried in Bladon churchyard.

Once a year, on January 24, his daughter Mary comes to place flowers on his grave, and throughout the tourist season, Churchill's voice still echoes through the palace he loved—on taped recordings of his wartime speeches that are played in the small museum filled with relics from his life, close by the room where he was born.

"We shall fight on the landing grounds, we shall fight in the fields and in the streets, we shall fight in the hills; we shall *never* surrender."

# SOURCE NOTES

In the notes I use the abbreviation CB, followed by the volume number, for references to the invaluable eight-volume official Churchill biography by Randolph Churchill and Martin Gilbert, *Winston S. Churchill* (Heinemann, 1966–1988): CV for the five volume companion of letters and documents, *Winston S. Churchill: Companion 1874–1939* (Heinemann, 1967–1988); and WSC for Winston Spencer Churchill. Full details of all the works referred to in the notes will be found in the Select Bibliography.

Chapter One.  FATHERS, SONS, AND OTHERS
    18    "What an amazing thing." Bruce Lockhart, vol. 1, p. 219.
    19    "Gentlemen, let us only hope." *Evening Standard,* 17 June 1932.
    19    "Had anyone told me." Randolph Churchill, *Twenty-one Years,* p. 117.
    22    "like a little fairy." Sarah Churchill, *Keep on Dancing,* p. 15.
    22    "my oldest and dearest friend." WSC obit in *Times* (London) 1 July 1934.

Chapter Two.  THE ANCESTOR
    25    "a private monument." Sitwell, p. 162.
    25    "a poor Cavalier knight." Macaulay, vol. I, p. 162.
    25    he cuckolded the King. *Ibid.* p. 225.
    27    "that wild unmerciful House." F. Martin, *Lady Randolph Churchill,* vol. I, p. 54.

**27**    "an auctioneer." Horace Walpole to G. Montague, July 1760, *Letters of Horace Walpole,* vol. IV.

**27**    "His greatest weakness." Montgomery-Massingberd, p. 51.

**27**    "a physical monument." WSC, *Marlborough,* vol. III, p. 370.

**28**    "What about God?" Green, p. 146.

**28**    five subsequent dukes. Moran, p. 745.

**29**    "the latter years of his life . . ." *Annual Register,* 1840.

**30**    "a full-blown Victorian prig." Rowse, *The Later Churchills,* p. 215.

**30**    close friends of Disraeli. Montgomery Hyde, p. 29.

## Chapter Three.  TWO BROTHERS

**31**    "I cannot be grateful enough." Rowse, *The Later Churchills,* p. 217.

**31**    "my dearest, dearest friends." Martin, *Lady Randolph Churchill,* p. 89.

**32**    "half a snipe for dinner." Montgomery-Massingberd, p. 104.

**34**    "I don't like ladies at all." Martin, vol. I, p. 64.

**34**    "until his tongue was sore." Rhodes-James, *Lord Randolph Churchill,* p. 33.

**34**    "Jeanette" Jerome. Anita Leslie, *Jennie,* p. 16.

## Chapter Four.  THE JEROMES

**35**    "poppy" Marlborough eyes. Rhodes-James, *Lord Randolph Churchill,* p. 48.

**36**    "From what I have heard." Martin, *Lady Randolph Churchill,* vol. I, p. 58.

**36**    "under any circumstances." *Ibid,* p. 60.

**36**    he brought his family back. Anita Leslie, *Jennie,* p. 2.

**36**    "that Wall Street Jungle." Anita Leslie, *Leonard Jerome,* p. 57.

**37**    a many-sided hedonist. *Ibid.* p. 91.

**38**    "I have found the Court I want." *Ibid.* p. 81.

**38**    Little Mondays. Martin, vol. I, p. 10.

**38**    "Gentlemen." Anita Leslie, *Jennie,* p. 22.

**39**    the Emperor's dinner service. *Ibid.* p. 20.

## Chapter Five.  A VICTORIAN TRAGEDY

**40**    "the test of time." Martin, vol. I, p. 34.

**40**    a settlement of £50,000. *Ibid.* p. 36.

**41**    a mountainous trousseau. Anita Leslie, *Jennie,* p. 56.

**42**    "I *loathe* living here." *Ibid.* p. 77.

**42**    "very little money." WSC, *Lord Randolph Churchill,* p. 70.

**43**    Sporting Joe had been in India. Anita Leslie, *Edwardians in Love,* p. 85.

**43** proclaimed her son by Blandford illegitimate. Proceedings of the House of Lords, September 1863.

**44** "Powerful enemies." WSC, *Lord Randolph Churchill,* p. 74.

**45** "a dark, lithe figure." WSC, *My Early Life,* p. 12.

**46** "the speech of a foolish young man." Rhodes-James, *Lord Randolph Churchill,* p. 54.

**46** "from tip-cat to tiger-shooting." *Ibid.* p. 255.

**47** two hundred of her lovers. Asquith, p. 444.

**49** "I like to be the boss." Rosebery, p. 34.

**50** "he is so mad and odd." Martin, *Lady Randolph Churchill,* p. 180.

**50** he suddenly objected. Foster, p. 314.

**50** "When I came down to breakfast." Martin, *Lady Randolph Churchill.*

## Chapter Six. FAMILY TROUBLES

**52** His granddaughter Mary Churchill Soames. Soames, *A Churchill Family Album,* p. 14.

**53** "one long yellow tooth." Harris, vol. II, pp. 532–3.

**53** a mistress he was keeping in Paris. Anita Leslie, *Edwardians in Love,* p. 195.

**54** treated by a Dr. Robson Roose. Foster, p. 218.

**55** "How long will your leadership last?" Rosebery, p. 46.

**55** he departed hurriedly. Martin, vol. I, p. 186.

**55** an affair with another woman. Churchill and Mitchell, *Jennie,* p. 42.

**57** strangers took off their hats. Cowles, p. 33.

**57** "Winston was taken to a pantomime." Churchill and Mitchell, p. 160.

**57** Winston had been an uncontrollable, aggressive child. CB, vol. I, p. 53.

**57** "The naughtiest little boy in the world." Cowles, p. 30.

**58** "dearest Winnie." CV, vol. I, p. 221.

**58** "Gave Winston his lessons." Lady Randolph Churchill's diary for 1882. Churchill College Collection.

**59** the terrifying "Boneless Wonder." CB, vol. V, p. 389n.

**59** "You never came to see me." CB, vol. I, p. 83.

**59** "Lord Randolph became chief mourner." Rosebery, p. 181.

**60** "inclined to abuse his wife." Anita Leslie, *Jennie,* p. 83.

## Chapter Seven. DEATH IN THE FAMILY

**63** "He was his own worst enemy." *The Times,* 12 November 1892.

**64** "charming and joyous." Montgomery-Massingberd, p. 113.

**64** "given no kindness." Anita Leslie, *Jennie,* p. 86.

**65**   "the structure of a British sentence." WSC, *My Early Life,* 25.

**65**   "this astonishing gift for writing" CB, vol. VIII, p. 343.

**65**   "with some resentment." Sir Oswald Mosley, p. 29.

**66**   "I mistook you for a fourth-form boy." WSC, *My Early Life,* p. 26.

**66**   "Precocious, bumptious and talkative." Meinertzhagen, p. 175.

**66**   "I cannoned." *Ibid.* p. 177.

**67**   "Plenty of Tin." Anita Leslie, *Leonard Jerome,* p. 280.

**68**   "They say." Balsan, p. 84.

**68**   looking "very peaceful." Churchill College Collection, November 1892.

**70**   "I am cursed with so feeble a body." CB, vol. I, 211.

**70**   "show-off exaggeration and make believe." CV, vol. I, p. 386.

**71**   "harum scarum style of work." CB, vol. I, p. 189.

**71**   someone has neatly snipped. Churchill College Collection, 5 October 1883.

**71**   "such information about Lord R's condition." CV, vol. I, p. 544.

**71**   "I shall never tell anyone." CB, vol. I, p. 238.

**72**   "I know instinctively." Churchill College Collection, 8 June 1894.

**72**   According to Dr. Buzzard's notes. Buzzard Collection, Royal College of Physicians.

**72**   "My Darling's Last Letter." Churchill College Collection, 22 November 1894.

**73**   "Physically he is better." Anita Leslie, *Jennie,* p. 173.

**73**   "I am not *quite* the meek creature." *Ibid.,* p. 173.

**74**   "masses of Churchills." CV, vol. I, p. 546.

**74**   "Lord Randolph had a quiet night." Buzzard Collection, Royal College of Physicians.

## Chapter Eight.  AMBITION

**75**   "All my dreams of comradeship." WSC, *My Early Life,* p. 70.

**76**   "like an Aladdin's Cave." *Ibid.* p. 74.

**76**   "a freak—always that." CB, vol. VIII, p. 562.

**78**   He reported. *Daily Graphic,* 15 July 1895.

**78**   "slough of despond." CB, vol. I, p. 260.

**79**   "the natural catharsis of accompanying grief." Styron, p. 79.

**80**   "many depressives deny themselves rest." Storr, p. 16.

**80**   "many of which I already know by heart." CB, vol. I, p. 260.

**80**   "I took my politics unquestioningly from him." WSC, *My Early Life,* p. 54.

**81**   "beat my sabre into an iron despatch box." CB, vol. I, p. 288.

**81**   "all the influential friends that you possess." CB, vol. I, p. 288.

**81**   "my stay here might be of value." CB, vol. I, p. 297

82  he seemed to be "of endomorphic structure." Storr, p. 11.

83  Bartlett's *Familiar Quotations*. Sir Oswald Mosley, p. 105.

83  "a good knowledge of the *Annual Register*." CB, vol. I, p. 333.

84  "all along the front of the skirmish line." CB, vol. I, p. 359.

85  "Vehement, high and daring." WSC, *Savrola,* p. 43.

86  "The struggle, the labour." *Ibid.* p. 42.

Chapter Nine.  FAITHFUL BUT UNFORTUNATE

88  "neither pretty nor ugly." Churchill College Collection, 25 August 1892.

89  Mrs. Willie K. sensed victory. Vanderbilt, p. 32.

90  her mother set about her with a riding crop. Balsan, p. 6.

90  the coming-out ball at The Breakers. Vanderbilt, p. 78.

91  "in tears and alone." Balsan, p. 53.

91  "The roof of the Marlborough Castle." *Washington Post,* 12 November 1896.

92  "How strange that in so great a house." Balsan, p. 84.

92  "pushed his plate away." *Ibid.* p. 79.

92  "Your first duty." *Ibid.* p. 72.

Chapter Ten.  POWER AND GLORY

94  "the rogue elements." Martin Green, p. 82.

95  "one more example of your slovenly, shiftless habits." CB, vol. 1, p. 378.

96  "If there is anything." WSC, *My Early Life,* p. 170.

97  "Life is very cheap." CV, vol. 1, p. 96.

98  "like a dream." CB, vol. I, p. 973.

98  "a Ripper." CB, vol. I, p. 957.

98  "the consolations of philosophy." CB, vol. I, p. 969.

98  "I do not accept the Christian or any other form of religious belief." CB, vol. I, p. 969.

99  "A great general he may be." CB, vol. I, p. 407.

100  "the most beautiful girl I have ever seen." CB, vol. I, p. 296–97.

101  "He was slim, slightly reddish-haired." Atkins, p. 57.

105  "bronzed by African sunshine." WSC, *Marlborough,* vol. I, p. 58.

Chapter Eleven.  POLITICS

106  "dry hair like a wax-work." Buckle, p. 270.

106  "a little, square-headed fellow." Blunt, p. 16.

106  "What was difficult to see." Rhodes-James, *Churchill: A Study in Failure,* p. 34.

107  "easy for the Boers to surrender." *Hansard,* 18 February 1901.

107  their mother's wedding. Anita Leslie, *Jennie,* p. 253.

**107** "A broad writing-table." WSC, *Savrola,* p. 40.

**109** "the passions of the multitude." CV, vol. I, p. 818.

**109** "Of all the talents." CV, vol. I, p. 816.

**110** "I loved to hear Lord Rosebery talk." WSC, *My Early Life,* p. 56.

**111** "startling" resemblances. *Pall Mall Gazette,* September 1903.

**111** "When the young member for Oldham addresses the House." *Punch,* 8 June 1904.

**111** "he gave himself entirely to work." Atkins, p. 135.

**112** "inclined to leave the Conservative leadership to Mr. Balfour." Warwick, p. 138.

## Chapter Twelve. LOVE AND THE PURSUIT OF POWER

**114** "Went into dinner with Winston Churchill." Webb, p. 269.

**115** "the simplicity of a child." Beaverbrook, *Politicians and the War,* p. 284.

**115** "His approach to women." Bonham-Carter, p. 148.

**117** "but please don't become converted to Islam." CV, vol. II, p. 672.

**117** "It is positively cruel of Fate." CV, vol. II, p. 672.

**117** "Dear Mr. Winston." CV, vol. II, p. 674.

**118** "the vitality of these brutes." CV, vol. II, p. 693.

**121** "We all swooped down in motor cars." CV, vol. II, p. 798.

**122** "her last laundered and starched dress." Soames, *Clementine Churchill,* p. 40.

**122** "I want so much to show you that beautiful place." CV, vol. II, p. 800.

**122** "people of the better sort." *The Times,* 13 September 1908.

**122** The bride wore ivory colored silk. *Ibid.*

**123** the father of the two elder girls was "the gallant Bay Middleton." Longford, p. 386.

**124** the horse-mad Empress Elizabeth. Haslip, pp. 286–9.

## Chapter Thirteen. LIGHT FADES FROM THE PICTURE

**125** "To her simple and rather austere taste." Soames, *Clementine Churchill,* p. 50.

**125** "Vain and frivolous." *Ibid.*

**126** "Lord Esher discovered Kat and Pug." Esher, vol. II, p. 462.

**126** "I am a solitary creature." CB, vol. II, p. 787.

**126** "Is she a pretty child?" *Daily Mail,* 21 October 1965.

**128** "Winston swept me off." Masterman, p. 122.

**129** "I confess," James wrote. Edel, vol. I, p. 500.

**129** "the light faded from the picture." Moran, p. 167.

**130** "Alas, I have no good opinion of myself." Soames, *Clementine Churchill,* p. 64.

**130** "The mere thought that he might trip up." Moran, p. 181.

**131** "He is his own superman." A. G. Gardiner, *Prophets, Priests, and Kings.*

**132** "What the hell have you been doing now, Winston?" Brendon, p. 58.

**132** "The Club." Colville, *The Churchillians,* p. 12.

**133** "I am sure I have the root of the matter." CV, vol. II, p. 893.

## Chapter Fourteen.  ADMIRALTY

**135** "small emotions." Soames, *Clementine Churchill,* p. 63.

**135** "from 1911 onwards, Churchill's delight was." Colville, *The Churchillians,* p. 7.

**136** rolling together down the steps of the Admiralty. Randolph Churchill, *Twenty-one Years,* p. 12.

**137** predicted in a paper. From "Military aspect of the Continental Problem," Cowles, p. 154.

**138** "suddenly become so melancholy." Morgan, p. 338.

**138** "sweetest of the sweets of office." Bonham-Carter, p. 261.

**139** "a kind of floating hotel." Searle, p. 123.

**139** "Dearest Mama, it would do you a great deal of good." CV, vol. II, p. 1639.

**139** "He is like no one else." Bonham-Carter, p. 18.

**139** "Those Greeks and Romans." *Ibid.* p. 262.

**140** "side by side against the taffrail." *Ibid.* p. 262.

**140** "How much coal." *The National Review,* August 1912.

**140** "Winston is for 4 ships." Young, p. 32.

**140** "excursions to the beach." John S. Churchill, p. 27.

## Chapter Fifteen.  GOD BLESS THE DARDANELLES

**142** According to Nellie. Moran, p. 601.

**142** "Upon this grave assembly." Stevenson, p. 38.

**143** "Everything tends towards catastrophe." CB, vol. II, 710–711.

**144** "I ought to have remained in London." WSC, *Thoughts and Adventures,* p. 16.

**145** "His mouth waters." Brock, p. 266.

**145** "rather disgusted with Winston." Stevenson, p. 251.

**145** "like sheep to the shambles." Brock, p. 275.

**146** "this is living history!" CV, vol. III, p. 400.

**147** "an *idea* enters his head." Rhodes-James. *Churchill: A Study in Failure,* p. 29.

**150** "from melodrama to megalomania." Wilson, p. 40.

**150** "You don't care." Stevenson, p. 275.

**150** "silent, despairing." Bonham-Carter, p. 402.

**151** "his head buried in his hands." Stevenson, p. 253.

**151** "found himself—like Lord Randolph." Rhodes-James, *Churchill: A Study in Failure*, p. 78.

**151** Jennie had been walking. Anita Leslie, *Cousin Clare*, p. 69.

**151** He alone possessed "the power." Soames, *Clementine Churchill*, p. 123.

**151** "dance on Asquith's grave." *Ibid.* p. 124.

**151** "God bless the Dardanelles." *Ibid.* Randolph Churchill, p. 14.

**152** "blazed away like hell." Hozier to WSC, CV, vol. III, p. 1182.

**152** "We live vy simply." CB, vol. III, p. 494.

**152** "Randolph will carry the lamp." Soames, *Clementine Churchill*, CV, vol. III, p. 1098.

**153** "The golden opportunity has gone." John Churchill in CV, vol. III, p. 1071.

**153** But potatoes were not enough. CV, vol. III, p. 1078.

**154** "the dirty dogs." CV, vol. III, p. 108.

**154** *"Malbruck s'en v'a."* Blunt, p. 132.

**154** "the whole household upside down." Beaverbrook, p. 276.

**155** "many years of luxury." *Politicians and the War* CV, vol. III, p. 1286.

**156** "I am superior to anything." Soames, *Clementine Churchill*, CV vol. III, p. 1317.

**156** "when next I see you." Soames, *Clementine Churchill*, p. 266.

**156** "I don't know how one bears such things." Anita Leslie, *Cousin Clare*, p. 78.

**156** "the Hammer of Thor." Soames, *Clementine Churchill*, p. 180.

**157** "depressed beyond the limits of description." Beaverbrook, *Politicians and the War*, p. 282.

**157** "like Beethoven deaf." Hassall, p. 340.

**157** "The worst part of our life together." Birkenhead, p. 392.

**158** "We are all worms." Bonham-Carter.

**158** "Like a sea-beast." *Painting as a Pastime*, p. 16.

**158** "a spasm of the emotion." *Ibid.* p. 8.

Chapter Sixteen. LULLENDEN

**161** "a shut Rolls at present." CV, vol. IV, p. 397.

**161** "a Mustard Gas fiend." Soames, *Clementine Churchill*, p. 187.

**161** "a country basket." Soames, *Clementine Churchill*, p. 785.

**162** "a small farm outside East Grinstead." Sarah Churchill, *Keep on Dancing*, p. 2.

**162** Everyday life at Lullenden. Peregrine Churchill to the author.

**163** "a most dreadful bully." Peregrine Churchill to the author.

**163** contents of his chamber pot. John S. Churchill to the author.

**165**  proud to have a father who "was a boss man." Randolph Churchill, *Twenty-one Years,* p. 17.

**168**  "like the weighty smell of locked-in history." John S. Churchill, p. 24.

**168**  "took such a passionate interest in the game." Smith, *Life's a Circus,* p. 83.

**169**  "slight, and frail-looking." *Ibid.* p. 126.

**170**  "I heard the fire crackling." Montgomery-Massingberd, p. 161.

**170**  "One day, at Blenheim." Smith, p. 163.

**171**  "Absolutely dependent upon feminine influence." WSC to Clementine, CV, vol. II, p. 800.

**171**  she was secretly approaching forty. Vickers, p. 165.

**172**  "a mannikin." Asquith, p. 313.

**172**  a fatal touch of melancholy. Rhodes-James, *Chips,* p. 22.

## Chapter Seventeen.  TO RUSSIA WITH LOVE

**174**  a bizarre encounter with Churchill. Sassoon, p. 77.

**175**  "Head thrust well forward." *Ibid.* p. 79.

**176**  "a plague bacillus." Rhodes-James, *Churchill: A Study in Failure,* p. 117.

**176**  "tingling with vitality." Beaverbrook, *Men and Power,* p. 142.

**177**  "If we don't put our foot on the egg." Oswald Mosley, *My Life,* p. 108.

**177**  "just home from school." John S. Churchill to the author.

**178**  "every woman I have ever enjoyed." Anita Leslie, *Cousin Clare,* p. 82.

**178**  "He adores Clare." *Ibid.* p. 118.

**180**  "I have no interest in art." *Ibid.* p. 120.

**180**  "even when your teeth are clenched." *Ibid.* p. 128.

**181**  "You're so like me really." *Ibid.* p. 132.

**181**  "My boys asked me to." Martin, *Lady Randolph Churchill,* vol. II, p. 301.

**182**  "those I regard as fiendish criminals." Anita Leslie, *Cousin Clare,* p. 138.

**183**  "a scientific expedient for sparing life" CV, vol. IV, p. 1695.

**185**  "Just becos' I am ordinary." Soames, *Clementine Churchill,* p. 194.

**185**  "build lovely garden cities." *Ibid.* p. 187.

**186**  "listless little old lady." Sarah Churchill, *Keep on Dancing,* p. 3.

**186**  "subordinate everything in yr life." Soames, *Clementine Churchill,* p. 194.

**187**  "Had she been a man." Grace Hamblin to the author.

**188**  "shrunk and small." Soames, *Clementine Churchill,* p. 199.

**188**  "Oh Winston my Dear, do come tomorrow." *Ibid,* p. 199

**189**   "She was still a handsome woman." Sermoneta, p. 243.

**189**   "a clear profit of £15,000." CB, vol. IV, p. 521.

**189**   "Please make sure you have cut high enough." Martin, vol. II, p. 305.

**189**   "I do not feel a sense of tragedy." CV, vol. IV, p. 1524.

**190**   "Clementine in her agony." Soames, *Clementine Churchill*, p. 202.

### Chapter Eighteen.  THE CHARTWELL DREAM

**192**   "slimed the walls with green." Tilden, p. 115.

**193**   perished in a railway accident. Soames, *Clementine Churchill*, p. 288.

**194**   "Now that the sharp edge of financial anxiety has been removed." CB, vol. V, p. 793.

**194**   "I think a great deal of the coming kitten." CB, vol. V, p. 1957.

**195**   "Let us beware." Soames, *Clementine Churchill*, p. 217.

**196**   "Do you like it?" Sarah Churchill, *A Thread in the Tapestry*, p. 22.

**197**   "a Cherub Peace Maker." Soames, *Clementine Churchill*, p. 208.

**198**   the conclusion of modern historians. Prior, p. 23.

**198**   "the Warrior-King-Statesman." Keynes, *Essays and Sketches in Biography*, p. 168.

**199**   "the sentimental appreciation of beauty." Tilden, p. 118.

**199**   "trying experiments with baths." Tilden, p. 120.

**201**   "Clementine was more deeply tied to her husband than to her offspring." Anita Leslie, *Cousin Randolph*, p. 2.

**202**   "I am enormously and unbelievably tired." Soames, *Clementine*, 326.

**202**   "The Pussy Cat who is their queen." CV, vol. V, p. 144.

### Chapter Nineteen.  PARADISE ON EARTH

**203**   "I am what I have always been." CB, vol. V, p. 57.

**204**   "Do you mind the smoke of a cigar?" CB, vol. V, p. 59.

**206**   "but also all the versatility of an actor." CV, vol. V, p. 473.

**206**   from economists like John Maynard Keynes. Keynes, *The Economic Consequences of Winston Churchill*.

**206**   "everyone said that I was the worst Chancellor of the Exchequer that ever was." Rowse, *The Later Churchills*, p. 439.

**209**   "We are both awfully poor." Vickers, p. 179.

**209**   his Duchess's face was starting to collapse before his eyes. *Ibid.* p. 123.

**210**   "Winston was so delighted with his house." Lees-Milne, vol. I, p. 235.

**211**   the rich, tennis-playing polymath from Oxford. Birkenhead, *The Prof in Two Worlds*, p. 127.

**211**   the even more improbable self-made financier and newspaperman Brendan Bracken. Boyle, pp. 99–100.

**211**   "life at Chartwell was continual chaos." Peregrine Churchill to the author.

## Chapter Twenty. THE HAPPY FAMILY

**214**   left the choice of school to his son. Randolph Churchill, *Twenty-One Years,* p. 27.

**215**   Sarah described Clementine as "formidable." Sarah Churchill, *Keep on Dancing,* p. 17.

**215**   "what a true mother, and grand woman." CB, vol. V, p. 445.

**216**   "the tallest of trees would bend." Colville, *The Churchillians,* p. 21.

**216**   "like a jaguar out of a tree." Soames, *Clementine Churchill,* p. 231.

**216**   "take no notice, keep his head down." Lady Avon to the author.

**216**   "Mrs. C. is highly friendly." Blakiston, p. 71.

**217**   "I feel far safer from worry." CV, vol. V, p. 434.

**217**   "the darling old schoolboy." Cooper, *The Light of Common Day,* p. 155.

**218**   "If you set yourself against Chartwell." Soames, *Clementine Churchill,* p. 223.

**218**   "something of a collegiate atmosphere." Rowse, *The Later Churchills,* p. 451.

**218**   "aide-de-camp extraordinary and Super Quartmaster." John S. Churchill, p. 143.

**219**   "always a glorious feast." Soames, *Clementine Churchill,* p. 246.

**221**   "I just can't stand it any longer." John S. Churchill to the author.

**221**   "I found Chartwell living hell." Peregrine Churchill to the author.

**222**   "I could grow up to be as beautiful and elegant as Cousin Clementine." Lady Diana Mosley to the author.

**222**   "To sit next to Winston was my *ideal.*" Lady Diana Mosley to author.

## Chapter Twenty-One. WILDERNESS

**224**   "What fun it is to get away from England." Young, p. 110.

**224**   "I think he has made a good impression." CV, vol. V, p. 342.

**225**   "Randolph, recite us something." John S. Churchill to the author.

**225**   "A white round face like a blister." Nicolson, vol. I, p. 41.

**226**   "I am Winston Churchill, a British statesman." Gilbert, *The Wilderness Years,* p. 41.

**226**   "the last decade of my existence." CV, vol. V, p. 394.

**227**   a boy scout jamboree, and a revivalist meeting. *Sunday Graphic,* 3 March 1932.

**227**   "Nothing can long delay their arrival." *Ibid.*

**228**   "seditious Middle Temple lawyer." CV, vol. V, p. 357.

**229**   "But what on earth would I talk to him about?" Hanfstaengel, p. 184.

**229**   "anti-Semitism may be a good starter." *Ibid.*"

**230**   "roaring like a bull." Lady Diana Mosley, p. 92.

**230**   Lady Castlerosse's pet name for his son. Leonard Mosley, p. 113.

**231**   "Lindemann, you are a professor of biology." Bruce Lockhart, vol. I, p. 229.

**232**   "beautiful and elegant" Clementine. Sarah Churchill, *Keep on Dancing,* p. 150.

**232**   "because Mummy is horrid to me." Anita Leslie, *The Gilt on the Gingerbread,"* p. 83.

**233**   "Mr. Churchill's daughter a film star?" *Daily Express,* 5 March 1932.

**233**   "to escape all the endless talk." Celia Perkins to the author.

**233**   embattled women. *Daily Telegraph,* 13 December 1932.

**234**   discovered that he drank so much. Dame Barbara Cartland to the author.

**235**   He liked particularly to try out ideas. Ashley, p. 32.

**238**   "Watch Sunny, he hates her guts." Anita Leslie, *Gilt on the Gingerbread,* p. 57.


Chapter Twenty-Two.   PSYCHIC DYNAMITE

**239**   "My dear Maxine!" Forbes-Robertson.

**240**   "Winston, how brave of you" *Ibid.*

**240**   "At meals he just banged on and on." P. Willes to author.

**240**   "God, it's a ghastly place!" Forbes, *The Spectator,* 23 June 1979.

**242**   Stanley Baldwin said how much he envied. CB, vol. V, p. 496.

**243**   "I feel so lonely." Soames, *Clementine Churchill,* p. 251.

**245**   "my heart is in the 18th century." CV, vol. V, p. 660.

**246**   "Every prophet." WSC, *Thoughts and Adventures,* p. 283.

**246**   "the front door was rarely locked." Grace Hamblin to the author.

**246**   "lunch was devoted to unrelieved gloom." John S. Churchill, p. 101.

**247**   "spent much of the time together in the ladies loo." Pryce-Jones, p. 24.

Chapter Twenty-Three.  DISTANT FRIENDS

**249**  "the Roman genius." CB, vol. V, p. 457.

**249**  Hitler's "long wearing battle for the German heart." WSC, *Great Contemporaries,* p. 265.

**250**  The mysterious colonel. Thompson, p. 21.

**250**  Unity's infatuation with all things German. Pryce-Jones, p. 159.

**251**  "the Darling leader." *Ibid.* p. 159.

**252**  "that surprising frankness often found in men at the top." Lady Diana Mosley, p. 149.

**252**  "you love *Parsifal* more and more." *Ibid.* p. 142.

**253**  this contact with Hitler that had ruined his life. Nicholas Mosley, p. 170.

**254**  "simply everyone, from Winston down." Lady Diana Mosley to the author.

**254**  "Winston only wanted to hear about Hitler." Lady Diana Mosley to the author.

**256**  "an extraordinary man, colossally rich." Rhodes-James, *Chips,* p. 396.

**257**  "sweet and darling Winston." CV, vol. V, p. 967.

**257**  Clementine fell romantically in love. Soames, *Clementine Churchill,* p. 266.

**258**  "a little depressed about politics." CV, vol. V, p. 1136.

Chapter Twenty-Four.  TWO LOVE AFFAIRS

**259**  "oh Dear, I want to start out." Soames, *Clementine Churchill,* p. 269.

**261**  "With her beautiful red hair." Sir Harry Llewelyn to the author.

**262**  Cochran was an old-style theatrical survivor. Harling, p. 64.

**262**  "I pointed out to her." CV, vol. V, Part 2, p. 1295.

**263**  "at this period of her life." CV, vol. V, p. 1296.

**263**  Born in Vienna thirty-eight years before. Part II, Oliver, p. 12.

**264**  he "could be marrying into a most unusual family." Ellen Pollock to the author.

**264**  "The well flows freely." CB vol. V, Part 3, p. 735.

**265**  Oliver was "common as dirt." CV, vol. V, p. 52.

**265**  "addressed like a public meeting." Sarah Churchill, *Keep on Dancing,* p. 36.

**266**  "I think I have put her off." *Ibid.* p. 36.

**269**  "I'm here to take Sarah home." *New York Times,* 17 September 1936.

**270**  " 'Queen Wally' would sound well." Pearson, *Façades,* p. 316.

**272**  wrote every word of it for him. Bradford, p. 202.

**272**  "hat in one hand, stick in the other." Winston, p. 267.

272 He delighted in her company. CB, vol. V, p. 810.

273 Clementine had had enough. Peregrine Churchill to the author.

### Chapter Twenty-Five. THE RETURN OF THE PROPHET

275 "Randolph, you've been drinking." Laura, Duchess of Marlborough, to the author.

275 "one strong young figure." CB, vol. V, p. 903.

276 the great ball thrown by the Duchess of Richmond on the eve of Waterloo. Fielding, p. 187.

276 "It was a strange experience." CB, vol. VII, p. 32.

278 "Randolph's adoration of his father." Nicolson, vol. I, p. 339.

278 Meeting his old friend Lady Mary Dunn. Lady Mary Dunn to the author.

278 "Red-headed and rather fat, but Mummy says the puppy fat will disappear." Anita Leslie, *Cousin Randolph,* p. 47.

279 "in action in the early spring." CB, vol. VII, p. 167.

279 "I had had no experience of life or men." Mrs. Averell Harriman to the author.

280 "Pam was not particularly beautiful." Alastair Forbes to the author.

280 "a preparation for this hour." WSC, *The Second World War,* vol. I, p. 527.

281 "I offer neither pay nor quarters nor provisions." Trevelyan, p. 231.

281 "How we despised his orations!" Amory, *Letters of Ann Fleming,* p. 364 n.

283 Extra "diplomatic" rations. Soames, *Clementine Churchill,* p. 391.

284 "There has to be a purpose to it all." Colville, *The Fringes of Power.*

284 "a purpose far beyond our simple reasoning." Moran.

### Chapter Twenty-Six. FAMILY AT WAR

285 "immaculately distinguishedly porcine." Vickers, *Cecil Beaton,* p. 244.

285 "a hard-bitten virago who takes drugs." *Ibid.* p. 245.

287 found her "abusive." Colville, *The Fringes of Power,* p. 273.

288 the swift rejoinder from the general. Soames, *Clementine Churchill,* 290.

288 "rough, sarcastic and overbearing manner." *Ibid.* p. 291.

289 She had tried to kill herself. Pryce-Jones, p. 232.

289 "typically British feature of the situation." Skidelsky, p. 458.

290 she and her husband had become "untouchable." Lady Diana Mosley, p. 177.

**291** "Of course, it was extremely difficult for him." Lady Diana Mosley to the author.

**291** "a kindly thought of Winston's." Lady Diana Mosley, p. 188.

**293** "One of the most objectionable people I have ever met." Colville, *The Fringes of Power*, p. 177.

**294** "he was primarily someone who loved his family." Mrs. Averell Harriman to the author.

**295** "champagne and tenantry on the lawns." Cooper, *Trumpets from the Steep*, p. 62.

**295** "But how does Pamela know that hers will be a boy?" Winston S. Churchill Jr., p. 12.

**296** "Poor infant." Cowles, p. 326.

## Chapter Twenty-Seven. POOR RANDOLPH

**297** One of the happiest Christmases I can remember." Soames, *Clementine Churchill*, p. 300.

**297** "naive and rather charming adoration." Colville, *The Fringes of Power*, p. 201.

**298** "Much the most courteous member of the family." Peregrine Churchill to the author.

**299** "the P.M. sang lustily." CB, vol. VI, p. 962.

**299** "Oh Randy . . . oh my darling." Winston S. Churchill, Jr. p. 14.

**300** "there was very high gambling." Amory, *The Letters of Evelyn Waugh*, p. 149.

**300** "to keep the British Isles afloat." Harriman and Abel, p. 3.

**301** "improved considerably after a shot or two of good Scotch whisky." Pimlott, p. 199.

**301** "Pamela and Averell Harriman also examining the devastation." Colville, *The Fringes of Power*, p. 375.

**301** "the most beautiful man I ever met." Isaacson and Thomas, p. 329.

**302** "mightily smitten by Randolph Churchill's glamorous young wife." Drogheda, p. 98.

**302** "if Randolph were killed." Colville, *The Fringes of Power*, p. 178.

**303** "I found him absolutely charming." Winston Churchill Jr., p. 28.

**304** "I hope he is going to be a gentleman." Sarah Churchill, *Keep on Dancing*, p. 58.

**306** "Are you a Communist?" Ingram, p. 205.

**307** "more than a carload of cops to get Decca into a church." Jessica Mitford to the author.

**309** "looking embarrassed and shy." Nicholson, vol. III, p. 208.

**309** "You called my son a coward." *Ibid.*, p. 209.

**310** "arm in arm and beaming." *Ibid.*

310   "the trouble between Randolph and his mother." Laura, Duchess of Marlborough, to the author.

311   "repelled her with his spotted face." Bruce Lockhart, vol. II, p. 158.

311   "a very tasty morsel." Amory, *The Letters of Evelyn Waugh,* p. 349.

312   "Pamela seems very well." CB, vol. VII, p. 101.

312   How typical of Randolph. Soames, *Clementine Churchill,* p. 315.

313   "it will cause you harrowing anxiety." *Ibid.* p. 315.

313   " 'Poor Randolph!' " Grace Hamblin to the author.

## Chapter Twenty-Eight. MASTER OF ALLIANCES

316   "Call me Winston." Moran.

317   "On my right sat the President of the United States." CB, vol. VII, p. 570.

318   Roosevelt, unimpressed by Churchill's gestures. Roosevelt, p. 182.

319   "Stupendous issues." Moran, p. 140.

320   not only a great statesman, but "a nice father." Sarah Churchill, *Keep on Dancing,* p. 71.

321   "wrapped in my towel." CB, vol. VII, p. 602.

321   "the fact that W. and I still don't get on." Letter to Laura, Lady Dudley, from Randolph Churchill, undated 1942.

321   "R's marriage is going wonky." Nicolson, vol. III, p. 397.

323   "an event so natural and indispensable." WSC, *Great Contemporaries,* p. 256.

323   "If I die, don't worry." CB, vol. VII, p. 606.

323   "a soporific Christmas lunch." CB, vol. VII, p. 622.

323   she "smiled whimsically." Moran, p. 152.

324   "Intimately as both my wife and I knew Lady Churchill." Colville, *The Fringes of Power.*

324   "Try ridding yourself of this microbe." Soames, *Clementine Churchill,* p. 314.

325   "hated one another's guts." *The Times,* 11 October 1982.

326   "There was our old baby in his rompers." Cooper, *Trumpets from the Steep,* p. 178.

326   "Clemmie said nothing." *Ibid.* p. 182.

## Chapter Twenty-Nine. THE SHADOWS OF VICTORY

326   "I think Winston will die when it's over." Cooper, *Trumpets from the Steep,* p. 152.

330   "No one dared pursue a topic." Cowles, p. 325.

330   "losing interest in the war." Colville, *The Fringes of Power,* p. 574.

**331**  "If you go on playing the fool like this." Boyle.

**332**  "glad our commanders are capable of running these sort of risks." CB, vol. VII, p. 795.

**333**  "old and ill." Colville, *The Fringes of Power,* p. 560.

**335**  dined *à deux* on weekdays on only four occasions. Soames, *Clementine Churchill,* p. 355.

**336**  "extraordinarily wholesome." Laura, Duchess of Marlborough, to the author.

**336**  "supposing anything happened to me." Soames, *Clementine Churchill,* p. 367.

**336**  "good stuff in this fellow." Moran, p. 539.

**337**  "a case of two people who had loved each other." Oliver, p. 146.

**337**  "brought her closer to her father." Paul Medlicott to the author.

**337**  "half way between Chequers and London." Sarah Churchill, *Keep on Dancing,* p. 60.

**337**  "how careful Sarah always was." Pauline Bretherton to the author.

**339**  "God! Wasn't God a shit!" Davie, p. 587.

**339**  "He is not a good companion." *Ibid.* p. 587.

**340**  "fighting with his last breath against Bolshevism." CB. vol. VII, p. 1325.

## Chapter Thirty. OPPOSITION

**342**  "It's absolutely monstrous." CB, VIII, p. 119.

**342**  "in Stygian gloom." Soames, *Clementine Churchill,* p. 386.

**342**  "I don't like sleeping near a precipice." Moran, p. 288.

**343**  the way one tiny grub, when fed the magical royal jelly. Moran, p. 757.

**343**  "What is there to stay up for?" Soames, *Clementine Churchill,* p. 391.

**344**  "In our misery." *Ibid.* p. 391.

**344**  "constant outbursts of childish petulance." Moran, p. 299.

**344**  the sudden appearance of a hernia. Moran, 297.

**345**  " 'I wish your mother were here.' " Sarah Churchill, *Keep on Dancing,* p. 278.

**346**  a dozen oysters, two good helpings of roast beef. Brendon, p. 202.

**346**  "cannot edge him aside." Nicholson, vol. III, p. 63.

**346**  "gloomy, grouchy, sullen." *Ibid.* vol. III, p. 79.

**346**  "'I'll tear their bleeding entrails out." Moran, p. 313.

**346**  finished finally and legally with Vic. Sarah Churchill, *Keep on Dancing,* p. 95.

**347**  "perfect for the part of the unhappy Elena." Mario Soldati to the author.

**348**  "only happy talking about old times." Colville, *The Fringes of Power*, p. 773.

**348**  "Britishly drunk all the time." Waugh. Amory, p. 248.

**348**  "I should use *The Name?*" Alastair Forbes to the author.

**349**  "to keep Sarah company." Soames, *Clementine Churchill*, p. 414.

**350**  "I was painfully affected." CB, vol. VIII, p. 267.

**351**  "The great thing about Christopher." Julia Amery to the author.

**351**  "couldn't follow Churchill's moods." Moran, p. 540.

**352**  "when my father began the death agony." John S. Churchill, p. 180.

**352**  "Do you think we shall be allowed to sleep?" CB, vol. VIII, p. 317.

**353**  her father was complaining of recurrent nightmares. Peregrine Churchill to the author.

**353**  "That's pretty good writing, you know." John S. Churchill, p. 181.

**353**  "just as I had seen him in his prime." CB, vol. VIII, p. 308.

**356**  "Her talents as an actress." Mario Soldati to the author.

**356**  "We have a deep animal love for one another." CB, vol. VIII, p. 308.

**356**  "without malice or intrigue." Colville, *The Churchillians*, p. 28.

**357**  "Fond as I was of Randolph." Laura, Duchess of Marlborough, to the author.

**358**  "a domestic and home-loving character." Amory, *The Letters of Evelyn Waugh*, p. 285.

**358**  "You can't seriously think of going through with it." Laura, Duchess of Marlborough to the author.

## Chapter Thirty-One.  THE SECRET BATTLE

**360**  "Very, very old, tragically old." Nicolson, vol. III, p. 212.

**361**  "You and I derive great pleasure." Boyle, p. 313.

**361**  "Go!" he shouted at Miss Hamblin. "Go!" Grace Hamblin to the author.

**362**  George VI's doctors had kept the King in ignorance. Bradford, p. 456.

**362**  "set his heart on seeing the young Queen crowned." Moran, p. 374.

**363**  "felt avuncular towards his orphaned niece." Colville, *The Fringes of Power*, p. 653.

**363**  "You are not the Cardinal Archbishop." Leslie, *Cousin Randolph*, p. 121.

**364**  "snubbed by the person one loves most in the world." CB, vol. VIII, p. 766.

**365**  "If you think that by insulting him." CB, vol. VIII, p. 451.

**366** "like disarming a butterfly." Laura, Duchess of Marlborough, to the author.

**366** "psychological troubles and their explanation quite beyond his ken." Soames, *Clementine Churchill*, p. 443.

**366** "He doesn't think the Old Man will ever go." Shuckburgh, p. 74.

**367** The surgeon's knife slipped, partially severing the bile duct. Rhodes-James, *Anthony Eden*, p. 362.

**368** Churchill genuinely fell in love with her. Colville, *The Churchillians*, p. 121.

**368** "why the BBC should have a better view of my monarch being crowned than me." Pearson, *The Selling of the Royal Family*, p. 72.

**368** "Boy, tell your mother to get your hair cut." Winston S. Churchill Jr., p. 76.

**369** "that great old relic, Winston Churchill." Buckle, p. 256.

**369** "Darling, Wow!" Sarah Churchill, p. 147.

**370** Churchill gave Colville "strict orders." Colville, *The Fringes of Power*, p. 669.

**370** "pacing the lawn in earnest conversation." *Ibid.* p. 669.

**371** "the place in Churchill's heart so long reserved for Randolph." *Ibid.* p. 669.

**371** "This decaying carcass." Graebner, p. 18.

**373** "safety will be the sturdy shield of terror." Hansard. 1 March 1955.

**373** the "cold hatred" he began to feel for Eden. Colville, *The Fringes of Power*, p. 706.

**373** "insisted on pursuing Clarissa with a derogatory article about Anthony Eden." *Ibid.* p. 708.

**373** "I feel that yr. Majesty is right." CB, vol. VIII, p. 1128.


## Chapter Thirty-Two. PAUSALAND

**374** a place of secret refuge and delight. Charles-Roux, p. 63.

**375** nine Renoirs, four Cézannes, three Degases, and his mistress. Evans, p. 156.

**376** purchasing his own abode in the South of France. CB, vol. VIII, p. 1215.

**376** "the charm and seclusion of 'private life' in private houses." Soames, *Clementine Churchill*, p. 460.

**376** "He was so *soft,* so very sweet," Mrs. Emery Reves to the author.

**377** very little in common with her hosts. Soames, *Clementine Churchill,*p. 462.

**377** "Clemmie was astonished." CB, vol. VIII.

**377** "Clementine thought her husband's least admirable characteristic." Colville, *The Churchillians*, p. 215.

**378**   "absolutely obsessed with a senile passion for Wendy Russell."
Payn and Morley, p. 323.

**378**   Churchill actually looked very fit "like a very healthy baby."
Buckle, p. 285.

**379**   "I still like work." Rowse, *Memories of Men and Women*, p. 6.

**380**   "Clementine's almost pitiful perfectionism." Alastair Forbes, *Spectator*, 1979.

**381**   "I'd kick him up the arse." Brendon, p. 220.

**382**   "quite ruined" his birthday. Soames, *Clementine Churchill*, p. 446.

**382**   "Filthy" he spluttered to Lord Moran. Moran, p. 620.

**382**   "These modern chaps. You're in their power." Buckle, p. 288.

**382**   one long heroic epic. Brendon, p. 222.

**383**   a gruesome evening at Chartwell. Davie, p. 732.

**384**   "Look here my girl, you'd better go home and have a shave."
Anita Leslie, *Cousin Randolph*, p. 126.

**385**   "All he really needed now was a spot of genuine success." Mrs.
Averell Harriman to the author.

**385**   "always drank treble whiskies." Alan Brien to the author.

**385**   "carrying on a feud against the world." Buckie, p. 288.

**385**   "Winston was the only person Randolph truly loved." Laura,
Duchess of Marlborough to the author.

**387**   making Randolph "Marquess of Toodle-do." Moran, p. 376.

**387**   Jane Doe was arrested for drunken and abusive behavior. *The
Times,* 12 January 1958.

**388**   "never discuss matters affecting members of my family with total
strangers." *Time* magazine, 28 January 1958.

**388**   "No one with Jerome blood should ever touch spirits." Anita
Leslie, *Cousin Clare,* p. 91.

**389**   "She absolutely *loved* to be photographed." Mrs. Al Parker to the
author.

**389**   "petrified before his greatness." Mrs. David Birkin to the author.

**390**   "Sober she was a golden girl." Ellen Pollock to the author.

**390**   "Love, love, love. Don't bite me." CB, vol. VIII, p. 1233.

**390**   "treated her very roughly at Liverpool." CB, vol. VIII, p. 1286.

**392**   "the courage to start it in the first place." Winston Churchill Jr.,
p. 90.

**392**   "a beastly profession." Rhodes-James, *Anthony Eden,* p. 600.

**392**   "greatest source of ill-luck had been Winston Churchill." *Ibid.*
p. 621.

**393**   "young people around him." Emma Soames to the author.

**397**   Clementine as "all billowing gown and broadened out with age."
Rowse, *Memories of Men and Women*, p. 22.

Chapter Thirty-Three. THE DARK ANGEL BECKONS

**398** "Throw in the corpse as well." CB, vol. VIII, p. 256.

**398** "he was very old and frail." Moran, p. 739.

**399** "How d'you think Winston is?" *Ibid.* p. 739.

**400** take the bier upstream by barge. Private source.

**400** "Operation Hope Not." CB, vol. VIII, p. 1347.

**400** "It was never like this in the past." Moran, p. 762.

**402** It was an uncomfortable evening. Evans, p. 156.

**402** "He made a good impression on me." CB, vol. VIII, p. 1174.

**402** "Oh, my dear, dear friend." Evans, p. 158.

**403** Onassis required acceptance. Nigel Neilson to the author.

**405** "Dear Sir Winston." CB, vol. VIII, p. 1315.

**405** "the months I spent at your charming house." *Ibid.* p. 1315.

**406** "I was in love with Randolph." Mrs. Natalie Barclay to the author.

**406** "I was delighted to see the old boy so happy." Laura, Duchess of Marlborough to the author.

**407** "What can you do with a woman who pronounces 'menu' as 'may-nyew?' " Alan Brien to the author.

**407** "You're not *writing* anything?" Grace Hamblin to the author.

**408** "He's asked me at last!" Anita Leslie, *Cousin Randolph,* p. 150.

**408** "Dearest Papa." CB, vol. VIII, p. 1313.

**408** rumored to spend $10,000 annually on flowers. *Vanity Fair,* July 1988.

**408** "they're all amoral." Brooke Hayward, *Haywire* (Knopf, 1977), p. 273

**410** "You did not drive yourself, did you?" Winston S. Churchill Jr., p. 183.

**410** "Take this for being a shit!" *Ibid.* p. 80.

**410** "carry the name Churchill . . . with honour into the future." *Ibid.* p. 175.

**411** "your bloody library's not a library." Laura, Duchess of Marlborough, to the author.

**411** "So Ari, we are related at last!" CB, vol. VIII, p. 1339.

**412** "nervous fatigue, depression, and anxiety state." Soames, *Clementine Churchill,* p. 480.

**412** "*Was* there an incident last night?" Ellen Pollock to the author.

**413** "Well, *that* puts the Marlboroughs in their place!" Sarah Churchill, *Keep on Dancing,* p. 194.

**413** "We stared silently at each other." *Ibid.* p. 204.

**413** "she was not prepared to become a mother to her husband." Anthony Montague Browne to the author.

**414** "room for two of a good thing." *Daily Express,* 18 April 1962.

**414** verdict of suicide. *Daily Telegraph,* 25 October 1963.

**415** "Just put them in a bucket for me, nurse." Lord Lambton to the author.

**415** "the only part of Randolph that was not malignant." Davie, p. 792.

**416** "trying to act as if nothing untoward had happened." Natalie Barclay to the author.

**416** "The Dark Angel beckons." Laura, Duchess of Marlborough, to the author.

**416** "My life is over but is not yet ended." CB, vol. VIII, p. 1317.

**416** "everything that he had done had ended in disaster." Montague Browne to the author.

**417** "I ought not, I must not, be held to account." Moran, p. 753.

**417** "a great deal to achieve nothing in the end." Sarah Churchill, *A Thread in the Tapestry,* p. 17.

**418** "I'm so bored." Soames, *Clementine Churchill,* p. 489.

**418** "In the midst of death." *Ibid.* p. 492.

**418** "It is the day that I shall die." Colville, *The Churchillians,* p. 19.

**418** "overwhelmed by the beauty." Emma Soames to the author.

**418** television's multiple insect-eye. Maurice Wiggin, *Sunday Times,* 3 February 1965.

## Chapter Thirty-Four. AFTERMATH

**421** "old and grey like a haggard hawk." Buckle, p. 387.

**422** she and Mary together laid a wreath. Soames, *Clementine Churchill,* p. 524.

**422** "I don't mind going." Idris Evans to the author.

**422** "She firmly slapped us children down." Emma Soames to the author.

**427** "Randolph would have turned incandescent." Laura, Duchess of Marlborough, to the author.

**428** His stepsister, Christina Onassis. Dempster, *Heiress, The Story of Christina Onassis,* p. 131.

**429** A policeman was assaulted. *Evening Standard,* 6 November 1986.

# SELECT BIBLIOGRAPHY

The literature on Winston Churchill forms an ever-expanding universe of its own, and it would be impossible to list all the sources I have relied on for this book. The following bibliography however may be useful for further reading, and includes full details of all the works mentioned in the chapter notes.

Amory, M. (ed.) *The Letters of Ann Fleming* (Collins, 1985)
  *The Letters of Evelyn Waugh,* (Weidenfeld, 1980)
Ashley, Maurice. *Churchill as Historian* (Scribners, 1966)
Asquith, Lady Cynthia. *Diaries 1915–1918* (Hutchinson)
Atkins, J. B. *Incidents and Reflections* (Unwin, 1921)
Balsan, Consuelo Vanderbilt. *The Glitter and the Gold* (Harper, 1952)
Beaverbrook, Lord. *Politicians and the War* (Oldbourne, 1959)
  *Men and Power* (Hutchinson, 1956)
Birkenhead, Earl of. *Churchill 1874–1922* (Harrap, 1990)
  *The Prof in Two Worlds* (Collins, 1964)
Blakiston (ed.) *The Letters of Conrad Russell* (John Murray, 1987)
Bonham-Carter, Lady Violet. *Winston Churchill As I Knew Him* (Collins, 1965)
Boyle, Andrew. *Poor Dear Brendan* (Hutchinson, 1974)
Bradford, Sarah, *George VI* (Weidenfeld, 1989)
Brendon, Piers. *Winston Churchill, A Brief Life* (Secker, 1984)
Brock, M. and E. (eds). *H. H. Asquith: Letters to Verchia Starle* (Oxford University Press, 1982)

Bruce Lockhart, Sir Robert. *Diaries* (Macmillan, 1973)

Buckle, R. (ed.). *Cecil Beaton: Selected Diaries* (Weidenfeld, 1979)

Charles-Roux, Edmond. *Chanel* (Cape, 1970)

Churchill, John S. *Crowded Canvas* (Odhams, 1961)

Churchill, Peregrine and Julian Mitchell. *Jennie, Lady Churchill. A Portrait with Letters* (Collins, 1974)

Churchill, Lady Randolph. *Reminiscences* (Arnold, 1908)

Churchill, Randolph S. *Twenty-one Years* (Weidenfeld, 1964)
   *Winston S. Churchill* vols I and II (Heinemann, 1966, 1967)

Churchill, Sarah. *A Thread in the Tapestry* (Deutsch, 1967)
   *Keep on Dancing* (Weidenfeld, 1981)

Churchill, Winston S. *Savrola* (Longmans, 1900)
   *Lord Randolph Churchill* (Macmillan, 1906)
   *The World Crisis and the Aftermath,* (Butterworth, 1923–31)
   *My Early Life,* (Butterworth, 1930)
   *Thoughts and Adventures* (Butterworth, 1932)
   *Marlborough: His Life and Times* (Harrap, 1938)
   *Great Contemporaries* (Butterworth, 1939)
   *Painting as a Pastime* (Odhams, 1948)
   *Second World War Memoirs* (Cassell, 1948–52)

Churchill, Winston S., Jr. *Memories and Adventures* (Weidenfeld, 1989)

Colville, John. *The Churchillians* (Weidenfeld, 1981)
   *The Fringes of Power* (Hodder, 1985)

Cooper, Lady Diana. *Trumpets from the Steep* (Hart-Davies, 1960)
   *The Light of Common Day* (Hart-Davies, 1959)

Cowles, Virginia. *Winston Churchill, the Era and the Man* (Hamish Hamilton, 1953)

Davie, M. (ed.). *The Diaries of Evelyn Waugh* (Weidenfeld, 1970)

Dempster, Nigel. *Christina* (Weidenfeld, 1989)

Drogheda, Lord. *Double Harness* (Weidenfeld, 1986)

Edel, Leon. *Henry James: A Life* (Harper and Row, 1987)

Esher, Lord. *Journals and Letters* (Nicholson and Watson, 1934)

Evans, Peter. *Ari: The Life and Times of Onassis* (Cape, 1986)

Fielding, Daphne. *Mercury Rising* (Hamish Hamilton, 1982)

Forbes-Robertson, Diana. *Maxine* (Hamish Hamilton, 1964)

Foster, R. F. *Lord Randolph Churchill. A Political Life* (Oxford 1981)

Gardiner, A. G. *Prophets, Priests and Kings* (Dent, 1908)

Gilbert, Martin. *Winston S. Churchill*. vols. III–VIII. (Heinemann, 1971–1988)
   *Winston S. Churchill: Companion; 1914–1939* (Heinemann, 1982)
   *Winston Churchill. The Wilderness Years* (Macmillan 1981)

Graebner, Walter. *My Dear Mr. Churchill* (Collins, 1972)

Green, David. *The Churchills of Blenheim* (Constable, 1984)

Green, Martin. *Children of the Sun* (Deutsch, 1978)

Hanfstaegel, P. *Hitler, the Missing Years* (Collins, 1957)

Harling, James. *Cochran* (W. H. Allen, 1982)

Harriman, W. Averell and Elie Abel. *Special Envoy* (Random House, 1972)

Harris, Frank. *My Life and Loves* (Richards, 1947)

Harrod, Roy. *The Prof: A Personal Memoir of Lord Cherwell* (Macmillan, 1959)

Haslip, Joan. *The Lonely Empress* (Weidenfeld, 1968)

Hassall, Christopher. *Sir Edward Marsh* (Longmans, 1959)

Ingram, Kevin. *Rebel: A Short Life of Esmond Romilly* (Weidenfeld, 1985)

Irving, David. *Churchill's War* (Veritas, 1987)

Isaacson, W. and E. Thomas. *The Wise Men* (Simon & Schuster, 1986)

Keynes, J. M. *The Economic Consequences of Mr Churchill* (Hogarth, 1926)
    *Essays and Sketches in Biography* (Hart Davies, 1951)

Lees-Milne, J. *Harold Nicolson* (Chatto, 1980)

Leslie, Anita. *The Fabulous Leonard Jerome* (Hutchinson, 1954)
    *The Gilt on the Gingerbread* (Hutchinson, 1960)
    *Cousin Clare* (Hutchinson, 1968)
    *Jennie* (Hutchinson, 1968)
    *Edwardians in Love* (Hutchinson, 1972)
    *Cousin Randolph* (Hutchinson, 1985)

Leslie, Seymour. *The Jerome Connection* (Hutchinson, 1964)

Longford, Elizabeth. *A Pilgrimage of Passion. The Life of Wilfred Scawen Blunt*
    (Weidenfeld, 1979)

Macaulay, Lord. *The History of England* (Longmans, 1889).

Martin, Ralph. *Lady Randolph Churchill,* vols I and II. (Cassell, 1969)

Masterman, Lucy. *C. F. G. Masterman* (Nicholson and Watson, 1939)

Meinertzhagen, Col. R. *Diary of a Black Sheep* (Oliver and Boyd, 1964)

Montgomery Hyde, H. *The Londonderrys: A Family Portrait* (Hamish Hamilton,
    1979)

Montgomery-Massingberd, Hugh. *Blenheim Revisited* (Bodley Head, 1985)

Moran, Lord. *Winston Churchill: the Struggle for Survival* (Constable, 1966)

Morgan, Ted. *Churchill: Young Man in a Hurry* (Simon and Schuster, 1982)

Mosley, Lady Diana. *A Life of Contrasts* (Hamish Hamilton, 1977)

Mosley, Leonard. *Castlerosse* (Hodder, 1968)

Mosley, Nicholas. *Beyond the Pale* (Secker, 1983)

Mosley, Sir Oswald. *My Life* (Nelson, 1968)

Nel, Elizabeth. *Mr Churchill's Secretary* (Hodder, 1958)

Nicolson, Nigel (Editor). *Harold Nicolson, Diaries and Letters 1930–1962,* 3
    vols (Collins, 1966–68)

Oliver, Vic. *Mr Showbusiness* (Harrap, 1954)

Payn, Graham and Sheridan Morley (eds.). *The Noël Coward Diaries* (Weiden-
    feld, 1982)

Pearson, John. *Façades* (Macmillan, 1978)

Pimlott (ed.). *The Hugh Dalton Diaries,* (Cape, 1986)

Prior, Robin. *Churchill's World Crisis as History* (Croome Helm, 1985)

Pryce-Jones, David. *Unity Mitford: A Quest* (Weidenfeld 1976)

Rhodes-James, Robert. *Chips: the Diaries of Sir Henry Charron* (Weidenfeld, 1967)

   *Churchill: A Study in Failure* (World Publishing, 1970)

   *Anthony Eden* (Macmillan, 1986)

Riddell, Lord. *Intimate Journal of the Peace Conference and After* (Gollancz, 1933)

Roberts, Brian. *Randolph* (Hamish Hamilton, 1984)

Roosevelt, Elliott. *As He Saw It* (Duell Sloane and Pearce, 1946)

Rosebery, Lord. *Lord Randolph Churchill* (Humphreys, 1906)

Rowse, A. L. *The Early Churchills* (Macmillan, 1956)

   *The Later Churchills* (Macmillan, 1958)

   *Memories of Men and Women* (Eyre Methuen, 1980)

Sassoon, Siegfried. *Siegfried's Journey* (Faber, 1946)

Scawen-Blunt, Wilfred. *My Diaries* (Secker, 1965)

Searle, G. R. *Corruption in British Politics* (Oxford, 1989)

Sermoneta, Duchess of. *Sparkle Distant Worlds* (Macmillan, 1926)

Sheridan, Clare. *To the Four Winds* (Deutsch, 1957)

Shuckburgh, Evelyn. *Descent to Suez* (Weidenfeld, 1986)

Sitwell, Sacheverell. *Great Houses of Europe* (Weidenfeld, 1961)

Skidelsky, Robert. *Oswald Mosley* (Macmillan, 1975)

Smith, Lady Eleanor. *Life's a Circus* (Collins, 1962)

Soames, Mary. *Clementine Churchill* (Cassell, 1979)

   *A Churchill Family Album* (Penguin, 1982)

Stevenson, F. *Lloyd-George: A Diary* (Hutchinson, 1971)

Storr, Anthony. *Churchill's Black Dog* (Collins, 1989)

Styron, William. *Darkness Visible: A Memoir of Madness* (Random House, 1990)

Taylor, A. J. P. *English History 1914–45* (Oxford, 1965)

Thompson, R. W. *Morton and Churchill* (Hodder and Stoughton, 1976)

Tilden, Philip. *True Remembrances of an Architect* (Country Life, 1954)

Trevelyan, G. M. *Garibaldi's Defence of the Roman Republic* (Longman's, 1908)

Vanderbilt, Arthur. *Fortune's Children.* (Michael Joseph, 1989)

Vickers, Hugo. *Gladys, Duchess of Marlborough* (Hamish Hamilton, 1979)

   *Cecil Beaton* (Weidenfeld, 1985)

Warwick, Frances, Lady. *Life's Ebb and Flow,* (Collins, 1920)

Webb, Beatrice. *Our Partnership* (Secker, 1938)

Wilson, K. (ed.). *The Rasp of War: The Letters of H. A. Gwyne of the Morning Post,* (Sidgwick & Jackson, 1988)

Windsor, Duke of. *A King's Story* (Collins, 1962)

Young, Kenneth. *Churchill and Beaverbrook* (Eyre, 1966)

# INDEX

# Photo Credits

1, 2, 5, 9, 10, 11, 16, 18, 19, 20, 21, 25: Hulton Picture Company.
3: British Library, London.
4, 7: National Portrait Gallery, London.
6: *Country Life*.
8: Courtesy Charles J. Sawyer, National Portrait Gallery, London.
12: Syndication International LTD.
13: Courtauld Institute of Art.
14: Associated Press.
15: Courtesy Gilbert Adams Collection, National Portrait Gallery, London.
17: Sotheby's, London.
22, 23: Popperfoto.
24: Camera Press.